Contemporary Strategic Marketing

Contemporary Strategic Marketing

ROSS BRENNAN
PAUL BAINES
PAUL GARNEAU

with Foreword by Phil Harris,
Chairman of the Academy of Marketing

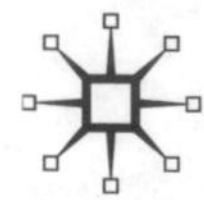

First published 2003 by
PALGRAVE MACMILLAN
Houndmills, Basingstoke, Hampshire RG21 6XS and
175 Fifth Avenue, New York, N.Y. 10010
Companies and representatives throughout the world

PALGRAVE MACMILLAN is the global academic imprint of the Palgrave Macmillan division of St. Martin's Press, LLC and of Palgrave Macmillan Ltd. Macmillan® is a registered trademark in the United States, United Kingdom and other countries. Palgrave is a registered trademark in the European Union and other countries.

ISBN 0–333–98118–9 hardback
ISBN 0–333–98119–7 paperback

This book is printed on paper suitable for recycling and made from fully managed and sustained forest sources.

A catalogue record for this book is available from the British Library.

A catalog record for this book is available from the Library of Congress.

Editing and origination by Aardvark Editorial, Mendham, Suffolk

10 9 8 7 6 5 4 3 2 1
12 11 10 09 08 07 06 05 04 03

Printed and bound in Great Britain by
J. W. Arrowsmith Ltd, Bristol

Contents

List of Figures and Tables

Figures

Tables

About the Authors

Ross Brennan is Chair of the Marketing Group and Principal Lecturer in Marketing at Middlesex University Business School in London. He holds a PhD in marketing from the University of Manchester Institute of Science and Technology (UMIST). His primary research interests lie in the fields of business-to-business marketing and strategic marketing. Prior to his academic career, Ross worked for 11 years in marketing and strategic planning positions in the telecommunications industry. Ross is the only member of the authorial team to have played chess against grandmasters.

Paul Baines is Director of Business Development and Senior Lecturer in Marketing at Middlesex University Business School. He also holds a PhD and MPhil in marketing, also from UMIST. His primary research interests are in marketing strategy for mass-mediated service organisations, particularly in the field of political marketing. Paul has conducted market research and strategic marketing projects for a number of household names. Paul is the only member of the authorial team to have been skydiving.

Paul Garneau is Programme Leader for the MA in Marketing Management and Senior Lecturer in Marketing at Middlesex University Business School. He has extensive experience of marketing as an academic, consultant and practitioner, both in the UK and in his native Canada. Paul's research interests lie in the fields of consumer behaviour and Internet marketing strategy. He is the only member of the authorial team tohave built his own house on the shores of the Pacific and to have braved wild brown bears while a supplier of specialist seafood to the citizens of Vancouver, British Columbia.

Foreword

Marketing as a distinct discipline is still relatively new and has only been actively researched and taught for the last fifty years. Early marketing theory and practice reflected a heavily structured and mechanistic society, which was managed on predominantly hierarchical lines and models. Much of early marketing reminds one of Orwell's *Animal Farm* characters or worse still, Gradgrind and his utilitarian reductionism in Dickens' *Hard Times*. Marketing moved on from this period of functionalism to a more modern and relationship orientated approach and has begun to move in the past decade to a more holistic, strategic and network-orientated approach. This book builds on that by looking at contemporary themes and issues in marketing. It is by three of the more interesting modern academics, consultants and researchers, Ross Brennan, Paul Baines and Paul Garneau and includes new case study material.

I particularly like the breadth of case studies reflecting the dynamics of the football business (sorry – for Americans, soccer) with material based on their contemporary work with Fulham Football Club. As somebody who lives in Manchester I can understand readily the major branding and marketing issues alongside club football. When I tell people in Australasia and, increasingly, America, that I am from Manchester they do not associate my home town with cotton mills but with Manchester United and Granada TV's Coronation Street.

The cases also have the boldness to reflect modern crises, such as demand in the airline industry post September 11th, and, more daringly, the impact of BSE on the British beef business. Both reflect the impact of the fear factor on consumption and the irrationality of consumer demand. As a member of the International Board of Trustees, I was particularly impressed with the knowledge and awareness of the internationalisation question reflected in the Chartered Institute of Marketing case. Besides these, the rest of the cases make good reading and are informed. They will be an asset to students and staff studying or leading courses on modern marketing.

The text is pleasing as it deals in a broad, yet detailed, way with the fundamentals and critical issues that the marketing practitioner has to face; consumption patterns, buyer behaviour, strategy, the planning process and effective e-marketing strategies. It is a book for our modern times and will serve students and tutors as a good quality text over the next decade. Enjoy.

DR PHIL HARRIS

Chairman of the Academy of Marketing, 1999–2002

Preface

This textbook is designed to provide a complete package for a course in strategic marketing. Successful decision-making in strategic marketing requires rigorous thinking, familiarity with current research in the field and an ability to make practical decisions under conditions of uncertainty. Reflecting this, the book is structured in three complementary parts – text, case studies and readings. Throughout each part we acknowledge the changing face of strategic marketing research and practice, while retaining much of the 'traditional' strategic marketing curriculum.

THE CHANGING FACE OF STRATEGIC MARKETING RESEARCH

The text includes much traditional material on the analysis of the marketing environment, strategic marketing analysis and the generation of alternative marketing strategies. In addition to this, however, we have included chapters dealing with the key recent developments of relationship marketing strategies, Internet marketing strategies and strategies for mass consumer services. The case study section provides cases dealing with 'traditional' businesses such as the newspaper industry and the car industry but we have also included more unusual cases such as one dealing with a major English football club, and another looking at the marketing of drugs for HIV/AIDS in South Africa. In the selection of readings on strategic marketing in Part Three we have concentrated on providing recent articles dealing with key contemporary issues in strategic marketing, rather than 'classic' articles that can be readily found elsewhere. The primary foci of the readings included are relationship marketing, the changing nature of competition and the need for marketers to demonstrate their contribution to shareholder value.

STRATEGIC MARKETING IN PRACTICE

It should be emphasised that strategic marketing is certainly not just an area of academic study. Rather, strategic marketing is a management practice. In addition to teaching and researching in the field of strategic marketing, all three authors have experience as practitioners and consultants. That is one reason why, throughout this work, we have concentrated on conveying the concepts and techniques of strategic marketing in a rigorous but easily comprehensible manner. Naturally, the field of strategic marketing includes a number of complex ideas and involves a certain amount of specialist vocabulary, which we introduce in a sympathetic manner. However, where possible, we have chosen to explain topics in straightforward language and have avoided the use of jargon for its own sake.

BALANCING SKILLS AND KNOWLEDGE

As academics, practitioners and consultants in the field of strategic marketing, we appreciate the need for strategic marketing plans to be based on rigour of thought and current research, and the needs of the marketing practitioner (or student) to have useful guidelines to facilitate management decision-making. We strike a balance throughout the book between these two requirements. When reading certain academic articles on strategic marketing, the student or practitioner might be excused for wondering how, if at all, they are connected to the realities of marketing decision-making. On the other hand, we are not fans of the 'checklist' approach that can be found in some popular management books, which suggests that every complex strategic decision can be reduced to a series of simple steps. The successful strategic marketer must be able to combine the skills of the researcher or analyst – to stand back from a problem and appraise the situation objectively on the basis of the data – with the skills of the practical manager or entrepreneur to make a decision and then implement it. When we teach a course on strategic marketing, we aim to develop all these abilities in our students, through a combination of academic knowledge and case study practice. It is our intention that this book will help students to develop the right balance of skills and knowledge to be able to contribute effectively to strategic marketing decision-making in the future.

USING THE BOOK

While it is quite possible to read this book through from beginning to end, the text is designed for the three parts to be used concurrently. The concepts that are explained in the text are then illustrated in practice through associated case studies, while the readings provide a deeper understanding of key areas. A guide to using case study analysis is provided in Chapter 12 along with a grid indicating which concepts are explored within each case study and reading.

To the lecturer using this book, or for the independent reader seeking the most effective route through the book, we would recommend that the material be sub-divided into five roughly equal components each comprising chapters, case studies and readings. First, read Chapters 1, 2 and 12, which provide an understanding of the subject matter and of the role of case studies in learning it. Case Studies 1 and 2 should be read in conjunction with this material. Second, read Chapters 3 and 4, which explain the role of buyer behaviour in strategic marketing. Case Studies 9 and 10, and Reading 1, should be read to illustrate and deepen this knowledge. Third, read Chapters 5 and 6 in order to understand the role of environmental analysis in strategic marketing. Case Studies 3, 11, 12, and 14, and Reading 2 provide support for these chapters. Fourth, Chapters 7 and 8 detail the key tools available for strategic marketing analysis and formulation. Case Studies 5, 6, 8 and 15 provide opportunities to practice these techniques, while Readings 4 and 5 provide additional conceptual material. Finally, Chapters 9, 10 and 11 explain key recent developments in strategic marketing thinking. Case Studies 4, 7 and 13, and Reading 3, support these chapters.

Lecturers who adopt this book can gain access to an accompanying website (at http://www.palgrave.com/business) which includes answers to chapter questions, full teaching notes for all of the case studies and slides featuring tables, figures and learning objectives.

ROSS BRENNAN
PAUL BAINES
PAUL GARNEAU

Acknowledgements

The authors and publishers wish to thank the following for permission to reproduce copyright material:

Sarah Brennan for Figure 3.2.

H. Hakansson (1982) *International Marketing and Purchasing of International Goods* pp. 15, 24, copyright © 1982 by John Wiley & Sons Limited. Reproduced with permission for Figure 4.2.

Michael E. Porter (1985) *Competitive Advantage: Creating and Sustaining Superior Performance* for Figures 5.6 and 8.5. Reproduced by permission of Simon & Schuster Adult Publishing.

Crown copyright material is reproduced with the permission of the Controller of HMSO and the Queen's Printer for Scotland, for Table 8.2.

NRS for Table 8.3.

The *Journal of Marketing Research*, published by the American Marketing Association, November 1999, for Table 9.7 by Hutt & Speh. Reprinted with permission.

The Directory of Multinationals (1997) Macmillan Press for Tables C2.1, C2.2, C2.3 and C2.4, reproduced by permission of Palgrave Macmillan.

Deloitte & Touche Sport for Table C4.2 and Figure C4.8.

The Meat and Livestock Commission for Figures C5.2, C5.3 and C5.4.

Market Research GB for Tables C3.1, C3.2, C3.3, C3.4 and C3.5. Reproduced by permission of Euromonitor International.

Soccer Analyst for Table C4.1 and Figure C4.7. Reproduced by permission of Soccer Investor Ltd.

D Steve White and David A Griffith (1997) 'Combining corporate and marketing strategy for global competitiveness', *Marketing Intelligence and Planning*, **15**(4): 173–8. Reproduced by permission of MCB University Press Limited.

Peter Turnbull, David Ford and Malcolm Cunningham (1996) 'Interaction, relationships and networks in business markets: an evolving perspective', *The Journal of Business and Industrial Marketing,* **1**(3/4): 63–79. Reproduced by permission of MCB University Press Limited.

Peter Doyle (2000) *Value-based Marketing,* pp. 18–23, copyright © 2000 by John Wiley & Sons Ltd. Reproduced by permission of John Wiley & Sons Limited.

Ross Brennan (1995) 'British Telecommunications plc: facing up to the 90s', *Cases in Marketing Management,* Pitman Publishing, copyright © 1995 by Ross Brennan. Reproduced by permission of Pearson Education Limited.

Christian Grönroos (1995) 'Relationship marketing: The strategy continuum', *Journal of the Academy of Marketing Science,* **23**(4): 252–4, copyright © 1995 by Academy of Marketing Science. Reproduced by permission of Sage Publications, Inc.

Jagdish N Sheth and Rajendra S Sisodia (1999) 'Revisiting marketing's lawlike generalizations', *Journal of the Academy of Marketing Science,* **27**(1): 71–87, copyright © 1999 by Academy of Marketing Science. Reproduced by permission of Sage Publications, Inc.

The authors are grateful for the assistance of Sukhbinder Barn in the preparation of the case study 'Fulham FC: Strategic Marketing for Football Clubs', and to Phil Harris for the case study 'Regaining the International Market for British Beef'.

Every effort has been made to trace all copyright holders, but if any have been inadvertently overlooked, the publisher will be pleased to make the necessary arrangements at the earliest opportunity.

part one

Text

chapter one

Introduction

It is only in recent years that the significance of customer expectations has come to be well understood in marketing. A wealth of research followed the initial revelation by Parasuraman et al. (1985) that, in the marketing of services, customer satisfaction was not solely determined by the objective quality of the service offered, but was also affected by the customer's expectations. This has some rather unexpected implications. For example, two businesses that deliver identical service to customers can achieve quite different customer satisfaction ratings, because one of them was expected to perform much better than the other. Rather ironically, it is the business that was expected to perform badly that would get better customer satisfaction ratings than the business that was expected to perform well. Customers are dissatisfied where there is a large gap between their expectations and the service actually delivered. For that reason, marketers have come to recognise the importance of actively managing customer expectations. In this chapter we aim to do two things. First, to manage your expectations concerning what this book can do. Second, to provide an overview of the book, which we do in the final section of the chapter. Your first expectation might have been that we would explain what we meant by 'strategic marketing' in this chapter – but you will have to wait until Chapter 2 for that explanation. Now, let us imagine that you have asked three very reasonable questions:

- Will this book provide me with the necessary tools to be able to develop and sustain a competitive advantage for my (future) organisation?
- Will this book give me the universal principles of strategic marketing?
- Will this book tell me how to plan my marketing strategy?

QUESTION 1: CAN THIS BOOK GIVE YOU A SUSTAINABLE COMPETITIVE ADVANTAGE?

One of the primary purposes of strategic marketing is to identify ways in which an organisation can create and sustain a competitive advantage over its rivals. In starting to read a book entitled *Contemporary Strategic Marketing* you might expect that, by reading it diligently, you would learn how to create and sustain such a competitive advantage. Is this a reasonable expectation?

At a number of points in this book you will find us making use of a medical analogy. For example, in Chapter 12 we discuss the process of identifying 'symptoms' in a case study and using these to 'diagnose the underlying disease'. While we think that the use of the medical analogy is legitimate, and will help you to understand what we are saying, it has to be admitted that there is a severe limitation with the analogy when we discuss strategic marketing. In medicine, the patient and the doctor are collaborating towards the common goal of curing a disease. The disease is not an intelligent adversary, it does not predict the likely strategies employed by the doctor and devise counter-strategies. Strategic marketing, however, is concerned with situations in which the adversary is intelligent, does predict the likely strategies that you will employ, and does devise counter-strategies to defeat you. As Varadarajan and Jayachandran (1999, p. 125) put it: 'Competitive behaviour, the actions and reactions of competitors, is central to marketing strategy research and practice.'

The fact that you are engaging with an intelligent adversary, who will predict and react against your strategies, creates something of a paradox. The fundamental purpose of strategic marketing is to achieve and sustain a competitive advantage over rival firms. Is it possible to achieve a sustainable competitive advantage by employing strategic marketing techniques that are publicly available to everyone through the medium of textbooks such as this one? In the past, when far fewer managers experienced formal training in marketing, the answer might have been 'yes' because your rivals did not have equivalent general knowledge of marketing strategy. Today this is far less likely to be the case. The acquisition of general strategic marketing knowledge and skills is unlikely to bestow a real competitive advantage. Does that mean, then, that such knowledge and skills are useless? Absolutely not. In a world in which more and more business people have experienced formal training in strategic marketing, a business (or an individual) that is ignorant of strategic marketing principles is clearly at a competitive *disadvantage*. We do not claim that the knowledge and skills acquired through using this book will enable you effortlessly to develop marketing strategies that offer competitive advantage over rival firms. More likely, it will put you on a level playing field with your rivals.

QUESTION 2: WILL THIS BOOK GIVE YOU UNIVERSAL PRINCIPLES OF STRATEGIC MARKETING?

If this book is unlikely to provide you with a sustainable competitive advantage over your rivals, then you might expect that it would, at least, provide the universal principles of strategic marketing. Is this a reasonable expectation? Let us take a considered look at the type of knowledge that has gone into the book.

Rossiter (2001) has argued that marketing knowledge can be conveniently classified into four categories:

- Marketing concepts – the building blocks of marketing knowledge
- Structural frameworks – checklists and non-causal marketing models
- Strategic principles – marketing models that present causal links between marketing variables, and so suggest plausible courses of action under given circumstances ('if this is the case, then you should do the following')
- Research principles – marketing models that suggest the appropriate research techniques to use to achieve defined research objectives.

This book is very largely concerned with the middle two categories, structural frameworks and strategic principles. Our assumption is that anyone reading this book will have previously studied an introductory course in marketing, or have read an introductory textbook, so that the reader is familiar with basic marketing concepts. Many people reading this book will also have studied marketing research, and so be familiar with 'research principles'. This knowledge will certainly help in tackling the case studies, but is not essential in order to understand the concepts that are explained in the main text.

The main emphasis in this book is upon what Rossiter calls structural frameworks and strategic principles. There is an interesting distinction between these two categories that may not be immediately obvious to the marketing student or practitioner. Structural frameworks are essentially descriptive lists of concepts. Probably the most famous is the marketing mix itself (product, price, promotion and place, with the addition of people, physical evidence and process for service products). They are useful as a means of organising the thinking process, and can serve as a useful checklist to make sure that nothing important has been left out. However, they do have certain disadvantages. For example, it is desirable that a checklist should be comprehensive, yet simple. In practice these desirable characteristics tend to be contradictory. The more comprehensive a checklist becomes, the more complicated it is to use. We return to this theme in Chapter 6, where we discuss the various structural frameworks that have been suggested to model the marketing environment.

Strategic principles are prescriptions for managerial action, recommending what should be done when faced with a particular set of circumstances. For example, in Chapter 9 we discuss the circumstances in which it is appropriate to implement marketing strategies based on the deepening of relationships with customers. However, a word of caution is in order concerning the 'strategic principles' of marketing. We would agree with Rossiter when he argues:

> All strategic principles will be conditional. The conditionality is the 'context' of the principle's applicability ... It has become increasingly clear that there are no *universal* principles in marketing, not even the Marketing Concept, Market Segmentation, the Product Life Cycle, or Relationship Marketing. (Rossiter, 2001, p. 16)

QUESTION 3: WILL THIS BOOK TELL YOU HOW TO PLAN YOUR STRATEGY?

While it may not be able to give you a sustainable competitive advantage, or even tell you what are the universal principles of strategic marketing, surely this book will be able to tell you how to plan your strategy? That, you would think, must be a reasonable expectation. However, as you will appreciate by now, things are not quite as simple as they seem.

The idea of a strategy is most commonly understood to be a plan for the future. Mintzberg (1994) reviewed the history of strategic business planning. He showed that the predominant view is that strategic planning is a controlled, conscious, formalised process, largely conducted by an organisation's top management team. In this view of business strategy there is a clear and logical process by which the strategy is formulated. The process begins with data gathering and analysis, which is an essential input into the process of formulating strategic options that the firm may pursue. The formulation of options precedes the process of strategic choice, where decisions are made about which of the options will be selected. Finally, the selected strategy is implemented. However, in an earlier work Mintzberg had already pointed to an apparent paradox in strategic planning:

> Ask almost anyone what strategy is, and they will define it as a plan of some sort, an explicit guide to future behaviour. Then ask them what strategy a competitor or a government or even they themselves have actually pursued. Chances are that they will describe consistency in *past* behaviour – a pattern in action over time. Strategy, it turns out, is one of those words that people define in one way and often use in another, without realizing the difference. (Mintzberg, 1987, p. 66)

Mintzberg argues that people tend to think of strategy *in the abstract* as a plan for the future, but they tend to think of strategy *in practice* as a consistency in past behaviour.

This brings us to the important distinction between 'intended' or 'deliberate' strategy and 'emergent' strategy. Mintzberg (1994) claims that the realised strategy of an organisation comes about as a result of both deliberate and emergent strategy processes. The deliberate strategy process is the one described in the previous paragraph, with a neat progression through the steps of data gathering, analysis, formulation, choice, and then implementation. Emergent strategy, on the other hand, can only be recognised retrospectively. Emergent strategy is a pattern that emerges from the behaviour of an organisation over time. It is the result of the accumulated effect of decisions taken by the members of an organisation. For example, Brennan and Turnbull (1997, 1999) found that a supplier of automotive components had adapted the organisational structure and operating systems of the business so that they addressed the needs of a single, large car manufacturer. It was not, and never had been, the explicit strategy of the company to become more and more adapted to the needs of this single customer. Indeed, the explicit strategy of the company was to become less dependent on the car manufacturer, and to develop new business opportunities outside the car industry. However, by a long sequence of operational decisions taken by a wide range of managers over an extended period of time, the car components supplier had, in effect, implemented a strategy of ever-increasing adaptation to the needs of a single customer. In Mintzberg's terms this was the 'realised strategy' of the components suppliers, while the 'intended strategy' – to develop new lines of business – had so far remained unrealised. The 'realised strategy' emerged as a pattern in a stream of management decisions, but was never actually adopted as the formal strategy of the components supplier. (You can explore the strategic marketing dilemma faced by this components supplier further in the 'BriCol Engineering Ltd' case study to be found later in the book.)

In this book we will accept Mintzberg's fundamental argument that strategy (in this case marketing strategy) can be both deliberate and emergent. The structure of the book, as we will see in the next section, is broadly organised around the structure of a formal, planned approach to strategy making. However, that is not meant to suggest that strategy is only created through formal, planned systems – such as the marketing planning process that is described in Chapter 7. Strategy development is not a simple formulaic process in which a set of well-defined tools is applied to a body of data, and out pops the ideal strategy. Creativity, flexibility and serendipity also play their part in successful strategy development. However, all other things being equal, we would contend that the careful application of formal planning procedures improves the process of marketing strategy development.

THE ORGANISATION OF THIS BOOK

The book is divided into three parts: text, case studies and readings. Much the largest part of the book is the text. Here we present our own perspective on the substantial body of knowledge that has come to be accepted as the core of strategic marketing, and we go beyond this accepted core to explain some of the most recent developments in strategic marketing thinking. We begin, in Chapter 2, with a discussion of the nature of strategic marketing. There is considerable scope for confusion in the use of terminology in this field. For example, how are we to distinguish strategy from tactics, or from budgeting? How are we to distinguish marketing strategy from corporate strategy? Questions such as these are addressed in Chapter 2.

In Chapters 3 and 4 we examine contemporary thinking on consumer behaviour and organisational buying behaviour. Many of the themes and concepts that are tackled later in the book (such as market segmentation and relationship marketing) depend upon an understanding of these principles of buyer behaviour. Chapter 3 deals with the processes used by private consumers when making decisions about their own purchases, or about purchases on behalf of a household. The concepts discussed in Chapter 3 are important inputs to the process of marketing strategy development in consumer markets. Chapter 4 is concerned with the processes used by members of organisations when making organisational purchasing decisions. These concepts are key inputs to the development of marketing strategies in industrial or business-to-business markets such as in marketing filtration systems to food or chemical manufacturers.

Chapters 5 to 8 deal with the commonly accepted heart of strategic marketing – the analysis of the environment and the development of marketing strategy. The marketing environment is usually subdivided into the competitive environment and the macroenvironment. Chapter 5 deals with the forces that shape the competitive environment, focusing particularly on the underlying conditions of demand and supply in the market, and the 'five forces' of competition (direct rivalry, new entry, substitutes, power of buyers, power of suppliers) identified by Michael Porter (1980). In Chapter 6 we introduce models that can be used to structure the macroenvironment and to allocate priorities to environmental forces, and discuss some key contemporary issues such as the increasing average age of the population and its implications for marketers. Chapters 7 and 8 then present a total of 15 'Key Concepts' of strategic marketing. These 'Key Concepts' range from elementary structural frameworks such as the SWOT (strengths, weaknesses, opportunities and threats), to quite complex technical analytical procedures, including discounted cash-flow analysis. It is unusual to find a discussion of discounted cash-flow analysis in a strategic marketing textbook. However, in order to understand certain other very important strategic marketing concepts (value-based marketing in Chapter 7, and the life-time value of a customer in Chapter 9) it is essential to have a grasp of discounted cash flow.

In Chapters 9, 10 and 11 we explore the application of strategic marketing in three particularly important contemporary contexts. Relationship marketing has been defined in many ways. The one feature that is stable is the focus of the marketer on retaining customers as well as attracting new customers – a focus that goes beyond one single transaction between a buyer and a seller. How this can be done and how effective such strategies are in different types of market are discussed in Chapter 9. Chapter 10 looks at the growing impact of the Internet on marketing strategy. Then in Chapter 11 we look at a characteristically modern phenomenon – the extension of formalised strategic marketing into aspects of life that until recently were considered to be outside marketing's scope. The particular foci of Chapter 11 are marketing by football clubs and marketing by political parties. Of course, both types of organisation have used elements of the marketing mix for many years, most notably marketing communications. However, what has emerged recently is a much more strategic approach to marketing, emphasising the use of marketing research, market segmentation and relationship marketing strategies.

Chapter 12 forms a link between the first part of the book (the text) and the second (the case studies). In this chapter we discuss the value of case studies as a method of learning about strategic marketing, present a structured approach to case study analysis, and provide guidance on the effective communication of case study analysis in writing and in face-to-face presentations.

As we explain in Chapter 12, one of the difficulties in learning about strategic marketing is that most students cannot practise what they learn in a real organisation. The 15 case studies that form Part Two of the book provide opportunities to practise the skills of strategic marketing. All but two of the case studies describe undisguised, real circumstances and real organisations. The remaining two case studies (BriCol Engineering Ltd and Trouble with the CPC100) are based on real circumstances and real organisations, but have been disguised to protect the anonymity of the people involved. We have striven to provide a wide range of case studies so as to illustrate strategic marketing in a wide range of contexts. The 'products' involved range across industrial goods (BriCol Engineering Ltd), business services (The Chartered Institute of Marketing), consumer services (Fulham FC) and consumer goods (A Tale of Two Wine Brands).

In Part Three we provide a small selection of readings that give more extensive treatment of some of the themes that we discuss in Part One. It should be emphasised that we have not aimed to provide a complete set of readings that would adequately support an in-depth course in strategic marketing. Rather, we have provided a small selection of readings that is clearly and directly related to major themes in our text, which will illustrate the benefits that can be obtained from engaging with the extensive literature that exists on strategic marketing. Those readers who are sufficiently enthused by this taster to want to explore further should use the references at the end of each chapter as a guide.

References

Brennan, R and Turnbull, P W (1997), 'The Process of Adaptation in Inter-firm Relationships', in Gemunden, H-G, Ritter, T and Walter, A (eds) *Relationships and Networks in International Markets*, Oxford: Elsevier/Pergamon, Chapter 5

Brennan, R and Turnbull, P W (1999), 'Adaptive Behavior in Buyer-supplier Relationships', *Industrial Marketing Management*, **28**: 481–95

Mintzerg, H (1987), 'Crafting Strategy', *Harvard Business Review*, (July/August): 66–75

Mintzberg, H (1994), *The Rise and Fall of Strategic Planning*, Hemel Hempstead: Prentice Hall

Parasuraman, A, Zeithaml, V A and Berry, L L (1985), 'A Conceptual Model of Service Quality and its Implications for Future Research', *Journal of Marketing*, **49**(Fall): 41–50

Porter, M E (1980), *Competitive Strategy*, New York: Free Press

Rossiter, J R (2001), 'What is Marketing Knowledge? Stage 1: Forms of Marketing Knowledge', *Marketing Theory*, **1**(1): 9–26

Varadarajan, P R and Jayachandran, S (1999), 'Marketing Strategy: An Assessment of the Field and Outlook', *Journal of the Academy of Marketing Science*, **27**(2): 120–43

chapter two

What is Strategic Marketing?

Learning objectives

By reading this chapter you will learn:

- The distinction between strategy and tactics
- The differences between corporate strategy and competitive strategy
- The differences between corporate strategy and marketing strategy
- What is meant by effectiveness and efficiency in marketing
- The defining characteristics of strategic marketing.

INTRODUCTION

In this chapter a number of important questions are addressed, starting with the very nature of strategy itself. Once we have an understanding of the nature of strategy, then we are in a position to address the nature of strategic marketing, and to differentiate strategic marketing from a simple 'forecasting and budgeting' approach. Having established a sound understanding of the nature of strategy and strategic marketing, in chapters that follow the elements of the strategic marketing planning process are introduced and explained.

WHAT IS STRATEGY?

> It is hard to imagine a business conversation today that does not include the word *strategy*. We talk about Microsoft's strategy in software, Coca-Cola's strategy in China, McDonald's human resource strategies, IBM's marketing strategies, Intel's technology strategy, and so on. Its frequent use would suggest that the term *strategy* is unambiguous and its meaning well understood. Unfortunately, it is not. (De Kluyver, 2000, p. 3)

De Kluyver is surely correct when he asserts that the word 'strategy' has become one of the most frequently used words in the business lexicon. Indeed, 'strategy' may well be one of the most overused words in the English language. It often seems as though the word is used simply to emphasise that the writer (or the speaker) thinks that something is important. When we talk about strategic marketing or strategic market planning, however, we are using the word in a more precise sense. The original meaning of strategy is derived from the military application of the word, where strategy is concerned with the overall disposition of forces in a military campaign. Tactical decisions are those decisions taken on the ground, by operational military commanders, often in the heat of battle and in direct response to an enemy manoeuvre. Strategic decisions concern the identification of high-level military objectives and the disposition of forces to achieve these; central to such decisions is the fact that there is an enemy who is also making strategic decisions and who can be expected to try to anticipate and thwart our strategy. In business strategy, and in marketing strategy, this military analogy can be helpful. Strategic marketing decisions are made away from the scene of marketing warfare, and concern the overall disposition of marketing 'forces'. Tactical marketing decisions are made in the heat of the marketing battle, often in direct response to a competitor initiative.

The analogy between military strategy and marketing strategy has been explored by John Saunders (1994). Some of the suggestions that emerge from the military analogy are of potential value to marketing strategists. For example, military strategy would suggest that you should not engage in a frontal assault on a powerful and well-entrenched enemy, since the chances of success are very poor. It makes more sense to adopt an outflanking strategy, or to engage in guerrilla warfare against such an enemy. These are useful analogies. The chances of achieving success by attacking a well-established market leader by adopting a similar marketing mix are slim. An outflanking strategy (developing a 'next generation' product) or a guerrilla strategy (picking off niche markets one by one) is more likely to succeed. However, it is possible to go too far with the military analogy. Increasingly, marketing strategists are finding that their competitors in one market are their collaborators in a strategic alliance in another market. Your competitor in one product area could be your supplier in another product area, and perhaps your customer in yet another area. Hence, naive military analogies focusing on the sole aim of destroying the enemy have only a limited role in marketing strategy.

Buzzell and Gale (1987, p. 18) defined strategy as: 'The policies and key decisions adopted by management that have *major* impacts on financial performance. These policies and decisions usually involve significant resource commitments and are not easily reversible.'

They made the distinction, which is today widely accepted, between *business unit strategy* and *corporate strategy*. Business unit strategy is concerned with how an individual business competes with its rivals, what it does and what it could do to stay in business and beat the competition. Corporate strategy is concerned with decisions made in an organisation comprising multiple businesses (often called strategic business units, or simply SBUs). Questions of corporate strategy concern the overall shape of the corporation, which SBUs should form part of the overall portfolio, and the way in which key resources (such as investment capital) should be divided between them. *Strategic marketing management is concerned with business unit strategy, also known as competitive strategy*.

Strategy is concerned with strategic decision-making. McDonald (1996) identified four characteristics of strategic decisions. First, they are concerned with the long-term orientation of the organisation, rather than day-to-day management issues. Second, strategic decisions define the scope of the organisation's activities, selecting what it will do and what it will not do. The third and fourth characteristics of strategic decisions both concern *matching* of the organisation's activities – they have to be matched to the external environment, and they have to be matched to its resource capacity. There is no point in setting objectives and devising strategies that are unconnected to the realities of the business environment, nor is there any point in pursuing strategies that cannot be implemented using the available resources.

WHAT IS THE DIFFERENCE BETWEEN STRATEGY AND TACTICS?

> A strategic decision involves the creation, change or retention of a strategy. In contrast to a tactical decision, a strategic decision is usually costly in terms of the resources and time required to reverse or change it. The cost of altering a wrong decision may be so high as to threaten the very existence of an organisation. Normally, a strategic decision has a time frame greater than one year; sometimes decades are involved. (Aaker, 1998, p. 18)

> Tactical manoeuvres tend to be sufficient to cope only with short-term and localised conditions and circumstances. They are only effective in the long term and on a large scale if they are co-ordinated and integrated within a more broadly based strategic framework. (Baker, 1992, p. 3)

There is no doubt that the distinction between strategy and tactics causes a lot of confusion. Yet the quotations from Aaker and Baker would tend to suggest that there is a clear distinction between the two concepts. While this is certainly true conceptually, there is little doubt that business people, students and scholars often become confused in practice. Broadly speaking, strategic decisions are important decisions, that will affect the direction of the business for a long time, and that have a considerable impact on the way in which organisational resources are allocated. Practical implications of this are that strategic decisions are usually taken by senior members of the organisation (in a large firm, by top executives, in a small firm, by the owner-manager), and that decision-making can be a lengthy process. For example, the decision by the German automobile group BMW to divest itself of the British manufacturer Rover Group was a strategic decision involving top managers and a great deal of information gathering and analysis. Clearly, this decision would have a major impact on the future of the BMW group. Tactical decisions, on the other hand, are made by members of the organisation at many different levels, and are often made quickly. For example, a sales executive may have to make a decision within seconds while sitting in a client's office – would the offer of a small additional discount be enough to win a substantial order?

McDonald (1999) made *time* the key factor distinguishing strategic planning from tactical planning. He defined a strategic plan as a plan that covers a period beyond the next fiscal year, usually three to five years, while a tactical plan goes into great detail about actions to be undertaken in the short term (usually one year or less). McDonald's conclusions about the depth of understanding of strategic marketing among marketing practitioners were not flattering (p. 31, emphasis in original):

> Few practising marketers understand the real significance of a *strategic* marketing plan as opposed to a *tactical*, or operational marketing plan ... Most managers prefer to sell the products they find easiest to sell to those customers who offer the least line of resistance. By developing short-term, tactical marketing plans first and then extrapolating them, managers merely succeed in extrapolating their own shortcomings.

Two key themes recur frequently in the extensive work done by Malcolm McDonald, Europe's leading expert on marketing planning. First, that strategic marketing makes a difference to company performance; second, that the level of understanding of strategic marketing is low among practising marketing managers. It follows from McDonald's analysis that an understanding of strategic marketing can create a career edge for the aspiring marketing practitioner.

WHAT IS STRATEGIC MARKETING?

According to the Chartered Institute of Marketing, marketing is the management process which identifies, anticipates and supplies customer requirements effectively and at a profit. Baker (1992, p. 20, emphasis in original) argued that marketing 'is concerned with the *establishment of mutually satisfying exchange relationships in which the judgements as to what is satisfying depend upon the perception of the parties to the exchange*'.

A great deal of practical marketing concerns the day-to-day tasks of ensuring that the product or service, as it currently exists, is delivered successfully to existing customers. Indeed, the day-to-day pressures of achieving this can very easily drive out of the heads of managers any concern for the products, services and customers of the day after tomorrow. Yet, as we all know, consumer tastes can easily change, and wider conditions affecting marketing success – such as competitors, government regulation and the state of the national economy – seldom stay the same for long. Strategic marketing is concerned with identifying changes in the market and the business environment, and then ensuring that the firm is well prepared to meet them. It involves looking beyond the day-to-day marketing battleground, reflecting upon the key changes that lie ahead and deciding how the firm will respond to them. However easy this may sound in principle, many firms, particularly small and medium-sized enterprises (SMEs), find it difficult to put into practice (McDonald, 1989; Lancaster and Waddelow, 1998).

Jain (2000) identified the salient features of strategic marketing:

- *Emphasis on long-term implications*. Since strategic marketing decisions take a long-term perspective, this makes it more likely that changes in the external business environment will affect such decisions. That is why monitoring the business environment is such a central element of strategic marketing planning.
- *Corporate inputs*. Day-to-day tactical marketing decisions can often be made without reference to the broader activities of the firm. Strategic marketing decisions have much wider-reaching implications, and so require a whole-firm perspective. Jain suggests that in making strategic marketing decisions, managers need to consider the corporate culture, the corporate stakeholders and corporate resources.
- *Varying roles for different products/markets*. Strategic marketing means looking at the whole of a company's portfolio of products and markets, and managing the portfolio to achieve the company's overall goals. The result could be that decisions are made not to invest in certain products or markets, in order to release resources to be invested elsewhere in the portfolio, where the opportunities are judged to be greater.

Lambin (1997, pp. 8–10) differentiated between *strategic marketing* and *operational marketing*. The role of strategic marketing is to 'lead the firm towards attractive economic opportunities; that is, opportunities that are adapted to its resources and know-how and offer a potential for growth and profitability'. On the other hand, operational marketing 'is an action-oriented process which is extended over a short- to medium-term planning horizon and targets existing markets and segments'. In other words, operational marketing (which is synonymous with tactical marketing) is concerned with doing what we already do as effectively and efficiently as we can. Strategic marketing is concerned with identifying important changes taking place in the market and in the business environment, and working out how the organisation should respond.

A brief digression at this point is worthwhile to look at the distinction between effectiveness and efficiency. In everyday language the two words mean roughly the same thing. In the language of marketing, however, they are used to differentiate two distinct concepts. A simple definition of effectiveness would be 'doing the right things'. For example, to be effective a marketing organisation must have a portfolio of products and services that are well designed to meet the needs of the market. A simple definition of efficiency is 'doing things right'. For example, to be efficient a marketing organisation must monitor the performance of the sales force against target, and take corrective action where underperformance is detected. It is quite possible to be effective but inefficient – for example, to have a poorly motivated or poorly trained sales force trying to sell an excellent portfolio of products. It is equally possible to be efficient but ineffective – for example, to have an excellent customer service department delivering exemplary speed of response to customer enquiries, but to have a poor product range. Naturally, marketing organisations will aim to be both efficient and effective, since long-term survival is threatened by the absence of either. As we will see in the chapters that follow, the principal realm of strategic marketing is marketing effectiveness. The main job of the marketing strategist is to make sure that the organisation is 'doing the right things'. However, even when developing marketing strategy it would be foolhardy to neglect issues of efficiency. Certainly, when conducting a strategic audit (see Chapter 7), the relative efficiency of one's own marketing operations compared with key competitors will be an important consideration. It remains the case, though, that strategic marketing is primarily concerned with marketing effectiveness.

WHAT IS THE DIFFERENCE BETWEEN PLANNING AND FORECASTING OR BUDGETING?

Many authors in the field of strategic market planning emphasise the gulf that separates planning from forecasting and budgeting. It is a common misconception that a forecast and budget constitutes a 'business plan'. The forecast projects demand for the organisation's products and services and can be used, with the addition of pricing assumptions, to project revenues. The budget is a projection of the direct and indirect costs that the business expects to incur based on the sales forecasts. Both the forecast and the budget are a proper part of the marketing planning process – it is essential to have a forecast and a budget for at least the next twelve months as a component of the marketing plan itself. However, the forecast and budget are not a substitute for the full plan and the planning process underlying it. The sales forecast and budget are the logical consequence of the planning process. After a careful analysis of the business environment, of market and competitive trends, and a process of matching the resources of the firm to those trends resulting in broad statements of marketing strategy, then it makes sense to think in terms of concrete sales forecasts and their budgetary consequences.

HOW DOES STRATEGIC MARKETING FIT WITH CORPORATE STRATEGY?

> Corporate strategy is concerned with an organisation's basic direction for the future: its purpose, its ambitions, its resources and how it interacts with the world in which it operates.
>
> Every aspect of the organisation plays a role in this strategy – its people, its finances, its production methods and its environment (including its customers). (Lynch, 2000, p. 5)

It is quite easy to confuse strategic marketing and corporate strategy. Both are concerned with *big* decisions – taking effect over a long period, having considerable resource implications, being made by top managers. However, strategic marketing is concerned with a narrower range of decisions than strategic management and is focused at the level of *business unit* or *competitive strategy*, rather than at the corporate level. Lynch (2000) explained the broader nature of corporate strategy in terms of six key points:

1. Corporate strategy involves the entire organisation.
2. Corporate strategy is likely to concern itself with the survival of the business as a minimum objective and the creation of value added as a maximum objective.
3. Corporate strategy covers the range and depth of the organisation's activities.
4. Corporate strategy directs the changing and evolving relationship of the organisation with its environment.
5. Corporate strategy is central to the development of sustainable competitive advantage.
6. Corporate strategy development is crucial to adding value.

Strategic marketing management shares several of these characteristics. In particular the development of sustainable competitive advantage is central to strategic marketing, and there is a very strong case that strategic marketing is crucial to adding value (see Chapter 7 and Doyle (2000) on value-based marketing). However, strategic marketing does not involve the entire organisation, nor does it cover the full range and depth of the organisation's activities. The focus of strategic marketing is on products, markets and the management of relationships with customers, both actual and potential. Of course, it can be argued that customers are so important to the organisation that all strategic decisions should spring from an understanding of customer wants and needs, and therefore from a marketing perspective. This is a powerful argument. Nevertheless, many important strategic decisions – for example the balance between debt and equity financing, sources of supply for critical inputs to the production (or service delivery) process, the recruitment and retention of key staff – are rather remote from strategic marketing. Such issues *are* proper considerations for corporate strategy.

SUMMARY

'Strategy' is an overused word. In marketing terms, its use should be restricted to important decisions that will have a major effect on the future of the organisation. Strategic marketing decisions are concerned primarily with ensuring the effectiveness of the marketing organisation in the competitive struggle. Effectiveness is about 'doing the right things', whereas efficiency is about 'doing things right'. Corporate strategy is a broader concept than strategic marketing, incorporating, for example, issues to do with finance, human resources and manufacturing or service operations, as well as marketing matters. Forecasting and budgeting are a logical component of the strategic market planning process, but should not be confused for the process itself.

Questions for discussion

1. What distinguishes strategic business decisions from tactical business decisions?
2. What is meant by competitive strategy, and how does it differ from corporate strategy?
3. What are the key characteristics of strategic marketing?
4. What is a 'forecasting and budgeting' approach to marketing planning, and how would you differentiate it from strategic marketing?

References

Aaker, D A (1998), *Strategic Marketing Management*, New York: Wiley

Baker, M J (1992), *Marketing Strategy and Management*, Basingstoke: Macmillan – now Palgrave Macmillan

Buzzell, R D and Gale, B T (1987), *The PIMS Principles: Linking Strategy to Performance*, New York: Free Press

De Kluyver, C A (2000), *Strategic Thinking: An Executive Perspective*, Englewood Cliffs, NJ: Prentice Hall

Doyle, P (2000), *Value Based Marketing: Marketing Strategies for Corporate Growth and Shareholder Value*, Chichester: John Wiley & Sons

Jain, S C (2000), *Marketing Planning and Strategy*, 6th edn, Cincinnati: South-Western College Publishing

Lambin, J-J (1997), *Strategic Marketing Management*, Maidenhead: McGraw-Hill

Lancaster, G and Waddelow, I (1998), 'An Empirical Investigation into the Process of Strategic Marketing Planning: Its Attendant Problems, and Towards a New Practical Paradigm', *Journal of Marketing Management*, **14**(8): 853–78

Lynch, R (2000), *Corporate Strategy*, 2nd edn, Harlow: Financial Times/Prentice Hall

McDonald, M (1989), 'Ten Barriers to Marketing Planning', *Journal of Marketing Management*, **5**(1): 1–18

McDonald, M (1996), 'Strategic Marketing Planning: Theory, Practice and Research Agendas', *Journal of Marketing Management*, **12**(1–3): 5–27

McDonald, M (1999), *Marketing Plans: How to Prepare Them, How to Use Them*, 4th edn, Oxford: Butterworth Heinemann

Saunders, J (1994), 'Marketing and Competitive Success', in Baker, M J (ed.) *The Marketing Book*, 3rd edn, Oxford: Butterworth Heinemann, pp. 11–32

chapter three

Understanding Consumer Behaviour

Learning objectives

By reading this chapter you will learn:

- What consumer behaviour is and why it is so important to strategic planners
- How an individual's psychological make-up affects consumption behaviour
- How consumer decisions are routinely affected not only by personal factors, but also by the consumer's social and cultural context
- Details of a variety of models that have been developed to help us better understand consumption behaviour
- The strategic implications of the study of consumer behaviour for the field of marketing.

INTRODUCTION

Effective strategic marketing requires business planners to be almost obsessive about understanding the needs of their customers. In today's highly competitive global environment, the success of any consumer-focused programme will almost certainly involve imaginative product development, integrated distribution methods, well-calibrated pricing and state-of-the-art communications. This chapter and the next deal with the key issues of how customers make buying decisions and what factors influence those buying decisions. In this chapter the focus is on the private consumer, making buying decisions on his or her own behalf, or on behalf of a private household. In the next chapter we will look at organisational buyers, who make buying decisions on behalf of a business or another kind of organisation (such as a charity or a hospital). Examples of private consumer decision-making (which we call 'consumer behaviour') include shopping decisions in supermarkets, clothes stores, restaurants, and the selection of where to go for the annual family holiday. Examples of organisational decision-making ('organisational buying behaviour') include decisions about which advertising agency to use, which company to give an office cleaning contract to and the bulk purchase of coffee beans for use in the manufacture of instant coffee.

In this chapter, we begin by considering a few fundamental definitions and then move on to consider the buying decision process itself. To do this well, first we need to investigate the inner-determinants or psychological dimensions of people's behaviour. Following that we turn our attention to the impact of social context on consumption behaviour. We move on to look at the evolution of useful models in this field, then we consider some of the more pivotal strategic marketing implications of this knowledge. The chapter concludes with a look into the future by considering some of the more interesting developments currently unfolding.

WHAT IS CONSUMER BEHAVIOUR AND WHERE DOES IT COME FROM?

For the purposes of this chapter a 'consumer' requires goods and services of all types for personal as well as household usage. Sometimes referred to as client, patron, shopper or simply customer, each consumer is something of an enigma to marketers. How does he or she perceive products, brands, stores or even entire organizations? How are individual product choices made? Is customer loyalty attainable? Is the consumer genuinely interested in engaging in a long-term buying relationship with a particular merchant? The field of consumer behaviour has emerged in recent years to help strategic marketers better understand critically important issues such as these.

Schiffman and Kanuk (2000) describe consumer behaviour quite simply as an investigation into the way individuals make decisions on how to spend their available resources (time, money, effort) on personal and household products. Sheth et al. (1999) add that the consumer may act as buyer, payer, user or any combination of these roles at any given time. An even more comprehensive view can found in Hoyer and MacInnis (2001). They suggest that a proper study of consumer behaviour ought to consider what occurs before people consume something, what goes on during the consumption period itself and how consumers handle the disposal of what they have consumed.

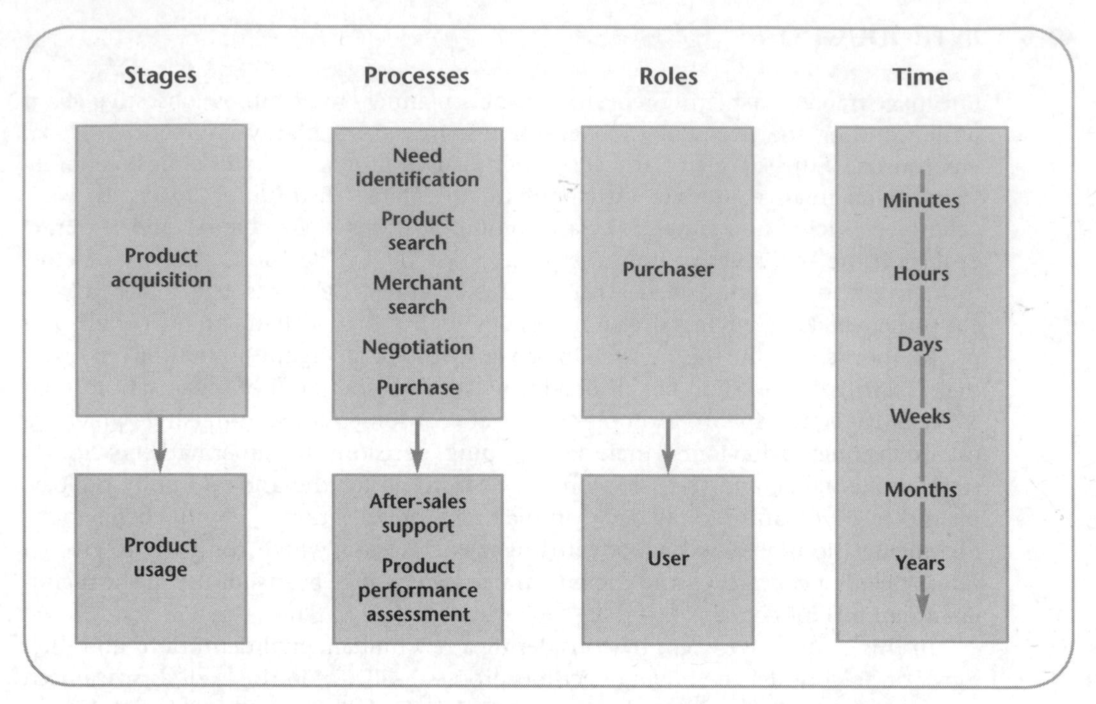

Figure 3.1 A consolidated view of consumer behaviour

Figure 3.1 represents an attempt to consolidate the views of the authors above into a single model. Here, the word 'products' is used in the largest possible sense to include goods, services, artistic works, events, ideologies and so forth.

This holistic view of consumer behaviour illustrates the truly multifaceted nature of this relatively new field of inquiry. A greater understanding of customers has become invaluable to market researchers and strategic decision-makers the world over.

THE CONSUMER BEHAVIOUR PROCESS

To begin unraveling the many mysteries of the consumer's mind, today's researchers typically draw from many fields: psychology (experimental, clinical, developmental, social), micro/macroeconomics, sociology, semiotics, demography, anthropology and so on. The central theme is simply to interpret human consumption behaviour so that marketers can improve their efficacy. Although a myriad of approaches have been tried over the past 50 years or so, current thinking in this field tends to focus on two interrelated behavioural dimensions, namely inner-determinants and social context. The following sections attempt to address elements of each of these in turn.

INNER-DETERMINANTS OF CONSUMER BEHAVIOUR

First we need to look at the consumer as a unique person whose psychological make-up has considerable effect on day-to-day consumption patterns. Each and every day we all have needs to be satisfied, we experience drives that condition our actions, we take in thousands of sensory perceptions that require interpretation, we learn, we formulate attitudes and beliefs, and somehow find time to develop an individual personality in the process. Researchers have found it useful to explore these inner-determinants of our behaviour in considerable detail.

Needs and motives

Simply put, needs are a lack of something useful. Human beings find many things useful, from a simple sandwich to spiritual wellbeing. Probably the most widely used model illustrating the range of human needs is psychologist Abraham Maslow's hierarchy of needs (Maslow, 1970). He believed that in much of the Western world people tend to satisfy their lower level needs first, then move on to satisfying higher needs. From lowest to highest his hierarchy of needs looks like this:

1. *Physiological needs* such as sustenance and reproduction.
2. *Safety needs* such as protection and shelter.
3. *Social needs* such as love and togetherness.
4. *Esteem needs* including recognition, status and self-esteem.
5. *Self-actualisation* needs leading to the full development of one's potential.

Depending on our age, degree of education, income, country of birth and so on, each of us tries to satisfy a number of needs each and every day. Because effective marketing is fundamentally about satisfying customer needs well, marketing scholars Sheth et al. (1999) have identified five sets of needs which underpin most of our consumption choices:

1. *Functional needs* are met by a product that simply does 'what it says on the tin' such as paint or shampoo.

2. More sophisticated *social needs* are satisfied by goods and services that provide associations with societal segments (for example the clothes you choose to wear may indicate membership of a certain social group); such 'branded' products are often selected on the basis of what they say about the consumer.

3. Consumers also buy products that help satisfy their *emotional needs*. We make purchases that help us express our love, regret, sympathy and so on.

4. *Epistemic needs* refer to our tendency to want to explore the unknown. We buy books, travel abroad and take classes for this reason.

5. Finally, *situational needs* are those contingent upon time and place. We often make unplanned purchases when unexpected events pop up.

Once we have a better understanding of the nature and variety of our needs, we ought to turn our attention to the relationship between needs and motivation. Motives are simply the inner drives that move us to act this way or that. Our physical activities (including shopping) are 'driven' by our desire to satisfy our needs. This process is illustrated by the example featured in Figure 3.2.

Figure 3.2 Satisfying needs

This cartoon character could be you. At first you are sitting comfortably in your favourite chair reading a highly engaging novel. You are alone for hours, uninterrupted. After some time you have trouble concentrating on the story because your stomach is starting to hurt. It gets worse and you put down the book. You realise that you are very hungry. You have not eaten for hours and hunger has now set in. You trot off to the kitchen and make yourself a quick meal. Once satiated you hurry back to your chair hopefully to finish the story before anyone comes home.

What we have here is a typical situation involving needs, motives, perceptions, consumption behaviour and the like. To start off you are in a situation of relative 'balance'; your needs (relaxation, entertainment, knowledge) are being met rather well. When hunger sets in, a very strong need (nutrition, sustenance) has become predominant and you are driven to satisfy it promptly. A merchant had sold you some frozen chips, burgers and cola a few days ago and you are driven to consume these to overcome your hunger. Satisfied, you then return to your chair to finish the book.

Perception

In addition to wanting to satisfy our various needs, our consumption behaviour is also influenced by the ways in which we perceive our world. At each waking moment, our senses – sight, hearing, smell, taste and touch – allow a steady stream of sensory inputs to penetrate our being. These sensations are then processed by the brain and, little by little, they contribute to the formulation of attitudes and beliefs we come to hold about our world and the product choices we make each day.

It is interesting to recall here that successful marketers are those who manage to 'position' their products favourably in our minds. They use every single component of their marketing programme (place, price, promotion and so on) to ensure we develop a positive mind-set about their product, their brand, their store, their organisation.

Learning and memory

We humans are fundamentally somewhat lazy! We prefer to save time and energy by storing information that might be useful to us down the road. As each day passes we process and reprocess information about our world. We 'memorise' useful information and experiences, and this in turn allows us to 'learn' about behaviours that are particularly helpful to us. Researchers have found that sometimes our learning is triggered by outside forces (behavioural learning) and that, at other times, we take full control (cognitive learning).

In marketing, a widely used form of behavioural learning is instrumental conditioning. For example, our shopping behaviour may well be 'shaped' by grocery retailer XYZ who regularly provides rewards such as discounts, vouchers and loyalty points for buying XYZ branded merchandise. Cognitive learning on the other hand is normally under the consumer's control. Rather than simply responding to behavioural incentives, the consumer acts as problem-solver. An automotive dealer, for example, may provide information, make suggestions and even offer a test drive but, ultimately, the buyer will consider all the facts intently and will probably make a choice based on internal reflections and feelings. Regardless of how we learn, if it were not for our memory we would not learn at all. Figure 3.3 illustrates the way behaviourists see our memory systems.

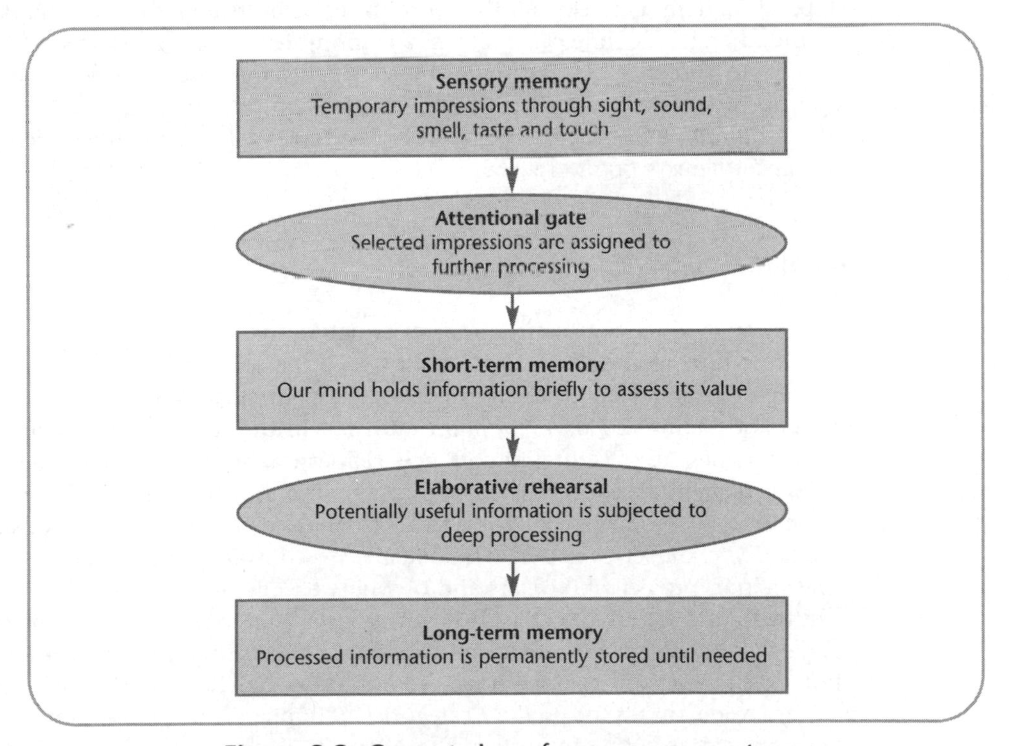

Figure 3.3 Current view of our memory systems

We can see that marketing messages must first make it through the consumer's 'attentional gate' (in competition with a lot of clutter). Once the information about a particular brand or store is in short-term memory, the consumer will quickly decide whether or not to place this information into long-term memory or not. The figure suggests that we go through a process of 'elaborative rehearsal' as we attach deep meaning to these inputs. This explains how we formulate, over time, certain positive (or negative) attitudes about products and organisations. Later on, when we need something, these favourable brands will be evoked in our minds and we will purchase the product with the most favourable position in our minds.

Attitudes

Favourable attitudes are important to marketers simply because it is much easier (and less costly) to maintain a customer's positive attitude rather than to try and turn around an attitude that may have gone sour. For example, many of the world's largest telecommunications firms (most being ex-monopolies) find themselves constantly battling to arrest the loss of market share to smaller, more nimble competitors. These new competitors are quick to exploit a new attitude among consumers in terms of their new freedom to switch to a supplier they consider to be more favourable. Peter et al. (1999, p. 117) suggest that: 'Today, most researchers agree that the one-dimensional concept of attitude, which defines attitude as a person's favourable or unfavourable feelings towards an object, is most useful.' The object can be, for example, a good, service, ideology or belief system.

At this point it may be useful to discuss briefly the notion of 'persuasion'. Dubois (2000, p. 124) attempts to explain this word in terms of its application to marketing: 'One could, therefore, define persuasion as a communication aimed at influencing the attitudes of an audience.' He continues by suggesting that there are two alternative strategies for persuading someone: through adaptation or by disruption. The former involves moulding a message to pre-existing attitudes, while the latter attempts to modify the audience's point of view.

Personality

To conclude our discussion concerning inner-determinants of consumption behaviour, we now turn to the idea of personality. As a 'person' each one of us enjoys a unique set of characteristics and attributes. These in turn delineate our identity. Schiffman and Kanuk (2000, p. 95) point out that 'In the study of personality, three distinct properties are of central importance: (1) personality reflects individual differences; (2) personality is consistent and enduring; and (3) personality can change.'

Our personality comes from within and is then projected outwards. As consumers, we tend to depict ourselves to the world outside. We constantly pick and choose products that help us project who we are and/or who we aspire to be.

Schiffman and Kanuk (2000, p. 109) also suggest that even brands can be said to have a personality. Exposed to clever and consistent advertising, consumers eventually 'attribute various descriptive "personality-like" traits or characteristics to different brands in a wide variety of product categories'. Shoppers will see certain products/ brands as rugged, exciting, sophisticated and so on. Such a 'position' in consumers' minds may be exploited repeatedly by marketing professionals skilled in new product development, package design, advertising, point-of-sale promotions and so on.

IMPACT OF SOCIAL CONTEXT ON CONSUMER BEHAVIOUR

We have seen that the behaviour of individual consumers is routinely influenced by inner-determinants such as our needs, drives, beliefs and personality. We now turn our attention to the many external forces that affect the way we shop. In particular marketing decision-makers need to understand the impact of culture, social class and groups.

Culture

Although, as we have seen, attitudes are typically personal in nature, researchers believe they are nonetheless formed primarily as a result of cultural influences. Rice (1997, p. 70) reminds us that culture can be defined as 'The values, attitudes, beliefs, ideas, artifacts and other meaningful symbols represented in the pattern of life adopted by people that help them interpret, evaluate and communicate as members of a society.' To illustrate this more clearly, Rice suggests we look at culture as originating in our institutions (religion, politics, language and so on) and culminating in a set of collective attitudes and behaviours, as illustrated in Figure 3.4.

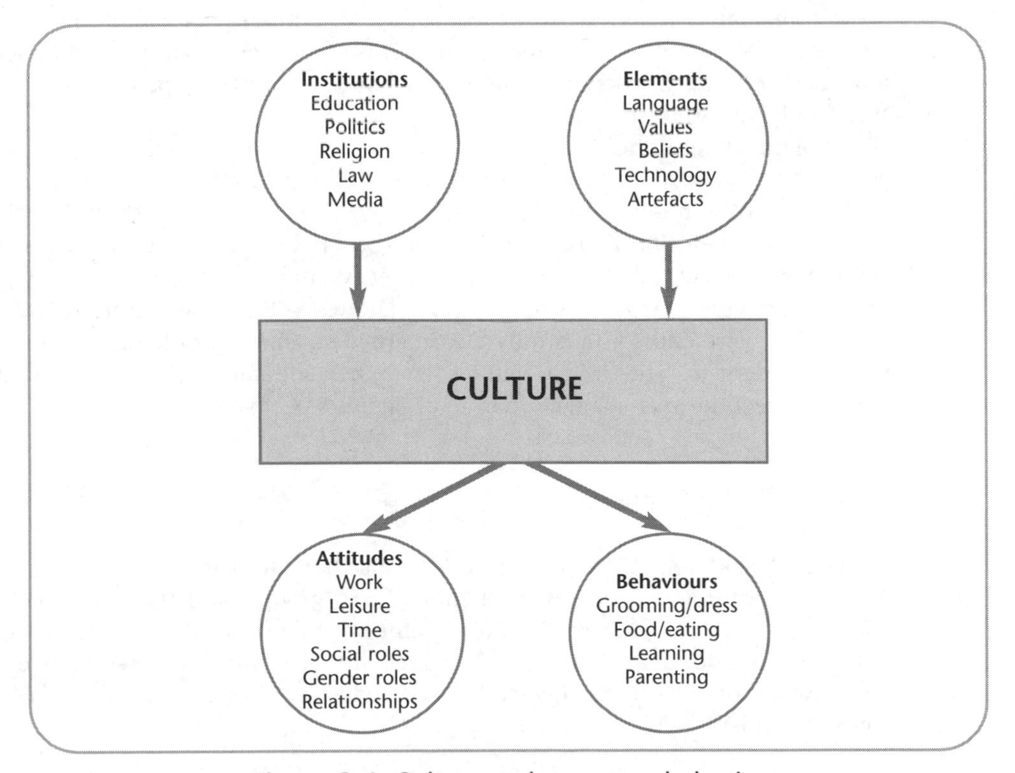

Figure 3.4 Culture and consumer behaviour

Accordingly, Solomon et al. (1999, p. 106) state that 'enculturation' can be described as 'learning the beliefs and behaviours endorsed by one's own culture'. The authors also define 'acculturation' as 'the process of movement and adaptation to one country's cultural environment by a person from another country' (p. 431). There is little doubt that in today's global environment, marketers can improve their retail effectiveness significantly by carefully analysing 'local' cultural circumstances.

Social class

Researchers have long understood that most humans the world over much prefer socialisation to a life of solitude. Everywhere we go we can see that people are grouped into distinct communities, each with its own characteristics and behaviours. A useful approach, particularly in the West, has been to regroup consumers into six categories according to a combination of three key factors, namely social standing, occupation and income:

1. Upper-upper class (old money)
2. Lower-upper class (nouveaux riches)
3. Upper-middle class (managers)
4. Lower-middle class (skilled workers)
5. Upper-lower class (unskilled workers)
6. Lower-lower class (not working/fixed income)

Marketing strategists can use this classification in a number of ways: one country or region can be compared with another in terms of market potentiality, product portfolio decisions can be better balanced, consumer aspirations can be observed more specifically and so forth.

Looking at consumers in this way leads us to the notion of 'lifestyle', defined by Assael (1998, p. 421) as 'consumers' modes of living as reflected in their attitudes, interests, and opinions'. Most marketers like to think of lifestyle simply as the way people spend their time and their money. In the UK, for example, a highly resourceful website operated by CACI Ltd (www.upmystreet.com) provides detailed lifestyle information for every postcode in the country. The way people eat, drink, spend leisure time, vote, work and so on is fully documented so that a profile of each postcode's typical resident may be easily obtained. These behavioural profiles are updated regularly to reflect the ever-changing nature of people's behaviour.

Social/group influences

Hoyer and MacInnis (2001, p. 387) inform us that social influences are essentially 'information by and pressures from individuals, groups, and the mass media that affect how a person behaves'. They also point out that some of these influences tend to be marketer-dominated (mass media advertising, company websites, store environment) while others are not (general mass media, word of mouth, opinion leaders, family, friends).

Non-marketer-dominated influences which manifest themselves as formal and informal groups regularly affect our consumption behaviour. Individual shoppers tend to 'refer' to such groups (their 'reference groups') prior to, during and/or after the act of buying. Solomon et al. (1999, p. 269) state that a reference group is 'an actual or imaginary individual or group conceived of having significant relevance upon an individual's evaluations, aspirations or behaviour'. The behaviour of each of us is frequently influenced by our circle of friends, family members, work colleagues, athletic team mates, celebrities, politicians and so forth.

INFLUENCE, PERSUASION AND INVOLVEMENT

We have seen how many consumer decisions are routinely influenced by the various individuals and groups in our lives. We now need to look at how marketers spend much time and money trying to influence our behaviour, and how they then try to persuade us, in an effort to get us inextricably involved with their product or brand.

For greater clarity let us consider a few definitions, all of which are taken from the *Oxford English Dictionary*:

> *Influence:* 'the effect a person or thing has on another'. Our attitudes and beliefs are always susceptible to the influence of others, and marketers know this well.
>
> *Persuasion:* 'the addressing of reasonings, appeals, or entreaties to a person in order to induce him to do or believe something'. Marketers try to convince us of their product's or brand's suitability. In this context we can refer to persuasion as an active attempt to alter some of the current beliefs and attitudes we hold.
>
> *Involvement:* to involve is to 'cause (a person or thing) to participate'. In marketing terms it can be described as the consumer's motivation to process product-related information and to act accordingly.

The bottom line is this: skilled strategic marketers devote every dimension of their marketing programme (product/package design, distribution network, pricing strategies, communications mix and so on) to get the very best positioning possible in customers' minds. Sometimes, as is the case with many deregulated utility companies, marketers need to reposition themselves in their customers' minds.

Useful models

Supported by a number of significant technological advances, the latter half of the twentieth century spawned a multitude of modelling practices in diverse fields of enquiry, including the behavioural sciences. Before looking at any of these models in detail, it may be useful to consider the typology of modelling approaches as shown in Table 3.1.

In the early days of consumer behaviour studies, researchers used rather elementary 'monadic' models, so-called because of their reliance upon a single discipline (economics, for example).

Table 3.1 Typology of research models

Micro	or	Macro
Data-based	or	Theory-based
Behavioural	or	Statistical
Generalised	or	Ad hoc
Qualitative	or	Quantitative
Static	or	Dynamic

Source: Adapted from Rice (1997, pp. 201–2)

Chisnall (1994) offers a useful overview of some of these models in his text on consumer behaviour. The basic 'black box' model, for instance, which can still be found in most current consumer behaviour textbooks looks like this:

Inputs (stimuli) ⟶ Consumer's mind (black box) ⟶ Outputs (responses)

We can see here that a psychological view is used to present humans as processors of information not unlike the computers we have today. First we experience a multitude of stimuli (visuals, sounds, smells and so on), we then process this in our minds (we use our mental computer to sort and store information) and, when an opportunity arises, we retrieve the relevant information when we are ready to make a purchase. This model falls short of actively considering the effects that other factors such as social context, economic conditions or cultural influences might also have on people's purchasing behaviour.

Towards the beginning of this chapter we noted that today's consumer researchers draw from many fields, using what is referred to as 'multi-variable approaches'. These studies differ from earlier monadic efforts in that they rely on a combination of elements from varying behavioural sciences. Here again Chisnall's analysis provides evidence of a progressively more elaborate string of models. Among these are the early efforts of Howard (1963), Nicosia (1968), Howard and Sheth (1969) and Howard and Ostlund (1973). The last of these models incorporates the role of 'exogenous' variables (those originating outside ourselves) in relation to our purchase behaviour. Such external variables include, for example, social setting, time constraints and type of information source.

Towards an integrated model

More recently, Sheth et al. (1999, p. 35) turned their attention to the different roles a consumer may fulfil. They look at consumer behaviour as involving 'role specialization', suggesting that we sometimes act as 'buyer', 'user' and/or 'payer'. This theme has been further developed by Dubois (2000) and others to include additional roles. Figure 3.5 represents an attempt to integrate earlier consumer behaviour models with more current views.

So far this chapter has been concerned with providing a clear overview of the important concepts and models from the field of consumer behaviour. The study of

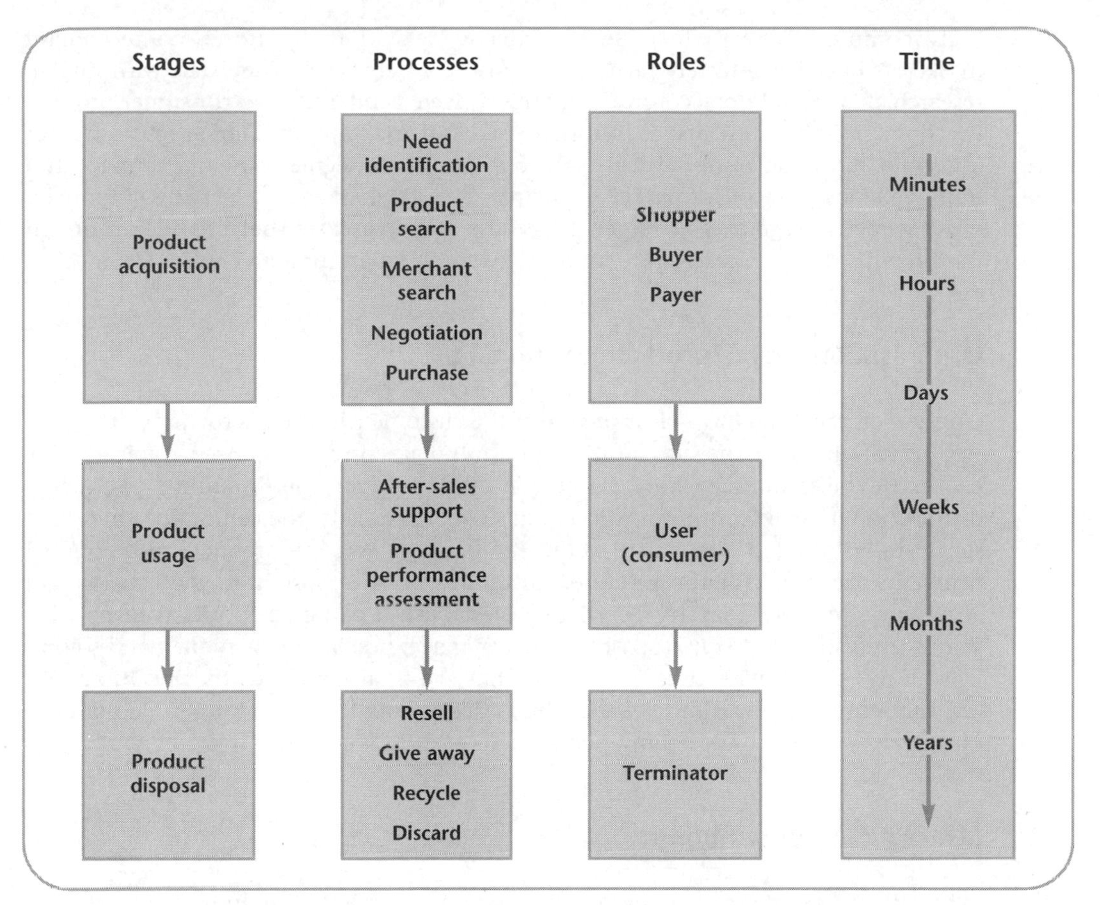

Figure 3.5 A modern view of consumer behaviour

consumer behaviour is a key foundation stone upon which to build effective marketing strategies. In the remainder of the chapter we look at the relevance of consumer behaviour to strategic marketing planning. In addition, we look at the ways in which developments and trends in the consumer behaviour field might affect the evolution of strategic marketing.

STRATEGIC IMPLICATIONS

From market aggregation to targeting

Strategically speaking, marketing is a relatively young field of study. Although the world has known selling, buying and advertising for many centuries, the concept of using a multidimensional, coordinated approach to commercialising products only came into practice during the twentieth century. The fact that marketing is 'coordinated' makes the whole difference. The days of aggregation – using a single strategy and a single product to satisfy the needs of all markets – are fast disappearing. The world is now a very complex place, and the people who inhabit it are living increasingly complex lives. To increase the effectiveness of their efforts, contemporary marketers have come to rely heavily on consumer behaviour. They start with market research that takes into account qualitative as well as quantitative consumer profiles. Psychographics are now just as routinely used as demographics. Market research findings then allow marketing strategists the opportunity to segment the marketplace into homogeneous groupings (market segments). Finally, marketers select the potentially most attractive segments to target. It is these target markets that provide an organisation with the very heart of its strategic marketing plan for a given year.

Organisation/brand/product positioning

Once an organisation has a clear picture of the customers it intends to attract, the next step usually involves the development of a full marketing programme. Typically this process involves thinking hard about the entire product line, branding, packaging, distribution, pricing, communications and so on. Essentially, the central idea here is to successfully 'position' the organisation, the brand(s) and the products to be offered firmly in the minds of the intended customers. It is important to note here that, although a marketer may try very hard to establish a particular position in people's minds (industry leadership, top of the quality range, best value for money and so on), it is always the individual consumer that has the final say about that position. You may present your new film release as the greatest thing to come along in decades but ultimately it is up the film-going public to decide whether or not it is any good.

Strategic use of symbolism

Typically, marketers rely heavily upon communications (including advertising, websites, packaging and so forth) to get potential customers interested in their products. An interesting development of late has been the increase in the use of semiotics in marketing communications. Lambkin et al. (1998, p. 348) point out that 'Generally defined as the science of signs, semiology or semiotics is primarily concerned with the investigation and explication of meaning, that is, how meaning is created, transmitted and interpreted in various situations.' Company logos, high-impact package designs, animated characters and the like are now widely used by organisations the world over to engage consumers as never before. Sometimes referred to as 'semiotics of consumption', these symbols have come to play an important role in helping to shape the way we perceive our world.

Product innovation/value decisions

All goods and services enjoy a certain 'position' in people's minds. Kardes (2002, p. 315) reminds us, however, that 'a brand is typically not perceived or judged in isolation', that 'it is judged relative to other brands'. Today's strategic marketers must ensure that their particular offering continues to provide that something special in relation to competing brands on offer. Perceptual maps have proved helpful in this regard. Consumers can be surveyed in terms of how they perceive a company's particular brand in relation to available alternatives. Decision-makers may then use this

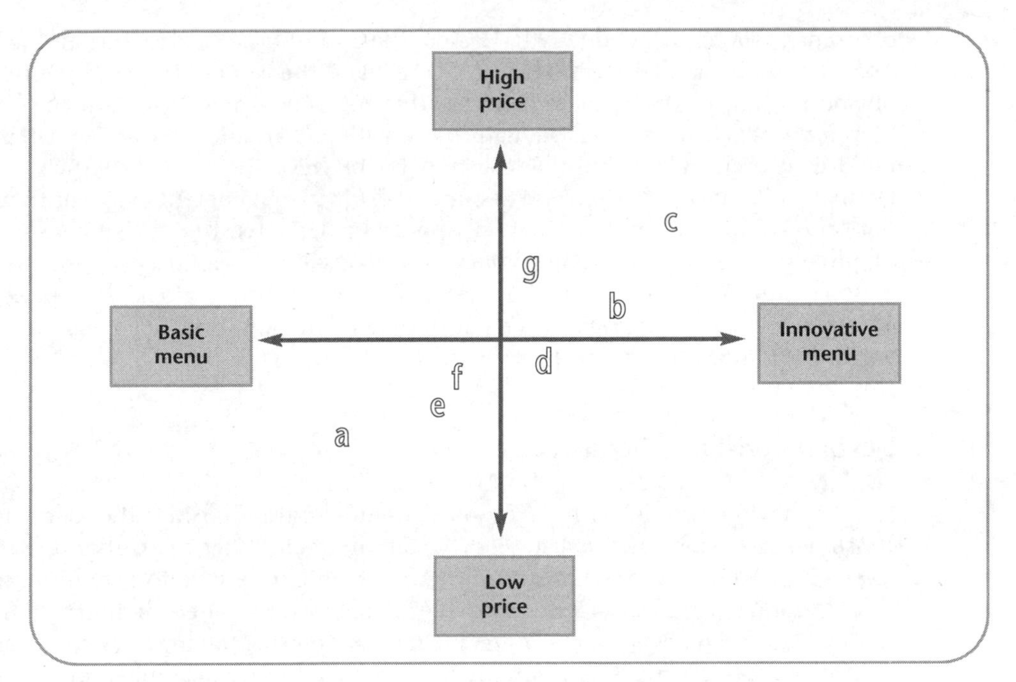

Figure 3.6 Positioning map for eight different restaurants

information to adjust their product's position, or possibly to reposition it altogether. Figure 3.6 provides an example of such a map.

DEVELOPMENTS TO WATCH

e-Shopping

The industrialised world is fast becoming an interactive world as well. Never before have consumers been able to shop for and purchase so many products through diverse non-traditional channels such as free-standing retail kiosks, interactive digital TV and Internet-based e-tail (electronic retail) websites. Although these are still early days for this phenomenon, consumer interest the world over can be expected to grow rapidly as the benefits of new technologies such as these become more apparent. The role of the Internet in strategic marketing is considered later in the book, in particular in Chapter 5 on the competitive environment and Chapter 10 on Internet marketing strategies.

Growth of international/global marketing

The widespread availability of information and communications technologies has opened up a wide range of new opportunities for marketers. Many established retailers have been busy capitalising on this by expanding their territory into neighbouring countries. In Western Europe, for example, we are witnessing the rise of the 'euro' consumer. Studies by Todd (1990), Hasson (1995) and others, the Value and Lifestyle Analysis classification system (known as VALS) and the work of the Research Institute on Social Change (RISC) support the view that consumers may have more in common than marketers had originally thought. Now, with globalisation, we are witnessing the rapid development of a truly planetary point of view. Global players such as Nike, Honda and Sony are now looking at our world with very different eyes. For them, the notion of a 'foreign' market is fast disappearing. They tend to see all consumers as essentially the same and their products as universally appealing. It appears that we may be witnessing the rise of what we might refer to as the 'global consumer'. This attractive yet potentially controversial development may well open up fresh challenges for tomorrow's marketing strategists.

Deviant consumer behaviour

Some behavioural scholars have found it useful to also consider the 'dark side' of consumer behaviour. Chisnall (1994), Solomon et al. (1999), Hoyer and MacInnis (2001) and others believe that strategic planners might be wise to take into account possible abnormalities, excesses and illegal behaviours when analysing markets. Examples of such deviant behaviours include compulsive buying, addictive/compulsive consumption (smoking, gambling and binge eating for example), buying on the black market, underage smoking/drinking and so forth. It is interesting to note that there can be no easy categorisation here, rather what we might call a spectrum of behaviours. Presumably a glass or two of wine each day may not seem excessive by most standards, yet a full bottle of whisky a day would most probably be seen as 'deviant'. But then, there are those who regard any alcohol consumption as 'deviant'. The same logic also applies to gambling, shopping, pornography, smoking and so forth. Hoyer and MacInnis (2001, p. 561) suggest that 'These behaviors are fairly pervasive in our consumer society, and although some of them (for example black markets) can offer consumer benefits, most others can have fairly negative effects on consumers and the social groups in which they operate.' Of course this raises significant ethical issues that strategic planners must grapple with head on.

Economic psychology

Another development of interest in the field of consumer behaviour involves 'the study of economic and psychological factors on economic behaviour, that is, all behaviour involving scarce resources such as money, time and effort' (Lambkin et al., 1998, p. 315). Also known as behavioural economics, this relatively new field of study examines areas of human behaviour such as anchoring, mental accounting, sunk-cost fallacy, choice conflict and loss/regret aversion. Let us now briefly consider some examples to illustrate each of these areas.

- *Anchoring*
  Buying and selling products can prove to be quite stressful, especially if a considerable sum of money is involved. To help reduce the risk of getting it wrong, we routinely fix a certain 'price' or 'value' (our anchor) in our minds prior to making a final purchase decision. This is how most people buy a home, bid at auctions or haggle at open-air markets.

- *Mental accounting*
  'In essence, this is the tendency to value some dollars less than others based on where the money comes from (salary vs. bonus, for example), how it is to be spent (down payment vs. vacation) or the size of the transaction' (Belsky, 1999). One might think that, logically, the consumer would value each unit of currency the same. However, Belsky points out that this is not always the case. For example, people are inclined to spend unexpected windfalls (such as a small lottery win) spontaneously on an 'extravagance', as though the money is of a different nature from their regular income.
- *Sunk-cost fallacy*
  The sunk-cost fallacy refers to the tendency of consumers to take account in their decision-making of expenditures that they have already made and that can never be recovered. For example, suppose a consumer made a poor decision and put money into an investment that then declined in value. Logically, the only consideration in whether to sell the investment or not is the consumer's expectation about the future performance of the investment. But, in practice, consumers are reluctant to sell loss-making investments even when this is clearly the correct decision. They are influenced by the losses they have made and can never recover. Clearly, the financial services marketing manager needs to be aware of this tendency in consumer decision-making.
- *Choice conflict*
  This conundrum is typically associated with our outlook towards branded products. If we need to choose between a popular brand and a lesser-known store brand (own label), we may well act quite decisively. If, on the other hand, we need to select from three equally reputable brands, our decision will be characterised by far more perplexity.
- *Loss/regret aversion*
  Consumers have a tendency to 'feel the pain that comes with loss more strongly than the pleasure that comes with an equal gain' (Belsky, 1999). People are prepared to pay comparatively high insurance premiums to ensure they are compensated for any unexpected material losses in their lives.

Today's consumers are confronted with an unprecedented array of branded and unbranded goods and services from all over the globe. A better understanding of how consumers approach everyday 'economic' decision-making can only help marketers do their job more effectively.

SUMMARY

Consumer behaviour is the study of the processes and factors that lie behind consumption decisions. A good understanding of consumer behaviour enables the marketer to design more effective marketing strategies. Determinants of consumer behaviour can be classified as individual (inner-determinants) or social. Inner-determinants of consumer behaviour are needs and motives, perception, learning and memory, attitudes, and personality. Social determinants of consumer behaviour are culture, social class, social and group influences, and influence, persuasion and involvement. Models of consumer behaviour aim to identify the stages through which a consumer passes on the way from identifying a need through to making a purchase and consuming a product or service. The field of consumer behaviour is by no means static, and a number of recent trends in the field – e-shopping, globalisation, deviant consumer behaviour and economic psychology – have been highlighted as being of relevance to the strategic marketing planner.

Questions for discussion

1. Distinguish between needs, wants and desires. Do marketers have the power to create any of these?
2. Discuss the effects of globalisation on culture. Is this becoming a matter of concern for all marketers and all product categories?
3. How can the models of consumer behaviour presented in this chapter be adapted to include the recent developments involving online shopping and consumption behaviours?
4. Appropriate positioning has been presented as an essential strategy for organisations wishing to prosper in the marketplace. Discuss the future prospects of unbranded goods and services in this context.
5. Discuss the ethical challenges faced by responsible marketers in terms of such deviant behaviours as compulsive buying, bingeing, addictive gambling and so forth.

References

Assael, H (1998), *Consumer Behavior and Marketing Action*, Cincinnati: South-Western College Publishing

Belsky, G (1999), 'Seven common mental money mistakes', *America's Community Banker*, October **8**(i10): 22

Chisnall, P M (1994), *Consumer Behaviour*, Maidenhead: McGraw-Hill

Dubois, B (2000), *Understanding the Consumer – A European Perspective*, Harlow: Financial Times/Prentice Hall

Hasson, L (1995), Monitoring Social Change, *Journal of the Market Research Society*, **37**(1): 69–80

Howard, J A (1963), *Marketing: Executive and Buyer Behaviour*, New York: Columbia University Press

Howard, J A and Sheth, J N (1969), *The Theory of Buyer Behavior*, New York: John Wiley

Howard, J A and Ostlund, L (1973), *Buyer Behaviour: Theoretical and Empirical Foundations*, New York: Alfred A Knopf

Hoyer, W D and MacInnis, D J (2001), *Consumer Behaviour* 2nd edn, Boston: Houghton Mifflin

Kardes, F R (2002), *Consumer Behavior and Managerial Decision Making*, Upper Saddle River, NJ: Prentice Hall

Lambkin, M, Foxall, G, Van Raaij, F and Heilbrunn, B (eds) (1998), *European Perspectives on Consumer Behaviour*, Hemel Hempstead: Prentice Hall Europe

Maslow, A H (1970), *Motivation and Personality*, New York: Harper & Row

Nicosia, F M (1968), 'Advertising Management, Consumer Behaviour and Simulation', *Journal of Advertising Research*, **8**(1)

Peter, J P, Olson, J C and Grunert, K G (1999), *Consumer Behaviour and Marketing Strategy*, European edn, Maidenhead: McGraw-Hill

Rice, C (1997), *Understanding Customers*, Oxford: Butterworth Heinemann on behalf of the Chartered Institute of Marketing

Schiffman, L G and Lazar Kanuk, L (2000), *Consumer Behavior*, Upper Saddle River, NJ: Prentice Hall International

Sheth, J N, Mittal, B and Newman, B I (1999), *Customer Behavior*, Fort Worth: Dryden Press

Solomon, M, Bamossy, G and Askegaard, S (1999), *Consumer Behaviour: A European Perspective*, Upper Saddle River, NJ: Prentice Hall Europe

Todd, E (1990), *L'Invention de l'Europe*, Paris: Seuil

chapter four

Organisational Buying Behaviour

Learning objectives

By reading this chapter you will learn:

- The key differences between business-to-business markets and consumer markets
- Why effective business-to-business marketing strategy must be built on a sound understanding of business purchasing processes
- How business purchasing can be analysed using the concepts of the decision-making process and purchasing decision criteria
- How to analyse the relationship between a buying firm and a selling firm as the basis for a marketing strategy.

INTRODUCTION

This chapter focuses on situations in which the customer is an organisation (for example an industrial firm, a commercial business or a governmental organisation) rather than a private consumer. Consumer marketing is the most visible form of marketing in modern economies. That is because there are many millions of consumers, often buying a homogeneous product, and it makes economic sense to communicate with as many of them as possible at the same time – often through the medium of television. Everybody fits into myriad different target markets, and therefore is the recipient of multiple different consumer marketing messages. On the other hand, most people are very unfamiliar with business-to-business marketing. The reason for this is that business-to-business markets usually have few buyers, who can be reached economically through precision marketing campaigns, and who respond to highly technical messages. Most of us would not cast a glance at a newspaper advertisement explaining how a new machine could reduce raw material wastage by 4.3 per cent in the manufacture of plastic pipe. That is why nobody wastes their money on such advertisements, and why the general public remains largely ignorant of business-to-business marketing.

To begin the chapter there is a brief discussion of the differences between business-to-business markets and consumer markets in order to explain further the context within which organisational buying decisions are made. This is followed by a discussion of the best-known approaches to organisational buying behaviour, which were developed in the 1960s and 70s. Next, more recent insights into organisational buying decisions – based on the idea that business-to-business buying and selling is an interaction process – are introduced. Finally the key messages for marketing strategy development are explained.

CHARACTERISTICS OF BUSINESS-TO-BUSINESS MARKETS

Business-to-business marketing is concerned with the marketing of products and services from one organisation to another. Examples include telecommunications equipment manufacturers selling systems to British Telecommunications plc, dairy product companies selling ice cream ingredients to Birds Eye Wall's, or a clothing manufacturer supplying Fulham FC with the football shirts that are then sold to fans. The point is that the customer is an organisation, with organisational goals. When organisations buy goods and services, they do so to pursue organisational objectives, not to derive pleasure or personal satisfaction from using the product. BT buys telecommunications systems to deliver phone and other services to customers, Birds Eye Wall's buys milk to manufacture ice cream and confectionery, Fulham FC buys football shirts to sell to fans. Business-to-business marketing is the process of trying to match a company's products and services to the organisational goals of its target customers. This fundamental difference makes business-to-business marketing different from consumer marketing. Gross et al. (1993) provide a list of 58 differences between business-to-business and consumer marketing. However, most of these differences are at the level of marketing tactics – for example the promotional emphasis in business-to-business marketing is on personal selling, to be contrasted with mass advertising in consumer markets. Such tactical differences between business-to-business and

Table 4.1 Characteristics of business-to-business markets

Dimension	Characteristic of business market	Explanation
Nature of demand	Derived demand	The demand from a business depends upon (is *derived* from) its own volume of sales
Buying influences	Many influences	There are often many interested parties who influence the buying decision
Market structure	Often concentrated demand	A small number of large customers often make up a substantial share of the market
Purchasing motives	Organisational, rational	Business products are purchased to contribute to the achievement of organisational objectives
Purchasing decision process	Often complex and lengthy	Major organisational buying decisions can involve long and complex analysis and negotiation processes
Purchasing skills	Professional, trained	Organisational buyers are often professionally qualified in purchasing

consumer marketing can be traced back to the underlying nature of business markets shown in Table 4.1.

The demand from businesses for products and services is derived from the demand for their own products and services (hence 'derived demand'). There are often multiple influences on organisational buying decisions, since organisational buying decisions are usually made by a group of skilled employees, each of whom brings professional expertise to the buying decision. Organisational purchases are made to pursue the goals of the organisation, and the purchasing decision process (the 'purchase cycle') can be very lengthy. Purchasing teams can include experts from a range of different professions (for example production managers, engineers, quality managers) and are often coordinated by a purchasing professional, that is, someone with a professional purchasing qualification who is employed to manage the purchasing process. Finally, and a key consideration in marketing strategy development, business markets vary enormously in terms of 'demand concentration'. In consumer markets, demand is dispersed among a large numbers of buyers, none of whom has substantial buying power. Some consumers are certainly more profitable than others, particularly those who buy repeatedly and in large quantities. However, no individual consumer wields real buying power. While this also holds true in some business markets, in many business markets there is a high degree of 'demand concentration', meaning that a small number of buyers make up a large percentage of sales. Examples include the supply of telecommunications equipment, automobile components and advertising services. Respectively, the major telecommunications providers (such as BT), a few large automobile manufacturers (such as General Motors) and a small number of major consumer goods manufacturers (such as Unilever) wield great buying power in these markets. To construct a marketing strategy in such markets as though 'all customers are equal' would be a recipe for disaster. Different marketing strategies are needed for the many small-scale buyers and for the 'vital few' major buying organisations.

APPROACHES TO ORGANISATIONAL BUYING BEHAVIOUR

Effective competitive marketing strategy in business markets depends on an understanding of the ways in which organisations buy. The firm that understands the organisational buying behaviour of a target industry better than its rivals will have a competitive advantage. There are many reasons for this, affecting all elements of the marketing mix. For example, by knowing the professional backgrounds of those involved in the buying process, one can develop more effective marketing communications messages – messages that address the concerns of the people involved in the buying decision. By understanding the key criteria that they will use to make their decision, one can design a product that is more likely to succeed. However, two different approaches to the analysis of organisational buying can be found in the literature on marketing. The first emphasises the need to understand in detail the processes of decision-making within the buying organisation, in order to develop a marketing mix that will bring the greatest chance of competitive success (let us call this the 'marketing mix approach'). The second emphasises the fact that buying and selling take place simultaneously as an interactive process, and so focuses on the analysis and management of the interaction process between the buying and selling organisations (this is usually called the 'interaction approach'). We will examine both these approaches and assess their contribution towards marketing strategy development. Before doing so, it is important to establish that both are legitimate approaches to the fundamental issues associated with business-to-business marketing strategy. They are essentially complementary ways of looking at the business world, and the business-to-business marketing strategist needs to appreciate both. When dealing with relatively dispersed markets, selling uncomplicated products with short purchase cycles, comparatively little buyer–seller interaction will be necessary and a marketing mix approach to strategy development is likely to be appropriate. In concentrated markets, with a few key customers, particularly where the product is complex and the purchase cycle long, far greater buyer–seller interaction will be required and an interaction approach to strategy development will be needed.

BUYCLASSES AND BUYPHASES

Robinson et al. (1967) made the striking discovery, based on primary research into real buying decisions, that organisational purchases could be usefully divided into three categories, which they called straight rebuy, modified rebuy and new task purchase. These three categories are each types of 'buyclass'. In order to establish which kind of buyclass is involved in a buying situation, three questions are asked. These are:

- How familiar is the buying organisation with this type of purchase?
- How extensive are the buyer's information requirements?
- How wide a set of alternatives will the buyer consider?

The buyclass framework is illustrated in Table 4.2.

A straight rebuy is the most common type of organisational purchase, involves negligible consideration of alternatives and very little information gathering, since the buyer reorders virtually automatically from the 'in-supplier' (the current supplier). For example, reordering general stationery supplies from an office supplies company

Table 4.2 The buyclass framework

Buyclass	Newness of problem	Information requirements	Consideration of alternative
New task	High	Maximum	Important
Modified rebuy	Medium	Moderate	Limited
Straight rebuy	Low	Minimal	None

Source: Based on Robinson et al. (1967, p. 14)

would usually be a straight rebuy. However, if there is some change of requirements then the purchase becomes a modified rebuy. The change of requirements, may be, for example, a desire for a better price or a minor change of product specifications. A certain amount of information gathering will take place, but the in-supplier retains a relatively strong position. Suppose that you suspect you could obtain your stationery supplies more cheaply from another firm, and so decide to evaluate alternative suppliers before placing an order – this would be a modified rebuy.

With both the straight rebuy and the modified rebuy, the buying organisation has some degree of familiarity with the buying task. This is not so in the case of a new task purchase. According to Robinson et al., it is in the 'new task' buying situation – where the organisation is buying something with which it is unfamiliar – that extensive problem-solving behaviour will occur. Many alternatives are considered, a great deal of information gathered and analysed.

The complexity of the buying process will be determined by the buyclass of a particular purchase decision. The degree of complexity in the buying process is shown by the number of steps in the buying process. These steps are called 'buyphases', and there are a maximum of eight buyphases:

1. Anticipation or recognition of a problem (need) and a general solution
2. Determination of characteristics and quantity of a needed item
3. Description of characteristics and quantity of needed item
4. Search for and qualification of potential sources
5. Acquisition and analysis of proposals
6. Evaluation of proposals and selection of supplier(s)
7. Selection of an order routine
8. Performance feedback and evaluation.

In the case of a new task purchase, the buyer will go through all eight of these steps. For a modified rebuy, the process is truncated, starting at step four, since the principal decision concerns the selection of the best supplier to meet a well-understood organisational need. For a straight rebuy, the process is truncated even further, being limited to the last two steps only. In the case of a straight rebuy, the buying organisation does not consider alternative suppliers, but simply reorders from the current supply firm.

The buyclass/buyphase model has stood the test of time remarkably well. Efforts have been made to test its validity or improve upon it (for example, Anderson et al., 1987; Bunn, 1993), but it remains a robust conceptual framework that is of considerable practical value. The business-to-business marketing strategist will aim to classify marketing opportunities as straight rebuy, modified rebuy and new task, and adapt the marketing strategy accordingly. For example, it is inappropriate to develop complex marketing communications and product development strategies, to provide extensive customer information and arrange substantial face-to-face sales contact when dealing with straight rebuy situations. This would be an extravagant waste of marketing resources. Once a straight rebuy becomes a modified rebuy, however, considerable expenditure of marketing resources may be justified – by the in-supplier seeking to retain an important customer, or by rivals ('out-suppliers') seeking new business.

THE BUYING CENTRE AND A 'GENERAL MODEL' OF ORGANISATIONAL BUYING

Webster and Wind (1972) aimed to provide a *general* model of organisational buying behaviour. They explicitly characterised organisational buying as a *process* involving several people – in contrast to the earlier conception of buying as the purchasing act, carried out by a purchasing executive.

The forces influencing the buying process were categorised by Webster and Wind as environmental factors, organisational factors, social factors and individual factors. The model is illustrated in Figure 4.1. The buying process, and ultimately the buying decision, will vary depending on the business environment and the organisation within which it takes place, and will vary with the social group involved in the process and the characteristics of the individuals within that group. At the environmental level, factors such as the level of competition and general economic conditions will affect a purchase decision. For example, an economic recession may cause buying organisations to be more cost-conscious, and to emphasise price as a decision-

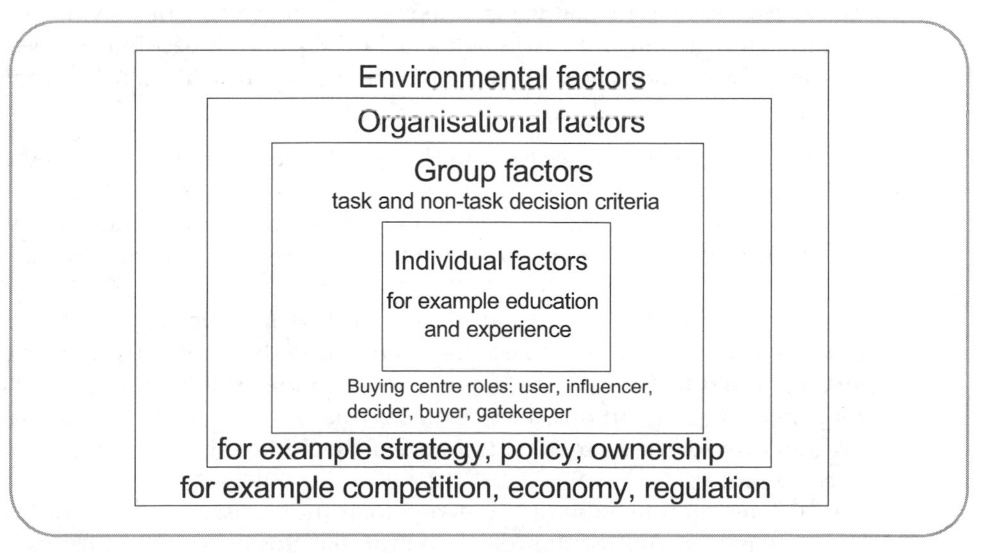

Figure 4.1 Organisational buying influences
Source: Based on Webster and Wind (1972)

making criterion more than they would if the economy were booming. At the organisational level, factors such as business strategy, purchasing policy and corporate ownership can make a difference to purchasing decisions. For example, a company that has a marketing strategy designed to achieve differentiation through highly innovative product design will want to do business with suppliers that can contribute towards this objective – purchase price will be a secondary criterion. Corporate ownership can affect buying decisions in a number of ways. Large Japanese manufacturing firms (such as Toyota) have well-established policies of building long-term relationships with suppliers, and offering them practical support to develop new products and quality systems. Comparable US firms have traditionally been less supportive, and less loyal, towards their suppliers.

Going beyond the environmental and organisational levels, the Webster and Wind model suggests that group dynamics within the purchasing team and individual characteristics of those involved in the decision-making process will influence the outcome of the buying decision. This means that it is not enough, in formulating business-to-business marketing strategy, to look at the relatively tangible factors associated with the buying organisation and the purchasing environment – one must also consider the less tangible factors associated with the people making the decision.

At the group level, five roles are commonly identified within the 'buying centre':

- *The user:* who will put the purchased item to work. For example, the estates or facilities manager would adopt the role of user if a new barrier system for the car park were being procured.
- *The influencer:* who is considered to have relevant expertise and therefore to have a valuable opinion on the purchase.
- *The decider:* who has the ultimate decision-making authority. If it is an important and costly purchase, then this will probably be a senior manager. For minor items, decision-making authority may be delegated to junior management.
- *The buyer:* who is the individual responsible for organising the buying process and ultimately dealing with the contractual details once a decision has been made. Large organisations usually have a purchasing department staffed by professional buyers.
- *The gatekeeper:* this is anyone who controls the flow of information to the buying centre. Often it will be the purchasing department representative, who has the overall responsibility for managing the purchasing process, and decides what is relevant information to be circulated to members of the buying centre.

A sixth buying centre role of *initiator* has also been suggested – someone who is responsible for identifying the need for a purchase in the first place. In many cases the initiator would be the same as the user. For example, the estates manager receives complaints that unauthorised use is being made of the company car park, and concludes that a new barrier control system should be introduced, so initiating the purchase process.

The buying centre (also often referred to as the 'decision-making unit' or simply 'DMU') may have five (or six) roles within it, but this does not mean that there are always five (or six) people in it. Clearly one person can fulfil more than one role. For example, often the purchasing department representative will fulfil the roles of buyer and gatekeeper. Equally, there may be more than one person fulfilling a single role. Suppose that a public utility company (such as a gas or electricity business) is purchasing a computerised billing system, which it will use to monitor customer usage, to generate periodic bills to be sent to customers and to check that customer payments are correctly received. The accounts department (the 'user department'), responsible for customer billing, may well want to involve more than one representative in the purchasing process. For example, one representative might focus on ensuring accuracy in the billing process, while another might focus on the customer relations aspects of billing (making the bills easy to understand, dealing with visually impaired customers and so on).

In considering the group and individual buying influences illustrated in Figure 4.1, it is useful to remember the distinction made by Webster and Wind between 'task-related' and 'non-task-related' factors in the buying decision. Task-related factors are decision criteria that are directly related to the explicit purpose behind the purchase. Examples that are frequently found include purchase price, product quality and reliability, after-sales service and speed of delivery. Non-task-related factors are decision criteria that are not directly related to the explicit purpose behind the purchase. Members of the buying centre might be motivated to make a 'safe' decision rather than objectively the 'best' decision; for example, choosing a better known supplier over one less well known simply because the decision will be easy to justify. This is summarised in the management aphorism that 'nobody ever got fired for buying IBM'. It should also be remembered that the members of the buying centre are human beings, as well as managers. Therefore they may carry their own personal prejudices (for example against suppliers from a particular country) and preferences into the organisational buying process.

THE INTERACTION APPROACH TO ORGANISATIONAL BUYING AND SELLING

Most of the ideas discussed in the preceding sections were developed in the 1960s. They retain considerable relevance today and provide a basis for business-to-business marketing strategy development, particularly where a market is dispersed, the purchase cycle short and the product relatively simple. Naturally these ideas have been subject to criticism. Two principal objections have been raised. First, that the models focus exclusively on the buying process, and implicitly assume that organisational buying and selling can be treated as though they were entirely separate processes. Second, that the emphasis is on understanding organisational buying in order to develop a marketing mix, on the implicit assumption that organisational buying is a response to a marketing stimulus. Both of these implicit assumptions have been challenged in more recent research into organisational buying and selling.

A stereotypical view of business, and the processes of buying and selling in particular, is to imagine that buyers and sellers meet only briefly to exchange money and goods, and that the seller is the more active participant in the process who makes a 'pitch' to which the buyer responds. The reality of business is more complex than this, particularly in many business-to-business markets. Investigations into the way in which buying and selling takes place between real companies (Hakansson, 1982; Wilson and Möller, 1995) have shown that in many cases firms do business with each other over a long period of time (often a decade or more). This leads to the idea that buying and selling organisations enter into 'relationships' with each other, and that each subsequent contract is influenced by what has gone before – by the history of the relationship. Furthermore, as often as not a specific contract will be initiated by a buying organisation, which has identified a need and then seeks out a supplier capable of satisfying it. More broadly, buying and selling between organisations does not take place in a series of simple, unconnected transactions. Buyers and sellers interact with each other in a complex fashion. Their interactions revolve around money, goods and services, certainly, but also involve exchanges of information and social meetings. These elements – long-term relationships, complex buyer–seller interaction, multifaceted exchange processes – were combined into a model of the organisational buying and selling process by a team of researchers known as the IMP (industrial marketing and purchasing) Group. In the next section we will examine their work and its implications for marketing strategy.

RELATIONSHIPS, INTERACTION AND NETWORKS

The main characteristics of the IMP interaction model are illustrated in Figure 4.2. The model uses the relationship rather than the transaction as the principal unit of analysis. This is justified on the basis that observed relationships between buyer and seller organisations are frequently long term, close and complex. Such relationships are characterised by numerous 'exchange episodes'. Exchange episodes may involve a product/service or money, but in many cases involve no more than information exchange or social contact. Social exchanges are important in the development and maintenance of the relationship to build and maintain trust between the parties. Within the relationship adaptations take place, involving one or both parties in relationship-specific investment in physical or human assets (for example specific

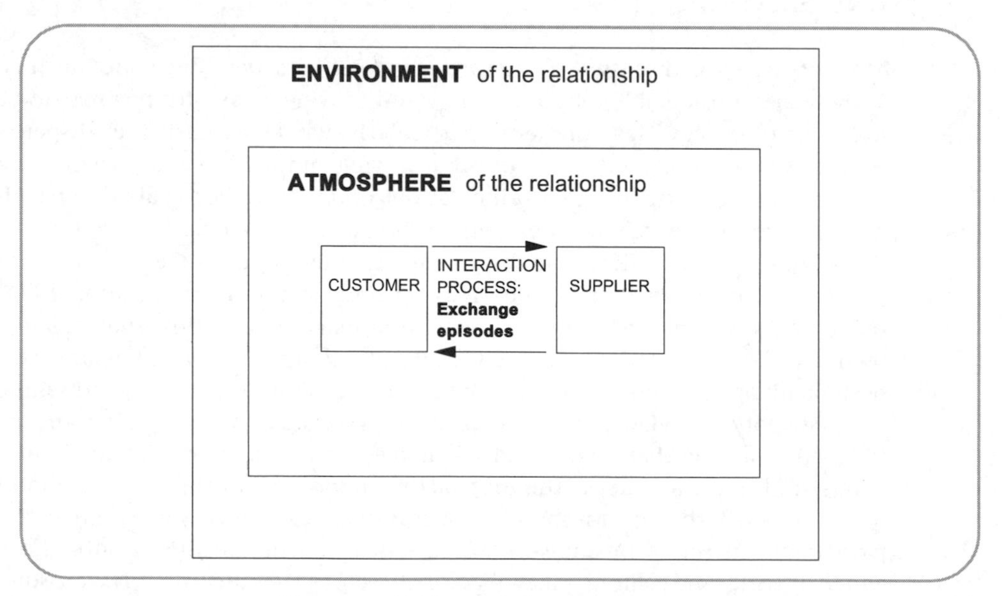

Figure 4.2 The IMP interaction model
Source: Adapted from Hakansson (1982)

training to operate the machinery manufactured by a particular supplier). Each relationship has a unique history, which has a considerable influence on current exchange episodes. The IMP Group formalised this idea into the concept of the relationship 'atmosphere'. Key factors in the development of the relationship atmosphere would include any conflicts that have occurred (for example over missed delivery dates), instances of effective cooperation (perhaps to overcome a technical or commercial problem), or occasions on which cooperation had been ineffective. Taken together, these factors affect what the business partners expect of each other, for example whether they will deliver on time, pay on time, be able to solve a technical problem, or provide useful commercial information unasked.

Very much like the Webster and Wind model discussed above, the IMP model acknowledges the importance of the wider business environment to organisational buying and selling. The broader business environment is regarded as affecting the relationship and exchanges which take place within it. The environment includes variables such as the structure of the markets in which the partners operate (for example the extent to which demand is dispersed among many customers or concentrated in only a few) and the dynamism (rate of change) of environmental factors. In the next section we will consider some key trends in the business environment and their implications for organisational buying and selling.

THE RELEVANCE AND APPLICATION OF ORGANISATIONAL BUYING THEORY

Much of the research into organisational buying behaviour is expressed in fairly esoteric language that may deceive the reader into thinking that it is purely academic abstraction, of perhaps limited relevance to the practical marketing strategist. However, most of these ideas have been developed through careful investigation of the real world of business, and they represent the best information we have about the broad processes involved in organisational buying and selling. Clearly, since these are general models that aim to provide insights into a wide range of market situations, it will be necessary for the marketing strategist to have more focused information on the specific buying processes, and interaction processes, that take place within particular markets of interest. But these general models will provide valuable clues to what the specific processes might look like within individual markets. It is surely better to start with a soundly based general theory of organisational buying, and then to investigate further exactly what happens within a specific industry, rather than to start from a position of total ignorance. It is reasonable to protest: 'but the marketing and sales managers I know don't talk about Webster and Wind or the interaction model'. However, even if the successful practitioner does not have explicit knowledge of these abstractions (although increasingly they do), he or she will certainly understand and apply the concepts implicitly. Handling the complex interactions between a large supplier and a key customer, for example, is what a 'key account manager' does for a living. The key account manager will certainly understand the importance of social interaction, of knowing who the key decision-makers are in the buying process, and of understanding the customer's business strategy and what contribution his or her firm can make to successful implementation. Knowledge of the conceptual abstractions can help the practitioner to make more sense of his or her professional world, and gives the student of marketing a head start in appreciating the realities of business-to-business marketing.

We have examined two broad approaches to organisational buying theory. The first concentrated on the buying process alone, the second extended this to look at buying and selling simultaneously as an interaction process. It may be confusing to find two distinct approaches to the study of a single aspect of marketing management. The temptation is to consider them as two competitive ways of describing the world, and to select one or other as the preferred view. For example, the 'marketing mix' approach may be preferred on the grounds that it is closer to the more familiar concepts that are to be found in the study of consumer marketing. Or the 'interaction approach' is preferred because of its emphasis on business relationships – and common sense tells us that relationships are important in business-to-business marketing. To treat the 'marketing mix' and the 'interaction approach' as competing alternatives in this way is not a helpful approach, in either theoretical or practical terms. A more legitimate approach is to suggest that the older models of organisational buying behaviour belong to an earlier era, that the business world has become more 'relational' in recent decades, so that the marketing mix approach is increasingly obsolete and the interaction approach increasingly relevant. Arguments very much like these have been deployed by Wilson (1996) and Sheth (1996). Wilson (1996) proposed that we were in an era when 'old model' organisational buying behaviour was being supplanted by 'new model' organisational buying behaviour. The buying function, she claimed, was evolving in a number of ways:

- Away from a win/lose negotiating orientation to a win/win orientation
- Away from a short-term orientation to a long-term orientation
- Away from transactional, price-based purchasing to partnership purchasing
- Away from the conventions of keeping suppliers at arm's length and avoiding close contact to increasingly intense communications and information sharing with supplier partners.

Sheth (1996) argued that such trends in the purchasing function could be traced to developments in the broader business environment. Quality has become an imperative in modern industries. Businesses have discovered that it is easier to achieve assured high levels of quality with a few carefully chosen and nurtured suppliers than with a constantly changing group of suppliers who are frequently asked to compete against each other to lower prices. Meanwhile, as businesses have focused on their core business operations and outsourced many of their other activities, so they have become increasingly reliant on suppliers, and the purchasing function as the interface with suppliers.

It is entirely reasonable to argue that broad trends in the business world have rendered the marketing mix approach to business-to-business marketing less relevant, and the interaction approach more relevant. However, business markets are heterogeneous. It would be wrong to suggest that there is a single 'correct' approach to marketing strategy in such markets. We prefer to believe that both the older models of organisational buying behaviour (and the marketing mix approach to strategy that they imply) and the more recent interaction approach (and the relational approach to strategy it implies) can be useful guides to strategy development. One company might have a homogeneous and straightforward product range, which is sold to a large number of largely undifferentiated customers. In such a case it is more appropriate to think in terms of the conventional marketing mix, employing conventional marketing communications methods, standard distribution channels, list pricing and a standardised product range. Another company might offer a range of complex products or services, which are sold primarily to a small number of large buyers. Then it makes more sense to develop relational strategies for the key customers or target customers, employing key account managers to coordinate interactions with the customer, developing tailored products for individual customers and negotiating with each customer over product specifications and price. Even within the same company, two divisions targeting different markets might have to adopt different strategies. And even within the same division, it is entirely possible that a differentiated marketing strategy will be required, with customer-specific relationship strategies developed for the top few customers, and a marketing mix for the remainder. For reasons such as these, some experts have suggested that business-to-business marketers should conduct 'customer portfolio analysis', that is, an assessment of the value of each customer against explicit criteria in order to rank customers, so that marketing resources can be directed at the most important customers or targets. We will return to customer portfolio analysis in Chapter 8.

SUMMARY

An understanding of organisational buying behaviour is fundamental to the development of effective business-to-business marketing strategy. Two principal approaches to the analysis of organisational buying processes have been identified. The first focuses on the decision-making process going on within the buying organisation. The aim is to identify what the stages are in the buying process, who is involved at each stage and what criteria are employed to select between competing offerings. By understanding these factors, the business-to-business marketer will be in a position to develop an effective marketing mix. The second approach focuses on the interactions that take place between buying and selling organisations. In this approach, each individual transaction can only be understood in the context of the broader relationship between the buying and selling organisations. The prior experience that the firms have of each other will influence their ability to do business together. By understanding the ways in which businesses, and people within business, interact with each other, the business-to-business marketer will be in a position to develop a coherent strategy for each customer relationship. It seems that, in recent years, trends in the business environment have favoured the development of a less confrontational approach to purchasing that encourages partnerships with key suppliers. This suggests that there might be a general trend in favour of marketing strategies based on relationships, rather than an impersonal marketing mix. However, business-to-business markets are very diverse. Both relationship strategies and marketing mix strategies are likely to be of use, depending upon conditions experienced in a particular market. The more complex the product, the longer the purchasing cycle, and the more that demand is concentrated in the hands of a small number of buyers, the more likely it is that a relationship-based strategy will be appropriate.

Questions for discussion

1. How does an understanding of the organisational buying process assist in the formulation of marketing strategy?
2. Organisational markets are very diverse. However, in many organisational markets demand is concentrated in the hands of comparatively few buyers. How does this affect marketing strategy?
3. Changes in the marketing environment have persuaded some influential commentators that business-to-business marketing strategies have to become more relationship oriented. What environmental changes have brought this about, and what does it mean to be more relationship oriented?

References

Anderson, E, Chu, W and Weitz, B (1987), 'Industrial Purchasing: an Empirical Exploration of the Buyclass Framework', *Journal of Marketing*, **51**(July): 71–86

Bunn, M D (1993), 'Taxonomy of Buying Decision Approaches', *Journal of Marketing*, **57**(January): 38–56

Gross, A C, Banting, P M, Meredith, L N and Ford, I D (1993), *Business Marketing*, Boston: Houghton Mifflin

Hakansson, H (ed.) (1982), *International Marketing and Purchasing of Industrial Goods*, Chichester: John Wiley & Sons

Robinson, P J, Faris, C W and Wind, Y (1967), *Industrial Buying and Creative Marketing*, Boston: Allyn & Bacon

Sheth, J (1996), 'Organizational Buying Behavior: Past Performance and Future Expectations', *Journal of Business and Industrial Marketing*, **11**(3/4): 7–24

Webster, F E Jr and Wind, Y (1972), 'A General Model for Understanding Organizational Buying Behavior', *Journal of Marketing*, **36**: 12–19

Wilson, D and Möller, K (eds) (1995), *Business Marketing: an Interaction and Networks Perspective*, Dordrecht: Kluwer

Wilson, E J (1996), 'Theory Transitions in Organizational Buying Behavior Research', *Journal of Business and Industrial Marketing*, **11**(6): 7–19

chapter five

Understanding the Competitive Environment

Learning objectives

By reading this chapter you will learn:

- The role of environmental analysis in strategic marketing
- The distinction between the competitive environment and the macroenvironment
- The importance of the underlying economic forces of supply and demand in the competitive environment
- How to classify and analyse factors in the competitive environment
- The impact of the Internet on the competitive environment
- How the 'resource-based view' of the firm can contribute to strategy development.

INTRODUCTION

Any form of business planning can be thought of as a process of understanding the current position (situation audit), deciding what we want to achieve (objective setting) and deciding how those objectives are to be achieved (strategy formulation). The first part of the process involves a process of gathering and analysing relevant information in order to understand the resources available to the firm, and the circumstances outside the firm that affect its ability to achieve objectives. When we talk about the marketing environment we are concerned with circumstances outside the firm. Every organisation, whether a profit-seeking business, or a non-profit organisation such as a charity or political party, is affected by a wide range of different environmental factors. For example, British Telecommunications plc has to evaluate advances in mobile Internet technology, assess new ideas for regulating the telecommunications industry developed by the government and consider new marketing strategies from rivals such as NTL, among a wide range of other environmental factors. The Conservative Party (Britain's principal rival to the ruling New Labour Party) has to consider the implications that an ageing British population will have on its membership and support, must evaluate new policies emerging from rival parties and regularly needs to monitor public opinion to see how the electorate is responding to issues such as immigration and education standards. Environmental scanning is not just a matter of importance to large organisations. The owner of a small, local shop will be aware of and concerned about local plans for traffic-calming measures or restrictions on parking that might affect business, and will be affected by the marketing decisions of other local competitors – for example promotional offers, changes to product portfolio (such as the acquisition of a liquor licence), or changes to opening hours.

The marketing environment consists of all the factors outside the organisation that may have an influence on the achievement of its marketing objectives. This is, of course, a very wide range of factors. In order to try to reduce the complexity involved in environmental analysis, it is customary to reduce the marketing environment to a relatively small number of categories and then to concentrate on each category in turn. The first step is usually to divide the marketing environment into the *competitive environment* and the *macroenvironment*, and then each of these is further subdivided. The *competitive environment* (or 'industry environment') comprises those factors with which the organisation comes into closest contact, factors that have a rather obvious and immediate impact on its success. The competitive environment is usually further subdivided using Porter's (1980) classification framework into direct competitive rivals, buyers, suppliers, substitutes, and new entry competition. The *macroenvironment* comprises factors outside the immediate competitive environment, some of which may have an obvious or immediate effect, but many of which have a longer term and more insidious effect on the success of the business.

In Chapters 5 and 6 we look at the ways in which the marketing environment can be classified and analysed, and examine a number of important trends in some key environmental variables. We start by looking at the competitive environment, where we examine the underlying logic of the market economy, and discuss Porter's (1980) suggested approach to analysing the competitive environment. Then, in Chapter 6, we move on to look at the macroenvironment, evaluating a number of classification frameworks, discussing the linkages between a number of key environmental variables and assessing their marketing implications. Given the large number of environmental factors that could be of significance in the design of a marketing strategy, some means of assessing the relative importance of environmental factors is clearly necessary. A method of ranking environmental factors in priority order is presented towards the end of the next chapter.

THE UNDERLYING LOGIC OF THE MARKET ECONOMY

Marketing is a flexible tool that can be applied in commercial and non-commercial settings, and in Western, market-based economies or alternative economic systems. However, there can be no doubting the logical connection between 'marketing' and 'the market economy'. We expect that virtually everybody reading this book will live in a country where 'the market' is the underlying principle for organising economic activity. By this we mean that most economic activity comprises voluntary exchanges between individuals and organisations that are pursuing their own economic interests. Of course, there is no such thing as a 'pure market economy'. Even in the USA, which is the closest of the major world economies to a pure market system, around 25 per cent of personal incomes are taken by government in tax, and spent in ways that the government decides rather than the individual. Clearly, the USA is a democratic country and it is expected that the government will spend tax revenues on the policies that were presented to the electorate and that command widespread support (such as the relief of poverty and public health provision). Nevertheless, government intervention of any sort in the private economic decisions of individuals is a move away from a pure market system.

The marketing environment encountered by businesses in most of the industrialised world has at its heart the logic of the market economy. Before moving on to consider the more practical tools for marketing strategy development that are presented in later sections of this chapter, we need to appreciate the market system, which underlies the majority of economic activity. By 'the market system', we mean the way in which the underlying forces of supply and demand cause resources to be allocated and prices to be determined. The logic of the market economy is an inescapable fact of economic life in the industrialised world and many of the environmental factors faced by businesses can be traced to fundamental shifts in demand and supply. We believe that an informed marketing strategy must be based on an understanding of these fundamental shifts, rather than more superficial or easily observed phenomena. Two rather old and overused analogies might help to explain this point. First there is the iceberg analogy – it is said that only a very small part of the iceberg can be seen above the surface of the water. If you change course only enough to avoid the tip of the iceberg, then you can easily run into the very much larger part of it that is hidden under the water. Second there is the medical analogy of symptom and disease. Doctors use symptoms (such as fever or pain) to diagnose disease, and then try above all to cure the disease, rather than simply alleviate the symptoms. If the doctor were to focus on the symptoms and ignore the disease, then in the case of serious illness the patient might die. Similarly, the easily observed 'symptoms' in the marketing environment (for example a rival firm decides to cease competing with you in a particular market) may hide a more important underlying 'disease' (for example that market will shortly be rendered unprofitable by the entry of overseas competition using low-cost, Eastern European labour).

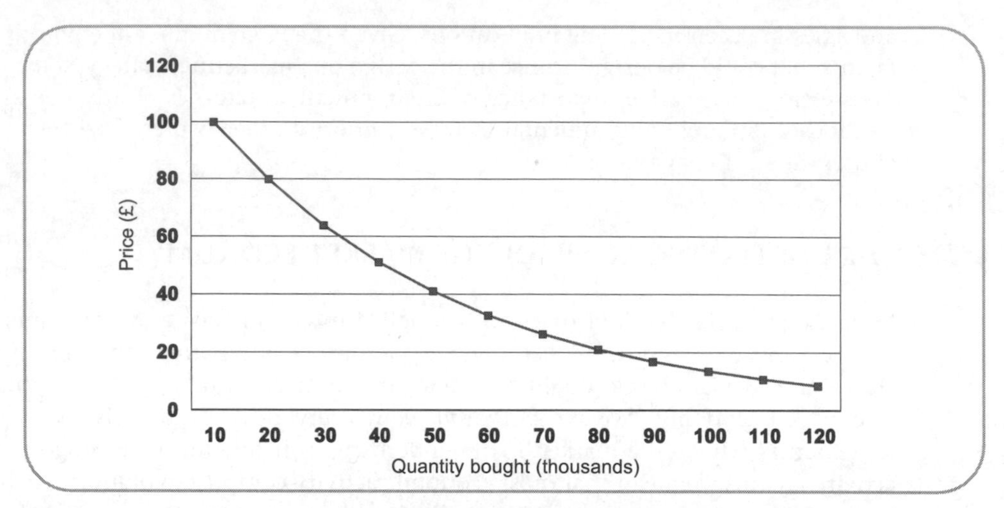

Figure 5.1 Demand function

The underlying logic of the market systems relies on the elementary analysis of demand and supply, which is illustrated in Figures 5.1, 5.2 and 5.3. Standard economic analysis is based on the idea that the price at which a good or service is sold, or offered for sale, will be the primary mechanism by which the amount that people want to buy and the amount that people want to sell are equalised.

Suppose that we are concerned with analysing the demand and supply for replica shirts for a prominent football (soccer) team. Figure 5.1 shows the relationship between the price of the shirt and the total number of shirts that people want to buy. Even at a high price of £100, there are 10,000 dedicated fans who absolutely *must have* the replica shirt of 'their team'. As the price of the shirt declines, the less dedicated fans also decide that they can afford one, and when the price drops below £20 maybe even some people who are not football fans think about buying the shirt – after all,

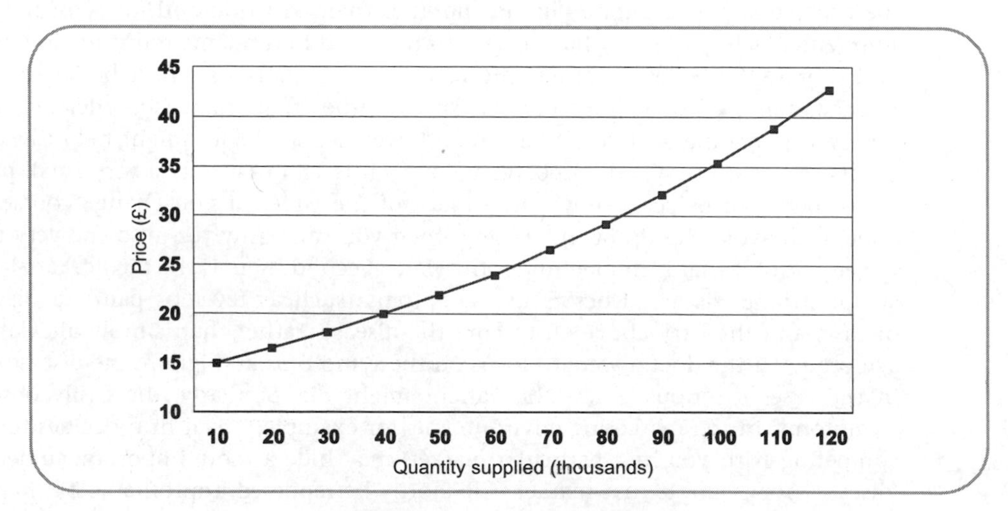

Figure 5.2 Supply function

it's a decent quality shirt manufactured in attractive colours! So we see a negative relationship between the price of the shirt and the amount that people want to buy.

Figure 5.2 shows the relationship between the price of the shirt and the total number of shirts that will be made available for sale. For the sake of simplicity, let us assume that the football shirts are supplied by a number of local clothing and sports retailers, all of which can buy the shirts at the same price from an international clothing manufacturer. The higher the price that the retailers think the shirt will command in the market, the greater the profit they will make on the sale of each shirt, and the more shirts they will want to sell. As it is shown in Figure 5.2, at a price of £15 the retailers would only want to sell 10,000 shirts, while at a price of £35 they would want to sell 100,000 shirts. As the price rises, so the profitability of this product line rises compared with other products and selling it becomes more attractive. So we see a positive relationship between the price of the shirt and the amount that suppliers want to sell.

Given many thousands of potential buyers, prepared to pay different prices, and several retailers competing to sell the shirts, how is it possible for a 'market price' to be established? Figure 5.3 shows the likely outcome of the many individual decisions taken by buyers and sellers. The market price of a shirt has stabilised at around £25, and about 73,000 shirts will be sold at this price. This is the point at which the demand and supply functions intersect. It is worth thinking, first, why there should be such a thing as a 'market price' anyway. In this case, we have a single product that is homogeneous (that is, every shirt is the same as every other shirt), it makes no difference where you buy it and all the shops are local so that customers can easily compare prices. One retailer could not sell at a higher price than the others because customers would simply go to a competitor. Given that there is a market price, why can it not be more than £25 per shirt? At a price above £25, the profitability of the shirt would encourage retailers to increase their stock, meanwhile some customers would be deterred by the higher price. The combination of increased stock and fewer customers would encourage retailers to bring prices down. Why can the market price of the shirt not be below £25? Retailers would then find that they were 'selling out' of

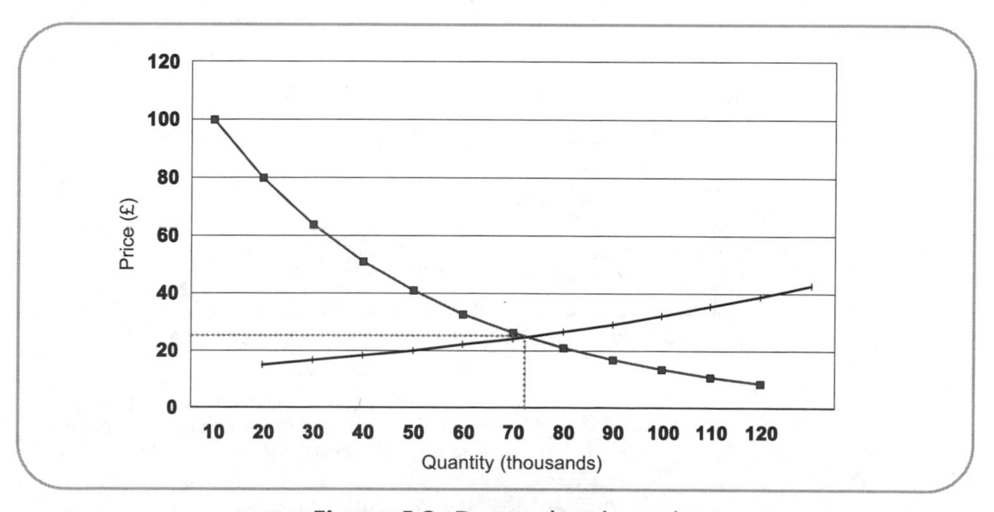

Figure 5.3 Demand and supply

replica shirts because more customers wanted to buy them. The shortage of shirts would encourage retailers to charge a higher price. There is only one price at which the number of shirts that football fans want to buy exactly equals the number of shirts that retailers want to sell and that is £25.

The analysis described above is a simplification of the complex realities of real markets. For example, the role of the football club itself in the market for replica shirts has been ignored. It was assumed that all the shirts were manufactured by the same clothing firm and were of the same quality. All the retailers are allowed to buy shirts from the manufacturer at the same price, whereas in practice we know that a small local retailer would probably have to pay more per shirt than the local branch of a national sports retail chain. Nevertheless, this simplified analysis can do a rather good job of explaining many underlying forces that affect strategic marketing decisions. If our football club were to be relegated to a lower division, what would happen to the price of replica shirts? Sadly, it is likely that fewer people would want to buy them at each possible price point, resulting in a shift downwards and to the left of the whole demand function. If we suppose that the supply function is unaffected by this, then Figure 5.4 shows what the likely outcome will be. Both the volume of shirts sold and the price at which they are sold decline.

What if the football club was to implement a successful marketing strategy? For example, they might develop a scheme in which their players visit local schools to give coaching sessions, enter into a deal with the local radio station to present a 'football focus' programme once a week, or many other things (see the case study on 'Fulham FC' for more possibilities). This would result in a shift of the demand function upwards and to the right, so that the volume of shirts sold and the price commanded would both increase.

In economic systems that give prominence to the market system, the underlying forces of demand and supply are a fundamental component of the marketing environment, which represent an underlying constraint on marketing strategy. These forces are remarkably easily forgotten. For example, during the last decade in several Western industrialised countries it seemed that share prices and property prices could only go up. Shares and property are characteristic 'speculative' commodities, in which

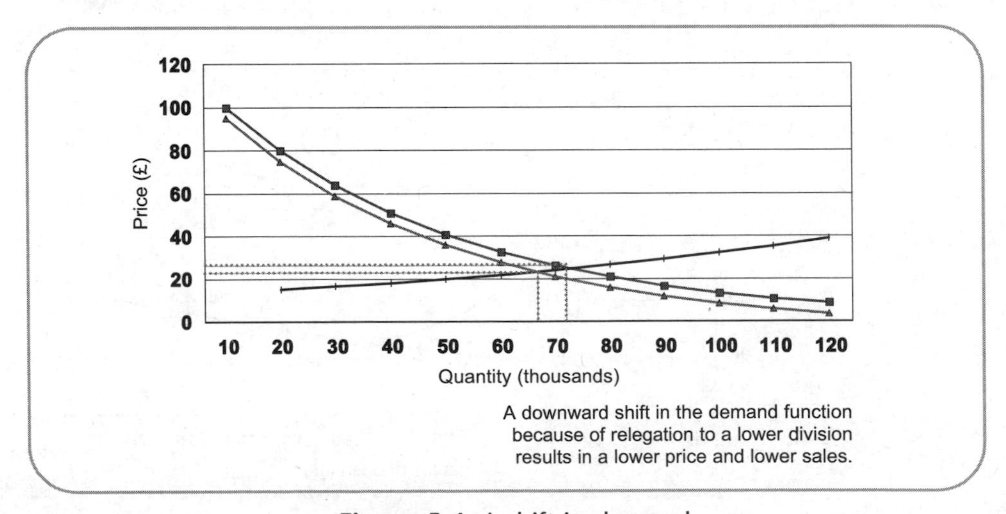

Figure 5.4 A shift in demand

some people invest simply for the opportunity to turn a profit. However, speculative investment can easily increase the price of a product far in excess of any underlying value. When the prices of shares in Internet businesses crashed, this was a case of underlying economic forces reasserting themselves.

Further examples are readily found. Consider the world market for diamonds, which is dominated by the De Beers diamond organisation. De Beers directly produces nearly half the world's high-quality diamonds by value, and aims to control the market by buying the diamonds produced by other mines. It sounds as though such a business should be immune to any underlying economic forces. In 2000 this proved no longer the case, and De Beers role in controlling the market had to change. As *The Economist* (3 June 2000, p. 112) put it: 'Simple economics, to which the cartel once thought itself immune, explains the change.' In this case, 'simple economics' meant that slow growth in the demand for diamonds made it no longer possible for De Beers effectively to control the world market price. Even businesses that have monopolies cannot ignore the underlying forces of demand and supply.

There was no denying the impact of the forces of supply and demand in the coffee market in July 1994 when it was announced that the Brazilian coffee harvest had been damaged by severe frost and would be 20 per cent less than expected. The price of coffee on the world commodity markets rose by 30 per cent in a single day, and retail prices began to rise almost immediately. However, in deciding to raise the price of a standard jar of instant coffee to wholesalers and retailers, the coffee manufacturers were not responding blindly to a market signal, but were carefully calculating the likely impact of a price rise on their competitive position in the market and on consumer demand. The underlying forces of supply and demand are important, but are only part of the picture.

For those of you who have not studied the economics of demand functions before (or who could use a refresher), we now move on to a more extended discussion of the marketing implications of the demand function. Subsequently, in the final section of the chapter, we deal with probably the best-known analytical framework for competitive analysis – Porter's five forces.

USEFUL THINGS TO KNOW ABOUT DEMAND FUNCTIONS

The characteristic shape of a demand function, showing that the volume of demand declines as price increases, should be familiar to all marketers. Even a seemingly simple concept such as this, however, can provide some valuable insights for strategic marketing. There are three key questions to ask about a demand function:

1. What is the slope of the demand function?
2. Is this a demand function for the whole industry, or for a single firm within the industry?
3. What is likely to make the demand function shift (as shown in Figure 5.4)?

A great deal of practical marketing strategy is concerned with trying to alter the slope of the demand function (usually with the aim of reducing customer sensitivity to price) or trying to shift the demand function to the right (so that more is bought at any given price).

The slope of the demand function

For most goods and services we would expect that a rise in price would provoke a decline in sales, and a fall in price would provoke a rise in sales. Obviously, the critical question is by how much will sales volume rise or fall when the price changes? The standard method of measuring sales volume changes which occur in response to price changes is the 'elasticity of demand with respect to price' (or 'price elasticity of demand'). In simple terms, the elasticity of demand can be gauged by the slope of the demand function, illustrated in Figure 5.5.

The steep demand function shown on the left of the diagram indicates that a large price change is needed to bring about much of a change in demand – this is known as 'inelastic demand'. The shallow demand function shown on the right indicates that even a small change in price brings about a large change in demand – known as 'elastic demand'. The concept can be made more rigorous.

Price elasticity of demand can be defined as the percentage change in quantity demanded for a 1 per cent change in price. To take an extreme example, if the price of something doubles (100 per cent increase) and there is only a 10 per cent reduction in demand, then elasticity of demand is –0.1 (that is –10 per cent change in demand divided by +100 per cent change in price). Demand for this product is inelastic with respect to price. When the percentage change in demand is less than the percentage change in price (elasticity is between 0.0 and –1.0), demand is said to be inelastic. When the percentage change in demand is more than the percentage change in price (elasticity greater than –1.0), demand is elastic.

There are certain types of product for which demand is usually inelastic, these are necessities such as basic foodstuffs and essential services such as gas and electricity. Demand for luxury goods and services, such as personal stereos and cinema tickets, would usually be elastic. It is also to be expected that the elasticity of demand for something will be affected by the number of alternative products that are available, and by the degree to which consumers regard the alternatives as good substitutes. For example, London Underground is the only company running underground trains in

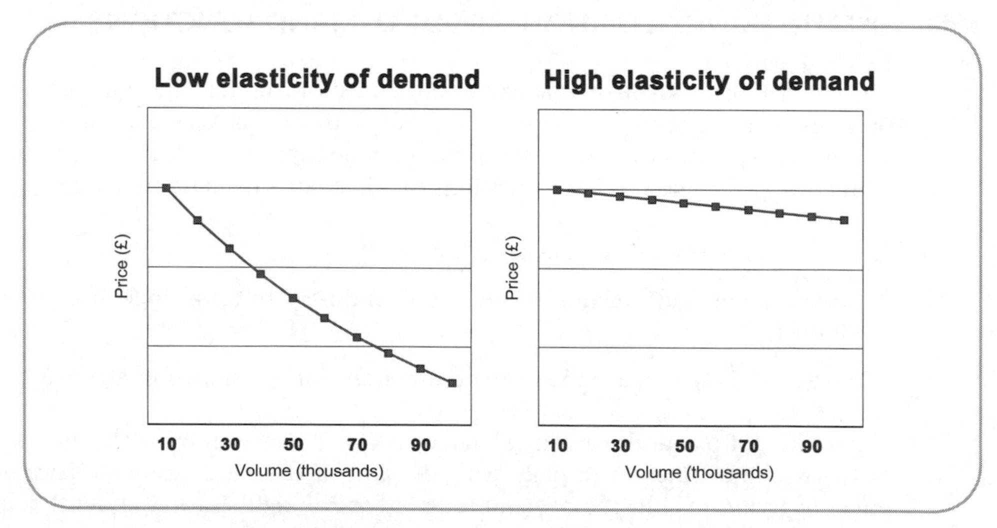

Figure 5.5 Elasticity of demand

London, and the demand for underground tickets is fairly inelastic – there is no really good substitute if you want to travel quickly and fairly cheaply around London. However, buses, taxis and walking are all partial substitutes for the underground. If London Underground raised their prices too far, some customers would walk (if their journey was short) and others would switch to the bus or the taxi.

The demand function of the firm and of the industry

Unless there is only one firm in the industry (a pure monopoly), there will be a difference between the demand function for the industry and the demand function for the firm. This has important practical consequences. It is no use looking at the impact of aggregate price changes in the industry and their impact on overall industry sales volume to estimate the elasticity of demand with respect to changes in your own firm's price. Normally demand will be more elastic with respect to the price of a single firm than it is with respect to the whole industry. The reason for this is easy to understand. The firms within an industry produce products that are reasonably good substitutes for each other. When one firm alone raises price, customers can easily move to the products of competitors, so that the sales of that firm experience a substantial decline ('highly elastic'). If all firms were to raise their prices simultaneously, then customers have no easy substitute to turn to and so sales will decline by a smaller proportion. This is easily seen in the case of petrol (gasoline) sold for private motoring. Petrol buyers do have some brand preferences but they are not particularly strong, since petrol is generally regarded as a rather homogeneous product. If a single company raises the price of petrol, it will experience a substantial drop in sales as customers switch to alternative brands, which they regard as more or less the same. However, if all petrol companies raise prices simultaneously, there will be a rather small decline in petrol sales (this is a product with low elasticity of demand). The important lesson is that you must not imagine that, because you are selling a product with low overall elasticity of demand, you have great latitude in pricing strategy.

Shifts in the demand function

Figure 5.4 illustrated the way in which a demand function could 'shift'. This occurs where the whole demand curve is moved to the right or the left. It means that the product or service has become more popular with consumers (a shift to the right, meaning that consumers want to buy more at all the different possible prices), or less popular (a shift to the left, meaning that consumers want to buy less at all different prices). In the discussion of Figure 5.4 we gave an example of how this could happen remarkably quickly. When a sports club is promoted or relegated, almost overnight there will be a shift in demand for the products and services that it sells (for example replica shirts, other merchandise, season tickets, tours of the ground). When a food scare occurs, the demand for the affected food product is affected in the same way. Our case study on the British beef industry (see cases section) illustrates how the demand function for British beef shifted very rapidly to the left when news of the human form of BSE ('mad cow disease') became known to the public. The marketer needs to be aware of the nature of shifts in the demand function, both to respond when factors external to the marketing mix bring them about – the marketing department can do little about a football team's performance on the field, or the behaviour of the rogue proteins that cause BSE – and to consider means of engineering them. Much consumer goods marketing is concerned with rendering a product more fashionable. If successful, such a strategy results in a shift of the demand function to the right. The strategies pursued by the British Meat and Livestock Commission in the wake of the BSE problem were designed to shift the demand function back to the right.

Final thoughts on demand functions and elasticity

The concept of price elasticity provides a rather comforting feeling that, by means of a simple calculation, the impact of a price change on demand and total sales revenue can be established. Unfortunately, life is seldom that simple. First, it is very difficult to disentangle the effect of price from the effects of the other marketing mix variables. For example, if there was a change in advertising activity alongside a change in price, it would be difficult to tell what proportion of a sales volume change should be attributed to price and what to advertising. Second, the price elasticity of demand for large price changes is likely to be different from the elasticity for small changes. So even if we know that a 2 per cent cut in price leads to a 1 per cent increase in sales volume, we cannot conclude that a 40 per cent cut in price will lead to a 20 per cent increase in sales volume. This was the type of situation described for London Underground above. A small price rise will not lead people to change their behaviour substantially, or to seek out substitute products very actively. A large price rise will motivate them, and may even force them, to look for alternatives. Small changes in the price of petrol have virtually no effect on demand, because the private car is much the most convenient means of transport available to many people. Large petrol price increases can have a significant effect on the buyer's disposable income, and make alternative forms of transport seem much more attractive.

ANALYSING THE COMPETITIVE ENVIRONMENT USING PORTER'S FIVE FORCES

Figure 5.6 illustrates a widely accepted method of classifying the key factors in the competitive environment, originally developed by Porter (1980) and often referred to as 'Porter's five forces'. The 'five forces' involved are direct competitive rivalry, the threat from new entry competition, the threat from substitutes, the power of buyers and the power of suppliers. The key feature of this framework is that it extends the concept of competition, and the competitive environment, beyond those businesses that supply products and services that are direct rivals with our own product range. Before examining each of the five forces in turn, it is worth spending a little time considering why we need to think beyond our direct competitive rivals.

Originally, industry analysis using the 'five forces' was developed as a method of analysing the relative profitability of different industries. Such analysis is of intrinsic interest to economists and also to marketing strategists who may wish to evaluate the attractiveness of different industries – either because they wish to enter that business themselves, or perhaps because they hope to sell products or services to firms in the industry. Initial expectations were that the profitability of an industry sector would be

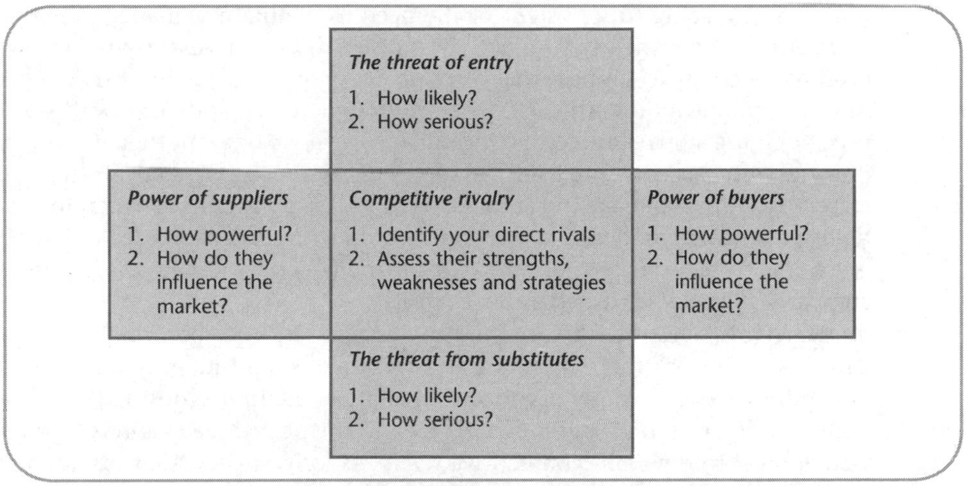

The threat of entry

1. How likely?
2. How serious?

Power of suppliers

1. How powerful?
2. How do they influence the market?

Competitive rivalry

1. Identify your direct rivals
2. Assess their strengths, weaknesses and strategies

Power of buyers

1. How powerful?
2. How do they influence the market?

The threat from substitutes

1. How likely?
2. How serious?

Figure 5.6 The competitive environment

Source: Adapted with the permission of The Free Press, an imprint of Simon & Schuster Adult Publishing Group, from *Competitive Advantage; Creating and Sustaining Superior Performance* by Michael E. Porter. Copyright © 1985, 1998 by Michael E. Porter

directly related to the intensity of competitive rivalry within it. The more fiercely firms within the industry compete with one another, the more aggressively one would expect them to set their prices, resulting in lower profit margins and lower overall profitability. However, it turns out that direct rivalry is not the whole story. The other four of the 'five forces' can also influence profitability, and so affect the competitive environment and thus the overall attractiveness of an industry sector. The intensity of competition within an industry increases under the following conditions:

- Where there is a high risk that one or more new firms will enter the market to compete with the incumbents
- Where there is a high risk that a new product technology – a 'substitute' – will be developed that provides the same benefits advantageously (for example at lower cost)
- Where supplier businesses exert considerable power over the industry
- Where customers (consumers or businesses) exert considerable power over the industry.

We now move on to consider the implications of each of these 'five forces' in turn.

Direct competitive rivalry

Direct competitive rivalry occurs between different firms producing a product or service that consumers consider to be similar. For example, direct competitive rivalry occurs between automobile manufacturers producing cars in the 'family car market', such as the Ford Mondeo, the Toyota Avensis and the General Motors Vectra. Clearly, few firms are going to lose sight of the need to maintain vigilance over their direct competitors. Nevertheless, it is not always easy to identify exactly who they are. For example, it is easy to suppose that firms operating in the same industry are necessarily in direct competition with each other. Although Ferrari and Ford both manufacture cars, they are not really competing directly against one another. Ferrari competes directly with Porsche, and Ford competes directly with General Motors. This is an extreme example to make the point clear. In less extreme cases (for example, are Ford's high specification models in direct competition with some Mercedes vehicles?), judgement has to be exercised, often based on industry experience, to determine which companies should be treated as direct rivals.

Having established who are the key direct rivals, it is appropriate to undertake a detailed analysis of their strengths and weaknesses, and identify and evaluate their marketing strategies. Many of the tools that are of use in diagnosing the strategic situation of one's own firm (described in this and the next three chapters) can be equally well applied to the main competitive rivals. As long as they are substantial, publicly owned businesses, there will be sufficient information in the public domain to make such analyses meaningful.

As a rule, the fewer direct rivals there are within an industry, the less intense will be competitive rivalry. The extreme case is a monopoly (industry with just one firm) where there is no direct rivalry at all. The degree of similarity or difference between the rivals also affects competitive rivalry. For example, where a domestic firm that relies wholly on the domestic market faces competition from a multinational firm – for which this is only one market out of many in which it competes – competition is likely to be more intense. The multinational may be prepared to accept low profits in this single market as it builds market share, and can finance this investment in market share out of profits made elsewhere in the world. The domestic rival has nowhere else to go, and no other markets to rely on, and will be forced to react aggressively if its market share is threatened.

The threat of new entry

Firms that do not currently compete in the market, but that may do so in the future, pose the threat of new entry competition. For example, in discussing the diamond market earlier we mentioned De Beers. One strategy open to De Beers is to exploit its reputation for diamonds (perhaps the ultimate luxury product) by entering other luxury goods markets, for example the market for designer clothing, handbags and cosmetics. This would represent a threat to the established competitors such as Louis Vuitton and Gucci. A key factor affecting the extent of the threat posed by new entry competition is the scale of the entry barriers in an industry. Entry barriers are those things that make it difficult for a firm to enter a new industry. For example, the substantial sunk-cost investments that automobile manufacturers have in plant and equipment would make it very expensive for a new entrant to achieve competitive parity. Legal barriers such as patent protection can also represent entry barriers. If the incumbent firms own well-known brands, then this can also create an entry barrier. In effect, the investment in the brand-building process is very similar to the investment in capital goods and equipment required for the production process. In order to compete effectively with the firms in the industry, a new rival would have to spend large amounts of money developing brand recognition. The risk that this expenditure would not pay off is a deterrent to a firm thinking about entering the market.

The firms within an industry can also deter potential entrants by making it clear that they would respond aggressively if a new competitive rival challenged them. For example, an industry in which there are frequent price wars between the incumbent firms is less attractive to new entry competition than one in which prices tend to remain stable for long periods.

The threat from substitutes

Beyond the firms with which you compete directly, and others that may enter the market, there is the threat that someone may develop a new product or service that renders your own product obsolete. This is the process of substitution, most frequently found where a new technological solution supersedes an older technology. For example, the manual typewriter was superseded by the electric typewriter, which was in turn rendered obsolete with the advent of word-processing equipment. In due course, the specialist word processor was replaced by the general purpose personal computer, which can run word-processing software, but has many other applications besides. For many years it has been expected that business travel would be replaced, to some extent, by new technologies – video conferencing services have been available from telecommunications firms for many years, and high-speed Internet access promises desktop video conferencing. This has not yet happened to any appreciable extent, nor do airline or rail companies regard it as a terribly serious threat, illustrating the difficulty involved in predicting change in the marketing environment.

The power of suppliers

Suppliers can also affect the dynamics of competition in an industry. The power exerted by suppliers will depend upon how many of them there are and the importance of the products or services that they supply. Where only a few firms, or in an extreme case a single firm, control the supplies of a key product or service, this can be the dominant factor in competitive success. If the supplier can also threaten to 'integrate forwards', that is, to become a direct competitive rival, then this is a serious strategic issue. Forward integration occurs when a company in your supply industry decides to enter into direct competition in your own market. This would happen, for example, if a supplier of mobile phone components (keypads, screens, circuit boards and so on) decided to manufacture and market complete mobile phones in competition with Nokia and Motorola.

The influence of a very powerful supplier has been debated in the American courts in the case of Microsoft and its domination of the market for personal computer operating systems. An anti-trust action was brought against Microsoft, which was accused of using its dominance in the supply of operating systems software to compete unfairly in the market for applications software (such as Internet browsers). To simplify a very complex legal argument, the contention was that when it supplied operating system software to personal computer manufacturers, Microsoft insisted on bundling it with applications software. The personal computer manufacturer might have preferred not to bundle the Microsoft applications software with the new

personal computer, but could not risk antagonising Microsoft and losing access to Windows – since this would have been commercial suicide. The Microsoft anti-trust case is a complex one and we have no intention of delving further into the detail here. The key point to extract from the case is the huge influence that a powerful supplier can exert on the competition within an industry under certain circumstances.

The power of buyers

Finally, we have the influence of buyers on competition within an industry. The power of buyers increases as buying is concentrated in only a few hands, particularly if the products bought are undifferentiated. As we saw in the previous chapter, high levels of demand concentration are not at all uncommon in business-to-business markets. In the extreme case there may only be a single buyer (this is known as a monopsony), but more commonly in business-to-business markets one finds the situation of only a few buyers (known as oligopsony). The global automotive components industry, for example, faces conditions of oligopsony, since there is only a handful of major automobile manufacturers. At this point we will not go into further detail on the implications of buyer power for marketing strategy, since this is a topic that is dealt with in detail in Chapters 4 and 9. In our discussion of organisational buying behaviour in the previous chapter we saw how the nature of buying behaviour is affected by the structure of the market. In Chapter 9, Relationship Marketing Strategies, we will explore the practical implications of dealing with concentrated markets (that is, markets dominated by a few buyers), compared with dispersed markets in which no single buyer has any substantial power.

THE IMPACT OF THE INTERNET ON THE COMPETITIVE ENVIRONMENT

We deal with the impact of the Internet on marketing strategy in Chapter 10. It is important at this point, however, to address a few of the issues that the Internet raises for the competitive environment. In the infancy of Internet-based commerce it was thought that the whole competitive environment might be radically altered. The Internet was seen as a means by which businesses could gain immediate and 'perfect' information about potential suppliers, and could gain direct access to their customers (Chaston, 2001; Timmers, 2000). Loyal, local suppliers would be thrown out in favour of lower cost suppliers discovered on the Internet. Customer loyalty would be substantially reduced. Rather than sticking to one supplier, the customer would be tempted to search the Internet every time they wanted to buy something, and select whichever supplier was offering the best price at the time. Similarly, it was thought that once firms could gain direct access to their customers through the Internet, they would no longer need to do business through conventional intermediaries, and that many of those intermediaries would cease to exist. Agents and brokers, in particular (such as travel agents and insurance brokers), were expected to suffer as firms used the Internet to sell direct to customers.

We can think about the changes that the Internet was expected to bring in terms of five forces analysis. The Internet was expected to intensify direct competitive rivalry by giving potential buyers ready access to virtually perfect information (enhanced buyer power). New entry competition would be facilitated since the barriers to entry into a market would be reduced – in particular the control over conventional channels of distribution by incumbent firms would be neutralised. To summarise, rather than operating in limited local markets, it was envisaged that the Internet would throw firms worldwide into direct competition with each other and improve the efficiency with which the underlying forces of supply and demand operated.

So far nothing so radical has happened. One fairly obvious reason for this is that the Internet has had no effect at all on the logistics and costs of transporting goods. For certain service products that can be *delivered* as well as sold over the Internet, it may make no difference if the supplier is in London, Cairo or Adelaide. But for goods that have to be physically transported and insured, it clearly does make a difference. A local supplier has a great advantage over a distant rival, since the costs of transport and insurance will be much lower. Another more subtle point is that there are certain types of information that the Internet cannot provide. No matter how many testimonials from satisfied customers may be posted at an Internet site, there are many products where only the act of meeting the supplier and visiting the supplier's premises can provide real reassurance of their ability to deliver.

The impact of the Internet on the competitive environment is clearly a factor that needs to be considered when conducting a competitive analysis. In some markets it will make (indeed has already made) a big difference. However, there are no grounds for any general claim that the Internet will revolutionise the competitive environment of business.

THE RESOURCE-BASED VIEW OF THE FIRM

The essential message of this chapter has been that to achieve above-average business performance a firm must gain a sustainable competitive advantage over its rivals, and that the analysis of the competitive environment is central to the identification of such a sustainable advantage. This focus on the market, and on competitive rivals, makes intuitive sense to marketing managers. It is logical to focus on direct rivals, and on the extended competitive environment, since it seems obvious that this is where a competitive advantage must be created. In recent years a slightly different approach to competitive strategy has been developed, summarised as the 'resource-based view' of the firm. In the resource-based view, the source of competitive advantage for an organisation is said to come from *internal resource advantages* rather than from *competitive positioning advantages*. The initial impetus behind the resource-based view arose from research showing that there were substantial, long-term differences in profitability between firms operating within the same industry at the same time (Rumelt, 1991). So the argument goes, if one firm manages to achieve a long-term performance advantage over its rivals even when operating under the same competitive circumstances, then surely the source of its competitive advantage must come from within – from the resources that it controls.

If the competitive advantage of the firm lies with the resources that it controls, then the next step must be to try to identify exactly which resources are commonly the source of that competitive advantage. A number of researchers have sought to classify resources in terms of their ability to generate a sustainable competitive advantage. Lynch (2000, pp. 280–2) provided a summary of this work in his 'seven elements of resource-based sustainable competitive advantage', which are as follows:

- *Prior or acquired resources.* Strategy is more likely to be successful if it is based on resources that the organisation already controls, rather than on resources that have to be newly acquired.
- *Innovative capability.* The capacity to innovate is itself a valuable resource, which companies do not share equally. Therefore, an organisation should actively seek to develop the capacity for innovation within itself.
- *Truly competitive.* For a resource to provide a competitive advantage, it must deliver something that is both relevant to the market and superior to the competition. It's not good enough to be good at something, that 'something' must matter in the market, and you must be better at it than your rivals (we will come back to this idea when we look at SWOT analysis in Chapter 7).
- *Substitutability.* The less easily a resource can be substituted, the more useful it is likely to be as the basis for a sustainable competitive advantage.
- *Appropriability.* The company must be able to 'appropriate' the advantages that arise from the resource – to appropriate something means to take possession of it. In the 'GlaxoSmithKline in South Africa' case study in Part Two, you will find a detailed discussion of the arguments surrounding patents in the pharmaceutical industry. Patenting is one of the ways in which a key resource can be effectively appropriated.
- *Durability.* The longer that a resource is capable of bestowing a competitive advantage on the firm, the better.
- *Imitability.* The less easily that a resource can be imitated by rival firms, the better. Both durability and imitability are illustrated in the two case studies of British Telecommunications plc (BT) to be found in Part Two. One vitally important resource for this company is the physical infrastructure that it owns (an extensive network of telephone exchanges and cables). This infrastructure has conferred a durable advantage upon BT that has proved very difficult to imitate. However, as mobile communications becomes ever-more sophisticated, so mobile networks represent an increasingly good substitute (see above, Substitutability) for BT's physical infrastructure.

For most of this chapter the focus has been upon competition, on the identification and analysis of relevant competitive forces that must be taken into consideration in marketing strategy development. There can be no doubt that the analysis of these competitive forces is fundamental to the strategic marketing process. However, the analysis of the external competitive environment is not enough. This final section has introduced the resource-based view of the firm, which is a complementary approach to strategy formulation that augments the analysis of competition. Having analysed the diverse forces that make up the competitive environment, the strategist should also ask what it is that the firm will do to achieve enhanced performance. The resource-based view provides some answers to this question.

SUMMARY

An understanding of the marketing environment is a necessary basis for marketing strategy development. The marketing environment can be conveniently classified into the competitive environment and the macroenvironment. Underlying any analysis of the competitive environment should be an appreciation of the way in which the market economy works. Understanding the fundamental forces of demand and supply within a market or industry is an important component of environmental analysis. The competitive environment is often further analysed using a 'five forces' approach – direct rivalry, new entry threat, threat from substitutes, power of suppliers, power of buyers. Radical suggestions that the Internet would revolutionise competition across a wide range of industries have not yet proved to be true. However, the Internet has had a substantial effect on the competitive environment of some industries, and will have a progressively wider and deeper impact on the competitive environment. While it is clearly essential to have a sound grasp of the competitive environment in order to develop an effective marketing strategy, the resource-based view of the firm emphasises that it is through the control of valuable resources that the firm will achieve a sustainable competitive advantage.

Questions for discussion

Consider the consumer market for petrol (that is, sales of petrol to private motorists rather than companies). Explain the significance of each of the following aspects of the competitive environment for the petrol marketing strategies of the oil companies.

1. World oil production is largely controlled by a small number of countries that are members of OPEC (the Organisation of Petroleum Exporting Countries), an organisation that aims to control world oil production and manage price fluctuations.
2. Suppose that petrol costs US$1 per litre. The government imposes a tax increase of 10 cents per litre, and all the oil companies simultaneously raise the retail price of petrol to $1.10 per litre. They notice that there is a 1.5 per cent reduction in demand as a result of this price increase.
3. Consumers regard petrol as close to a commodity product – competing products are regarded as good substitutes for each other.
4. Governments frequently impose high levels of duty on petrol.

References

Chaston, I (2001), *e-Marketing Strategy*, London: McGraw-Hill

Lynch, R (2000), *Corporate Strategy*, Harlow: Financial Times/Pitman

Porter, M E (1979), 'How Competitive Forces Shape Strategy', *Harvard Business Review*, March–April

Porter, M E (1980), *Competitive Strategy*, New York: Free Press

Porter, M E (1985), *Competitive Advantge*, New York: Free Press

Rumelt, R (1991), 'How Much Does Industry Matter?', *Strategic Management Journal*, March

Timmers, P (2000), *Electronic Commerce: Strategies and Models for Business-to-Business Trading*, Chichester: Wiley

chapter six

Understanding the Macroenvironment

Learning objectives

By reading this chapter you will learn:

- More about the role of environmental analysis in strategic marketing
- How to classify and analyse factors in the macroenvironment
- How to assess the impact of macroeconomic, demographic and 'green' issues on marketing strategy
- A method of assessing the relative importance of environmental factors.

INTRODUCTION

In this chapter we continue our discussion of the marketing environment, with a focus on the macroenvironment. The macroenvironment was defined in the previous chapter as those factors outside the immediate competitive environment that may have an influence on the organisation's achievement of its marketing objectives. The chapter begins with a discussion of the different methods that can be used to classify the macroenvironment. This can be a confusing area. You might wonder why there are so many different suggestions for classification schemes for environmental factors. As we will see, they all represent different approaches to the problem of devising a classification scheme that is sufficiently broad to ensure that all key environmental factors are included, without including so many categories that the system becomes too complex to use. An extended example from the construction industry is included to demonstrate the application of an environmental classification scheme. Further illustrations of the impact of prominent macroeconomic trends are illustrated with detailed discussions of the implications of macroeconomic factors, demographic change and 'green' issues for marketing strategy development. Finally, at the end of the chapter, we provide a method of allocating priorities to environmental issues.

CLASSIFYING THE MACROENVIRONMENT

One of the best known acronyms in marketing is 'PEST', standing for **P**olitical, **E**conomic, **S**ocial and **T**echnological factors in the business environment. This mnemonic has the merit of being very simple to remember and to apply. If you so wish, you can even remember it as 'STEP' instead! However, there are disadvantages associated with this simplicity. Essentially, PEST is a system of classification. It is to be used to classify all environmental factors that are considered potentially important under the four headings. Any good classification system should meet two important criteria. First, the categories should be exhaustive – in other words, it should be possible to classify every instance of a phenomenon into one of the headings. Second, the categories should be mutually exclusive – it should be clear into which box a specific example goes. PEST fails on both of these counts. It is by no means exhaustive of the types of environmental phenomena that businesses could face. The political category is often extended to include political, legal and regulatory factors. It is not entirely clear where factors from the 'green environment' should be located – global warming, for example, or deforestation. On the other hand, the PEST headings are not mutually exclusive either. The introduction of a statutory minimum wage, for example, is a substantial political issue that has economic and social effects. When the UK introduced a statutory minimum wage, there was clear political polarisation of opinion, with debate raging about the impact of a minimum wage on the economy (particularly the effect on unemployment and the viability of small businesses) and on social welfare. The minimum wage example illustrates that the categories used in the PEST mnemonic are 'leaky boxes'.

Nevertheless, there are good reasons to use a system for classifying environmental factors, and just about any usable classification system is likely to suffer from some of the same defects as PEST. Finlay (2000) suggested another memorable mnemonic, DEEPLIST, standing for:

- Demographics
- Economic
- Environmental
- Political
- Legal
- Informational
- Social
- Technological.

Brooks and Weatherston (2000) came up with the rather less memorable 'LE PEST C', which is simply PEST with the addition of Legal, Ecological and Competitive categories. All frameworks of this type can be of use to managers by providing a checklist of key headings, to make sure that no major and obvious aspect of the business environment has been neglected in the analysis. Most of the frameworks suggested by authors in the field (for example Aaker, 1998; Jain, 2000; Baker, 1992; Lynch, 2000; McDonald, 1999) are some simple variation on the PEST mnemonic, augmenting the scheme just a little to make the classification more nearly exhaustive. In our illustration from the UK construction industry we have drawn upon an industry report that used just such an augmentation, STEEP, standing for social, technological, economic, environmental and political factors. Of course, a confusion that can arise here is that the word 'environmental' is being used in two slightly different senses. First, we use the word to refer to the marketing environment, that is, all the factors that could affect the firm's achievement of its marketing objectives. Second, we often use the word in the specific sense of the world ecosystem, that is, 'a biological community of interacting organisms and their physical environment' (*Concise Oxford Dictionary*).

It must be borne in mind, however, that the point of the exercise is to identify the key factors in the business environment that are likely to affect the strategic marketing decisions of the organisation. Whatever mnemonic, framework or classification scheme may be used, it is simply a means to an end. It is the incautious manager who argues that he does not need such tools because he already knows very well what are the key trends in the business environment. Woodside (2000, p. 2) proposed the first 'sensemaking principle', that 'we are not very good at sensemaking but we think we are'. By 'sensemaking', Woodside means the activities of scanning the environment, interpreting what we see, making effective decisions and evaluating the outcomes. He provides persuasive evidence of an unfortunate human misconception, namely, human beings are not very good at predicting or interpreting the environment, but think they are. This applies at least as much to managers as to anyone else, and can easily result in overconfidence. Overconfidence is the first step on the road to being overwhelmed by a new competitor we either didn't see coming or believed to be no threat, or by a new technology that didn't seem to have any bearing on our products and markets. Meanwhile, entrepreneurs are seeking their fortunes by trying to find the right way to outflank established businesses and take away their markets. Many new opportunities to outflank established businesses have been created by information technology, with the Internet a focal point for new, entrepreneurial business solutions.

Analysing the Macroenvironment of the British Construction Industry

This analysis was conducted using a variation of the PEST framework, STEEP, standing for social, technological, economic, environmental and political.

Social

- Increasing age profile of the UK population
- Increasing number of households in the UK
- Increasing average personal affluence, perhaps with associated increased inequality and social exclusion
- Greater self-sufficiency among people in work, with declining welfare support from the state and a reduction in long-term employment security.

The most obvious social driver of the construction industry is demographics, particularly the number of households. Among other factors, increasing life expectancy and increased levels of divorce are expected to lead to changes in the volume of demand for housing and in the type of housing required.

Technological

- Computer technology will allow designers and architects to improve the design and specification of buildings
- Other technologies, such as robotics, will reduce the need for people to perform dangerous or repetitive tasks
- Information technology will alter patterns of employment and travel, more and more people will be able to work away from a conventional workplace (including working from home)
- New technologies will improve building materials – materials will become simultaneously stronger, lighter and easier to work with.

It is to be expected that the demand for both residential space and commercial office space will be affected by 'teleworking', and that the pattern of demand for urban and suburban transport infrastructure will change. Teleworking refers to employees doing work that was traditionally done on the employer's premises somewhere else. Often this is 'working from home', where the employee uses workspace at home to conduct their paid employment. Usually such employees have the use of information and communication technologies to enable them to keep in touch with colleagues, whether those employees are in a central office or are also teleworking.

Economic

- The threat of a general economic recession hangs over the industrialised world in the early years of the new century
- The British economy is in many ways more robust than its Western European neighbours, and may be better placed to withstand a recession
- The expansion of the European Union (EU) is likely to bring membership to low-wage economies in Eastern Europe.

The construction sector depends heavily upon the general economic wellbeing of other industries. When other industries cut back on investment expenditure, this can have a disastrous effect on construction. The expansion of the EU may provide British construction firms with access to a pool of cheap labour in Eastern Europe, since labour mobility is legally guaranteed within the EU.

Environmental

- Global warming is widely accepted as a fact of life, and the ecological impact of global warming is regarded as unavoidable
- Emissions from burning fossil fuels are of increasing concern, since they create a number of health risks – emissions will decline in the UK but are likely to continue to rise in the developing economies of the southern hemisphere
- Increasing numbers of people are either active or tacit supporters of the environmental movement, the aims of which will have increasing support in the UK and elsewhere.

The construction industry is often directly in the firing line over environmental issues, for example major road building projects have encountered well-organised and highly publicised disruption. However, there are clearly opportunities for construction firms to innovate, for example by providing more energy-efficient buildings and through more environmentally sympathetic treatment of construction waste.

Political

- Further European integration and EU enlargement are the political factors that will have the greatest impact on the construction sector
- There remain unanswered questions concerning the economic policies of the British government; some commentators think that industry can expect to shoulder an increased burden of taxation over the next few years
- Whatever government is in power, it is clear that new road building projects will be severely constrained for the indefinite future.

If the plans for further development of the EU stalled (for example if the single European currency area failed to expand, or if planned EU enlargement failed to occur) then the prospects for the European economy would be damaged, and the UK construction industry would suffer as a result.

Sources: Based on CIRIA (1999) and CIC (1998)

KEY FORCES IN THE MACROENVIRONMENT

Classification schemes, such as those discussed above, are a useful starting point for environmental analysis. The construction industry example has introduced some of the factors that might apply within each category, and begun to illustrate the impact on business that they might have. In conducting an environmental analysis for a specific firm, it is important to tailor the analysis to the specific circumstances of that organisation at that time. However, in this section we spend some time discussing a number of environmental factors that have a broad effect on business, and which are clearly important variables in the marketing environment of a great many firms. This will provide a starting point for the detailed analysis of particular businesses, whether in case studies or in reality. We will discuss the following 'key forces' and their implications:

- The macroeconomy
- Demographic change
- The 'green' environment.

The macroeconomy

The analysis of demand, supply and the interplay of competitive forces within a single market is known as 'microeconomics'. Businesses are also concerned about 'big' economic trends. Analysis that is concerned with change at the level of the whole economy is known as 'macroeconomics'. It is certainly not our intention in a book on marketing strategy to attempt to give an introductory course on macroeconomics! The interested reader is referred to an appropriate text (for example Macintosh et al.,

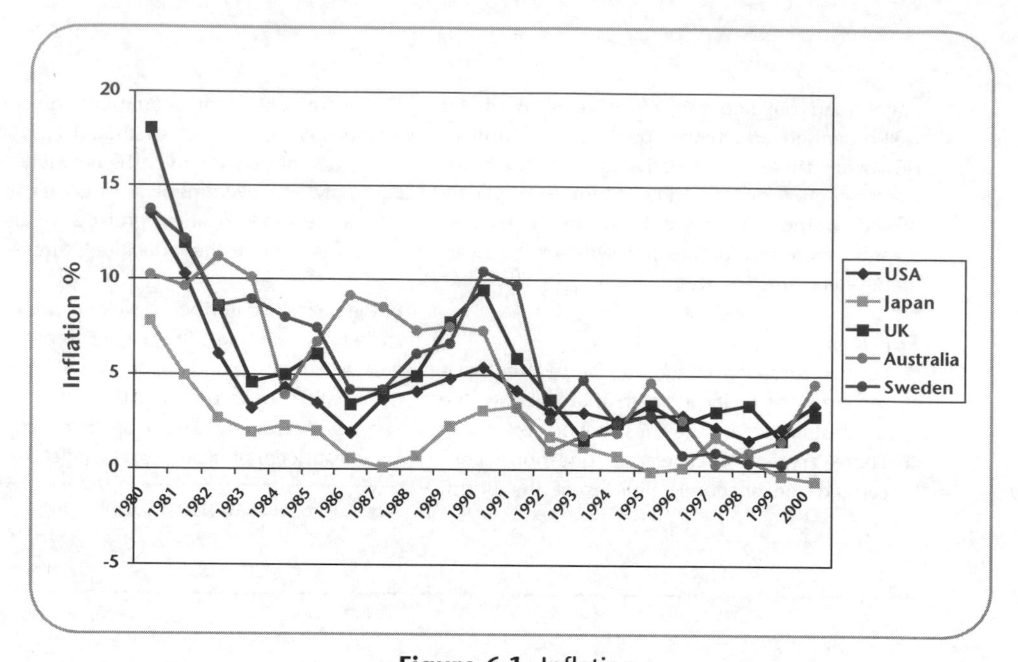

Figure 6.1 Inflation

Source: Based on data from OECD (1999, 2001)

1996). What we want to provide is sufficient knowledge to be able to appreciate the likely implications of macroeconomic changes for business and marketing strategy.

Until comparatively recently the control of *inflation* was regarded as the key macroeconomic priority by governments worldwide. Inflation can be defined very simply as a rise in the general level of prices. Figure 6.1 illustrates recent trends in inflation for five countries.

The inflation rate here is being measured using the annual percentage increase in general consumer prices. The rate of inflation in the world economy has declined substantially during the last two decades, and inflation is now regarded as a lower economic policy priority. However, Figure 6.1 shows that until quite recently inflation was running at more than 10 per cent per year in several countries and it is only in the last decade that inflation has dropped consistently below 5 per cent.

Inflation matters to businesses for a number of reasons. General rises in consumer prices lead to demands for wage increases from employees, since if wages do not increase in line with prices employees will gradually become worse off. The impact of inflation is not equal across all industry sectors, however. While all employees are affected (as consumers) fairly equally by inflation, firms differ considerably in their ability to raise their own prices. We discussed the reasons for this in the previous chapter (the underlying logic of the market economy). Businesses that operate in highly competitive markets may not be able to raise their prices, so that when wage costs rise they find their profits squeezed. Alternatively, they may choose to resist pressure from employees for wage rises. This, in itself, may damage the ability of the firm to recruit and retain employees, and so adversely affect the operations and marketing strategy of the firm. In Chapter 9, Relationship Marketing Strategies, we will see that marketing experts such as Reichheld (1996) and Grönroos (1991) emphasise the importance of retaining and motivating staff as a key component of marketing strategy, particularly in service markets. High levels of inflation, particularly where the rate of inflation is variable and unpredictable, pose problems for the formulation and implementation of marketing strategies.

Before moving on from the topic of inflation, it is worth comparing the performance of the different economies in Figure 6.1. The rate of inflation in Japan has almost always been below that of the other countries, while the UK and the USA have had relatively high rates of inflation. Clearly, if one country experiences high levels of inflation while another does not, then a businesses in the high inflation country could very easily find themselves at a competitive disadvantage relative to business in the low inflation country. For example, with high British inflation leading to rapid rises in the price of British goods and low Japanese inflation, surely British firms would become increasingly unable to compete with Japanese rivals? Were it not for exchange rate movements, this would almost certainly be true.

The *exchange rate* measures the relative value of currencies, and is often described as the price of one currency in terms of another (for example the number of US dollars that can be bought for one pound sterling). Figure 6.2 shows an exchange rate index for the same five countries that we used to examine inflation. The index is a measure of the value of the currency compared with its value in 1995 (the 'base year'), with the value in 1995 being set at 100. One thing that is immediately obvious is the way in which the Japanese currency increased rapidly in value over the period 1986 to 1995. From 1995 onwards currencies have deviated less in value than in the preceding period, and the Japanese yen has been much weaker. Much of this can be explained by the relative inflation rates. For example, the pound sterling declined substantially in value against the yen between 1986 and 1995, since otherwise British

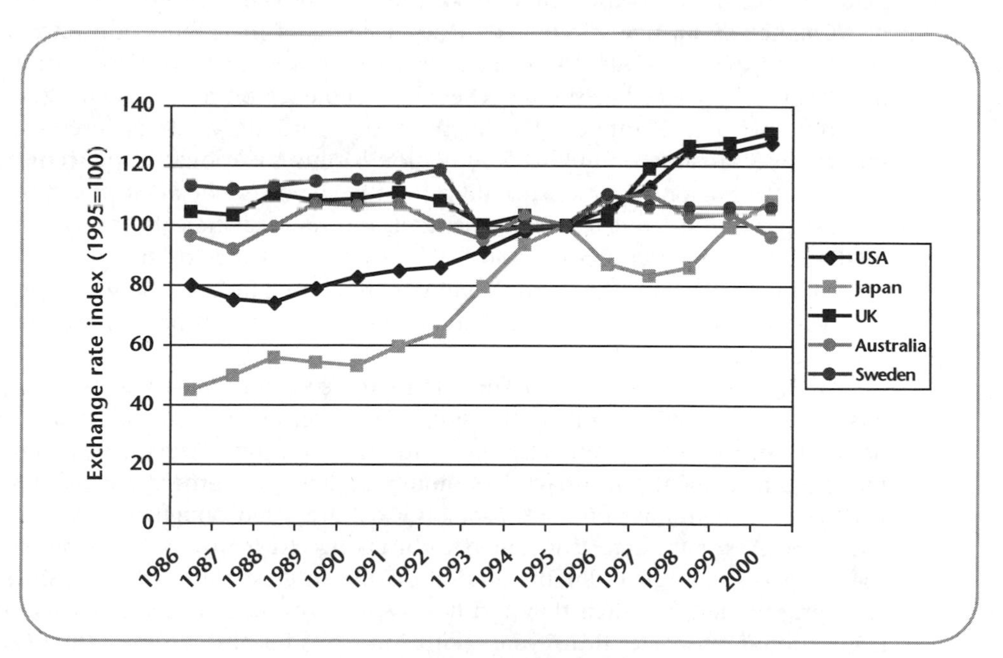

Figure 6.2 Exchange rate

Source: Based on data from OECD (1999, 2001)

firms would have been unable to compete with Japanese firms on world markets. They would simply have been 'priced out of the market' because of relatively high rates of British inflation. The decline in the value of sterling made British goods cheaper in terms of other currencies (particularly the yen), making it possible for British businesses to compete.

The implications of exchange rate movements for marketing strategy are considerable. Businesses selling in overseas markets, and receiving payment in foreign currency, can see expected profits vanish if the exchange rate changes after a contract is signed but before payment is made. If a contract price is agreed in foreign currency, and our own currency then appreciates (increases in value), then we will obtain less of our own currency for a given amount of foreign currency – we will make less profit than expected. It is possible to avoid this kind of exchange rate risk (for example by operating in the forward market for foreign exchange, or by insuring against exchange risks), but this will inevitably incur extra cost. The extra cost will either reduce profit margins, or will lead to higher prices and so a reduction in competitiveness. The underlying idea behind the creation of single currency areas, such as the euro zone in Europe, is to avoid such extra costs, and so to make international trade more efficient. This is why many British business leaders believe that their country should adopt the euro (the single European currency) as soon as possible. The adoption of the euro would make doing business with European firms easier, and would represent a significant improvement in the marketing environment for all businesses that export into the euro zone. Of course, there are many other arguments besides this one both in favour of, and against, the adoption of the euro by the UK – these arguments apply wherever single currency areas are found. A key argument concerns the role of interest rates.

The interest rate can be thought of as 'the price of money'. It is the price that is paid to use money owned by someone else. Figure 6.3 shows the comparative performance of our five selected countries in terms of their long-term interest rates. We can see that, as a rule, those economies that have had higher levels of inflation have also had higher interest rates. There is a simple reason for this. Our figure shows the 'nominal' rate of interest, that is, the actual percentage rate of interest paid on money owed. In an economy where inflation is running at over 15 per cent per year (Britain in 1980, for example), a creditor (that is, the owner of a debt) must receive at least 15 per cent interest merely to maintain the value of the debt in 'real terms'. So in high inflation economies people will only be prepared to lend money at high interest rates. Not surprisingly, the nominal interest rate in Japan has been lower than the other four countries throughout the period shown. Japan has almost always had the lowest inflation rate.

Interest rates play an important role in the economy for a number of reasons. First, they influence consumer spending. Many consumers also owe debts on their homes (mortgage debts). When interest rates rise, consumers have to spend more on mortgage repayments, and have less money available for other goods and services. Furthermore, consumer durables (notably cars) are often bought using bank loans. Higher interest rates deter consumers from taking out loans, and so tend to reduce spending on consumer durables. Additionally, interest rates affect businesses by changing the rate at which they can borrow to invest in new plant and equipment. High interest rates deter firms from taking out loans for business investments. A firm considering whether or not to borrow money to acquire new premises might decide against if borrowing costs are too high. A firm considering whether to replace its stock

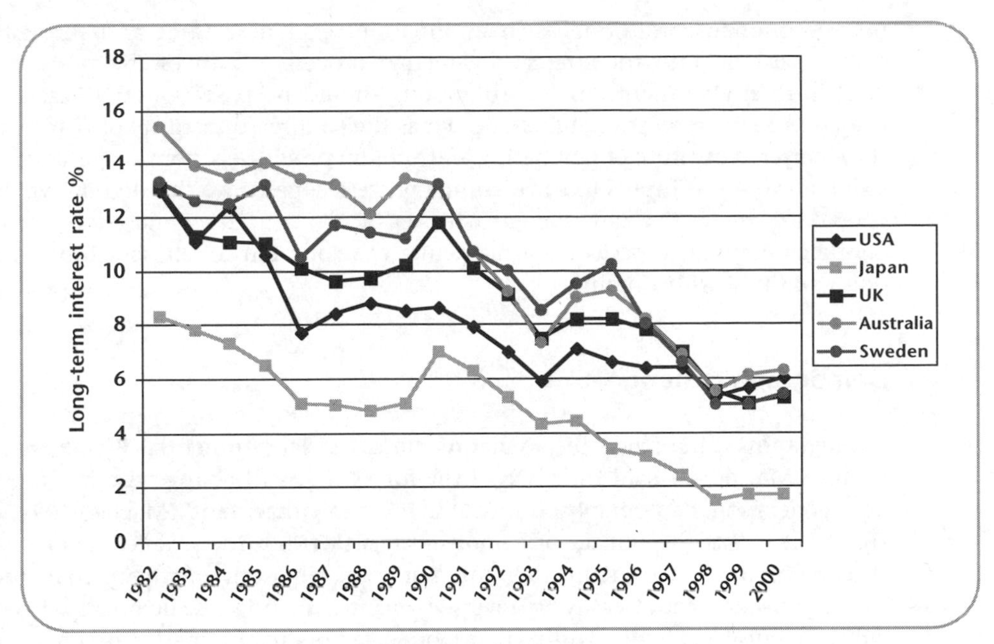

Figure 6.3 Interest rates

Source: Based on data from OECD (1999, 2001)

of vehicles might decide to maintain the existing fleet for another year for the same reason. All these decisions, by consumers and businesses, have considerable implications for marketing strategy. For example, a business-to-business marketer who unadvisedly launches an expensive new piece of construction equipment just as interest rates rise steeply will probably find that demand falls far below expectations.

Interest rates, inflation rates and exchange rates are key economic variables in the debate in the UK over adoption of the euro. Within the euro zone (as within any single currency area), there is a single interest rate. The different countries within the euro zone cannot each have its own interest rate, since there would be nothing to stop borrowers from simply choosing to borrow their euros in whichever country had the lowest interest rate. Of course, the adoption of a single currency also removes at a stroke the problems associated with currency fluctuations and business transactions. You can export within the single currency area, and be completely certain that the value of the currency you receive will be what you expected. However, we saw above that there is a key link between interest rates and the inflation rate, and that a country with a high inflation rate cannot also have a low interest rate. It follows that membership of the euro zone also requires that the British inflation rate should be roughly in line with European inflation. If it is expected that British inflation will be far out of line with Europe, whether much lower or much higher, then the economic argument for Britain's adoption of the euro is weakened – despite the advantages for exporters.

This discussion of macroeconomic factors has shown how influential such forces can be over the success or failure of marketing strategy. A marketing strategy that is developed without careful consideration of the likely macroeconomic conditions could easily run into difficulties. That is why the creation of assumptions about macroeconomic conditions, such as inflation, exchange rates and interest rates, should be built into the strategic marketing process as part of the analysis of the marketing environment. Such assumptions should be based on the best available evidence. Many professional bodies (such as the Chartered Institute of Marketing and the Chartered Institute of Purchasing and Supply) provide economic forecasts for their members to use as inputs to the planning process. Finally, we should observe that the decision of the British government whether or not the UK should adopt the euro is another important aspect of the marketing environment for British firms and firms doing business with Britain.

Demographic change

Demography is the study of population statistics. The influential British economist Hamish Macrae has said that: 'Of all the forces that will change the world over the next generation, demography is probably the most important' (Macrae, 1994, p. 97). His point is that the impact of demography is slow but inexorable. While a sudden shift in interest rates might alter the marketing environment for certain products overnight – and could easily be reversed within a fortnight – demographic changes will take effect gradually. Unlike many other factors in the marketing environment, population data can be forecast with a high degree of accuracy over quite long periods. Barring major disasters (such as a nuclear war or a major asteroid strike), forecasts of population up to 20 years into the future are highly reliable. There is a large pool of people alive, which grows as people are born and shrinks as people die. In the world as a whole the birth rate exceeds the death rate, so that the number of human

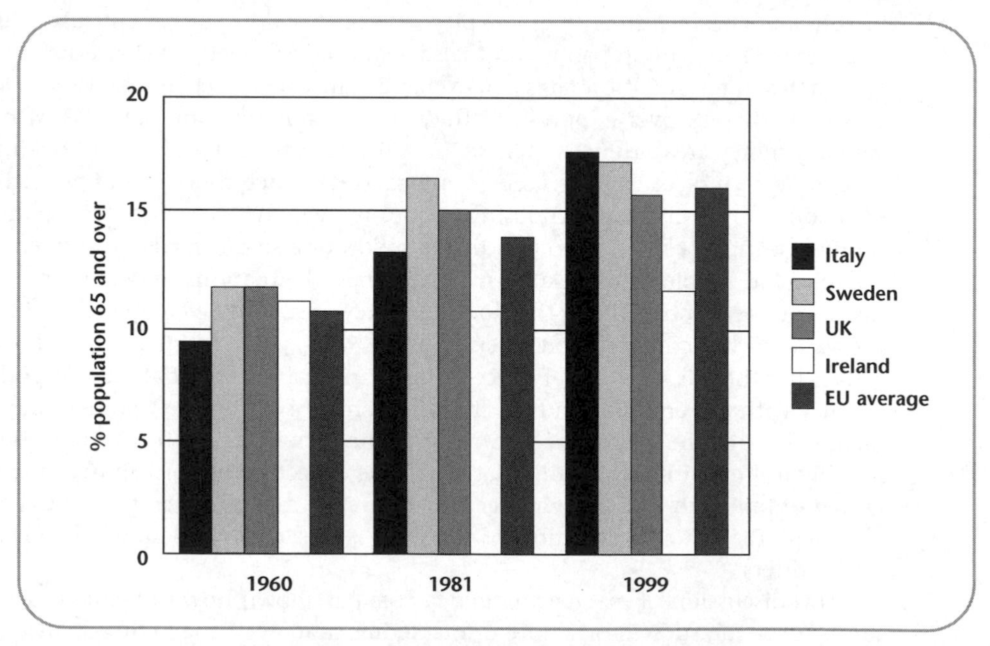

Figure 6.4 The ageing population of Europe

Source: Based on data from Eurostat

beings on the planet increases every day. In many countries of the industrialised world the picture is different, as we shall see. However, the key point is that the birth rate and the death rate are stable through time, changing only slowly in response to wider social and economic factors. One of the most important empirical facts about population growth is that, as a nation grows richer, so both the birth rate and the death rate decline.

Figure 6.4 gives us the first inclination of the way in which demographic change will affect the marketing environment. This shows, for four selected European countries and the European Union overall, the way in which older people have made up an increasing proportion of the population for several decades. This picture applies to other major industrialised nations, such as the USA and Japan, as well. Indeed, Japan is the country that is growing old fastest, considerably ahead of Italy, the fastest-ageing country in Europe (Macrae, 1994).

Table 6.1 fills in more detail on these recent demographic trends. The first thing to notice is that the world population is ageing overall. That is to say that over the last four decades the proportion of older people in the world population has increased. However, the world population is not ageing evenly. The industrialised world is ageing much more rapidly than the developing world. The data on Japan are particularly striking. Between 1960 and 1999 the proportion of the population aged 19 and under virtually halved, from 40.2 per cent to 21.0 per cent. Much the most rapidly growing category in Japan is those aged over 60 – who have increased from 8.9 per cent to 22.6 per cent of the population. While similar trends are taking place in the European Union, the effect is less marked. The trend is still there in the developing world, but much less pronounced. It was only in the late 1980s that the category 0–19 ceased to be the largest age group in these countries.

In Figure 6.5 we take a more detailed look at the population profile of the UK, and show forecasts of the age profile extending up to 2021. Two trends are very clear and quite marked. The proportion of the population that is aged under 18 will decline inexorably, and the proportion of the population that is of pensionable age will

Table 6.1 The ageing population

	European Union			Japan			Less developed countries		
	Age categories (years)			Age categories (years)			Age categories (years)		
Year	0–19	20–59	60+	0–19	20–59	60+	0–19	20–59	60+
1960	31.7	52.7	15.6	40.2	50.9	8.9	49.8	44.0	6.2
1970	32.1	50.3	17.6	32.8	56.6	10.6	52.1	41.8	6.1
1980	29.9	52.2	17.9	30.6	56.5	12.9	50.0	43.6	6.3
1990	25.3	54.8	19.9	26.5	56.1	17.4	46.1	47.0	6.9
1999	23.1	55.4	21.5	21.0	56.4	22.6	42.6	49.8	7.6

Note: Table shows percentage of the population in each age category

Source: Based on data from the European Commission (2000, Tables A-7, A-8 and A-9, pp. 42–3)

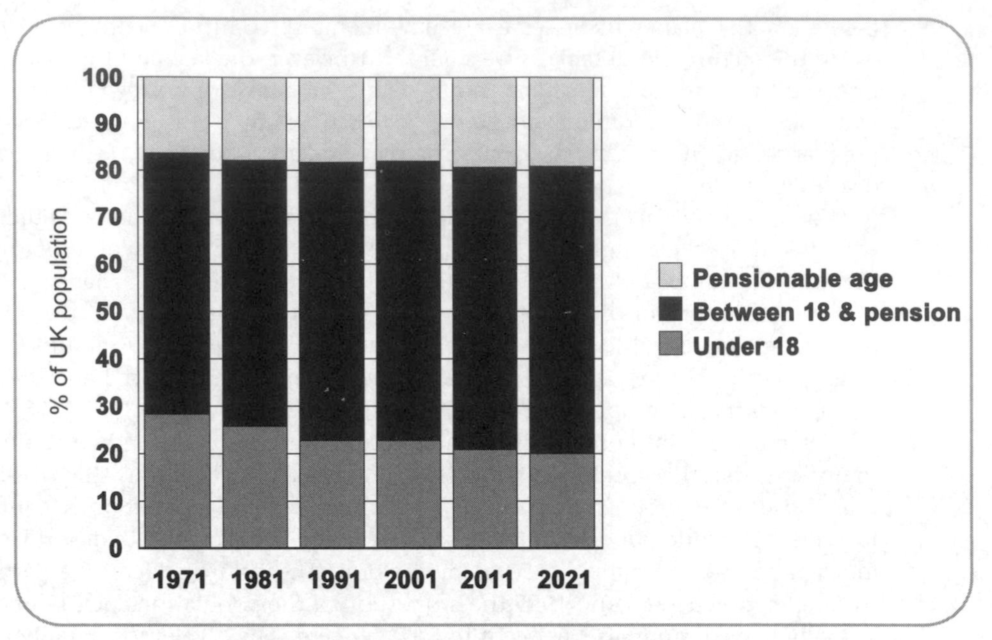

Figure 6.5 The ageing population of the UK
Source: Based on data from the Annual Abstract of Statistics

increase equally inexorably. These outcomes can be attributed first to choices made by people of child-bearing age to refrain from having children (a declining birth rate), and second to the ability of old people typically to survive much longer than previous generations. In turn, this second point can be put down not only to improved medical care (obviously an important factor) but also to increased affluence – many old people will benefit from occupational pension schemes and will avoid the poverty that was once a characteristic of old age.

Barring unforeseen disasters, we can look forward to an increasingly aged industrialised world. In our earlier analysis of the construction industry, we mentioned this as an important matter in the marketing environment. Older people have different housing needs from younger people. As the percentage of older people in the population increases, so the pattern of demand for housing will change. However, it must be emphasised, this is not the kind of change that will have much effect within a single year, or even within five years, it is the kind of change that takes effect very slowly. The impact of demographic change will affect just about every sector of the economy. For example, it is not difficult to see that the demand for transport (both private cars and public transport), healthcare, financial services, education, consumer goods and entertainment services will be affected as the population ages. What is less predictable is the way in which patterns of demand will change. It would be erroneous simply to take the patterns of demand that we find among today's elderly and suppose that this is how tomorrow's elderly will behave. First, more of tomorrow's elderly will be relatively affluent, so their spending will be less constrained. Second, there is an acknowledged social trend in the industrialised world for the 'baby boom' generation (that is those people born in the aftermath of the Second World War) to be less accepting of old age than previous generations. In other words, they are less inclined to emulate their parents and more inclined to exhibit 'youthful' buying behaviour.

The 'green' environment

Issues such as global warming, the depletion of the ozone layer, the destruction of the rain forests and environmental pollution became matters of general knowledge and concern in the 1980s. Although the effects that were involved were acknowledged to be long term, the impact on the marketing environment was quite rapid. The reason for this apparent paradox is that consumers were encouraged to make quite radical changes to their consumption behaviour in order to reduce the adverse effects of man's activities on the planet. Concerned consumers could buy books such as *The Green Consumer Guide* (Elkington and Hailes, 1989) and learn what were the key issues for the 'green consumer'. The 'green consumer' was encouraged to avoid products that were likely to:

- Endanger the health of others
- Cause significant damage to the environment during manufacture, use or disposal
- Consume a disproportionate amount of energy during manufacture, use or disposal
- Cause unnecessary waste, either because of overpackaging or an unduly short, useful life
- Use materials derived from threatened species or threatened environments
- Involve the unnecessary use of – or cruelty to – animals
- Adversely affect other countries, particularly developing countries.

Models of the interaction between man's consumption and the capacity of the Earth's resources to sustain life have a long history. For example, the English economist Malthus (in a work originally published in 1798, although here we refer to a 1987 edition) predicted over two centuries ago that population growth would increasingly outstrip the ability of mankind to grow more food, so leading eventually to starvation and death. He argued that population grows exponentially (that is, a constant percentage rate of increase), while the ability to grow food grows arithmetically (that is, with the constant addition of an absolute amount). Figure 6.6 illustrates this kind of model. Population growth is shown as a rising exponential curve, growing at a constant percentage rate, while food production is shown as a rising straight line, growing at a constant arithmetic rate. The figure has been drawn to show how exponential growth outstrips arithmetic growth through time. At first the effect is difficult to see (the gap between the lines is hardly visible), but as time goes on the two lines diverge from each other increasingly quickly. The third curve on the figure, the curve that falls from left to right, shows the effect on food production per head. This kind of Malthusian model was later applied, in a much more sophisticated form, to an analysis of the interaction between mankind and the entire resources of planet Earth (Meadows et al., 1974, 1992) in the 'limits to growth' studies. These studies used computer model-building, and included a much wider set of variables, but came to very similar conclusions. We may summarise this position as follows:

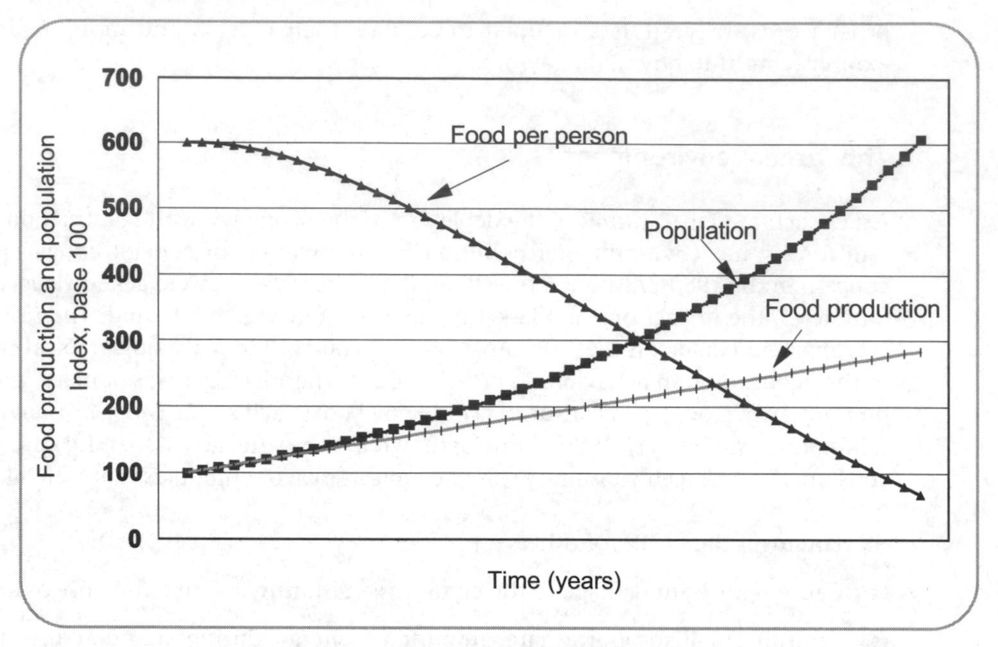

Figure 6.6 A Malthusian model

1. The resources of the Earth are finite.
2. The demands placed on the Earth by mankind grow at an exponential rate.
3. Therefore, eventually the demands of mankind will exceed the ability of the Earth to provide, with catastrophic consequences.
4. The symptoms associated with the catastrophe will not become obvious until it is too late to take effective action, because exponential growth is deceptive (over quite long periods it can look like linear growth).
5. Therefore, concerted political action is necessary *before* the symptoms become obvious, to reduce the damage that mankind does to the Earth.

In the 1980s and early 1990s, this broad analysis had achieved a degree of acceptance. This environmental argument had achieved respectability and exerted considerable influence over the marketing environment. Consumers who once gave no thought to such issues were now aware of the energy efficiency score of their fridge, the volume of water consumed by their washing machine and the proportion of recycled paper in their roll of kitchen towel. The marketing community was busily attaching 'green' labels to products, since this was perceived to be an attractive market position with consumers.

However, it is by no means clear that the near consensus on the 'green' environment will survive the first few years of the third millennium. Marketing strategists would be well advised to keep a keen eye on this aspect of the marketing environment. The anti-environmentalism lobby, once the preserve of oil company bosses (who quite reasonably were perceived to have a vested interest) is acquiring growing intellectual and political support. The American economist Julian Simon (1995) has argued, on the basis of extensive data analysis, that:

- Human life expectancy has risen enormously in the last two centuries and continues to rise.
- Raw materials (including energy and food) have become, and continue to become, less scarce rather than scarcer.
- The average standard of living of the world population shows a long-term, continuing increase, which is not restricted only to the 'rich' countries.
- The cleanliness of the environment is not deteriorating.
- The impact of global warming, damage to the ozone layer and acid rain on human welfare is uncertain and probably much less than the impact of radical policies to deal with them.

The former environmental activist and professional statistician Bjorn Lomborg (2001) has reconsidered his views on environmentalism and suggests that international political action to 'protect the environment' may cost far more than is justified by the likely benefits. He finds that the available reserves of many important natural resources (such as oil, aluminium and copper) have increased, not declined. World population growth has declined sharply, and food is becoming more abundant rather than scarcer. Pollution is not the problem that was once thought (the air is cleaner in London today than it has been since 1585). Finally, Lomborg contends that the costs of implementing the Kyoto Protocol on climate change would far outweigh the benefits. The US government has retreated from the Kyoto Protocol, and without the cooperation of the USA (the biggest economy and the biggest polluter) the agreement is seriously damaged.

The 'green' environment is a matter of great concern to us all. Responding appropriately to 'green' issues is, and will remain, an important component of marketing strategy for many firms. Our illustration (above) from the construction industry showed how the common assumption still is that becoming more 'green' will be a feature of the next decade. However, the marketing strategist would be wise to consider the possibility that an anti-environmentalism backlash will alter the features of the marketing environment, demanding a new strategic response.

ALLOCATING PRIORITIES TO FACTORS IN THE MARKETING ENVIRONMENT

So far we have explained a number of frameworks to be used in identifying and classifying potentially important environmental factors, and have discussed a number of factors that are likely to be important to a wide range of organisations. By applying these ideas, you should have confidence that you are unlikely to forget about anything important in the marketing environment. However, by contrast, you may find yourself drowning in potentially important environmental factors, and having difficulty discriminating between them. Which of these is really important? Which of them should we develop action plans to deal with? Which of them should we continue to monitor, and only take action if they seem to become more serious? Are there any that we can simply ignore? Clearly, environmental forces differ greatly in their impact and importance. For example, global warming and environmental damage (such as the hole in the ozone layer and damage to the Great Barrier Reef) may have a long-term effect on the tourist industry of Australia. These are important but rather long-term phenomena. However, if an increase in global terrorism were to deter tourists from flying, this could reduce Australian tourism from key overseas markets in Europe and North America almost overnight. Obviously, the latter factor would demand rapid action, while the former factors can be managed over time.

Environmental factors can be assessed using a number of different dimensions to determine the appropriate organisational response (Bates, 1985; Murphy, 1989; Camillus and Datta, 1991):

- *Clarity* – how much information is available on this factor and how reliable is that information?
- *Impact* – how seriously would the firm be affected if this environmental event occurred?
- *Probability* – how likely is it that this environmental event will occur?
- *Urgency* – how soon does a decision have to be made about the organisational response to this environmental event?

Clarity affects the organisational response in terms of the appropriate form of response. The clearer an issue becomes, the more it is possible to put in place a concrete action plan for it. Where an issue is very unclear, the appropriate response may be to seek out and analyse additional information.

The other three dimensions (impact, probability and urgency) can be combined to provide an overall impression of the *seriousness* of an environmental event. This can be achieved as follows:

1. Use the various tools discussed earlier in the chapter (such as PEST or STEEP, and five forces analysis from the previous chapter) to develop a 'long list' of potentially important environmental factors.
2. For each environmental factor estimate the likelihood that it will occur on a scale from 1 (unlikely) to 5 (very likely). If you want formally to apply probability analysis, then 1 would signify a probability of up to 0.2, and 5 a probability of over 0.8.
3. For each environmental factor estimate the impact on the organisation on a scale from 1 (relatively minor impact) to 5 (a fundamental effect on the future of the organisation).
4. Estimate the urgency of each environmental factor in terms of how soon a management decision needs to be made, using a scale from 1 (distant horizon) to 5 (decision must be made within the current planning cycle).
5. For each environmental factor estimate its *overall seriousness* by calculating the sum of the scores for likelihood, impact and urgency. This will be a score of between 3 (minimum seriousness) and 15 (maximum seriousness).

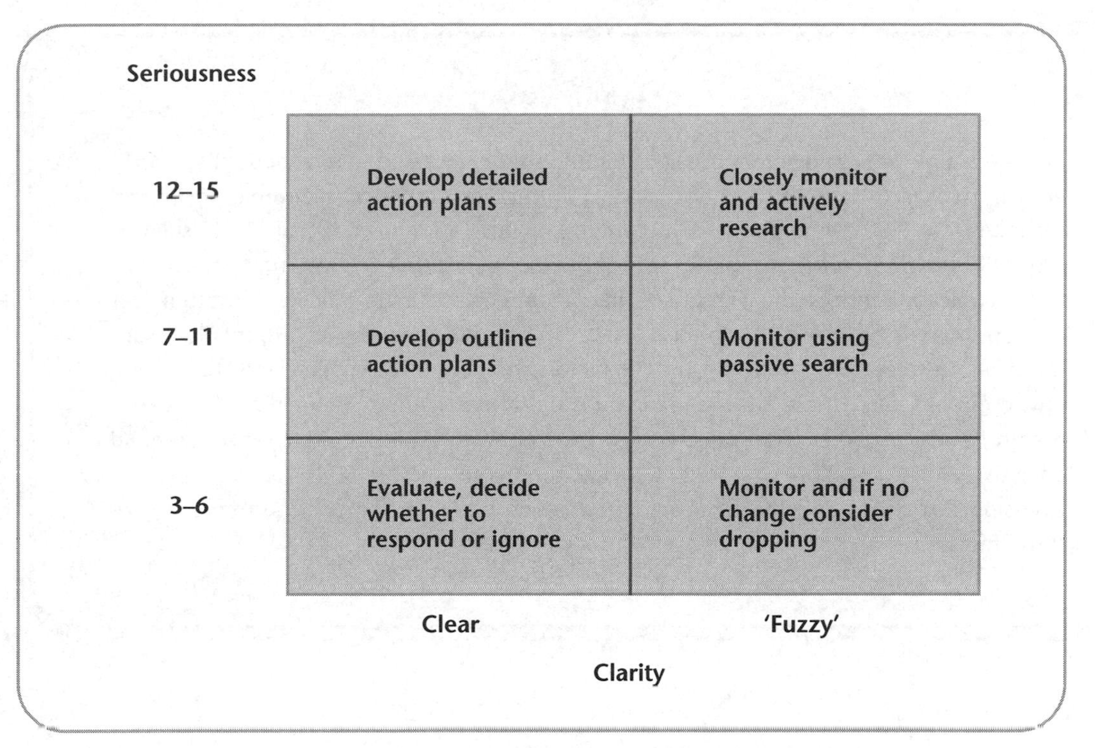

Figure 6.7 Environmental priorities

Sources: Based on Bates (1985), Murphy (1989) and Camillus and Datta (1991)

By mapping the clarity and the seriousness of environmental factors on a matrix such as that shown in Figure 6.7, we can identify in broad terms what response the organisation should take.

Environmental factors that are very serious require immediate management attention. If there is sufficient well-defined information on the issue, then detailed action plans to respond should be put in place. If there is insufficient information, or if the available information is unclear ('fuzzy' is the evocative word used by Camillus and Datta), then active research should be undertaken to improve the situation and enable action plans to be developed. Environmental factors of intermediate seriousness should be handled with care. If there is plenty of good information, then outline action plans can be put in place. If information is insufficient, then the issue can be monitored 'passively', that is to say, by regular scanning of relevant media (for example newspapers, industry or trade reports, appropriate Internet sites). Environmental issues that achieve low scores on the seriousness scale can probably be ignored – management time is a limited resource and it is not possible to keep a watch on every possible factor that might affect the organisation. If, having conducted the analysis, there are issues in the 'low seriousness' category that it does not seem intuitively right to ignore, then it would be appropriate to ask 'why?' Further evaluation of the issue might indicate that it was scored unduly low in terms of likelihood, impact and urgency, in which case it will move up to the 'intermediate seriousness' category and can be dealt with accordingly.

SUMMARY

There are a number of different classification tools that can be used to analyse the macro-environment, most of which are elaborations on the basic political, economic, social and technological (PEST) framework. A more comprehensive framework than PEST, such as DEEPLIST (demographic, economic, environmental, political, legal, informational, social, technological), reduces the likelihood that an important issue will be forgotten just because there is no 'box' for it. In this chapter we selected three key environmental issues for in-depth treatment – macroeconomic factors, demographic change and the 'green' environment – since these are wide-ranging issues that will affect the marketing environment of most organisations, in one way or another. A key element of any environmental analysis is the allocation of priorities to environmental factors. This can be done by assessing the clarity and the seriousness (based on likelihood, impact and urgency) of those factors.

Questions for discussion

1. What is the likely impact of the ageing population on organisations operating in the health sector?
2. The managing director of a medium-sized manufacturer of industrial lighting systems, based in Newbury (England), wants to know how her business would be affected if the UK adopted the euro. Her firm exports over 50 per cent of its output, mostly to European Union countries. Advise the managing director.
3. The managing director is so impressed by your advice that she now wants you to help her to assess the importance of a number of environmental factors, as set out in Table 6.2. Prepare an environmental priorities matrix from this information and suggest what the firm should do next.

Table 6.2 Environmental priorities

Issue	Clarity	Likelihood	Impact	Urgency
1. A sudden sharp increase in interest rates	Clear	1	2	2
2. Pan-EU legislation requiring businesses to improve lighting conditions for employees	Fuzzy	3	4	2
3. Entry into the European market by a major American competitor	Clear	4	4	4
4. Substitution of current industrial lighting technology by a new, more cost-effective and energy efficient technology	Fuzzy	2	4	1
5. A sudden sharp increase in the price of the raw materials for lighting systems	Clear	1	3	1
6. A sudden sharp decline in the value of the £ sterling	Clear	2	3	1

References

Aaker, D A (1998), *Strategic Marketing Management*, New York: Wiley

Annual Abstract of Statistics, 2001 edn, No. 137, London: The Stationery Office

Baker, M J (1992), *Marketing Strategy and Management*, Basingstoke: Macmillan – now Palgrave Macmillan

Bates, C S (1985), 'Mapping the Environment: an Operational Environmental Analysis Model', *Long Range Planning*, **18**(5): 97–107

Brooks, I and Weatherston, J (2000), *The Business Environment: Challenges and Changes*, Harlow: Pearson Education

Camillus, J C and Datta, D K (1991), 'Managing Strategic Issues in a Turbulent Environment', *Long Range Planning*, **24**(2): 67–74

Construction Industry Council (CIC) (1998), *State of the Construction Industry*, (www.cic.org.uk)

Construction Industry Research and Information Association (CIRIA) (1999) *UK Construction 2010 – Future Trends and Issues*, (www.ciria.org.uk)

Elkington, J and Hailes, J (1989), *The Green Consumer Guide*, London: Guild

European Commission (2000), *European Social Statistics: Demography*, Luxembourg: Office for Official Publications of the European Communities

Eurostat Yearbook – A Statistical Eye on Europe, 2000 edn, Luxembourg: Office for Official Publications of the European Communities

Eurostat Yearbook – The Statistical Guide to Europe, 2001 edn, Luxembourg: Office for Official Publications of the European Communities

Finlay, P (2000), *Strategic Management: An Introduction to Business and Corporate Strategy*, Harlow: Pearson Education

Grönroos, C (1991), *Strategic Management and Marketing in the Service Sector*, Lund: Studentlitteratur & Chartwell-Bratt

Jain, S C (2000), *Marketing Planning and Strategy*, 6th edn, Cincinnati: South-Western College Publishing

Lomborg, B (2001), *The Skeptical Environmentalist*, Cambridge: Cambridge University Press

Lynch, R (2000), *Corporate Strategy*, 2nd edn, Harlow: Pearson Education

McDonald, M (1999), *Marketing Plans: How to Prepare Them, How to Use Them*, 4th edn, Oxford: Butterworth Heinemann

Macintosh, M, Brown, V, Costello, N, Dawson, G, Thompson, G and Trigg, A (eds) (1996), *Economics and Changing Economies*, London: International Thompson Business Press.

Macrae, H (1994), *The World in 2020*, London: HarperCollins

Malthus, T R (1987), *An Essay on the Principle of Population: or a View of its Past and Present Effects on Human Happiness*, Cambridge: Cambridge University Press

Meadows, D H, Meadows, D L, Randers, J and Behrens, W W (1974), *The Limits to Growth*, London: Pan Books

Meadows, D H, Meadows, D L and Randers, J (1992), *Beyond the Limits: Global Collapse or a Sustainable Future?* London: Earthscan

Murphy, J J (1989), 'Identifying Strategic Issues', *Long Range Planning*, **22**(2): 101–5

OECD (1999), OECD *Economic Outlook* 66, Paris: OECD Publications

OECD (2001), OECD *Economic Outlook* 69, Paris: OECD Publications

Reichheld, F F (1996), *The Loyalty Effect: The Hidden Force Behind Growth, Profits, and Lasting Value*, Boston, MA: Harvard Business School Press

Simon, J L (1995), 'Introduction', in Simon, J L (ed.) *The State of Humanity*, Cambridge, MA: Blackwell, pp.1–28

Woodside, A G (2000), *Advances in Business Marketing and Purchasing* (vol. 8): *Getting Better at Sensemaking*, Stamford, CT: JAI Press

chapter seven

Strategic Marketing Analysis

Learning objectives

By reading this chapter you will learn:

- What are the key tools available to marketers for strategic marketing analysis
- How those tools are defined
- How those tools can be applied, their strengths and weaknesses
- The limitations to a formal, analytical approach to marketing strategy formulation.

INTRODUCTION

In this chapter and the next we discuss 15 Key Concepts in the strategic marketing planning process. We have divided those concepts into two categories, strategic marketing analysis (this chapter) and marketing strategy formulation (the next chapter). These are not hard and fast categories. However, they broadly subdivide our Key Concepts into those that are primarily to be used for purposes of understanding what is going in a particular strategic marketing situation (or case study), and those that are primarily to be used to identify plausible strategic alternatives. Some concepts can be used for both purposes, for example the SWOT, the Boston Consulting Group matrix and customer portfolio analysis. The concepts that we deal with are as follows:

Strategic marketing analysis

- The marketing planning process
- Objectives and gap analysis
- Cost concepts: the experience effect and economies of scale
- SWOT analysis
- Sales variance analysis
- Discounted cash-flow analysis
- Value-based marketing.

Marketing strategy formulation

- Market segmentation
- Targeting and positioning
- The product life cycle
- The Boston Consulting Group growth/share matrix
- PIMS (profit impact of marketing strategy)
- Porter's generic competitive strategies
- Ansoff's growth vector matrix
- Customer portfolio analysis.

These concepts provide the firm with tools to assist in the process of analysing its current situation, determining its objectives and developing appropriate marketing strategies. They will provide insights, but they cannot provide answers. There is no straightforward, formulaic approach that can be applied to the development of marketing strategy. Nevertheless, there is evidence that a structured approach to strategic marketing planning is associated with enhanced commercial success – those companies that adopt a formal approach to marketing planning are, on average, better performers than those that do not (McDonald, 1996). It would be naive to suppose that this observed correlation between company performance and the adoption of marketing planning demonstrates that marketing planning *causes* improved performance. Just because two variables are correlated does not mean that either of them necessarily *causes* the other. In the case of marketing planning and firm performance, it certainly seems to make sense to argue that a structured approach to marketing planning will cause improved company performance – there is good reason to suppose that structured marketing planning will yield a competitive advantage over rival firms. However, one could also argue that a firm that achieves above-average performance has more resources available to spend on the relative luxury of formal planning (this is called a 'reverse causality' argument). Alternatively, one might argue that a firm with an above-average management team would be expected both to achieve above-average performance and implement more structured planning. The ticklish problem of causality need not detain us for too long here. We do know that formal marketing planning is correlated with improved firm performance, and it is a reasonable proposition that improved performance is the result of formal planning. So let us investigate the elements of the formal marketing planning process.

KEY CONCEPT 1 The Marketing Planning Process

What it is

The marketing planning process consists of a series of managerial steps by which an organisation identifies its marketing objectives (what it is aiming to achieve) and marketing strategies (how the objectives will be achieved).

What it looks like

1. Mission
2. Corporate objectives
3. Marketing audit
4. SWOT analyses
5. Assumptions
6. Marketing objectives and strategies
7. Estimate expected results
8. Identify alternative plans and mixes
9. Budget
10. First year detailed implementation programme.

Tell me more

This is Malcolm McDonald's (1999) version of the marketing planning process. It is probably the most widely accepted model of the marketing planning process. McDonald calls steps 1 and 2 'goal setting', steps 3–5 'situation review', steps 6–8 'strategy formulation' and steps 9 and 10 'resource allocation and monitoring'. During the goal-setting process, the members of the organisation are involved in a process of identifying what are the feasible, yet stretching objectives that will be pursued during the plan period (which is often 3 or 5 years). The situation review process involves extensive data gathering and analysis on the company, key competitive rivals and the broader business environment. From the data gathered, a relatively small number of key issues are identified, which are summarised in the SWOT analysis (Key Concept 4). The strategy formulation stage consists of identifying and evaluating the broad strategies that the organisation could pursue, leading to the choice of the most effective marketing strategy. The most effective strategy is the one that is most likely to bring about the desired organisational objectives, given the current state of the market, the competitive environment and broader business environment trends. Once a strategy has been selected, the way in which it will be implemented using marketing tactics must be specified (step 8). Finally, the resource allocation and monitoring stage details exactly who will do exactly what, and what resources they will need, to put the strategy into practice for the first 12 months of the plan period. There will be periodic reviews to see whether or not the plan is on target, and to take remedial action if needed.

Where to find out more

McDonald, M (1999) *Marketing Plans: How to Prepare Them, How to Use Them*, 4th edn, Oxford: Butterworth-Heinemann.

KEY CONCEPT 2 Objectives and Gap Analysis

What they are

Objectives specify what the organisation expects to achieve as a result of the successful implementation of its marketing strategy. Strategic objectives are relatively long term, decided at top management level, and have considerable resource implications. Marketing objectives are concerned with products and markets. An objective can be defined in terms of the thing that the company wants to achieve (for example market share), a measure of that thing (percentage of the served market) and a target specified using that measure.

Gap analysis is the process of estimating the gap between what would be achieved on current trends (with no change of marketing strategy) and the specified objective.

What they look like

See Figure 7.1.

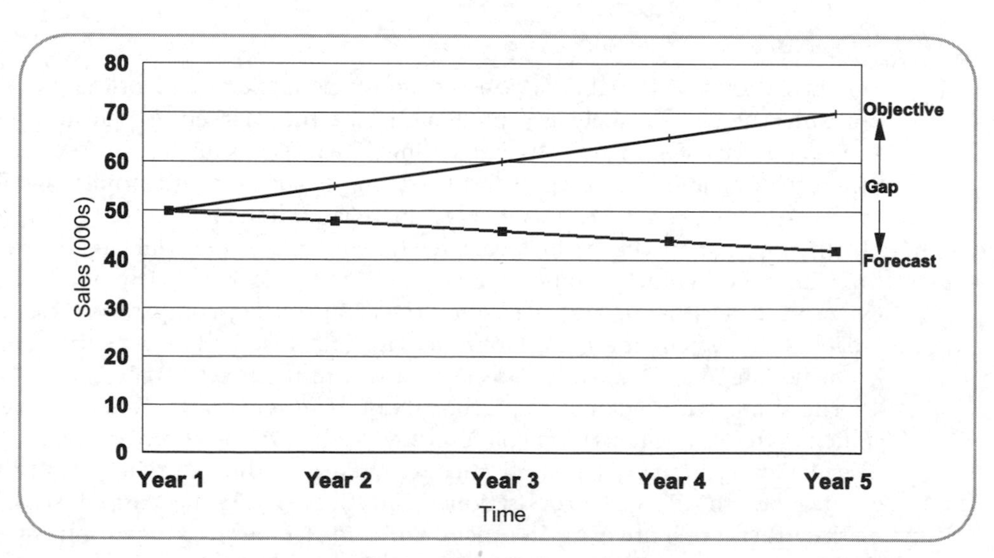

Figure 7.1 Gap analysis

Tell me more

Figure 7.1 shows the elements of a gap analysis. The lower line on the chart shows how sales volume is forecast to grow on the basis of the current state of the marketing environment and the continuation of the current marketing strategy. The upper line shows the firm's objective for sales growth. Clearly, there is a growing gap between what will be achieved with current strategies and what the firm wishes to achieve. The fundamental purpose of a revised marketing strategy will be to specify the ways in which this gap can be reduced and, if possible, eliminated. If the objectives set are stretching but realistic, then by the development of a new marketing strategy the firm should just be able to fill the gap between expected sales and the sales objective.

Objectives can be aspirational or realistic. Aspirational but unrealistic objectives are not uncommon and suggest a 'wishful thinking' approach to marketing strategy. While the members of an organisation may have aspirational objectives, in the absence of a situation analysis such as the marketing audit it is not possible to formulate realistic objectives. Suppose that a national charity aspires to increase revenue from private donations by 15 per cent within a year. However, the marketing audit identifies that other charities have greater skills in direct marketing and promotions, that personal disposable incomes are expected to remain static over the period, and that charitable donations have been negatively affected by the National Lottery. The charity may conclude that its original aspiration was unrealistic and revise the objective downwards. As a general rule, objectives should be realistic but still demanding. In other words, the members of the organisation should feel that they can achieve the objective if they perform to the best of their abilities. Objectives should also, as far as possible, be stated in quantitative terms. While 'to achieve a successful launch of new product X' is, in general terms, a desirable objective, it would be difficult to say whether or not it had been achieved. Such an objective could be restated as 'to achieve for new product X a 10 per cent share of the national market within one year', and it would then be possible to establish whether or not the objective was achieved. A mnemonic that is often used to help in the formulation of useful objectives is 'SMART'. An objective is SMART if it is:

- Specific: clearly defined and unambiguous
- Measurable: quantified and readily evaluated
- Attainable: demanding, but ultimately capable of being achieved
- Realistic: in line with the resources available
- Timely: to a specified schedule or deadline.

While such a mnemonic is clearly not the whole answer to the problem of setting good objectives, it serves to remind the marketing manager of a number of the key factors to bear in mind and may prevent some common errors, such as setting an objective without a timescale.

Where to find out more

Billsberry, J (1998) 'Gap Analysis' in Ambrosini, V, Johnson, G and Scholes, K (eds) *Exploring Techniques of Analysis and Evaluation in Strategic Management*, Hemel Hempstead: Prentice Hall, pp. 219–28.

KEY CONCEPT 3 Cost Concepts – The Experience Effect and Economies of Scale

Economies of large-scale production are thought to be a pervasive feature of modern industrial society. Automation, assembly lines, and sophisticated machinery often reduce production costs dramatically. (Baumol and Blinder, 1998, p. 148)

What they are

The experience effect is concerned with the relationship between unit cost of production and cumulative production volume. It postulates that the firm with the greatest accumulated experience will have a unit cost advantage over its rivals. Economies of scale are concerned with the relationship between unit cost of production and production volume per time period. In many cases a firm will find that increasing production volume will result in lower unit cost of production.

What they look like

See Figures 7.2 and 7.3.

Tell me more

It is probably fair to say that marketing people are not usually very interested in the cost side of the business. However, many people would argue that these concepts – the

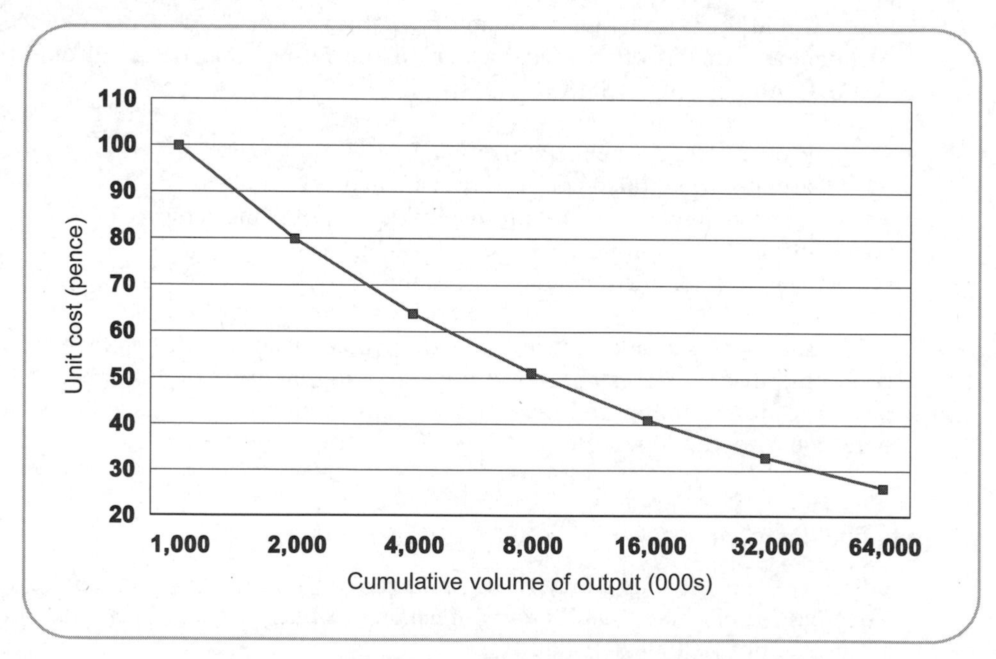

Figure 7.2 Experience effect

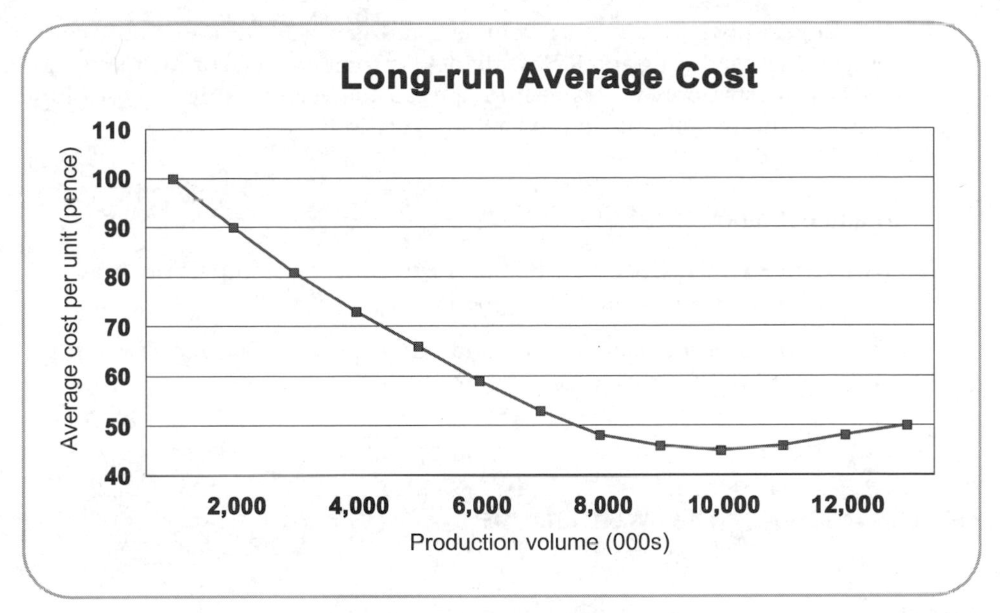

Figure 7.3 Economies of scale

experience effect and economies of scale – are important underlying determinants of the competitive strength of a company and its rivals.

It is well known that the more often a person does a thing, the better they become at that task. So, for example, when you first learn how to use a new piece of computer software, it takes a long time to make it do what you want. As you grow used to the software, you can do things faster and you learn new tricks for doing what you want to do more efficiently. The longer you use the software, the better you become, but after a while your rate of improvement slows down, until eventually any improvement comes only very slowly. The experience effect says that the same thing happens to organisations. It is not just a theoretical idea, but is based on concrete measurement of the unit cost of producing something, as a business increases its cumulative volume of production (that is, it's 'experience'). This suggests that the firm that has the greatest cumulative experience of a particular task – for example manufacturing a component or delivering a service – will do that task more efficiently than a rival with less experience. The experience effect can be illustrated through an experience curve, which shows the average cost of carrying out a task at different cumulative volumes of production. Empirical studies have shown that each time the volume of production doubles there is a consistent percentage reduction in average cost. For example, if there is a 20 per cent reduction in average cost for a doubling of cumulative production, then this is known as an '80 per cent experience curve' (80 per cent = 100 per cent – 20 per cent). The idea of the experience curve underlies the expectation that profitability will be positively associated with market share (see next chapter: PIMS and the Boston Consulting Group growth/share matrix).

While the experience effect proposes that a firm with greater *cumulative experience* will have a cost advantage over its rivals (particularly in a manufacturing industry), economies of scale refer to the cost advantage that a firm with *a high current volume of production* is expected to have. Firms with higher volumes have a number of advantages over those with smaller volumes, and can achieve lower unit costs in their purchasing, marketing and R&D activities. In some manufacturing industries, notably the car industry, only very large firms are capable of competing because of the considerable economies of scale in production operations.

Where to find out more

Experience effect: Hedley, B (1976), 'A Fundamental Approach to Strategy Development', *Long Range Planning*, (December) 2–11.

Economies of scale: Baumol, W J and Blinder, A S (1998), *Economics: Principles and Policy*, Fort Worth: Dryden Press, Chapter 7.

KEY CONCEPT 4 The SWOT Analysis

What it is

SWOT stands for **S**trengths, **W**eaknesses, **O**pportunities and **T**hreats. The SWOT analysis is a summary of the marketing audit, and contains an explanation of the key factors affecting an organisation's marketing activities at a specific time.

What it looks like

See Figure 7.4.

Tell me more

> A SWOT should be conducted for each segment that is considered important in the company's future. These SWOT analyses should, if possible, contain just a few paragraphs of commentary focusing on *key* factors only. They should highlight internal *differential* strengths and weaknesses *vis-à-vis* competitors and key external opportunities and threats. (McDonald, 1999, p. 48, emphasis in original)

Strengths and weaknesses are the outcome of an analysis of the organisation's resources compared with the resources of key competitive rivals. Organisations can be thought of as 'bundles of resources' – market resources, human resources, physical resources and financial resources. Market resources include, for example, products, brands and distribution channels. Human resources are the people who are associated with the organisation. Physical resources are tangible things that the organisation controls, such as buildings, vehicles, plant and equipment. Financial resources include all the financial assets upon which the organisation can draw, for example cash, loans and equity (share capital).

It is important to understand the difference between improving organisational performance in a particular area, and *obtaining a competitive strength* in that area. For

STRENGTHS *Relative to key competitors,* what differential strengths does the organisation have?	WEAKNESSES *Relative to key competitors,* what differential weaknesses does the organisation have?
OPPORTUNITIES *On the basis of an analysis of the organisation's external business environment,* what are perceived to be the key opportunities open to the organisation during the plan period?	THREATS *On the basis of an analysis of the organisation's external business environment,* what are perceived to be the key threats facing the organisation during the plan period?

Figure 7.4 SWOT analysis

example, in the provision of services such as a telephone helpline for an Internet Service Provider (ISP), the speed with which calls from customers are answered would be considered an important factor in customer satisfaction. If the average length of time that a customer is kept waiting is reduced from 2 minutes to 1 minute, then it is tempting to suppose that this is a 'strength'. However, if a rival ISP achieves an average call-waiting time of 30 seconds, then – despite the improvement – this factor may still be a weakness. A complicating factor is *customer perception*. Objective measurement may tell us that we achieve an average call-waiting time better than our rival (a strength), but customers may not perceive this to be the case. For example, customers may still be influenced by our performance from last year, and may not have registered the big improvement that we have made. In this case an *objective strength* is in fact a *subjective weakness* in the marketplace. This suggests immediate action to correct the false perceptions that consumers have of our service level – some form of marketing communications action, in the example cited.

From the preceding discussion of service levels of ISPs you can immediately see the way in which the SWOT analysis can suggest constructive strategies – pointing to a gap between customer perception of service level and the objective service level, suggesting a communications strategy to correct false perceptions. The SWOT is the starting place for the development of strategic marketing options. In some cases, strategic options might simply 'jump out' of the SWOT, and be so obvious that no further analysis is needed. For example, 'our customer service level is so far below all our rivals that if we don't do something about it we will go out of business'. However, it is a good idea to examine the SWOT in a disciplined manner. First, evaluate each of the factors in the SWOT to see whether, independently, they suggest a strategic option. The questions to ask are:

- How can we exploit this strength?
- How can we eliminate (or ameliorate) this weakness?
- How can we exploit this opportunity?
- How can we avoid (or minimise the effects of) this threat?

It is important to go beyond this kind of elementary approach and explore interactions between factors within the SWOT analysis. If it has been done properly, the SWOT has identified the vital few internal and external factors affecting strategy formulation. Our internal strengths and weaknesses compared with competitive rivals are of strategic significance where they influence our ability to respond to key factors in the business environment. The following combinations of factors need to be evaluated as part of the SWOT analysis.

1. *S/O interactions.* In turn, compare each strength with each opportunity. Does the strength facilitate the organisation in its efforts to exploit that opportunity? For example, pressure from the marketing environment (from regulators and customers) is persuading car manufacturers to produce vehicles with ever-lower exhaust emissions. This is a particularly valuable opportunity for a vehicle exhaust system manufacturer with strength in exhaust catalysers (the bit that removes many of the pollutants from exhaust gases).
2. *S/T interactions.* In turn, compare each strength with each threat. Does the strength facilitate the organisation's efforts to cope with that threat? The case studies on British Telecommunications plc in Part Two show how BT has struggled to cope with tremendous environmental upheavals, which could easily have brought the company to its knees, because of the power of the BT brand in the UK market and very high market penetration.
3. *W/O interactions.* In turn, compare each weakness with each opportunity. Does the weakness impair the organisation in pursuing that opportunity? For example, China represents one of the biggest marketing opportunities for Western firms today. Few of these firms employ people with the linguistic and cultural skills to develop business partnerships with Chinese enterprises, or conduct marketing campaigns in China.
4. *W/T interactions.* In turn, compare each weakness with each threat. Does the weakness impair the organisation's ability to cope with that threat? Returning to BT plc, the firm's strategic dilemma was intensified by the fact that both revenue and profits were heavily reliant on UK business customers and international telephone calls; these were exactly the markets in which new competition was most intense.

Where to find out more

Smith, G D, Arnold, D R and Bizzell, B G (1991) *Business Strategy and Policy*, 3rd edn, Boston: Houghton Mifflin, pp. 191–7.

KEY CONCEPT 5 Sales Variance Analysis

What it is

Sales variance analysis is the process of calculating the deviation of actual sales revenue from forecast sales revenue, and then allocating that deviation ('variance') arithmetically to its constituent parts – market size, market share and net price.

What it looks like

See Figure 7.5.

Tell me more

Sales variance analysis is a tool that is used routinely in the control process for marketing planning, and will also be of use in putting together a realistic assessment of the firm's strengths and weaknesses (SWOT analysis). It is a rigorous arithmetic technique, which is designed to assist the marketing manager in answering the question: 'why is our actual sales revenue different from what we forecast it would be?' Sales variance analysis breaks down the difference between actual and forecast sales revenue (the 'sales revenue variance') into its logical components. Sales revenue can be calculated as the product of price and quantity sold; if you take how many units you have sold and multiply by the average price you received, then you will end up with sales revenue. The number of units sold (sales volume) can be calculated as the product of the market share you achieved and the overall market size; if you take your market share (say 10 per cent) and multiply it by market size (say 1000 units), then you get sales volume (100 units). So the logical components of sales revenue are price, market size and market share. The sales revenue variance can be readily broken down into these components: price variance, market size variance and market share variance. This enables the marketing manager to ask more penetrating questions about current marketing strategy and performance.

Sales variance analysis is illustrated in Figure 7.5 and Table 7.1. Figure 7.5 illustrates graphically the concept of sales volume variance. The firm expected to achieve a 15 per cent share of a market of 100,000 units, so expected sales were 15,000 units (area *abcd* in the diagram). In fact the market was considerably larger than expected (125,000 units), but the firm only picked up a market share of 11 per cent, so actual sales were 13,750 units (area *aehi* in the diagram). The optimistic marketing manager

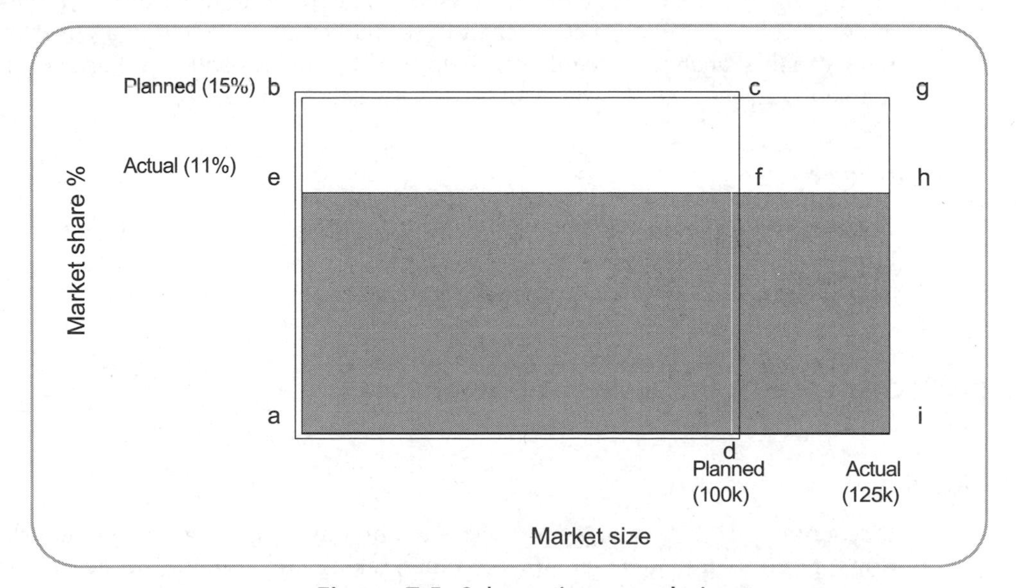

Figure 7.5 Sales variance analysis

Table 7.1 Sales variance analysis

	Actual	Forecast	Variance	Variance %
Market size (units)	125,000	100,000	25,000	25
Market share (%)	11	15	(4)	(26.7)
Sales volume (units)	13,750	15,000	(1,250)	(8.3)
Net price (£)	24.75	25.00	(0.25)	(1)
Sales revenue (£)	340,313	375,000	34,687	(9.2)

Note: Negative values are shown in brackets

may reflect that if they had achieved their target market share in the unexpectedly large market, then sales would have been well above forecast (area *abgi*). The pessimistic marketing manager, however, may imagine what a disaster it would have been if market share had been only 11 per cent and their market forecast accurate (sales volume of only *aefd*). The prudent marketing manager will start asking crucial questions. Why have we failed so badly to meet our market share target? What has happened in the market to make our forecast of market size so badly wrong? How can we improve our forecasting in the future? In Table 7.1 the dimension of price is added to the analysis, so that the overall effect on sales revenue can be established. For the example presented, it turns out that a small negative price variance has to be added to the negative sales volume variance, so that overall sales revenue is 9.2 per cent below forecast. Price variances generally arise when firms give bigger or smaller discounts than were expected in the marketing plan. For example, the entry of a new competitive rival may mean that salespeople have to offer larger than expected discounts to trade customers to motivate them to maintain their stocks.

It is important to appreciate that sales variance analysis alone cannot explain anything. The explanations for variances are to be found in other forms of marketing analysis, for example competitor analysis or market environment analysis. However, sales variance analysis certainly can help in the process of identifying key strategic marketing issues that are worthy of further investigation.

Where to find out more

Dyson, J R (2001), *Accounting for Non-accounting Students*, 5th edn, Harlow: Financial Times/Prentice Hall, pp. 324–48.

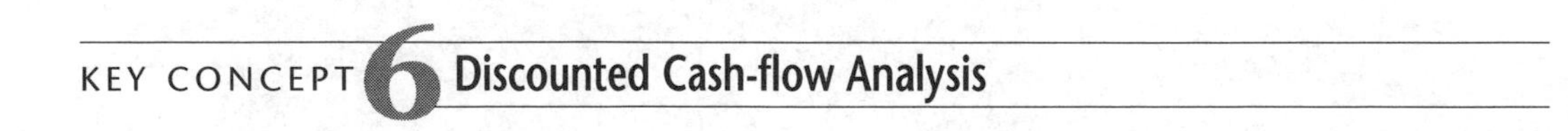

KEY CONCEPT 6 Discounted Cash-flow Analysis

What it is

Discounted cash-flow analysis provides a method of comparing sums of money (cash flows) received or paid out at different times, taking into account the fact that money 'now' is worth more than money 'later'.

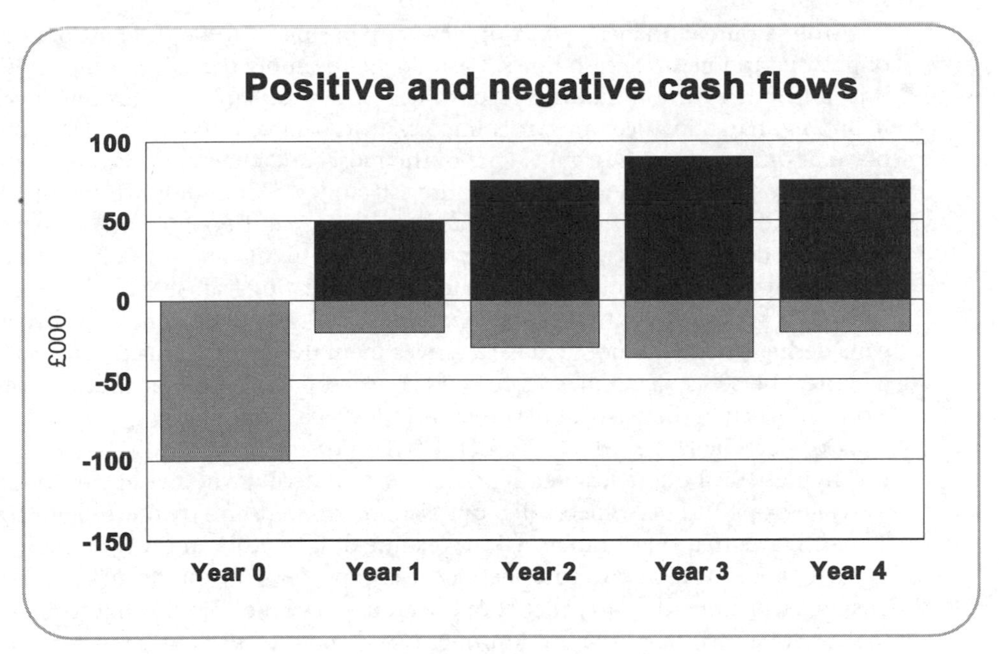

Figure 7.6 Discounted cash-flow analysis

What it looks like

See Figure 7.6.

Tell me more

Writing in the *Journal of Marketing*, Srivastava et al. (1999, p. 178) said:

> A new and unavoidable challenge for marketing managers is the need to assess the cash flow consequences of their decisions, commitments and investments ... Managers must learn both cash flow analysis methodology and the underlying thought process.

Key Concepts 6 and 7 are concerned with understanding cash-flow analysis and its application to strategic marketing decisions.

There was a time when discounted cash-flow analysis was considered to be a technique of interest only to financial managers. However, recent developments in strategic management and marketing mean that marketing managers also need to be familiar with the concept. The 'shareholder value approach' to strategic management, which is today very influential among business people and academics, relies upon an understanding of discounted cash-flow analysis. The emerging concept of 'value-based marketing' (Key Concept 7) applies exactly the same ideas to strategic marketing management. In any event, familiarity with the concept of discounted cash flows is of use to the marketing manager to understand a range of other contemporary marketing concepts. New product development decisions will normally involve discounted cash-flow calculations, and the concept of brand equity is based on the discounted value of future cash flows accruing from brand ownership.

From a purely financial point of view, any business can be thought of as a series of positive and negative cash flows. Cash flows are simply the sums of money flowing into and out of the business. For purposes of a wide range of business decisions, including marketing decisions, it is important to be able to compare cash flows that occur at different points in time. One of the most fundamental decisions that a business has to make is whether or not to invest money. Commonly we might think of investments in equity (stocks and shares) or in physical equipment (for example a new computer). However, it is equally appropriate to talk about marketing expenditure as investment spending, with the aim of creating valuable brands and loyal customers who will continue to generate positive cash flows for years to come. In considering whether or not to make an investment decision, the manager has to judge whether the series of positive cash flows received over the life of the investment is worth more than the series of negative cash flows paid out.

Consider Table 7.2, which shows the data presented graphically in Figure 7.6. In this hypothetical example an entrepreneur is considering whether or not to invest in a business opportunity which will require an initial, start-up expenditure of £100,000. She estimates that this business will have a life of four years, and will bring in a total of £290,000 of revenue over the period. It is expected that the running costs of the business will amount to 40 per cent of the annual revenue, and this figure is shown in the negative cash-flow column. Running costs amount to £116,000 in total, making total expenditure of £216,000 over the four years to bring in £290,000 revenue. At first sight this is simply a good business proposition, with a profit of £74,000. However, so far we have neglected the time value of money. Money 'now' is worth more than money 'later'. The simplest way to understand this is to think of the interest on a savings account. At a compound interest rate of 5 per cent per annum, £100 today will be worth £105 (which is 1.05 times £100 or, equivalently, 105 per cent of £100) in one year's time, and £110.25 (£100 × 1.05 × 1.05 or equivalently, £100 × 1.05^2) in two years. Simply put, £110.25 in two years is worth the same as £100 today at an interest rate of 5 per cent. A 'discount rate' is simply a reverse interest rate. We can 'discount' the value of £110.25 received in two years back to its present day value by *reversing* the compound interest calculation:

£100 = (£110.25 divided by 1.05^2), which can also be written as $\frac{£110.25}{1.05^2}$

Note that 1/1.05 is called the *reciprocal* of 1.05.

Table 7.2 shows how discounted cash-flow analysis can be applied to our entrepreneur's decision. Suppose that she can borrow the money she needs to make the investment at 10 per cent per annum. This is then the appropriate discount rate to use. Each annual net cash flow (the difference between the positive and negative cash flows) is discounted back to the time of the initial investment using this discount rate. In year one the discounting factor is the reciprocal of 1.1 (0.909), in year two it is the reciprocal of 1.1^2 (0.826), in year three the reciprocal of 1.1^3 (0.751), and in year four the reciprocal of 1.1^4 (0.683). One way to think of this is that £1 received in four years is worth 68.3 pence today.

With all the net cash flows discounted back to the start point (usually referred to as 'year zero'), we can see that even after the time value of money is taken into account the business proposition looks attractive. The discounted net cash flows for years one to four amount to roughly £136,000, which is considerably larger than the initial investment of £100,000. The surplus of income over expenditure is now much

Table 7.2 Discounted cash-flow analysis (using 10% discount rate)

Period	Negative cash flow	Positive cash flow	Net cash flow	Discount factor	Discounted net cash flow
0	100,000	0	(100,000)	1	(100,000)
1	20,000	50,000	30,000	0.909	27,270
2	30,000	75,000	45,000	0.826	37,170
3	36,000	90,000	54,000	0.751	40,554
4	30,000	75,000	45,000	0.683	30,735
Total	**216,000**	**290,000**	**74,000**		**35,729**

Note: Negative values are shown in brackets

less than the profit of £74,000 that was calculated above when no account was taken of the time value of money. Nevertheless, the discounted value of the positive cash flows exceeds the discounted value of the negative cash flows, so that this business opportunity is said to have a 'positive net present value' at a 10 per cent discount rate. If, however, the entrepreneur had to borrow money at a much higher rate of interest, the opportunity would soon cease to be attractive.

Where to find out more

Dyson, J R (2001) *Accounting for Non-accounting Students*, 5th edn, Harlow: Financial Times/Prentice Hall, pp. 397–421.

KEY CONCEPT 7 Value-based Marketing

Marketing is the management process that seeks to maximise returns to shareholders by developing and implementing strategies to build relationships of trust with high-value customers and to create a sustainable differential advantage. (Doyle, 2000, p. 70)

What it is

Value-based marketing is based on the concept of *shareholder value*. Shareholders are the owners of the firm, and the shareholder value perspective holds that the fundamental purpose of the business is to maximise the value of the company to its shareholders. The fundamental principle of value-based marketing is that marketing strategies should be judged on the basis of their net contribution to shareholder value.

Tell me more

Peter Doyle (2000) has recently advocated this new approach to strategic marketing that starts with the concept of shareholder value. He argues that there is something of a paradox in the perception of marketing in contemporary businesses. On the one hand, chief executives will certainly accept that a focus on the customer is crucial to business success, on the other hand the marketing profession is not generally held in very high esteem. Perhaps this is because the justifications that marketing managers give for their strategies are insufficiently focused on the central objective of the business. Such justifications are often framed in terms of customer awareness, sales volume and market share. Marketing managers are prone to suggest that these measures are valid objectives in themselves. Chief executives increasingly focus on the maximisation of shareholder value as their central corporate goal, and are not convinced that such marketing measures have a clear and consistent link to shareholder value. Shareholder value is certainly not the same thing as profit, and it is entirely possible to increase profits while damaging shareholder value. For example, cutting costs in service centres by reducing staffing levels would increase profits, but may well reduce customer loyalty and so adversely affect the long-term value of the company. Shareholder value is a discounted cash-flow concept (see Key Concept 6). The shareholder value in a company is the discounted value of all future cash flows expected to accrue to that company.

The increasing influence of shareholder value analysis in corporate headquarters represents a considerable opportunity for marketing managers. Marketing in general, and strategic marketing in particular, is concerned with the achievement of a sustainable competitive advantage. Strategic marketing is concerned with adapting the firm to meet the needs of a changing environment. Businesses today have to respond to increasingly rapid change, and they seek their competitive advantage in the marketing function rather than in their manufacturing or service operations. Many businesses have largely subcontracted their manufacturing operations so that they can concentrate on the key tasks of analysing customer needs and developing new technologies and new products to meet them. The only way in which firms can hope to realise the shareholder value aspirations of their investors is by pursuing strategies to achieve sustainable competitive advantage. This is the task of the strategic marketing manager.

In applying shareholder value logic to strategic marketing decisions, there are four ways in which marketing can contribute to increased shareholder value (Srivastava et al., 1999):

1. *Acceleration of cash flows*. The logic of discounted cash-flow analysis dictates that money received 'sooner' is worth more than money received 'later'. So if marketing decisions can bring forward positive cash flows, for example by convincing customers to buy sooner rather than later, this will improve shareholder value.

2. *Enhancement of cash flows by increasing revenues and reducing costs*. Most marketing strategies are directed towards increasing revenues. Customer relationship marketing (see Chapter 9) is directed at increasing customer profitability by reducing the costs associated with customer turnover, increasing sales per customer, and identifying opportunities for selling new products to loyal customers ('cross-selling').

3. *Reducing the vulnerability and volatility of cash flows*. Projected cash flows can be vulnerable to competitive action and subject to fluctuations in demand. Strategic marketing is concerned with identifying and responding to both competitor

actions and marketplace trends. A key function of marketing is to reduce cash-flow volatility by predicting and planning for important changes in the business environment.

4. *Augmentation of the long-term value of the business through investments in tangible and intangible assets*. Srivastava et al. (1999) see this as the logical outcome of the successful implementation of the first three actions. The key intangible assets that are created through successful marketing strategy are brands and customer relationships.

While the value-based marketing approach is undoubtedly an important development in strategic marketing thinking, it would be wrong to suppose that it constitutes some kind of 'general theory' of strategic marketing. First, one can dispute whether the single overriding aim of a business organisation should be the creation of shareholder value. Businesses have many stakeholders, including, for example, employees, customers, members of the communities in which they conduct their business, as well as shareholders. Should a business not strive to balance the interests of shareholders with the interests of other stakeholders? One response to this argument is to say that it is only the shareholders who actually *own* the business, and that they have a clear legal right to be regarded as the primary stakeholder of the organisation. Another response is to argue that the ultimate success of the business depends upon delivering value to shareholders. A firm that does not deliver shareholder value will end up either going out of business or being taken over. However, the underlying debate about the appropriate purposes of business in a capitalist economy is an enduring one, to which there is certainly no simple answer. A second critique of 'value-based marketing' is that it can only ever be applied to privately owned, profit-seeking organisations. While marketing by such organisations is of huge importance, there are large parts of the world economy where the approach is simply inapplicable. One could not offer strategic marketing advice to the international environmental charity Greenpeace, or to the British political party the Liberal Democrats based on value-based marketing. Public sector organisations, including the majority of schools and hospitals even in capitalist economies such as the UK and the USA, simply cannot adopt value-based marketing. However, in the free enterprise sector of the economy, value-based marketing offers a great deal to marketers as a means of demonstrating the importance of marketing to the fundamental purpose of the firm.

SUMMARY

In this chapter we have discussed seven Key Concepts that are of use in analysing the current situation of the organisation, and in deciding what it will set out to achieve. The marketing planning process provides an overview of the steps involved in developing a strategic marketing plan. Gap analysis, objective setting and value-based marketing are means by which the organisation can clarify exactly what it intends to achieve. The SWOT matrix can be used as a bridge between analysis and strategy formulation, since it is both a succinct method of summarising the marketing audit, and a tool for generating strategic options. The experience effect and economies of scale are potential sources of competitive advantage, and in the next chapter we will see how they can be used to underpin marketing strategies. Sales variance analysis and discounted cash-flow analysis are technical procedures that can be useful in analysing the effectiveness of our chosen marketing strategies.

Questions for discussion

1. Companies that adopt a formal approach to marketing planning tend to perform better in terms of key marketing and financial indicators than companies that do not. Does this prove that the adoption of formal marketing planning causes improved financial performance?
2. The marketing director of a local firm explains the following to you: 'We have invested a lot of money in improved customer service. Over the last six months we have cut the average length of time customers have to wait on the phone to speak to a customer service representative in half, from two minutes to one minute. I would say that customer service was obviously a key strength of ours.' What else would you need to find out to establish whether customer service is really a strength?
3. The marketing director goes on to explain that sales revenue for the last six months was very close to target, even though the company has lost several market share points over the period. Explain how this could have happened, using the language of sales variance analysis.
4. Our enthusiastic marketing director goes on to explain that he has recently invested in a customer database system which will allow him to track customer demand and improve his direct mailing effectiveness considerably. All the costs associated with the system were incurred last month, and amounted to £75,000. It is expected that additional business generating profits of £35,000 for each of the next three years will be created by using the system – which will then be obsolete and have no residual value. Does the system look like a good investment? (Use a 10 per cent discount rate.)

Where to find out more

Doyle, P (2000), *Value Based Marketing: Marketing Strategies for Corporate Growth and Shareholder Value*, Chichester: John Wiley & Sons.

References

Baumol, W J and Blinder, A S (1998) *Economics: Principles and Policy*, Fort Worth: Dryden Press, Chapter 7

Billsberry, J (1998) 'Gap Analysis' in Ambrosini, V, Johnson, G and Scholes, K (eds) *Exploring Techniques of Analysis and Evaluation in Strategic Management*, Hemel Hempstead: Prentice Hall, pp. 219–28

Doyle, P (2000) *Value Based Marketing: Marketing Strategies for Corporate Growth and Shareholder Value*, Chichester: John Wiley & Sons

Dyson, J R (2001) *Accounting for Non-accounting Students*, 5th edn, Harlow: Financial Times/Prentice Hall, pp. 324–48

Hedley, B (1976) 'A Fundamental Approach to Strategy Development', *Long Range Planning*, (December): 2–11

McDonald, M (1996) 'Strategic Marketing Planning: Theory, Practice and Research Agendas', *Journal of Marketing Management,* **12**(1–3): 5–27

McDonald, M (1999) *Marketing Plans: How to Prepare Them, How to Use Them*, 4th edn, Oxford: Butterworth Heinemann

Smith, G D, Arnold, D R and Bizzell, B G (1991) *Business Strategy and Policy*, 3rd edn, Boston: Houghton Mifflin, pp. 191–7

Srivastava R K, Shervani, T A and Fahey, L (1999) 'Marketing, Business Processes, and Shareholder Value: An Organizationally Embedded View of Marketing Activities and the Discipline of Marketing', *Journal of Marketing* (special issue), **63**: 168–79

chapter eight

Marketing Strategy Formulation

Learning objectives

By reading this chapter you will learn:

- What key tools are available to marketers for marketing strategy formulation
- How those tools are defined
- How those tools can be applied, their strengths and their weaknesses.

INTRODUCTION

In the previous chapter we dealt with those Key Concepts of strategic marketing that are primarily concerned with analysing the current situation, deciding what objectives the organisation should pursue and assessing success in achieving objectives. The primary emphasis in this chapter is on concepts that are of assistance in the process of generating strategic alternatives. Remember, however, what we said in the introduction to the previous chapter. While we have chosen to classify these concepts into the 'analysis' and 'formulation' categories, these categories are not hard and fast. The following sections discuss eight more 'Key Concepts' of strategic marketing.

KEY CONCEPT 8 Market Segmentation

Decision-oriented segmentation research tends to start with the assumption that individual differences in consumption do in fact exist. The problem then becomes:

1. How may the heterogeneous individuals that comprise the market be grouped into relatively homogeneous cells or segments?
2. How should marketing resources be allocated to the cells? (Frank et al., 1972, p. 11).

What it is

Mass marketing, addressing a large and heterogeneous market with an undifferentiated market offering, is less and less effective as a marketing strategy. Market segmentation is the process of identifying groups of customers who are relatively homogeneous in their response to marketing stimuli, so that the market offering can be tailored more closely to meet their needs.

Tell me more

Central to marketing is the idea that by developing the right mix the marketing manager will achieve the desired objectives – consumers will buy the product, donors will give more to the charity, citizens will adopt a healthier diet, for example. The ultimate aim of marketing is to affect the behaviour of a group of people. The marketing concept says that these behavioural changes will be achieved by understanding what people want, and then developing products or services to satisfy those wants. Where marketing is employed for purposes of improving public health, the marketing concept is extended to include things which people may not even know themselves that they need, such as a reduced intake of fatty foods or alcohol.

Since affecting the behaviour of consumers (or others) is central to marketing, it is not surprising that the study of buyer behaviour is regarded as the first step in the development of successful marketing plans. The behaviour of each individual consumer is unique. However, research into almost any market will show that consumers can be grouped together so that the behaviour of group members is similar to each other, and noticeably different from the behaviour of other groups. Groups of this nature – groups of consumers showing common patterns of consumption behaviour – are called market segments, and the process of dividing the market up into groups is called segmentation.

If segmentation is carried out effectively, then each segment will respond uniquely to a given marketing mix. In order to achieve the best possible response from the market, a different marketing mix will have to be developed for each segment. Typically, some segments will be found to be more sensitive to the price of a product than others, some will be more concerned about quality, some about after-sales support and so on.

Since segmentation is essentially about dividing consumers up on the basis of their behaviour, a logical basis for segmentation would be the 'psychological profiles' of consumers. We can reasonably assume that people who think about the world in a similar way will respond similarly to the marketing mix. This is the basis used in 'psychographic' or 'lifestyle' segmentation. The main advantage of this approach to segmentation is the attempt that is made to understand the basis for consumer behaviour in underlying psychology. The major disadvantage is that it is based on complex information – consumer psychology – which cannot readily be observed, but which must be analysed using psychometric profiling techniques. Psychographic segmentation can be contrasted with demographic segmentation in which a market is divided into subgroups (segments) on the basis of readily observable personal characteristics such as age, gender, occupation and ethnicity. Occupation is the normal method of defining 'social grade'. Demographic segmentation is much more straightforward to implement than psychographic segmentation, since demographic data on most populations are readily available in published form. In the UK there are two methods of social grade classification in common use. The method most frequently employed for marketing purposes is the National Readership Survey classification, shown in Table 8.1. An alternative approach is the 'national statistics socioeconomic classifications', which is adopted for government data, and is illustrated in Table 8.2.

Intuitively it seems that demographic segmentation should be a fairly good method of dividing consumers into groups with common behaviour patterns. We might expect to see differences in behaviour between, for example, men and women,

Table 8.1 British social grade categories (National Readership Survey)

Social grade	Occupational descriptions	Examples
A	Higher managerial, administrative or professional	Lawyers, doctors, senior managers
B	Intermediate managerial, administrative or professional	Teachers, shopkeepers
C1	Supervisory, clerical, junior managerial, administrative or professional	Nurses, shop assistants
C2	Skilled manual workers	Electricians, plumbers
D	Semi and unskilled manual workers	Lorry drivers, fitters
E	Unskilled manual workers	Labourers, barmen

Table 8.2 British social grade categories (national statistics socioeconomic classification)

Social grade	Occupational descriptions	Examples
1	Higher managerial and professional occupations	
1A	Employers and managers	Senior managers, senior police officers
1B	Professionals	Doctors, lawyers, teachers
2	Lower managerial and professional occupations	Nurses, lower ranks of police and armed forces
3	Intermediate occupations	Clerks, secretaries
4	Small employers and own account workers	Publicans, farmers
5	Lower supervisory, craft and related occupations	Plumbers, television engineers, train drivers
6	Semi-routine occupations	Shop assistants, bus drivers
7	Routine occupations	Couriers, labourers
8	Never worked and long-term unemployed	

Source: Adapted from Office for National Statistics (2002), Table 2, p. 8

young people and older people, people in manual jobs and people in managerial jobs. Consider the different readership profiles of two popular British newspapers shown in Table 8.3. Obviously there are significant demographic differences between the readership profiles of the two newspapers. The *Express* appeals equally to men and women, draws over 58 per cent of its readership from social categories B and C1, and 60.8 per cent of readers are aged over 45. The *Daily Star* appeals much more to men than to women, draws over 70 per cent of its readership from social categories C2 and D, and only 27 per cent of readers are aged over 45. The point could have been made even

Table 8.3 Newspaper readership profiles

	Express	Daily Star
Circulation	2,784,000	2,132,000
Readers by gender		
Men	50.4%	69.9%
Women	49.6%	30.1%
Readers by age		
Aged 15–44	39.2%	73%
Aged 45 and over	60.8%	27%
Readers by social group		
A, B, C1	58.8%	29%
C2, D, E	41.2%	71%

Source: NRS

more strongly by comparing a 'quality' newspaper such as the *Daily Telegraph* (84 per cent of readers in social groups A, B, C1) with that epitome of British popular newspaper culture, The *Sun* (27 per cent A, B, C1).

Segmentation of organisational markets

The aim of consumer market segmentation is to identify subgroups within the overall market who will respond in a similar fashion to the marketing mix. When addressing organisational markets the aim is the same, but rather than groups of individuals or families, the marketing manager must identify coherent groups of organisations. The parallel with consumer market segmentation can be taken somewhat further. As in consumer markets, the easiest method of segmenting organisational markets is on the basis of observable and well-documented characteristics. In the case of organisational markets, there are three easy to observe segmentation characteristics:

- *Organisational size.* This might be measured in terms of annual sales turnover, number of employees, or even volume of production, depending on the specific application. For example, if you are interested in selling training courses, then employee size might be used, while if you are selling an input to the production process (such as in-car entertainment systems to a car manufacturer) then volume of production might be a more useful segmentation variable.
- *Industry sector.* This can be measured in an informal way, simply by referring to 'the banking sector' or 'manufacturing industry'. However, such informality can easily lead to confusion (where, for example, one person thinks that an insurance company is in 'the banking sector' and another does not). Therefore industry sector segmentation is usually formalised using a standard industrial classification (SIC) system. Such systems were devised by governments as a means of collecting reliable economic data on industrial production, but turn out to be very useful to marketing managers whose customers are other businesses. This means that aggregate sector data are often available, organised using SIC codes, which can be of use to the marketer.
- *Geographical location.* At its simplest, geographic segmentation might simply allocate customers to 'domestic' and 'export' markets. Clearly both of those categories can be further subdivided. Nationally defined economic regions can be used for the domestic market, and countries or economic trading blocs (such as the European Union, or the North American Free Trade Area) for the export market.

Often these easily observed characteristics of businesses are referred to as 'business market demographics'. Just as in consumer markets, the major strengths of such characteristics as a basis for segmentation are that they are easy to understand, and that extensive data can be found already analysed under these headings.

However, in the discussion of consumer market segmentation, it became clear that the most convenient method of classifying consumers (demographics) was not necessarily the most meaningful way of dividing them up for marketing purposes. Similarly, it has been proposed that more sophisticated tools should be applied in the segmentation of organisational markets. The distinction has been drawn between macrosegments, which are groups of organisations classified together using business demographic measures, and microsegments, which are groups of organisations which have similar product or service needs. One microsegment might be relatively insensitive to price, for example, but demand the very highest quality, while another microsegment might demand particularly high levels of after-sales service. Organisations can be easily allocated to macrosegments on the basis of published information, but in order to identify microsegments it is necessary to carry out detailed market research studies. Furthermore, some doubt has been cast on the usefulness of microsegmentation for practical marketing purposes by Dibb and Simkin (1994). They found that highly sophisticated market segmentation techniques could not clearly be demonstrated to improve upon the elementary business practice of allocating business customers to industry sectors.

Where to find out more

Dibb, S and Simkin, L (1996), *The Market Segmentation Workbook – Target Marketing for Marketing Managers*, London: Routledge.

KEY CONCEPT 9 Targeting and Positioning

What it is

Targeting is the process of assessing the relative worth of different market segments and selecting one or more segments in which to compete – these become your target segments. Positioning is the identification of a particular appeal that the firm can make to customers in each target segment, which is designed to convince customers to choose that firm over its rivals.

What it looks like

See Figure 8.1.

Selection criteria	Segment 1	Segment 2	Segment 3	Segment 4
Size				
Growth				
Competitiveness				
Competence compatibility				
Mission compatibility				

Each segment can be ranked against each criterion. For example, segment 4 might be the largest (rank 1), the slowest growing (rank 4), the second least competitive (rank 2), the most compatible with the firm's competences (rank 1) and the second most compatible with the firm's mission (rank 2). This would yield a "sum of ranks" of 1+4+2+1+2 = 10. The sums of ranks of the segments can be used as an initial indicator of segment attractiveness. The segment with the lowest sum of ranks is the most attractive.

Figure 8.1 Target segment selection

Tell me more

The process of market segmentation (Key Concept 8) is concerned with identifying relatively homogeneous groups within the overall market, so that the marketing mix can be tailored to their preferences. Segmentation is the first step towards a target marketing strategy. Target marketing consists of *segmentation*, followed by *target selection* and then *positioning*. From the market segments identified at the segmentation stage the firm must select those in which it intends to compete. Typically, the criteria for selecting appropriate target markets are:

1. Segment size
2. Segment growth rate
3. Segment competitiveness
4. Segment compatibility with the firm's competences
5. Segment compatibility with the firm's mission and objectives.

Figure 8.1 illustrates how these criteria could be used to rank four market segments in terms of their overall attractiveness.

All other things being equal, a larger segment offers more opportunities than a smaller segment, and a fast-growing segment more than a slow-growing segment. However, all other things are seldom equal. Large and fast-growing market segments typically attract more competitors, perhaps larger and more powerful competitors, than small and slow-growing segments. Furthermore, the abilities of the firm and its competitive rivals are different. The SWOT analysis (previous chapter) should have highlighted key strengths and weaknesses compared to rivals. Market segmentation analysis will have identified the specific characteristics of demand in each market segment. It is important to try to match the firm's strengths to the requirements of the target segments. There is no point in targeting a highly price-sensitive market segment if the SWOT revealed that your cost position is far worse than that of your key rivals. There is no point in targeting a highly quality-sensitive market segment if your production department cannot match or better competitors on product quality. Target market segments must be compatible with the firm's competences. Finally, target market selection should take account of the strategic direction that the firm intends to take, not just its current position. If the firm has a reputation for low cost and mediocre quality, but has put in place a concrete strategy to make it an industry leader on quality, then over an appropriate timescale it will adjust its target market selection away from the low-cost segment towards the high-quality segment. Naturally, this will require the implementation of some creative marketing communications strategies to convince customers in the target segment of the quality of the products.

The third element of the target marketing process is positioning. It is not enough just to define and then select target market segments. It is also necessary to give customers in the target market one or more good reasons to select your company rather than one of your rivals. This is the essence of the positioning problem. The clue to solving the positioning problem lies in the very nature of a market segment. In some important ways, customers within a market segment are like each other and are different from customers in other market segments – otherwise it would not be a segment. Those differences between customers in different market segments can be addressed using marketing stimuli – the marketing mix. In order to differentiate our market offering from that of our rivals, we have to convince customers in the target market that we are offering something of value that competitors are not offering.

The valuable differentiating characteristic that we offer must be defined in terms of the specific preferences of our selected target market segment. For example, the German car manufacturer Mercedes targets upscale consumers with expensive but well-engineered and prestigious motorcars. The Korean car manufacturer Daewoo targets price-sensitive consumers with value-for-money vehicles. The two manufacturers hardly compete with each other at all, targeting different market segments and holding very different positions in the market. Mercedes competes with companies such as BMW and the Jaguar brand (a business unit of the Ford Motor Company). Daewoo competes with companies such as Proton and the Skoda brand (a business unit of the Volkswagen group). An automotive components company seeking to target Mercedes, BMW and Jaguar might seek to establish a market position based on engineering excellence and quality – a market position based simply on low cost would be entirely pointless. However, establishing a low-cost position would probably be the number one priority for an automotive components firm seeking to win business from Daewoo and its rivals. This is *not* to say that cost is irrelevant to Mercedes and other top range manufacturers, nor that quality is irrelevant to budget car manufacturers. However, in each case they have clear priorities for the cost and quality of purchased components, based on their own selected target markets and chosen market positions.

Figure 8.2 illustrates the way in which the positioning decision can be depicted in terms of a two-dimensional display (a perceptual map). In this case, the criteria used to differentiate products are price and quality – characteristics that are often important in consumer decisions about packaged groceries. The standard, market-leading brands occupy the middle ground of the map, since they define the 'average' levels of price and quality. Indicative names have been attached to each of the quadrants, suggestive of the type of brand that might occupy that position in the market. Premium brands are priced above average and are perceived by consumers to be of above-average quality. Budget brands occupy the low-price, low-quality quadrant.

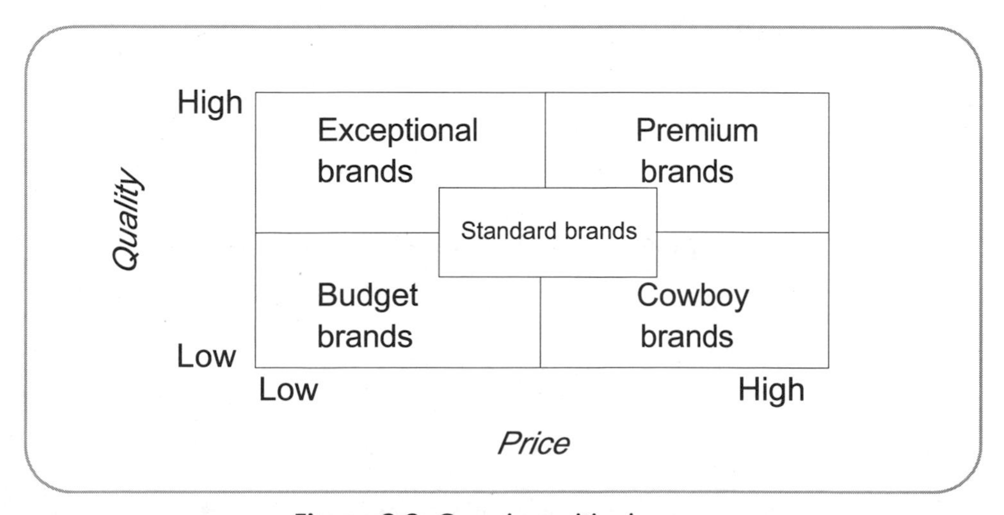

Figure 8.2 Generic positioning map

Comparatively few exceptional brands are to be found offering above-average quality at an average or below-average price. Finally, it is unlikely that a brand perceived to offer below-average quality at an above-average price ('cowboy brand') will be able to survive in the long term.

Where to find out more

Malhotra, N K and Birks, D F (2000), *Marketing Research: An Applied Approach*, European edn, Harlow: Financial Times/Prentice Hall, Chapter 23.

KEY CONCEPT 10 The Product Life Cycle (PLC)

As a confirmed supporter of the validity of the PLC I reject outright the claim that there is no empirical support for the concept and would argue that the fact that managers have made wrong decisions when seeking to apply the concept is due to their misinterpretation of it rather than an intrinsic deficiency in the concept itself ... the PLC may be regarded as an important tool for planning at the strategic level always recognising that it is not of itself deterministic and may be influenced significantly by environmental changes and/or marketing action. (Baker, 1992, p. 100)

What it is

The product life-cycle hypothesis postulates that a successful new product will pass through a series of stages – introduction, growth, maturity and decline – on its way from birth to death.

What it looks like

See Figure 8.3.

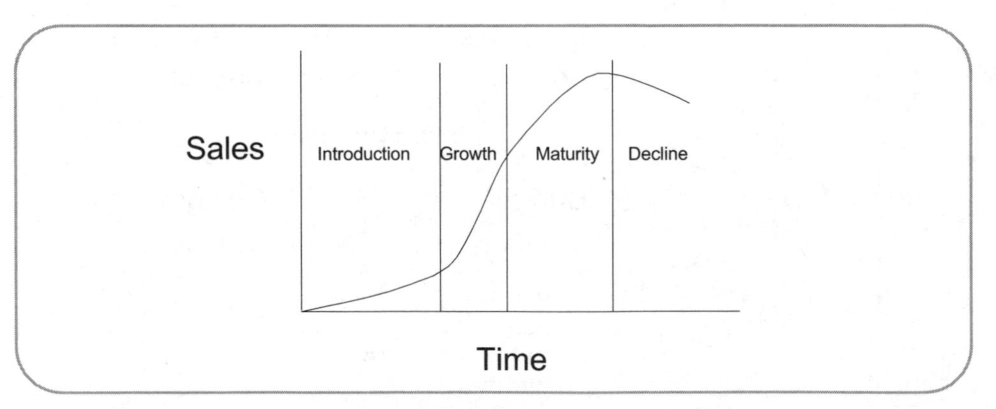

Figure 8.3 Product life cycle

Tell me more

A new product is launched and, if successful, enjoys a period of sales growth which would normally be followed by a gradual decline in the rate of growth as the market saturates. This idea has been formalised as the *product life-cycle* concept, in which it is proposed that all successful products move inexorably through four phases – introduction, growth, maturity and decline. Attempts have been made to demonstrate that marketing management decisions can be guided by an understanding of the position of a product in its life cycle. For example, John Smallwood (1993) provided a matrix showing how elements of the marketing mix should be adapted to the life-cycle stage of the product. There is an intuitive appeal about Smallwood's recommendations. In general terms, it would make marketing management easier if there was some kind of formula that could be applied. In specific terms, much of what Smallwood proposes looks sensible. For example, as the product goes from the introduction to the growth phase it should become more sophisticated, in the maturity phase the market should be segmented and multiple product variations offered, while in the decline phase the number of product variations on offer should be reduced.

There is some debate over the worth of the product life-cycle concept. The general opinion today is that the idea of the product life cycle is of value as a general statement of the inevitability of product decline, as a spur to new product development and as protection against the complacency which rapid sales growth can bring. However, there are grave problems involved in using the product life cycle as a practical marketing tool. It is difficult to tell exactly which of the stages a product is in at any one time, and many products have gone into apparent decline only to be revived through the application of creative marketing.

Managing the Product Life Cycle

In the 1980s the market for durable, metal razors was in decline because consumers preferred plastic, disposable razors. The process at work in the market seemed to be one of 'commoditisation', which is where marketers find it increasingly difficult to differentiate products on the basis of such factors as features or quality, because consumers begin to choose more and more on the basis of price alone. In a commodity market, there is a strong temptation to cut back on advertising and product development spending to keep costs down in order to maintain competitive prices. Gillette took the bold step of developing and launching an innovative new metal razor (Sensor) which proved enormously popular and reversed the decline in demand for durable razors. According to *The Economist* (15 August 1992) Sensor was:

> that rarity in today's supermarket: a product that is demonstrably better than its competitors.

Had Gillette acted naively on the basis of product life-cycle theory, on seeing that durable razors were in the decline phase of the life cycle, they would have cut back on advertising, product development and channels of distribution and might also have increased prices. The result would have been to reduce the demand for durable razors even further, providing further evidence that the product was in its decline phase.

The Gillette example illustrates the most damning criticism leveled at the product life cycle, namely that the life cycle is the *result* of rather than the *precursor* to marketing actions. This point was argued strongly by Dhalla and Yuspeh (1976), who also pointed out that it is unclear just what is meant by the 'product' part of the product life cycle. Does it mean a product class (for example motor cars), a product form (for example family saloon cars) or a brand (for example Ford Focus)? On the basis of evidence from an analysis of consumer goods brands in the UK, Mercer (1993, p. 274) concluded of the product life cycle that:

> this (PLC) theory cannot any longer be justified in terms of general applicability – and should be relegated to usage (albeit valuable usage) in special circumstances.

Where to find out more

Smallwood, J (1973), 'The Product Life-cycle: A Key to Strategic Market Planning', *MSU Business Topics*, Winter.

KEY CONCEPT 11 The Boston Consulting Group Growth/Share Matrix

What it is

Simply known as the BCG matrix or 'Boston box' this is a method of representing the strategic business units of a company, or the products of a firm, in terms of their market share and market growth rate. The purpose of the analysis is to identify priority areas (SBUs or products) for marketing investment by the organisation.

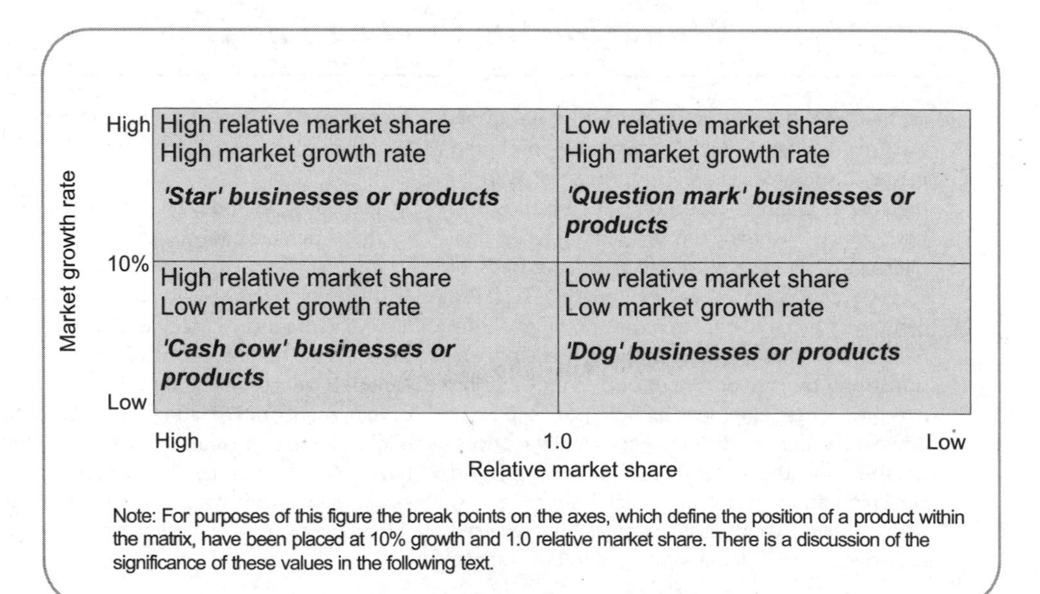

Figure 8.4 BCG growth/share matrix

What it looks like

See Figure 8.4.

Tell me more

The BCG matrix is the best known of the portfolio models used in strategic management and strategic marketing planning. Such portfolio models are attempts to provide a useful insight into complex business problems through the use of a two-dimensional representation, a matrix. The types of business problem to which portfolio models apply are those in which scarce resources have to be allocated to multiple competing applications. Originally, portfolio models were designed for use in *corporate strategy* by diversified firms running multiple strategic business units in different markets. For the purposes of *competitive strategy*, such models, including the BCG matrix, are more likely to be of use in analysing a product portfolio. The BCG matrix has also been adapted for use in the analysis of a firm's portfolio of customers, to assist in the allocation of scarce resources (such as technical development expenditure) between key customers (Campbell and Cunningham, 1983). This is an application of particular relevance in business-to-business marketing, which is further explored in Key Concept 15.

For the moment, let us focus on the use of the BCG matrix to analyse a product portfolio. The horizontal axis measures the relative share of the market controlled by the company. This is the company's market share, divided by the market share of the largest rival in the market, expressed as a ratio. For a market leader, the relative market share ratio is greater than 1.0, since it has greater market share than has its nearest rival. For a market follower, the relative market share ratio is less than 1.0. For example, if we think of a market in which there are only three competitors, then their absolute sales, market share and relative market share can be illustrated as in Table 8.4.

Relative market share means your share of the market divided by the share of your largest competitor, for example:

- if you have 25 per cent of a market, and your largest competitor has 20 per cent, then your relative market share is 1.25
- if you have 10 per cent of a market, and your largest competitor has 30 per cent, then your relative market share is 0.33
- if you have 30 per cent of a market, and your largest competitor has 30 per cent, then your relative market share is 1.00.

Table 8.4 Calculating relative market share

Competitor	Sales £m	Market share %	Relative market share
Rival 1	100	50.0	50/37.5 = 1.33
Rival 2	75	37.5	37.5/50 = 0.75
Rival 3	25	12.5	12.5/50 = 0.25
Industry total	**200**	**100.0**	

Market growth rate means the annual rate of growth of the market in which you are competing, and might be quite different from the rate of growth of your SBU. Suppose that market sales grew from £15 million to £20 million last year, while you increased your sales from £1 million to £2 million. The market grew at a healthy 33 per cent, but your business grew by 100 per cent (incidentally, you increased your absolute market share from 6.6 per cent to 10 per cent, but we don't have enough information to calculate your relative market share). The vertical axis measures the growth rate of the market in 'real terms'. That is to say, the growth rate of the market is measured after account has been taken of any general inflationary effect.

The axes are measured in this way to try to identify the competitive strength of the product, and the attractiveness of the market in which it is sold. Relative market share is used to measure competitive strength, and market growth rate is used to measure market attractiveness. All other things being equal, it is supposed that a firm with greater market share will be a more powerful competitor than one with less market share – and PIMS (Key Concept 12) provides evidence that market share is positively associated with performance. All other things being equal, it is assumed that a faster growing market will be more attractive than a slower growing market. Of course, both of these are simplifying assumptions and in both cases exceptions can be found to the 'rule'. Nevertheless, the underlying logic of the BCG matrix holds that the economic performance of a product can be linked to the two variables, relative market share and market growth rate. In particular, it is expected that the net cash flows associated with products will be related to their position in the matrix. 'Cash cows' are so named because, as strong products in stable markets, they are expected to be substantial net generators of cash, which can be invested in growth businesses. Those growth businesses are either 'stars', in which the company should invest to protect its strong position, or 'question marks'. 'Question marks' (also known as 'problem children') could become 'stars' with sufficient investment, but risk becoming 'dogs' as their market matures and its growth rate declines. 'Dogs' tend not to be large net users or generators of cash.

The BCG matrix was a technique developed by a major consulting organisation for use by its clients and was used by many large corporations in the 1970s (Morrison and Wensley, 1991). It remains a potentially valuable tool of strategic marketing planning, but is certainly not a panacea. There are a number of difficulties associated with the model. For example, different sources give different market growth rate 'break points' between high- and low-growth markets, and the 'break point' between high and low relative share products is sometimes shown as 1.0 (Day, 1977) and sometimes as 1.5 (Hedley, 1977). Morrison and Wensley argue that the most problematic criticism of the model is the definition of 'market'. In order to calculate the relative market share and the market growth rate it is first necessary to define precisely 'the market'. This may raise awkward questions in terms of geographical definition (town, region, country or world market) and in terms of product substitutes (in measuring the market for laptop computers, how does one decide when an electronic personal organiser from Psion or Palm becomes a computer?). In conclusion, it is a technique worth using, but only as an interesting input to the planning process, and to be interpreted with care.

Where to find out more

Morrison, A and Wensley, R (1991), 'Boxing Up or Boxed In? A Short History of the Boston Consulting Group Share/Growth Matrix', *Journal of Marketing Management*, 7(2): 105–29.

KEY CONCEPT 12 PIMS

What it is

'PIMS' stands for *Profit Impact of Market Strategy*. The philosophy of the PIMS approach is that it should be possible to relate marketing strategy consistently to organisational performance. So, the characteristic marketing strategies employed by successful companies can be identified.

Tell me more

Starting in 1972, the PIMS project was designed to gather quantitative information relating company performance to marketing strategy. This research study was designed to establish what strategies made a real difference to company performance, by gathering a vast amount of data on the performance and strategies of real companies. This enabled the PIMS researchers to suggest some general principles of strategy (Buzzell and Gale, 1987, pp. 7–14):

- In the long run, the most important single factor affecting a business unit's performance is the quality of its products and services, relative to those of competitors
- Market share and profitability are strongly related
- High investment intensity acts as a powerful drag on profitability
- Many so-called 'dog' or 'question mark' businesses generate cash, while many 'cash cows' are dry
- Vertical integration (that is, operating business units at consecutive stages of the production process, such as an integrated circuit factory and a personal computer manufacturer) is a profitable strategy for some kinds of business, but not for others
- Most of the strategic factors that boost return on investment (that is, profit measured as a percentage of capital employed) also contribute to long-term value.

These six key principles say some things that are expected and some that are unexpected. Today, most organisations acknowledge the importance of quality to their business. PIMS concludes that it is the number one factor for successful long-term business performance. The positive relationship between profitability and market share is not a surprise. It is important to recognise that this positive *relationship* does not automatically mean that higher profitability is the *result* of higher market share – the statistical relationship could equally well be explained by saying that high market share is the result of high profitability. However, there are good reasons to suppose that high market share brings the business certain advantages over its rivals (for example economies of scale and experience cost advantages – see Chapter 7) which lead to superior performance. This positive association between profitability and market share has been used elsewhere in strategic marketing to develop tools for strategic analysis – the BCG growth/share matrix is an important example. The PIMS results provide interesting data relating to the BCG growth/share matrix (see Key Concept 11). That model suggests that low-share/low-growth businesses ('dogs') will have negative cash flows, while high-share/high-growth businesses ('cash cows') will have positive cash flows. PIMS showed that 59 per cent of 'dog' SBUs were generating positive cash flows, while 26 per cent of Cash Cow SBUs were generating negative cash flows. This does not mean that the matrix is 'wrong'. In general, the data demonstrate that 'cash cows' are much more likely to be cash-generating businesses than 'dogs'. However, it does illustrate that it is important to appreciate the limitations on the kind of useful generalisations that can be made about business strategy. Normally, these generalisations are not clear-cut, unambiguous 'facts'. Rather, they are 'tendencies', often true, but subject to important exceptions. That is why strategic marketing cannot be reduced to a simple technical process of applying techniques and models.

Where to find out more

Buzzell, R D and Gale, B T (1987), *The PIMS Principles: Linking Strategy to Performance*, New York: Free Press.

KEY CONCEPT 13 Porter's Generic Competitive Strategies

What it is

Porter's generic competitive strategies are a means for understanding the fundamental basis of competitive strategy for a business unit. A business unit can achieve competitive advantage either through cost leadership or through differentiation, across either a broad or a narrow target market.

What it looks like

See Figure 8.5.

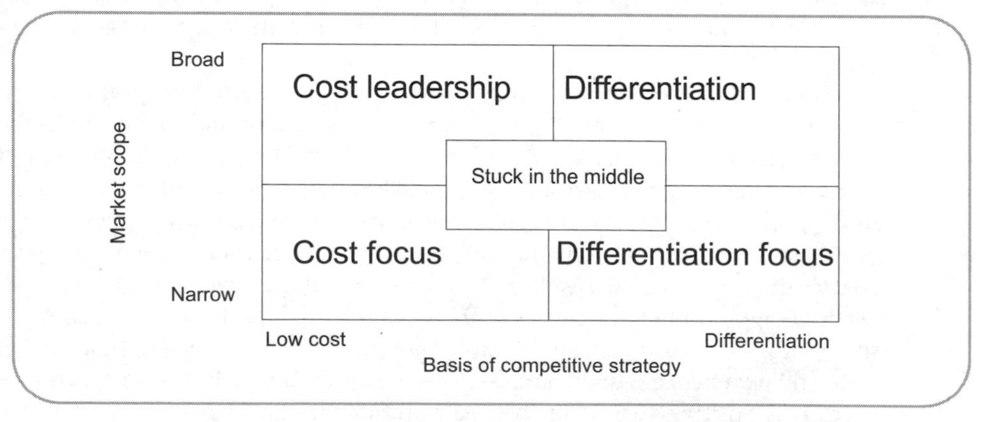

Figure 8.5 Porter's generic competitive strategies

Source: Adapted with the permission of The Free Press, an imprint of Simon & Schuster Adult Publishing Group, from *Competitive Advantage: Creating and Sustaining Superior Performance* by Michael E. Porter. Copyright © 1985, 1998 by Michael E. Porter

Tell me more

In his book *Competitive Strategy*, Michael Porter (1980) concentrated his attentions on diagnosing the forces shaping competitive strategy within an industry, identifying the famous 'five forces' of competitive rivalry, substitutes, new entrants, customers and suppliers. In the later work *Competitive Advantage*, Porter (1985) asked how it is possible for a firm, operating in its competitive environment, to build a sustainable competitive advantage over its rivals. This has proved to be an enduring question, and there are people who would argue that the pace of change in technology, in competitive conditions and in consumer tastes makes it difficult or even impossible today to build a genuinely sustainable competitive advantage. Nevertheless, Porter's argument – that a firm can only achieve competitive advantage along two possible dimensions, namely cost *or* differentiation – still deserves serious attention. The second half of Porter's argument, that this competitive advantage can either be applied to a broad or a narrow market, is an easy point for marketers to understand, since the subdivision of the market into segments has been a fundamental principle of marketing for a long time. Strategies of undifferentiated marketing (addressing multiple segments with the same marketing mix) and targeted marketing (developing tailored strategies for individual segments) are similar to Porter's ideas about a broad and a narrow target market.

It is important to realise that Porter was arguing for the mutual exclusivity of cost leadership and differentiation strategies. If a company pursued a cost leadership strategy, then the objective was to have lower average costs than any competitive rival, so that superior profits could be generated by charging the market average price while holding costs down. This is not a 'cheap and cheerful' strategy. Cost leadership need not imply 'lowest price', although the true cost leader certainly has the advantage that, should the need arise, it will be able to cut prices further than its rivals without making losses. Low cost must be the obsession of a company pursuing a cost leadership strategy, and there can only be one true cost leader in any single market. The obsession with low cost implies that in all its activities, production, customer service, distribution, marketing and so on, low cost is the primary criterion driving managerial decision-making. Porter argued that this was incompatible with simultaneously pursuing a differentiation strategy. By no means everyone would agree with this. Many business people would argue that it is imperative simultaneously to pursue low cost *and* differentiation. Indeed, customers in some industries have become used to receiving improved quality and better value year after year (this is most obvious in high-technology markets such as personal computers and mobile phones, but also applies to mature products such as cars and clothing). This dispute – whether cost leadership and differentiation are mutually exclusive or not – remains largely unresolved.

Unlike cost leadership, multiple companies in the same market can achieve differentiation. Differentiation means delivering something of value to the customer that competitive rivals are not delivering. There are many ways of differentiating the company's offering in the market. Depending upon the nature of the product, and the tastes of consumers, successful differentiation might be based upon, for example, excellence in service quality, excellence in product design, speed of delivery, brand exclusivity, or many other factors. In essence, successful differentiation requires the company to identify a criterion of importance to customers, for which they will be prepared to pay a premium price, to integrate that into the market offering, and then to communicate that benefit to the market. Superior profitability in a company pursuing a successful differentiation strategy comes from the price premium that customers are prepared to pay for the extra value that they perceive. In some cases, it will be possible to identify a differentiation strategy that will appeal to a wide target market, but in many cases it will only be a segment of the market that values a specific benefit enough to pay a price premium for it – the 'differentiation focus' strategy.

Where to find out more

Porter, M E (1985), *Competitive Advantage*, New York: Free Press.

KEY CONCEPT 14 Ansoff's Growth Vector Matrix

What it is

The Ansoff matrix itemises the four ways in which a firm can develop its portfolio of products and markets – market penetration (current products/markets), product development (new products/current markets), market development (new markets/current products) and diversification (new products/new markets).

What it looks like

See Figure 8.6.

Tell me more

Igor Ansoff (1987) suggested four 'growth vectors' for a firm's future business – that is to say four directions that future growth could take.

A firm pursuing a *market penetration strategy* aims to increase its market share in its existing markets and with broadly the same product range. Should this prove insuffi-

Market		Product	
	New	Market development	Diversification
	Present	Market penetration	Product development
		Present	New

Figure 8.6 Ansoff growth vector matrix

Source: Adapted from Ansoff (1987)

cient to achieve the firm's objectives, then it may consider a *product development strategy* or a *market development strategy*. In the former case new products are developed, but they are sold into markets which the firm already addresses – so much of the existing database of marketing research is relevant. Market development means that the firm pushes into new markets, but with broadly the same products. In this case it needs to research the new markets, but understands the product technology involved. Finally, if the firm decides to enter new markets with new products, this is known as a *diversification strategy*. By definition, both the market and the product are unfamiliar when diversification is pursued, so that the managers of the firm have to gain experience of both new markets and new products simultaneously. In consequence, diversification can be regarded as a relatively high-risk strategy.

Where to find out more

Ansoff, I (1987), *Corporate Strategy*, revised edn, Harmondsworth: Penguin Books.

KEY CONCEPT 15 Customer Portfolio Analysis

What it is

Customer portfolio analysis is a method of classifying individual customer accounts in order to assess the degree of 'balance' in the customer portfolio and inform the process of allocating resources to customer account development.

What it looks like

See Figure 8.7.

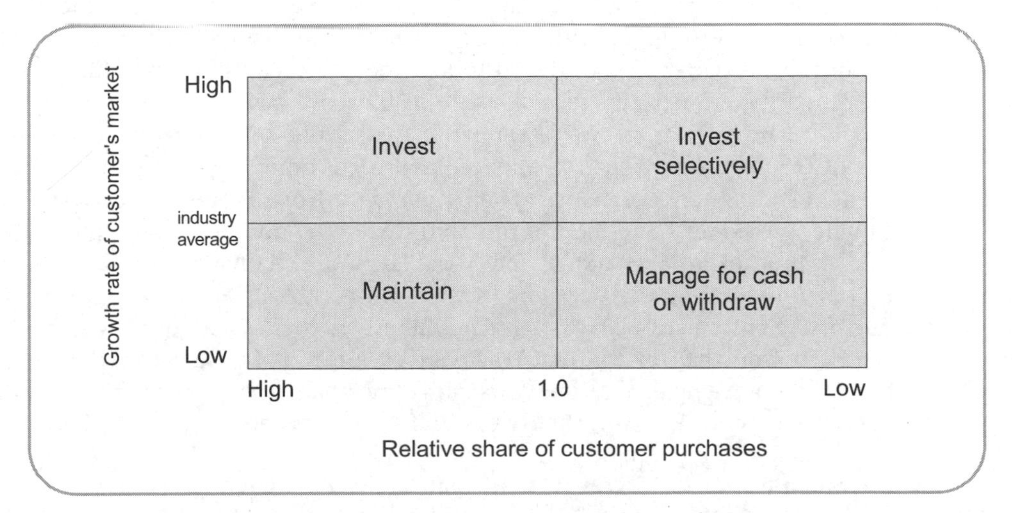

Figure 8.7 Customer portfolio analysis

Tell me more

The concept of portfolio analysis is, of course, familiar from Key Concept 11, the growth/share matrix. Figure 8.7 illustrates the application of the same portfolio technique to a company's customer accounts. This is a technique that can only be of use in business-to-business marketing, since it assumes that the customer is an organisation that has its own markets to serve. Customer portfolio analysis is closely related to the ideas discussed in Chapter 4 about organisational buying behaviour. This technique can be of great assistance to business-to-business marketers in identifying the appropriate marketing approach for a customer or group of customers (Chapter 4 provides a fuller explanation of why this is).

In Key Concept 11 we explained how the growth/share matrix could be applied to business units or products to assist in the process of allocation of scarce marketing resources. Customer portfolio analysis applies the same process to the firm's customers. An important starting point for the analysis is the realisation that such decisions have to be made, one way or the other. While in marketing rhetoric we may claim that all customers are of vital importance to our business, marketing reality is rather different. Some customers are clearly more important than others. We cannot afford to lavish marketing resources (for example hospitality, customer account planning, regular review meetings, senior management involvement) on customers that are unlikely ever to generate much (if any) profit. If decisions about the allocation of marketing resources are not made using some objective technique, such as that described here, then they will be made in some other way. One problem that can arise, where decisions are made subjectively, is that resources are allocated on the basis of historical factors that no longer apply. This could easily be the case where a customer has been loyal over a long period, was once a leader in its own market, but has now been overtaken by new competitors. Such a customer may retain a much higher proportion of our marketing expenditure than is strictly justified in commercial terms, as a result of inertia in the budgeting process. The hidden cost of such overinvestment in one customer could be underinvestment in another customer, perhaps one that has recently been improving its market position and could represent a long-term sales growth opportunity.

These ideas are formalised through an objective customer portfolio analysis technique, such as that shown in Figure 8.7. The two axes are designed to measure, first, our competitive strength with the customer (the horizontal axis) and, second, the commercial attractiveness of the customer (the vertical axis). Competitive strength is measured in terms of our relative share of the customer's purchases of a particular product. The calculation is very similar to the calculation of relative market share in the BCG growth/share matrix. Suppose that a customer buys, in total, £5.5 million worth of automotive exhaust systems per year from four suppliers. The leading supplier provides £2.5 million of this, and we are the number two supplier providing £1.5 million of exhaust systems per year. Then our relative market share is 1.5/2.5, that is, 0.6, locating the customer in the right-hand half of the matrix. The growth rate of the customer's market then determines whether this account is located in the top or bottom half of the matrix. If our customer is in a relatively slow-growing industry (for example, in recent years sales of new cars have grown very slowly or stagnated in Western Europe), then we would locate this account in the bottom right-hand quadrant of the matrix.

Much like the BCG growth/share matrix, this technique can be used both to look for 'balance' in the portfolio and provide broad strategic guidance about the treatment of particular customers. 'Balance' is difficult to define concretely. Clearly a customer portfolio that only has customers in the bottom right-hand quadrant would be unbalanced and problematic. However, it would be incorrect to suppose that a portfolio showing approximately equal numbers of customers in each quadrant would be in some sense optimal.

Again, like the BCG growth/share matrix, the customer portfolio matrix can provide no more than vague generalisations about the treatment of the accounts located in each quadrant. In the bottom right-hand quadrant, that advice is to 'manage for cash or withdraw'. The key here is to avoid expensive investments of marketing resources that are unlikely to be recouped in future years (see Key Concepts 6 and 7, discounted cash-flow analysis and value-based marketing). In the upper right-hand quadrant, a judgement has to be reached, whether we can gain an extra share of this customer's business and move it leftwards, or if this is unlikely to be possible because of the strength of the competition. Only if a leftward shift were possible would we consider substantial marketing investment. Customers in the upper left-hand quadrant are very valuable – customers in fast-growing markets to which we are the leading supplier. This means that they are likely targets for our competitors, and that ongoing marketing investment will be required to maintain our position. Finally, in the lower left-hand quadrant, we find the equivalent of the BCG 'cash cow' – a customer in a slow-growth market, to which we are the leading supplier. While clearly these are valuable customers, they may not have quite the same growth potential as 'top-left' customers, and although it is important to maintain good relations with such customers, strategic marketing investment (for example, extensive new product development) may be less justified.

It is not difficult to criticise such an approach to customer portfolio analysis. The measures used for each axis are only one possible indicator of competitive strength and customer attractiveness. In practice it may be quite difficult to calculate the relative share axis anyway, since you need to know the share of a customer's business held by at least one other competitor – although this difficulty should not be overstated, since such information can often be obtained from the customer itself. The rather alarming vagueness of the strategic recommendations from this technique is a weakness that was also noted with the BCG growth/share matrix. To some extent, however, this illustrates a misconception of the purpose of the analysis. Such broad analysis cannot possibly provide a detailed strategy for each individual customer account. Only detailed information gathering and analysis at the customer level can do that. But this form of analysis does provide a basis for making judgements across customer accounts, identifying those that are prime candidates for substantial investments of marketing resources, and those that are not.

Where to find out more

The technique discussed in this Key Concept has been developed from the ideas of Campbell and Cunningham: Campbell, N C G and Cunningham, M T (1983), 'Customer Analysis for Strategy Development in Industrial Markets', *Strategic Management Journal*, **4**: 360–80.

McDonald and Rogers (1998) discuss a similar approach to customer portfolio analysis in Chapter 4.

SUMMARY

In this chapter and the last we have investigated a wide range of analytical tools that have been developed to assist in the process of developing marketing strategy. We know that formal methods of marketing planning are associated with above-average company performance, and it is reasonable to suppose that there is causal effect at work, that is, marketing planning helps bring about improved performance. It follows that familiarity with the tools described in these chapters can enable the marketing manager to make a more effective contribution to his or her firm. However, marketing strategy and planning should not simply become an obsession with the application of formal tools and techniques. In strategic marketing, we use formal methods of analysis to assist in the process of decision-making, not as a substitute for the judgement of the professional marketer. Thoughtful application of these tools is likely to improve company performance.

Questions for discussion

1. Market segmentation is often based on directly observable characteristics of customers and potential customers, such as the age and sex of consumers, or the turnover size and industry sector of companies. What are the advantages and disadvantages of such segmentation methods when compared with segmentation based on buying behaviour characteristics?
2. A friend of yours, who is a successful entrepreneur, says to you: 'You're wasting your time with all this strategic marketing theory. I don't know a dog from a cash cow, and I wouldn't know a differentiation focus strategy if I tripped over it in the street. But my business seems to be doing fine!' What arguments would you use to persuade your friend that strategic marketing models can play a valuable role in business?
3. Table 8.5 shows data relating to the product lines of an office equipment company. Draw up an accurate BCG growth/share matrix for this product portfolio. What observations do you have about the balance of this portfolio?
4. Autobits Ltd manufactures speedometers and tachometers for use in motorcycles, selling these directly to Japanese bike makers Honda and Suzuki. The firm's management has identified a number of alternative strategic options to develop the business. The sales director wants to generate more sales by investing greater efforts in developing the relationships with Honda and Suzuki. The marketing director advocates developing new relationships with Harley Davidson in the USA and the UK firm Triumph. The managing director joined the company from General Motors, and is inclined to look for new business from automobile manufacturers. The production director believes that it would make sense to sell additional equipment, such as fuel gauges, to Honda and Suzuki. Explain all these options using the Ansoff growth vector matrix.

Table 8.5 Applying the BCG growth/share matrix

Product line	Market size £k 2001	Market size £k 2002	Own market share	Rival market share
101A (photocopier)	5,500	5,600	10%	25%
102A (home laser printer)	45,000	50,000	30%	15%
102B (business laser printer)	95,000	95,000	12%	30%
103A (home scanner)	25,000	26,000	5%	40%
103B (professional scanner)	10,000	12,000	10%	15%

References

Ansoff, I (1987), *Corporate Strategy*, revised edn, Harmondsworth: Penguin Books

Baker, M J (1992), *Marketing Strategy and Management*, Basingstoke: Macmillan – now Palgrave Macmillan

Buzzell, R D and Gale, B T (1987), *The PIMS Principles: Linking Strategy to Performance*, New York: Free Press

Campbell, N C G and Cunningham, M T (1983), 'Customer Analysis for Strategy Development in Industrial Markets', *Strategic Management Journal*, **4**: 360–80

Day, G S (1977), 'Diagnosing the Product Portfolio', *Journal of Marketing*, (April): 29–38

Dhalla, N K and Yuspeh, S (1976), 'Forget the Product Life Cycle Concept', *Harvard Business Review*, January/February, 102–12

Dibb, S and Simkin, L (1994), 'Implementation Problems in Industrial Market Segmentation', *Industrial Marketing Management*, 23

Dibb, S and Simkin, L (1996), *The Market Segmentation Workbook – Target Marketing for Marketing Managers*, London: Routledge

Frank, R E, Massy, W F and Wind, Y (1972) *Market Segmentation*, Englewood Cliffs, NJ: Prentice Hall

Hedley, B (1977), 'Strategy and the 'Business Portfolio', *Long Range Planning*, **10**(February): 9–15

Malhotra, N K and Birks, D F (2000), *Marketing Research: An Applied Approach*, European edn, Harlow: Financial Times/Prentice Hall

McDonald, M and Rogers, B (1998), *Key Account Management*, Oxford: Butterworth Heinemann

Mercer, D (1993), 'A Two-Decade Test of Product Life Cycle Theory', *British Journal of Management*, **4**(4): 269–74

Morrison, A and Wensley, R (1991), 'Boxing Up or Boxed In? A Short History of the Boston Consulting Group Share/Growth Matrix', *Journal of Marketing Management*, **7**(2): 105–29

Office for National Statistics (2002) The National Statistics Socio-economic Classification User Manual, London: Office for National Statistics

Porter, M E (1980), *Competitive Strategy*, New York: Free Press

Porter, M E (1985), *Competitive Advantage*, New York: Free Press

Smallwood, J (1973), 'The Product Life-cycle: A Key to Strategic Market Planning', *MSU Business Topics*, Winter

chapter nine

Relationship Marketing Strategies

Learning objectives

By reading this chapter you will learn:

- The distinction between discrete transactions and relational exchange
- The nature of the relationship life cycle
- What is meant by relationship marketing
- Methods of implementing relationship marketing
- The application of relationship marketing in consumer goods markets, consumer services markets and business-to-business markets
- A range of criticisms that have been levelled at relationship marketing.

INTRODUCTION

One of the most important developments in both the theory and practice of marketing during the last two decades has been the emergence of the concept of 'relationship marketing'. Relationship marketing is the umbrella term for a wide range of marketing practices that have, as one common facet, a focus that goes beyond the single transaction between a buyer and a seller. Table 9.1 illustrates the breadth of terminology that has been used to describe this field.

One problem that has arisen in discussions of this field is a lack of clarity, or a lack of agreement, on the meaning of fundamental terms. Buttle (1996) argued that the notion of marketing as simply being concerned with developing, selling and delivering products was obsolete. Increasingly, he claimed, marketing was more concerned with the development and maintenance of mutually satisfying long-term relationships between buyers and sellers. This argument raises a number of important issues, around which the rest of the chapter will be organised:

1. Exactly what do we mean by a 'long-term buyer–seller relationship'? To investigate this we will examine the concept of the 'relationship life cycle'.
2. What is meant by 'relationship marketing', and how can this concept be defined?
3. How can relationship marketing be put into practice, and does it have to be adapted according to the nature of the market (for example, are service markets different from goods markets)?
4. What challenges have been raised to this relatively new approach to marketing?

LONG-TERM BUYER–SELLER RELATIONSHIPS AND RELATIONSHIP LIFE CYCLES

Fundamental to the notion of relationship marketing is the concept of relational exchange. The best way to think of this is as one end of a spectrum of possible behaviours. At the far end, as far away from relational exchange as it is possible to get, lies

Table 9.1 Related terms to relationship marketing

Micromarketing	Relational contracting
Database marketing	Relational marketing
One-to-one marketing	Working partnerships
Loyalty marketing	Symbiotic marketing
Wrap-around marketing	Strategic alliances
Customer partnering	Co-marketing alliances
Symbiotic marketing	Internal marketing
Interactive marketing	

Source: Based on Morgan and Hunt (1994) and Buttle (1996)

the 'discrete transaction'. A discrete transaction occurs where an exchange occurs with the absolute minimum of communication between the buyer and the seller. It is a one-off event, and neither party to the exchange is concerned with the possibility that they might do business with this person again. Many exchanges at a fruit and vegetable market are close to 'discrete transactions'. Cash is tendered, the buyer takes the produce, and that is that. Even at such a market, the possibility of some 'relational' characteristics entering the equation cannot be ignored. The same vendors and customers are often to be seen in the marketplace, and one customer may begin to patronise a particular vendor more than the others – perhaps because that vendor offers better produce, or because of better customer service (even a cheery smile). This is a move away from the 'discrete transaction' a small way in the direction of 'relational exchange'.

In the extreme, relational exchange describes a situation in which the buyer and the seller are tied together by social and economic 'bonds', where the act of exchanging goods for money is but a small part of the extended interaction between the two parties. Social bonds could be of various types, including friendship and kinship (belonging to the same extended family), or bonds of mutual esteem developed over a period of successfully transacting business together. Economic bonds arise where the two parties to the exchange are better off doing business with each other than with a third party. While comparatively unusual in consumer marketing, this is a common circumstance in business-to-business marketing, where customer and supplier firms often invest in equipment and processes that are specific to an individual exchange partner (Brennan and Turnbull, 1999). In relational exchanges, prior transactions leave a 'trace' that affects subsequent dealings between the parties. If a supplier does something out of the ordinary (for example manages to meet an unusually tight deadline, or delivers a poor quality batch of products), it is remembered and taken into account in future business. The same is equally true for customer behaviour – for example where a customer delays payment on a big order for no tangible reason, or recommends the supplier to another potential customer, these events will affect future relations, and future transactions, between the firms.

In principle, all marketing exchanges can be conceived to lie at some point along the relational spectrum. Where exchanges typically lie more towards the relational end of the spectrum, some kind of relationship marketing strategy is likely to be suitable. Where exchanges are typically more of the nature of discrete transactions, a conventional 'marketing mix' approach is indicated. However, it is clear that many firms have concluded that strategic action to move customers along the spectrum more towards the relational end is desirable as a means of trying to cement customer loyalty and improve their own long-term profitability. Relationship marketing strategies can either be a response to the nature of the exchange, or an attempt to increase the relational element in the exchange in order to achieve a competitive advantage.

The concept of the relational spectrum gives rise to the related idea of the relationship life cycle. The essence of this idea is that the two parties to an exchange process (which could be individuals or companies) gradually develop bonds (economic, social, or both) over a sequence of repeated transactions, so that their exchange process moves progressively away from discrete transacting and towards relational exchange. The relationship life-cycle idea has never acquired the same popularity as the product life-cycle idea, but two substantial attempts have been made to produce a general model of the development processes associated with marketing relationships – relationship life cycles. These are described in the next section.

FORMAL RELATIONSHIP LIFE-CYCLE MODELS

The first relationship life-cycle model we examine emerged from the field of industrial marketing, more specifically from the interaction approach that was described in Chapter 4. This model (Ford, 1980) proposes a five-stage relationship development process – pre-relationship, early stage, development, long-term and final. Each of these stages is characterised by variations in five key variables:

1. The mutual experience of the parties.
2. The uncertainty of the parties.
3. The 'distance' between the parties, subdivided into:
   - social distance
   - geographical/cultural distance
   - technological distance
   - time distance.
4. The commitment of the parties to the relationship.
5. Adaptations carried out by the parties specifically for their partner within this relationship.

Broadly, as two firms do more and more business together, their *experience* of each other increases, their *uncertainty* about the behaviour of the other party diminishes, the *psychic distance* between them declines, while their *commitment* to the relationship and their *adaptation* to meet the needs of the other party increase. Table 9.2 elaborates on this basic description.

Table 9.2 Ford's (1980) relationship life-cycle model

Pre-relationship stage	The early stage	The development stage	The long-term stage	The final stage
Evaluation of new potential suppliers	Negotiation of sample delivery	Contract signed or delivery build-up	After several major purchases or large-scale deliveries	In long-established stable markets
Conditioned by prior experience	Low experience	Increasing experience	High experience	Extensive institutionalisation
Zero commitment	High uncertainty	Declining uncertainty	Minimum uncertainty	
	High distance	Declining distance	Minimum distance	
	Low perceived and actual commitment	Increasing commitment demonstrated through informal adaptations	Maximum actual commitment, perceived commitment may be reduced	
	High investment of management time	Increasing formal and informal adaptations	Extensive adaptations	

Source: Adapted from Ford (1980)

In this five-stage model, the first transactions occur at the early stage, building up during the development stage. As increasing amounts of business are transacted between the two firms, so there is an increasing amount of direct contact (to negotiate contracts, organise delivery, discuss future requirements, deal with problems and so on), which leads to increasing levels of social contact and information exchange. It is important to observe that this model does not include a relationship termination stage, which is rather surprising, and that the 'final stage' does not imply the end of the business relationship. Rather, the final stage refers to a point at which the relationship carries on almost through inertia, with few new ideas emerging. The term 'institutionalisation' was coined for this type of relationship. In practice, of course, marketing relationships often do come to an end. Later research using the Ford relationship life-cycle model suggested that a *termination* stage (Rosson, 1986) or a *declining* stage (Knox and White, 1991) was necessary to cover the full range of possible relationship stages.

Dwyer et al. (1987) developed a different conceptual framework to illustrate the process of marketing relationship development. They based their relationship development model explicitly on social exchange theory, using the metaphor of a marriage to illuminate the concept of a marketing relationship. It is by no means uncommon to use metaphors from personal relationships to explain marketing relationships (O'Malley and Tynan, 1999), but such metaphors should not be used naively. For example, one can metaphorically suggest that a good swimmer is like a fish or that a strong person is made out of iron, but any literal interpretation of the metaphor would court disaster (fishes *can* breathe under water, iron *is* capable of withstanding a shotgun blast). Similarly, overgeneralisation of the marriage metaphor (or friend-

Table 9.3 Dwyer et al.'s (1987) relationship development model

Phase 1:	Awareness	The parties recognise that they may be suitable exchange partners. Tentative interaction takes place.
Phase 2:	Exploration	Trial purchases may take place. The relationship is fragile. Five sub-phases are proposed: – attraction – communication and bargaining – development and exercise of power – development of relationship norms – development of expectations.
Phase 3:	Expansion	The range and depth of mutual dependence increases. The five sub-phases at phase 2 also operate in this phase.
Phase 4:	Commitment	Customer (or seller) loyalty has been achieved. The parties cease active search for alternative partners. Three measurable criteria of commitment are: – inputs – durability – consistency.
Phase 5:	Dissolution	Dissolution may take place at any phase of the relationship (that is, the 'relationship' need develop no further than *awareness*). The processes of relationship dissolution are poorly understood.

Source: Based on Dwyer et al. (1987, pp. 15–20)

ship, kinship or other personal relationship metaphors) to marketing relationships would be dangerous. Nevertheless, the judicious application of the metaphor results in the development of an interesting model of the relationship life cycle, illustrated in Table 9.3.

That this is a rather different model from the Ford relationship life cycle is not surprising. Ford's model was developed inductively (that is, by observing real business relationships) and is designed to explain business-to-business relationships only. The model shown in Table 9.3 was developed deductively (that is, based on fundamental theories of human behaviour) and is designed to apply to all marketing relationships.

Although at first sight both are five-stage (phase) models, Dwyer et al.'s model is perhaps more accurately characterised as a four-phase development model, with dissolution possible at any point within the development process. Indeed, this model may comprise anything from two phases (awareness–dissolution) to five (awareness–exploration–expansion–commitment–dissolution). This could be regarded as an advantage over the Ford model, which can easily be misinterpreted as signifying that all buyer–seller relationships are expected to pass through all five stages. In fact, of course, only successful relationships within which buyer and seller each realise benefits in excess of the relationship costs will pass through all five stages. It does appear to be a clear weakness of the Ford model that it does not explicitly allow for the ending of a relationship. Ford's final stage is one in which the partners have become so used to each other that they just carry on doing what each other expects, without questioning the value of continuing the relationship

However, the two models do share common features. Successful business relationships develop through a period of mutual recognition (pre-relationship/awareness), a period of tentative business development (early/exploration), a period of rapid development (development/expansion), into a period of high mutual commitment (long term/commitment).

Before moving on to discuss relationship marketing itself, a few final words are in order concerning the concept of the relationship life cycle. Two important questions arise. First, does anything like a relationship life cycle exist in reality? Second, if it does, what are the implications for strategic marketing management? In answer to the first, it should be observed that any life-cycle model in the field of marketing or management is designed to be a helpful simplification of a complex reality. We cannot expect to allocate marketing relationships to a few categories (such as 'long-term' or 'expansion') quickly, easily and with a high degree of certainty. But the existence of these categories (the life-cycle models) and the observation that there seems to be a reasonably high degree of consistency in the development of marketing relationships is both interesting and potentially useful. If there is some degree of consistency in relationship development, then that suggests that there is a degree of predictability, which can certainly be a useful input to the marketing planning process (particularly in business-to-business markets where account plans may be drawn up for individual customers). However, it would be wrong to suppose that the existence of a broad, general pattern of relationship development can tell us exactly how any one relationship will change over a given period of time. The life cycle is a metaphor. We are thinking of the marketing relationship as though it were a biological organism. While biological organisms are programmed genetically to develop from an embryonic state to full maturity and then finally to die, the same is clearly not true of marketing relationships – no matter how powerful the metaphor, marketing relationships certainly do not have genes!

RELATIONSHIP MARKETING

A starting point for the definition of relationship marketing is the way in which marketing is conventionally defined. The UK-based Chartered Institute of Marketing (CIM) defines marketing as 'the management process of identifying, anticipating and satisfying customer requirements profitably'. The American Marketing Association (AMA) asserts that: 'Marketing is the process of planning and executing conception, pricing, promotion and distribution of ideas, goods and services to create exchanges that satisfy individual and organizational objectives.' Both these definitions contend that marketing is a management process. The CIM definition emphasises the centrality of customer requirements, saying little about what goes on within the marketing management process. The AMA definition goes quite a lot further, putting successful exchange at the heart of the definition of marketing, and including what we would recognise as the marketing mix in the body of the definition. These definitions constitute the foundations of what we will call 'conventional marketing'. Conventional marketing is a management process that develops a marketing mix (product, price, promotion, place, with the addition of people, physical evidence and service delivery processes for services marketing) designed to persuade potential customers to engage in exchanges with the firm, in order to achieve the firm's objectives. It is assumed that if a customer enters voluntarily into exchanges with the firm, which usually means buying something, then that customer must consider himself or herself better off as a result of the exchange. The various definitions of relationship marketing challenge this conventional view of marketing in a number of different ways:

1. In conventional marketing, the marketer is seen as active and the buyer as passive. The marketer develops a proposition (the marketing mix) which is communicated to the customer, who then responds to that proposition. This is known as the stimulus–response approach to marketing. Relationship marketing allows for much greater involvement by the customer in the proposition development process. In the extreme, in some industrial markets, it is the buyer who is active, who specifies exactly what is required of the seller, and the seller who is passive.
2. The aim of conventional marketing is to bring about an exchange – a transaction. The exchange should meet the objectives of the marketer (usually that means it should turn a profit) and is assumed to meet the aims of the customer, since the customer entered the exchange voluntarily. Relationship marketing does not focus on an individual exchange event. The aim becomes the maintenance and development of an exchange *relationship* that meets the aims of both parties. A clear implication is that the marketer must be more concerned with whether or not the aims of the customer are genuinely met by the exchange, since if they are not, the exchange relationship will be damaged.
3. The tools of conventional marketing are predominantly impersonal mechanisms, that is, the marketing mix, designed to bring about the desired outcomes without engaging in any real dialogue with the customer. The tools of relationship marketing necessarily involve much greater direct interaction between the buyer and the seller. In conventional marketing, the selling process (development of the proposition to be put to the customer) and the buying process (the consumer or organisational buying decision process) are considered separately. Relationship

marketing blurs the edges between the selling and buying processes. In some cases the buying and selling processes become simultaneous and interactive.

Defining relationship marketing

There have been many attempts to define relationship marketing. We have selected just six of these, spanning a period of 14 years, which we present in chronological order:

> Relationship marketing is attracting, maintaining and – in multi-service organisations – enhancing customer relationships ... Cementing the relationship, transforming indifferent customers into loyal ones, serving customers as clients – this is marketing too. (Berry, 1983, p. 25)

> A distinction is made between interactive marketing (sometimes called relationship marketing) and non-interactive (mass) marketing. The interactive relationships are not only marketing interactions they are also interactions during which the service is produced. (Gummesson, 1987, pp. 13–14)

> Relationship marketing has as its concern the dual focus of getting and keeping customers. (Christopher et al., 1991, p. 4)

> Relationship marketing concerns attracting, developing, and retaining customer relationships. (Berry and Parasuraman, 1991, p. 33)

> Relationship marketing refers to all marketing activities directed towards establishing, developing, and maintaining successful relational exchanges. (Morgan and Hunt, 1994, p. 22)

> Relationship marketing involves the identification, specification, initiation, maintenance and (where appropriate) dissolution of long-term relationships with key customers and other parties, through mutual exchange, fulfilment of promises, and adherence to relationship norms in order to satisfy the objectives and enhance the experience of the parties concerned. (O'Malley et al., 1997, p. 542)

A common problem with definitions of relationship marketing, which we see in several of those above, is the inclusion of the word 'relationship' as part of the definition (see the definitions by Berry, Gummesson, Berry and Parasuraman, and O'Malley et al.). Obviously there is a risk of circular reasoning (Audi, 1995) when a part of what is being defined is included in the definition. It would be entirely unhelpful to define the meaning of 'a tall man' by using the words 'tall' and 'man' – one must define tallness using other concepts, such as formal measures of height (feet or metres). If necessary, one could similarly find an independent way of defining 'man'. Morgan and Hunt (1994) refer instead to 'relational exchange'. This is certainly an improvement, since relational exchange is a concept that can be separately defined – and we have already discussed it earlier in the chapter.

You will see a development in thinking about relationship marketing expressed in the chronological sequence of the definitions. The earlier definitions emerged from research in the field of services marketing (the authors of these definitions are acknowledged experts in services marketing), and had either a customer retention focus, or, in Gummesson's definition, a focus on the interaction between human beings as part of the service delivery process. The later definitions have extended the concept of relationship marketing further, and make the relationship development and relationship management processes the central foci of relationship marketing.

Such attempts to define relationship marketing reinforce the idea that we introduced above that there are two types of marketing, namely relationship marketing and conventional marketing. In the discussion above on the nature of marketing relations, the concept of a spectrum was introduced, stretching from one-off discrete transactions to full relational exchange. Obviously there are difficulties in trying to define all the positions on such a spectrum while using only two categories. Brodie et al. (1997) differentiated between the transactional and the relational 'perspectives' on marketing, and then described four different types of marketing along the discrete/relational spectrum. Their four marketing types were transaction marketing, database marketing, interaction marketing and network marketing. The characteristics of these four types of marketing are summarised in Table 9.4.

Table 9.4 Four types of marketing

Marketing type	Characteristic features
Transaction marketing	■ Focus is the exchange/transaction ■ One-off transactions ■ Communication is from the firm to the customer ■ Communications are impersonal ■ Seller takes the initiative, buyer responds to seller's stimuli ■ Focus is on attracting new customers ■ Orientation is short term
Database marketing	■ Focus is on information acquisition and the exchange/transaction ■ Repeated transactions ■ Communication is from the firm to the customer ■ Communications are personalised but distant ■ Seller takes the initiative, buyer is more involved than in transaction marketing ■ Focus is on customer retention ■ Longer term orientation
Interaction marketing	■ Focus is on the individual customer relationship ('dyad') ■ Continuing transactions with mutual adaptation ■ Two-way communications ■ Communications are personalised and often face to face ■ Both exchange partners are active participants ■ Focus is on relationship development ■ Orientation is both short and long term
Network marketing	■ Focus is on network of connected relationships ■ Continuing transactions with network adaptation ■ Communications between multiple parties ■ Communications are of many types and at multiple layers ■ All parties are active and adaptive ■ Focus is on multi-party coordination ■ Orientation is both short and long term

Source: Based on Brodie et al. (1997)

This is clearly a more complex approach to defining and classifying types of marketing than the dichotomy between conventional marketing and relationship marketing that we discussed earlier in this chapter. It accords much better with the underlying idea of a spectrum from discrete transactions to relational exchange.

Transaction marketing is very similar to what we have previously described as conventional marketing, with a short-term focus, impersonal communication and the initiative for the exchange coming solely from the seller.

Database marketing introduces the concept of customer retention, implying a longer term perspective, and an element of personalisation in the communications process. The seller is still the more active party in the exchange but the buyer is no longer simply a passive responder to marketing stimuli.

Interaction marketing is similar to our prior definitions of relationship marketing. Both the buyer and the seller participate actively in the exchange process, with the primary focus on managing and developing the relationship rather than bringing about individual exchanges.

Finally *network marketing* extends beyond a narrow definition of relationship marketing to encompass a much wider range of potential business relationships. This is akin to Morgan and Hunt's (1994) proposition that in order to compete successfully in global markets the firm must be a member of an effective network of partnerships, including supplier partnerships, buyer partnerships, internal partnerships and lateral partnerships. Morgan and Hunt developed a theory of relationship marketing using commitment and trust as the core concepts. They argued that to be an effective competitor in a global market required the firm to be a trusted collaborator, which has given rise to the axiom 'collaborate to compete'. Global competition is conducted between networks of competing firms, and in order to succeed it is as important to build strong relationships within the network as it is to outperform the rival network. Relationship commitment exists where an exchange partner believes that an ongoing relationship with another firm is so important that maximum effort will be exerted to maintain it. Relationship trust is defined as having confidence in an exchange partner's reliability and integrity. Commitment is the glue that binds the relationship together. Trust is the key factor that enables commitment to develop. Where we trust an exchange partner, we expect them to behave in a manner that promotes our interests. When we believe this to be the case, we can take the risk of making a tangible commitment to the relationship.

PUTTING RELATIONSHIP MARKETING INTO PRACTICE

In the preceding sections we have introduced some fundamental concepts and looked at various attempts to define relationship marketing. This is important, since it provides us with a set of concepts that will underpin any attempt to introduce a relationship marketing strategy. Nevertheless, none of this has addressed the question of exactly what is involved in implementing a relationship marketing strategy. In this section we consider some of the practical issues of implementing relationship marketing. First we look at Buttle's (1996) requirements for successful relationship marketing, then we examine Reichheld's (1996) approach to loyalty-based marketing, and finally we consider the implications of implementing relationship marketing in different market sectors.

REQUIREMENTS FOR SUCCESSFUL RELATIONSHIP MARKETING

Table 9.5 summarises Buttle's (1996) five requirements for successful relationship marketing.

1. *A supportive culture*. Relationship marketing represents a change in the conduct of marketing, and more or less any change in business conduct threatens the position of some members of the firm. The implementation of relationship marketing might mean, for example, that 'account managers' are employed rather than 'sales executives'. The nature of the account management task is rather different to that of the sales executive, it demands different aptitudes and skills, and the reward structures may well be different (Weitz and Bradford, 1999). Members of the existing sales force may feel threatened by the changes and create resistance.

2. *Internal marketing*. This follows from the first point. It is not enough simply to expect every member of the organisation to go along with the proposed changes in culture and conduct associated with a relationship marketing approach. Internal marketing is the process of applying explicit marketing practices to the goods and services that are exchanged *within a single firm*, and involves treating departments within the firm as though they were 'real customers'. It was a key idea in the 'total quality management' revolution of the 1980s. Departments were encouraged to identify their internal customers and suppliers, to conduct explicit discussions with them regarding expected levels of customer service, to develop an internal marketing communications mix, and to monitor performance against explicit targets. The underlying principle was that by applying marketing principles all the way along the internal chain, from the customer-facing departments to the back room or support departments, the products and services delivered to the external customer would be improved. Despite the strong intuitive plausibility of this idea, Lings and Brooks (1998) found no evidence to support the prediction that internal marketing can increase the quality of service provided to the external customer. In the context of a relationship marketing strategy, internal marketing will usually be used in a more limited sense, anyway. The emphasis is much more on communicating the benefits of the relationship marketing strategy to the 'internal market' (which obviously includes permanent employees, but may also include, for example, subcontractors and casual staff) in order to win support for it.

Table 9.5 Five requirements for successful relationship marketing

Five requirements for successful relationship marketing
1. A supportive culture
2. Internal marketing
3. Understand customer expectations
4. Sophisticated customer database
5. New organisational structures and reward schemes

Source: Based on Buttle (1996)

3. *Understand customer expectations.* This rather general marketing exhortation is arguably of even more importance where a relationship marketing approach is adopted than where a conventional marketing approach is used. It is a marketing platitude to say that we must understand customer expectations. However, where the explicit objective is to get closer to the customer, to engage the customer in a 'relationship' rather than simply to provide a product offering to which the customer may or may not respond, the importance of genuinely understanding customer expectations is greater. Research in the area of services marketing has shown that managers do not have a particularly good intuitive grasp of what customers expect (Parasuraman et al., 1985). Specific market research designed to understand customer expectations is recommended.

4. *Sophisticated customer database.* One related term to relationship marketing is 'database marketing' (see Tables 9.1 and 9.4). Database marketing is a sophisticated form of direct marketing in which detailed information on the customer is accumulated in a computer database, which is then used to generate personalised communications that make offers based on the known characteristics of the customer. Even where there is no intention to implement database marketing, the logic of any relationship marketing strategy requires that customer-specific information be gathered, stored, analysed and used for marketing purposes. In part, this may then be used for traditional activities such as marketing communications. However, customer-specific information has much wider application in relationship marketing, particularly in the analysis of customer retention and customer profitability. The implementation of customer loyalty marketing, discussed below, depends upon the maintenance of a sophisticated customer database.

5. *New organisational structures and reward schemes.* This issue was referred to briefly above when discussing the need for a supportive culture. The example used there was the likely reorganisation of the sales force. A little elaboration of that idea will help. The conventional role of the sales force has been the task of winning orders. Salespeople have been recruited for their aptitude and skill in performing that task, and sales force rewards have been substantially based on success in winning new business. The priority of the sales executive has been to make a sale, rather than the long-term satisfaction of the customer. To move towards a relationship marketing strategy, one that emphasises the development of longer term relationships with customers, the priority has to become satisfying the customer rather than making any one individual sale. The point of relationship marketing, after all, is that the focus is upon the buyer–seller relationship, rather than the individual transaction. The nurturing of customer relationships ('account management' rather than 'personal selling') requires different recruitment, training and reward systems for the sales force. Rewards should not only be based on the achievement of targets for selling new business (sales commission and bonus), but also on the retention of customer goodwill and the development of the customer relationship. Clearly these are much more difficult to measure than 'units sold'. However, a reward structure that emphasises only 'units sold' is not compatible with a relationship marketing strategy. One simple solution is to reduce the proportion of the account manager's remuneration that depends on sales performance and increase the base salary.

IMPLEMENTATION THROUGH LOYALTY MARKETING

Reichheld (1996) based his approach to customer relationship development on extensive experience as a management consultant. He observed that there seemed to be a 'missing factor' in corporate success. Otherwise similar companies experienced widely different levels of performance for reasons that conventional analyses could not discern. The 'missing factor' identified by Reichheld was loyalty. First of all customer loyalty, which is why we consider Reichheld's work to be in the field of relationship marketing. However, beyond customer loyalty, Reichheld identified employee loyalty and investor loyalty as key corporate success factors. Indeed, these three forms of loyalty are inextricably linked, as Figure 9.1 suggests.

It is customer loyalty with which we are concerned here, but Reichheld argues strongly that greater customer loyalty brings about enhanced employee satisfaction and improved returns for shareholders. These outcomes bring about increased employee and shareholder loyalty, which themselves bring about desirable outcomes that improve the value that the firm generates for the customer. Thus, business loyalty can become a virtuous cycle for the firm that successfully implements customer loyalty programmes. Equally, a firm can become enmeshed in a vicious cycle as low customer loyalty breeds dissatisfied employees and disloyal investors. The reason that such a vicious cycle is easily created is because, in the short term, there is clearly a negative relationship between creating value for customers and employees, and creating value for shareholders. In the short term, the quickest way to boost profits (returns to shareholders) is to cut employee remuneration and increase prices. The lesson of Reichheld's research is that such short-termism will, in all likelihood, damage the ability of the business to generate long-term value for all stakeholders. There is clearly a parallel here with the ideas of Peter Doyle on value-based marketing, and the reader is recommended to refer back to these ideas in Chapter 7 (Key Concept 7) if this parallel is not clear.

It is with Reichheld's proposals to improve customer loyalty that we are concerned here. In a typical company, the rate of customer defection each year runs at between 10 per cent and 30 per cent, which means that the business has to recruit between 10 and 30 per cent new customers each year just to maintain the customer

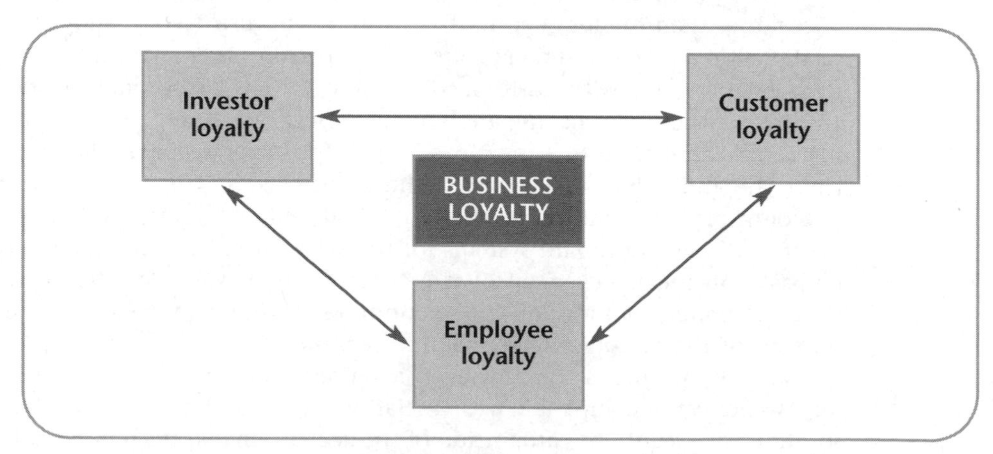

Figure 9.1 Business loyalty

Source: Original, based on Reichheld (1996)

Table 9.6 Customer loyalty – the customer volume effect

	Company 1	Company 2
Customer retention rate (per year)	95%	90%
New customers acquired (per year)	10%	10%
Net customer growth (per year)	5%	0%
Increase in customers in 14 years (at same annual rate)	100%	0%

base. Evidence suggests that there is a consistent relationship between customer retention and long-term profitability. The best performing companies are those that succeed in retaining their existing customers. There are two reasons for this. First is the 'customer volume effect', illustrated in Table 9.6.

Company 1 retains 95 per cent of its customers from one year to the next, while rival company 2 retains only 90 per cent. Let us suppose that both companies are equally successful with their 'traditional' marketing activities of generating new customers (through advertising, sales effort, public relations and so on), and manage to create 10 per cent new customers each year. This is just sufficient to maintain company 2's volume of customers, but it leads to an annual 5 per cent increase in customers for company 1. In a surprisingly short length of time, this difference in customer volume growth will lead to a big difference in customer numbers. After 14 years company 1 will have doubled its customer base, while company 2 will have remained static.

The second reason why firms with high customer retention rates achieve better long-term economic success is the 'profit per customer effect', illustrated in Figure 9.2. This shows the profit (revenues less costs) associated with an individual customer account. In the year of acquisition of the customer (year 1), costs substantially outweigh revenues, owing to the costs of acquiring a new customer and setting up a new customer account. In later years, revenues outweigh costs by increasing amounts for a number of reasons:

- Acquisition costs are non-recurring, they occur only once.
- Customers tend to spend more the longer they are with the business, because they are familiar with the business and buy additional products from it, and because they are inclined to 'trade up' to enhanced products or services. For example, someone who initially buys only home contents insurance from an insurance company will be more inclined to take other forms of insurance from that company if it is perceived to offer a high level of service.
- The longer a customer is with the company the more efficiently he or she can be served. For example, once the insurance company has acquired a range of basic information on the client, this need not be duplicated for all subsequent transactions.
- Satisfied customers are known to recommend their supplier to other potential customers, and so can become a source of 'referral business'.
- In some businesses, long-term customers pay a price premium compared to newly acquired customers. For example, newly launched magazines often have an

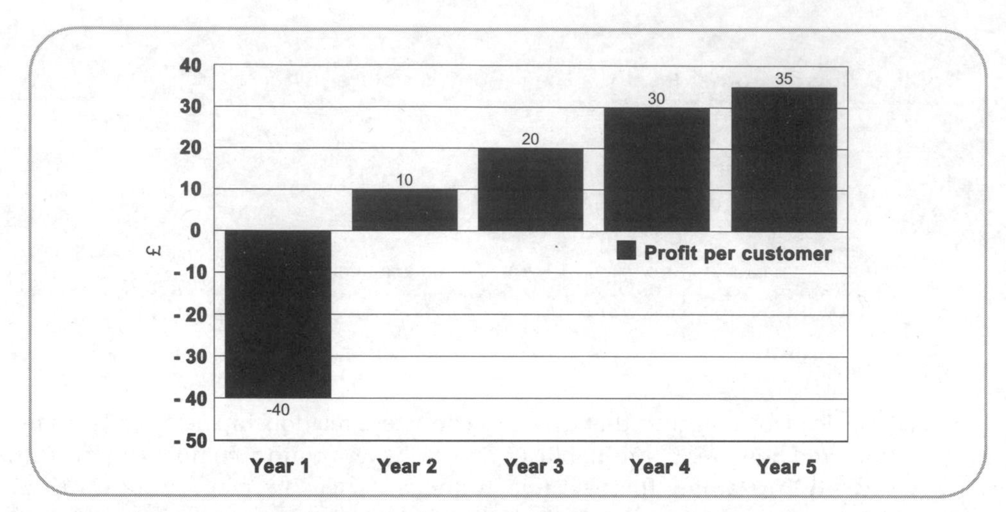

Figure 9.2 Profit per customer effect

initially low cover price to attract readers – the loyal customer will continue to buy at the standard price.

We are already aware that the calculation of the economic value of the customer to the business cannot be done simply by adding up the totals of the columns in Figure 9.2. If we were simply to add up the year by year totals, it would appear that the customer became profitable overall during year four. However, this is to ignore the time value of money, and to calculate the profitability of the customer we should apply discounted cash-flow analysis (see Chapter 7, Key Concept 6) to the data shown in Figure 9.2.

Analysis such as that shown in Figure 9.2 is fundamental to virtually all approaches to relationship marketing. It provides a method for calculating the life-time net present value of a customer to the business. Such an analysis provides the justification for a customer retention marketing scheme, and provides the basis for discriminating between customers, or groups of customers, on the basis of their long-term profitability. Once a company has gathered and analysed the data necessary to understand customer profitability for a substantial cross-section of customers, it is in a position to identify the common characteristics of loyal customers and defectors. Customers may have defected for reasons that were within the control of the firm (such as poor service or non-availability of a desired product), in which case the analysis of defections provides useful information to improve customer satisfaction and avoid further defections. It is also important to understand that some customer defections may have nothing to do with the firm's performance, for example a change in tastes or lifestyle (a simple example is that women frequently give up alcohol and smoking when they become pregnant).

SECTORAL VARIATIONS

In this section we consider the applicability of relationship marketing strategies to three different types of market, namely consumer goods markets, consumer services markets and business-to-business markets.

In consumer goods markets, the practice of relationship marketing is heavily orientated towards the creation of repeat customers. The principal means of implementing relationship strategies in consumer goods markets has been through the development of detailed customer databases. These enable the marketer to produce carefully targeted marketing communications that are designed to appeal to the consumer on the basis of his or her individual prior buying behaviour. There is a strong element of 'technology push' in this kind of marketing. Until comparatively recently, the technology simply did not exist to capture, store, analyse and then use data at the level of the individual customer. Rapid improvements in computer technology, and the availability of high-capacity data storage at low cost, make tailored communication with the customer possible. Whether the application of technology in this way really constitutes 'relationship marketing' is a debatable point (O'Malley et al., 1997), which we will explore a little further in the next section. It is easy to see that the use of sophisticated technology to produce carefully tailored marketing communications and sales promotional devices could simply be considered as an augmentation of the 'promotional' element of the marketing mix, rather than a fundamentally different approach to marketing.

In consumer services markets (for example personal care such as hair stylists and beauticians, educational services and healthcare), the idea that marketing is 'different' from the conventional marketing mix approach has been around for a long time (Berry, 1983). The intangibility of services increases the importance of the people factor in service delivery. People are intrinsically involved in many service delivery acts; for example you cannot take the nurse out of nursing, the beautician out of a manicure, or the counsellor out of counselling. Many services are high personal contact activities in which the opportunity exists to build genuine human relationships. The Scandinavian researchers Grönroos (1991) and Gummesson (1987) have explored the implications of these fundamental differences between service characteristics and physical product characteristics for marketing organisation and marketing strategy. Their primary conclusion is that, for services, the most important marketing activities are those that take place in direct contact with the customer (which Gummesson originally described as 'interactive marketing'). These activities are usually not performed by professional marketers, rather they are performed by 'part-time marketers', such as the beautician and the nurse. In organisations delivering such services, the full-time professional marketer must not focus exclusively upon conventional marketing activities, such as the design of the impersonal marketing communications mix, rather they must develop a marketing strategy that incorporates the important marketing tasks performed by the part-time marketers. Internal marketing, which was discussed above as one of Buttle's five requirements for successful relationship marketing, is an important task for the professional marketer. The part-time marketers should be informed of the importance of their role in *marketing* the organisation and its services, need to be kept up to date with the organisation's strategic marketing priorities, and may need training from a professional marketer in the marketing aspects of their work.

We have already explored the fundamental differences between business-to-business markets and consumer markets, and their implications for buying behaviour, in Chapter 4. A distinction was drawn between 'organisational buying behaviour' models, which focus on the buying process alone, and the 'interaction approach', which looks at the processes of interaction between buyer and seller involved in business-to-business exchanges. With the new terminology that we have introduced in

Table 9.7 Buyer preference as a basis for business-to-business strategy

Buyer preference for transactional purchasing	Decision criterion	Buyer preference for collaborative purchasing
Many	Availability of qualified suppliers	Few
Stable	Rate of change of the market	Volatile
Low	Importance of the purchase to the customer	High
Low	Complexity of the purchase	High
Low	Amount of information buyer and seller need to exchange	High
Few	Required operational linkages between buyer and seller	Many

Source: Based on Hutt and Speh (2001)

this chapter, we can now recognise organisational buying behaviour models as having a transactional focus, while the interaction approach has a relational focus. There is no doubt that many business-to-business markets require an approach to marketing strategy that emphasises the development and management of supplier–customer relationships. Hutt and Speh (2001) suggest a contingency approach to business-to-business marketing strategy, which is illustrated in Table 9.7.

The starting point for the determination of appropriate marketing strategy is the buyer's strategic purchasing preference. The buyer's preference will lie on a spectrum between transactional purchasing and collaborative exchange. Relationship strategies are appropriate for collaborative customers, but inappropriate for transactional customers who do not wish to be tied into a longer term relationship.

Clearly, in order to determine the appropriate marketing strategy, it is necessary to establish where the customer lies on the relational spectrum. The greater the number of suppliers that are capable of meeting the customer's specifications (qualified suppliers), the greater the preference for a transactional approach. Buyers will also prefer a transactional approach in a stable market, that is to say, a mature industry in which technological change is slow and there are few market entries or exits (for example the supply of car tyres). In a highly volatile market, the buyer is more likely to want to seek out a highly qualified supplier and use the competence of the supplier to keep up with, for example, rapid changes in technology (for example the supply of tailored electronic commerce solutions). Purchase importance refers to the extent to which the purchase affects the core business of the buying organisation. Some purchases are of critical importance (for example the computer system bought by an Internet business which it will use to deliver its service), others are not (screen wipes used to clean the computer displays), and many are somewhere in between (uniforms worn by service delivery personnel). The remaining three criteria are linked. The complexity of the purchased item (buying a large computer system is complex, buying work boots generally is not) dictates to a large extent the amount of information that will be exchanged between buyer and seller, and affects the number of 'operational linkages' that will occur during the buying and selling processes. Buying a large computer system requires the active involvement of many people from both the buying and the selling organisation. Buying a batch of work boots requires a clear specification of requirements, such as weight, size, degree of hazard protection and relevant international standards to be met, but does not require complex operational linkages.

Having established the buyer's strategic preference, the marketer can establish the appropriate marketing strategy. Relationship strategies are appropriate for collaborative customers. The marketer seeks to build the commitment of the customer to the relationship by investing resources (for example a key account manager), by developing operational linkages, by tailoring products especially for the customer, and by developing a customer strategic plan. Such an approach is inadvisable in the case of a transactional customer. The transactional customer can readily switch between suppliers, so is a relatively easy customer from whom to win some business. However, it is not possible to build the commitment of a transactional customer to a relationship (if it was possible, they would not be a transactional customer!), so time and money spent on relationship development is very likely to be wasted. Conventional marketing strategy, using a marketing mix approach, is recommended for such customers.

CHALLENGES TO RELATIONSHIP MARKETING

We asserted at the start of this chapter that relationship marketing was one of the most important developments in both the theory and practice of marketing to emerge during the last two decades. Naturally, such a development has brought about debate. While the pioneers of relational approaches in marketing might be accused of taking a rather uncritical approach to the emerging field, there has been no shortage of subsequent criticism. The first criticism we have touched upon already in examining a few definitions of relationship marketing. We criticised several of these definitions for using 'relationship' as part of their proposed definition, arguing that this tends to lead to a circular argument – 'relationship marketing is marketing conducted through the medium of relationships' would be the ultimate absurdity of this type. Despite the proliferation of definitions (and we have only touched on a small sample), there is still no clear and universally accepted understanding of exactly what relationship marketing is. Mattsson (1997, p. 156) put this point very neatly: 'When RM researchers talk about RM as a paradigmatic shift in marketing it is thus not very clear what the shift is from and even less clear what the shift is to.' The expression 'paradigmatic shift' refers to the concept of a scientific paradigm, which is a set of scientific beliefs that make up a theoretical framework within which scientific theories can be tested, evaluated and, if necessary, revised (Audi, 1995). In this case the paradigm in question is the body of accepted knowledge about marketing. Mattsson suggests that it is not clear what the pre-existing body of accepted marketing knowledge was, and even less clear what the new body of accepted marketing knowledge – relationship marketing – is. A key question in the debate over the definition of relationship marketing is whether it is a relatively narrow concept, referring to the usefulness of customer retention strategies as a component of a marketing strategy, or a much broader redefinition of marketing itself.

Closely related to these arguments about definition is a class of arguments that we will refer to as 'change the name and do the same'. This expression is well known in marketing circles. For example, a 'shop assistant' becomes a 'customer service consultant', and a 'salesperson' is transformed first into a 'sales executive', then a 'sales consultant' and finally, perhaps, a 'key account manager'. Yet the fundamental job remains the same, it is only the name that has changed. Blois (1997, p. 370) put it this way:

> Just as Molière's Monsieur Jourdain was surprised to learn that he had been talking prose all his life, so many firms will be surprised to learn that they are involved in 'relationship marketing'!

His argument here is that academic terminology has simply gone through a process of catching up with management practice. A slightly different example of 'change the name and do the same' is Brown's (1998) attack on relationship marketing. The essence of Brown's argument is that relationship marketing is above all a rhetorical trick. The marketer has not adopted any fundamentally new approach to marketing, nor even a new marketing strategy, but wishes to give consumers the impression that a new, caring, sharing form of marketing is being used. Used in such a way, relationship marketing would be manipulative and would probably contribute to a rapid decline in consumer confidence in all marketing activity. The irony here, of course, is that an approach that claims to put the relationship with the customer first would, through dishonesty, be contributing directly to a breakdown of trust, and thus relationships, between customer and vendor.

The final criticism of relationship marketing that we will explore is an extension of the argument that relationship marketing is a rhetorical trick. O'Malley et al. (1997) suggested that relationship marketing practices in consumer markets, implemented through direct and database marketing technology, might be interpreted by consumers as an invasion of their privacy. They argued that a 'relationship' must involve the two-way flow of information between the parties, based on mutual consent. There is clear evidence that consumers believe information is gathered about them without their consent and in a manner that intrudes into their privacy. Consumers feel that they lack control, and do not believe that the mutual benefit of both parties is the goal of technologically mediated 'relationship marketing' practice. Once again, as in the previous paragraph, a practice that has sometimes been referred to as 'relationship marketing' seems likely to bring about a reduction in trust and commitment, and so cause a reduction in the relational content of exchanges. This is not, however, to claim that direct and database marketing necessarily reduce trust and commitment. Rather, it is to point out that an implementation of such methods that is not sympathetic to the interests of the consumer in terms of mutual benefit and respect for privacy is likely to be counterproductive.

SUMMARY

The idea that there is a spectrum of exchange behaviour between discrete transactions and relational exchange is the basis for relationship marketing strategies. Long-term exchange relationships between buyers and sellers do exist, and management action can be taken to develop and manage these relationships. Some researchers have suggested that buyer–seller relationships might develop through a series of well-defined stages, so that we can think of a relationship having a life cycle. Relationship marketing strategies are based on the idea that exchange transactions need not always be initiated by the seller (the stimulus response model) and that the relationship can be an appropriate focus for marketing activity, rather than the transaction. Many definitions of relationship marketing have been suggested, and there is no one definition that has achieved widespread acceptance. The implementation of relationship marketing requires that attention be paid to culture change, internal marketing and patterns of remuneration, as well as the development of a sophisticated customer database. Loyalty-based marketing focuses on the customer as an asset, and calculates the discounted present value of the customer as a key input into the marketing planning process. The implementation of relationship marketing strategies will be affected by the nature of the market concerned, since relationship strategies mean rather different things in consumer goods markets, consumer services markets and business-to-business markets. Relationship marketing has been subject to a number of critiques, including unclear definition, 'change the name and do the same' and invasion of consumer privacy. When implemented purely as a technological solution, and without due care for consumer sentiment, relationship marketing in consumer markets can be counterproductive and destructive of trust and commitment.

Questions for discussion

1. Would you say that relationship marketing was either a philosophy of marketing or a marketing strategy, or both these things, or neither?
2. Suggest a number of examples of marketing exchanges, starting with a discrete transaction and moving progressively towards a relational exchange.
3. What problems might you have to overcome, as a full-time professional marketer in a service organisation, in engaging the 'part-time marketers' fully in your marketing strategy?
4. Taking the example of business-to-business marketing, explain how the decision whether or not to use a relationship marketing approach is based on an understanding of buying behaviour.

References

Audi, R (ed.) (1995), *The Cambridge Dictionary of Philosophy*, Cambridge: Cambridge University Press

Berry, L (1983), 'Relationship Marketing', in Berry, L, Shostack, G L and Upah, G D (eds) *Emerging Perspectives on Services Marketing*, Chicago: American Marketing Association, pp. 25–34

Berry, L and Parasuraman, A (1991), *Marketing Services: Competing Through Quality*, New York: Free Press

Blois, K (1997), 'Are Business-to-Business Relationships Inherently Unstable?', *Journal of Marketing Management*, **13**(5): 367–82

Brennan, R and Turnbull, P W (1999), 'Adaptive Behavior in Buyer-Supplier Relationships', *Industrial Marketing Management*, **28**: 481–95

Brodie, R J, Coviello, N E, Brookes, R W and Little, V (1997), 'Toward a Paradigm Shift in Marketing? An Examination of Current Marketing Practices', *Journal of Marketing Management*, **13**(5): 383–406

Brown, S (1998), *Postmodern Marketing Two: Telling Tales*, London: International Thompson Press

Buttle, F (ed.) (1996), *Relationship Marketing: Theory and Practice*, London: Paul Chapman

Cannon, J P and Perreault, W D (1999) 'Buyer-seller Relationships in Business Markets', *Journal of Marketing Research*, **36**: 439–60

Christopher, M, Payne, A and Ballantyne, D (1991), *Relationship Marketing: Bringing Quality, Customer Service and Marketing Together*, Oxford: Butterworth Heinemann

Dwyer, F R, Schurr, P H and Oh, S (1987), 'Developing Buyer-seller Relationships', *Journal of Marketing*, **51**(April): 11–27

Ford, D (1980), 'The Development of Buyer-seller Relationships in Industrial Markets', *European Journal of Marketing*, **14**(5/6): 339–54

Grönroos, C (1991), *Strategic Management and Marketing in the Service Sector*, Lund: Studentlitteratur & Chartwell-Bratt

Gummesson, E (1987), 'The New Marketing – Developing Long-term Interactive Relationships', *Long Range Planning*, **20**(4): 10–20

Hutt, M D and Speh, T W (2001), *Business Marketing Management: A Strategic View of Industrial and Organizational Markets*, Fort Worth: Dryden Press

Knox, S D and White, H F M (1991), 'Retail Buyers and their Fresh Produce Suppliers: A Power or Dependency Scenario in the UK?', *European Journal of Marketing*, **25**(1): 40–52

Lings, I N and Brooks, R F (1998), 'Implementing and Measuring the Effectiveness of Internal Marketing', *Journal of Marketing Management*, **14**(4): 325–52

Mattsson, L-G (1997), '"Relationship Marketing" and the "Markets-as-networks Approach" – a Comparative Analysis of Two Evolving Streams of Research', *Journal of Marketing Management*, **13**(5): 447–62

Morgan, R M and Hunt, S D (1994), 'The Commitment–trust Theory of Relationship Marketing', *Journal of Marketing*, **58**(July): 20–38

O'Malley, L and Tynan, C (1999), 'The Utility of the Relationship Metaphor in Consumer Markets: A Critical Evaluation', *Journal of Marketing Management*, **15**(7): 587–602

O'Malley, L, Patterson, M and Evans, M (1997), 'Intimacy or Intrusion? The Privacy Dilemma for Relationship Marketing in Consumer Markets', *Journal of Marketing Management*, **13**(6): 541–60

Parasuraman, A, Zeithaml, V A and Berry, L L (1985), 'A Conceptual Model of Service Quality and its Implications for Future Research', *Journal of Marketing*, **49**(Fall): 41–50

Reichheld, F F (1996), *The Loyalty Effect: The Hidden Force Behind Growth, Profits, and Lasting Value*, Boston, MA: Harvard Business School Press

Rosson, P J (1986), 'Time Passages: The Changing Nature of Manufacturer-Overseas Distributor Relations in Exporting', *Industrial Marketing and Purchasing*, **1**(2): 48–64

Takala, T and Uusitalo, O (1996), 'An Alternative View of Relationship Marketing: A Framework for Ethical Analysis', *European Journal of Marketing*, **30**(2): 45–60

Weitz, B A and Bradford, K D (1999), 'Personal Selling and Sales Management: A Relationship Marketing Perspective', *Journal of the Academy of Marketing Science*, **27**(2): 241–54

chapter ten

e-Marketing Strategies

Learning objectives

By reading this chapter, you will learn:

- The context in which e-marketing operates
- The relative advantages and disadvantages of using different interactive tools
- The impact of information and communication technologies (ICTs) upon the business-to-consumer (B2C) and business-to-business (B2B) marketing mixes
- The qualities of an effective web page
- The most appropriate business model for a traditional retailer wishing to go online.

INTRODUCTION

In this chapter, we are interested in the responses of marketing strategists to the challenges posed by the emerging information and communication technologies. Although we examine many facets of e-marketing, our focus is primarily on recent developments and opportunities involving the World Wide Web in particular. The chapter begins with an in-depth examination of the electronic marketing context. We then turn our attention to online shopping behaviour and present a profile of e-consumers. This is followed by two sections of practical importance to marketers: one on B2C and another on B2B e-marketing mix considerations. This leads on to a section on strategic planning, which examines e-marketing models and related strategic issues. The chapter concludes with an all-important look at some of the strategic challenges presented by our digital age.

THE WORLD OF e-MARKETING

e-Marketing, short for electronic or online marketing, is essentially about conducting marketing activities through interactive online computer systems. Virtually unheard of a decade ago, this new field has captured the interest of countless organisations the world over. Small and medium enterprises (SMEs), not-for-profit societies, government agencies and huge multinational corporations have come to view e-marketing as an essential strategic tool. Many well-established organisations such as Nike or Ikea incorporate online approaches in their more traditional marketing efforts, while some new businesses such as Amazon and Egg have opted for e-marketing approaches more or less exclusively. Using new technological tools, such as automatic teller machines (ATMs), retail kiosks (such as movie rental machines, for example), e-mail messaging or interactive television (iTV), companies and institutions throughout the globe are turning to e-marketing strategies in record numbers. We will explore these and other such tools more fully later in the chapter. Before we do, it is important to remember that e-marketing is much more than simply setting up a website on the World Wide Web (WWW). We define an 'e-business' as any *virtually* active commercial organisation, and 'e-commerce' as 'technology-mediated exchanges between parties (individuals, organisations, or both) as well as the electronically based intra- or inter-organisational activities that facilitate such exchanges' (Rayport and Jaworski, 2001, p. 3). Thanks to e-commerce, many, if not most, marketing activities may now be 'technology enabled' (O'Connor and Galvin, 2001, p. 25); for example relationship marketing, marketing research, data mining, promotion/communications, supply chain management, sales and purchasing and after-sales support.

Two seminal papers by e-marketing pioneers Donna Hoffman and Thomas Novak of Vanderbilt University are credited by many of today's e-marketers to have laid the conceptual foundations for this young, fast-growing field. The first paper, entitled *Marketing in Hypermedia Computer-Mediated Environments: Conceptual Foundations,* was released in the summer of 1995. In it, the authors present a network navigation model intended to help us understand the very foundations of interactive marketing.

The central construct of their model is *flow*. When flow is positive, it is more likely that the visitor will respond to the site in the desired manner. Flow is indirectly determined by indiv-

> idual, site, and situational characteristics. Individual characteristics include the relationship between skills and challenges. Site characteristics include interactivity and vividness. Situational characteristics include motivation and benefits sought. (Richardson, 2001, p. 35)

This is the paper that launched an entire field of inquiry into computer-mediated environments, now widely known as CMEs.

The second important Hoffman and Novak paper *A New Marketing Paradigm for Electronic Commerce* was released in February 1996. In this the authors point out that traditional marketing communication strategy based on the 'one-to-many' model (with its heavy reliance on the use of mass media) no longer represents the only option available. A new 'many-to-many' model, made possible by hypermedia CMEs like the Web, is developing very rapidly. 'Empowered' participants (buyers and sellers) create and experience information interactively. The authors see the Web as 'not a simulation of a real world environment, but an alternative to real world environments'. Participants are said to experience 'telepresence' – the perception of being present in the mediated, rather than real-world, environment. The authors argue that 'successful Web marketing efforts will require an evolution in the marketing concept to where the firm not only attempts to discover and meet customer needs profitably, but also engages in marketing activities that contribute positively to the development of the emerging medium itself, by developing new paradigms for electronic commerce'. For example, interactive customers may well choose to participate in the marketing process itself by generating new product ideas, helping with product design, and perhaps even 'test driving' goods and services in a virtual context before making purchase decisions. The paper suggests that emerging paradigms must consider issues such as cooperation and competition in very different lights. Interactive customers are no longer passive customers. Hoffman and Novak conclude that 'the traditional model, with its attendant implications and consequences for marketing theory and practice, has only limited utility in emerging many-to-many media like the World Wide Web'.

To place the above in perspective, we now turn to the relationship between electronic commerce and the 'trade cycle'. According to Whiteley (2000, p. 6), business customers (B2B) and consumers (B2C) alike typically go through four basic phases when purchasing products. During the 'pre-sale' phase, customers search for suitable goods/services and sometimes enter into negotiations about features, price, delivery terms and so on. The 'execution' phase involves ordering and taking possession of the products. This is inevitably followed by the 'settlement' phase when payment is made. The final 'after-sale' phase usually involves continued interaction between vendor and buyer. Whitely makes the point that electronic commerce, being an interactive approach to doing business, can be applied to all, or different, phases of the trade cycle. The main purpose here is to explore the strategic implications of this for marketing decision-makers.

Although most readers will be familiar with many of today's high-technology terms and expressions, it may be useful to refer to a glossary of the relatively new words used by e-marketers. You will find such a glossary at the end of this chapter.

> e-Commerce involves applying a wide range of technologies to streamline business interactions. Examples of these technologies include the Internet, EDI [Electronic Data Interchange], e-mail, electronic payment systems, advanced telephone systems, hand-held digital appliances, interactive televisions, self-service kiosks and smart cards. (Jobber, 2001, p. 459)

Increasingly, communication technologies are converging. As a result, when discussing this new technology, it is safer not to restrict any assessment of opportunity to the role of the Internet (Jobber, 2001; Chaston, 2001; Richardson, 2001). Instead, the debate should be expanded to cover all aspects of information exchange. This is increasingly being recognised by organisations who are moving to exploit the huge diversity of opportunities now offered by online marketing. A good example of this would be the recently released Nokia 5510. It is a personal stereo (plays FM and digital music), text machine, gaming console, WAP browser and – it is easy to forget – a mobile phone as well.

Let us now turn to the technologies themselves. Should marketers talk about the Web or the Net when discussing e-marketing strategy? The former may be described as 'a software application that runs on the Internet' (Whiteley, 2000, p. 2). The latter refers to the actual electronic network of communication equipment and links that support the World Wide Web, e-mail, ftp (file transfer protocol – used for exchanging files between computers), chat rooms, bulletin boards (news/discussion groups), telnet (for logging on to remote computers) and so forth. From their modest beginnings about a decade ago, these tools have evolved into a vast, increasingly user-friendly virtual interface. Marketers need to know that the Web and other interactive technologies such as mobile telephony, iTV, retail kiosks, ATMs and gaming consoles provide almost limitless opportunities to interact meaningfully with potential customers all over the world.

Interactive tools provide marketers with a number of distinct advantages such as:

- *Global reach.* As the Net grows and grows it allows marketers to access marketspaces just about anywhere (in the virtual world a marketplace is known as a 'marketspace' – Kotler and Armstrong, 2001, p. 637).
- *Speed and flexibility.* Although the Internet is not (yet) an instantaneous medium, it provides the opportunity for buyers and sellers to interact swiftly, around the clock, 365-days a year (known as the '24/7' feature). Users can interact when and where it is most convenient for them to do so, providing them with maximum flexibility, while allowing sellers to save on call centre expenses.
- *Low cost.* After the initial costs required to put the necessary technology in place (computers, modems, software, training and so on), the actual cost of each virtual interaction is typically a fraction of what it would be in the physical world. For this reason, we are witnessing the rapid development of online marketing research activities, not only for quantitative but also for more time-consuming qualitative enquiries.
- *Interactivity.* By its very nature, the Net allows each and every user to engage in a two-way 'multimedia' exchange process that traditional marketers can only dream of.

On the other hand, one also needs to consider some of the points which can provide certain obstacles to even the most determined market researcher, namely:

- *Clutter and congestion.* Users have access to literally millions of websites, countless discussion groups and chat opportunities, and exchange several billion e-mail messages each day. Marketers wishing to exploit such a virtual world are indeed faced with very daunting challenges in order to steer clear of potential cyber-space traffic jams!

- *Anonymity and statelessness.* On the Net it is often quite difficult to determine a user's exact physical location on the planet. From the customer's point of view this relative anonymity can be a double-edged sword. On the one hand, she or he is free to navigate on an equal footing with everyone else but, on the other, it may be extremely difficult to pinpoint the source of any unethical behaviours or practices (privacy of information is a prime example here). For e-marketers, on the other hand, although the prospect of trading with customers in every corner of the globe can seem irresistible, very few organisations can in fact realise this profitably.
- *Cost.* e-Marketers need to remember that today's online customers want it all: high-quality branded goods and services, at very low prices and delivered flaw-lessly. It comes as no surprise that so many well-established 'bricks and mortar' businesses are taking their time in building their Internet operations, so as not to waste money on costly yet potentially unprofitable e-strategies.
- *Sensory limitations.* Over the past decade or so, the virtual world has mostly been about words, colour, and images. More recently, motion and sound have been added to the mix and, sometime soon, online scents may also be common-place (DigiScents, for example). Touch and taste are not yet on the cards, as e-marketers need to consider each of the Net's 'special' sensory circumstances very carefully indeed.

For a taste of e-marketing success stories, readers might find it useful at this stage to get on the Net and sample what some of the sites listed in Table 10.1 have to offer.

Table 10.1 Examples of successful e-marketing websites

Product Category	Marketer	URL
Auctions	eBay	http://www.ebay.co.uk
Financial services	Egg	http://www.egg.com
Books/CDs	Amazon	http://www.amazon.com
Computing hardware	Dell	http://www.dell.com
Computing software	Tucows	http://www.tucows.com
Education/Scholarship	e-Lab	http://www2000.ogsm.vanderbilt.edu
Music	Grand Central	http://www.mp3grandcentral.net/signup.html
Flowers	FTD	http://www.ftd.com
Gaming	Sony	http://www.sonyps2.com
Groceries	Tesco Direct	http://www.tesco.co.uk
Investing	Schwabb	http://www.schwabb.com
Online publications	Ziff-Davis	http://www.ziffdavis.com
Travel	easyJet	http://www.easyjet.com

- Automatic teller machines (ATMs)
- Cyber cafes
- Digital/interactive television (mostly by either cable or satellite)
- e-Mail messaging
- Gaming consoles
- Mobile personal devices such as PDAs and palm tops
- Mobile telephony (mostly 'text messaging' and WAP phones)
- Personal computer access (facilitated by an ISP) to e-commerce websites on the WWW (home pages + linked Web documents in html format)
- Portals maintained by information service providers (ISPs)
- Retail kiosks

Figure 10.1 B2C e-marketing information and communication technologies

REACHING e-CONSUMERS

In this section we look at what characterises online business to consumer (B2C) marketing. Often referred to as electronic retailing – or simply 'e-tailing' – this form of marketing has come to rely upon a growing number of information and communication technologies (ICTs). A list of some of the more popular ICTs currently in vogue among e-tailers can be found in Figure 10.1

The e-consumer is an empowered consumer. According to Windham and Orton (2000, p. 29):

> The Internet is an empowerment tool, providing customers with myriad options they never had before – countless brands to choose from, searchable databases, unique personalization features, numerous shopping options, built-to-order merchandise, instant access/downloads of electronic content, close-out items, items up for auction ... The list goes on.

The authors also suggest that: 'The Web is a tool that strengthens their shopping intelligence.' To improve their chances at online success, e-marketers must appreciate that these 'new' customers typically value their time immensely, know what they want, insist on meaningful content and refuse to be disappointed or exploited. Chaston (2001, p. 39) supports this view by suggesting that:

> As e-commerce represents a very different environment for the customer in most consumer goods markets, probably the importance of understanding *on-line behaviour* will be critical in the effective implementation of Web-based marketing.

This may be somewhat of an understatement, given that today's online customer seems to want it *all*: 24/7 convenience, brand name goods and services, fast/efficient home delivery, and all this at rock-bottom prices.

Shopping/buying online

Because online B2C purchase transactions are still relatively rare, it is important to consider two distinct categories of consumers: those who rely on new technology simply to look, browse and compare, and those who actively buy online. At this point, it helpful to recall the six traditional stages of the consumer buying process identified in Figure 3.1:

1. Need identification
2. Product search
3. Merchant search
4. Negotiation (optional)
5. Purchase
6. After-sales support and product performance assessment.

These stages are essentially the same for *online* shopping except that ICTs are more likely to be involved in all but the need identification stage. Intelligent agents (also known as software agents), such as AuctionBot or BargainFinder, are now able to operate on behalf of a consumer to perform tasks such as information gathering, information filtering and even mediation. Schneider and Perry (2001a, p. 110) describe the process as follows:

> Because software agents are always running in the background, ready to help you when you need them, they can help reduce the workload that people normally take on in locating, thinking about, negotiating, and purchasing goods and services on the Internet.

Agents can help identify the best utility rates available in a homeowner's neighbourhood, and automatically purchase or sell shares and other investments when the market is at its peak. As we explore the elements of the e-marketing mix later on in this section, we will see how other ICTs such as mobile telephony and e-mail are relied upon more and more by consumers and marketers alike.

Profiling online consumers

Who shops/buys online? Are the patterns the same all over the world, for all consumer products? How fast are these patterns changing? Where can we look for reliable information about online consumption? Questions like these relate to the field of consumer psychographics (a blend of demographics and psychological data). To draft an up-to-date profile of e-consumers of particular interest, readers are encouraged to consult some of the excellent Web resources assembled in Table 10.2.

Although we cannot go into much detail here, your findings will reveal that, in general terms, online consumption is still in early development. e-Consumers are relatively young, reasonably affluent, well educated and typically have a good working knowledge of English. While men have been dominating e-shopping for some time now, this trend is changing rapidly. You will also find that reliable figures are easier to find for Web consumers rather than those who prefer to shop using iTV or retail kiosks, for example.

Table 10.2 Useful sources of e-consumer psychographic data

Website	Universal Resource Locator (URL)
CommerceNet Research Center	http://www.commerce.net/research/stats/
CyberAtlas	http://www.cyberatlas.com/
eMarketer	http://www.emarketer.com/
InternetTrack	http://www.ziffdavis.com/marketresearch/internettrack.htm
Media Metrix	http://mediametrix.com/
Nielsenmedia	http://www.Nielsenmedia.com/
NOP Research Group	http://www.nopres.co.uk/internet.htm
NUA Internet Surveys	http://www.nua.ie/surveys/
Online Shopping Survey	http://user.aol.com/commxtra/survey971.html
SRI Consulting	http://future.sri.com/VALS/survey.html
The Internet Index	http://www.openmarket.com/intindex/index.cfm
The World Factbook	http://www.odci.gov/cia/publications/factbook/index.html
Web Marketing Information Center	http://www.wilsonweb.com/webmarket/demograph.htm
Yahoo! Internet Statistics and Demographics hierarchy	http://www.yahoo.com/Computers_and_Internet/Internet/Statistics_and_Demographics/

B2C E-MARKETING MIX CONSIDERATIONS

In this part of our analysis, we turn our attention to the various dimensions of a typical marketing mix. For each of the variables, we need to examine what is different when e-commerce is involved. Kardes (2002, p. 269) highlights e-tailing's appeal for both buyers and sellers as follows:

> High levels of interactivity enable retailers to provide exactly the type of information about products, services, and pricing that the individual customer wishes to receive. High levels of interactivity also encourage customers to provide exactly the type of information about themselves that retailers want – including credit card numbers, e-mail addresses, shipping addresses, personal preferences, and purchase histories.

Product strategies

As offline consumers, we purchase impulse items, shopping goods and occasionally speciality items. Some of these purchases require little concentration (low involvement) while others demand much more mental and/or emotional investment (high involvement). Up until now, e-tailers have been reasonably successful selling middle-of-the-road shopping goods (for example CDs, books, travel bookings) and also relatively low-involvement speciality goods (for example computer games, software and auctions). As technology develops further and e-consumer confidence inevitably builds, we may well witness a significant rise in the availability and purchase of impulse items as well as high-involvement shopping and speciality products. Buying lottery or cinema tickets online or even a new automobile or home may be quite commonplace a few short years from now.

Not very long ago, brands were categorised as pure offline or online brands. Brands such as Coca-Cola, UPS and Sony enjoyed a very distinct position in relation to Yahoo!, AOL and Amazon. But:

> as the Internet expanded, we began to observe the crossover of offline brands into the online world, and the transition of online brands into the offline world. The end result is a blurring of the distinction between pure offline and pure online brands. (Rayport and Jaworski, 2001, p. 188)

Brands such as Netscape, Microsoft and Nintendo are promoted across all available media, the world over.

Place strategies

Although many products may not always be deliverable online, e-consumers are now requiring the use of more non-traditional logistical solutions for non-shop commerce. Increasingly, these customers will want to collect their purchases at tube/rail stations, the workplace, the post office and the petrol station.

e-Marketers, sometimes called 'electronic stallholders', have already seen that automatic cash machines (ATMs), automated kiosks (used for selling CDs, videos or performance tickets, for example) and other online technologies can provide excellent alternatives to traditional distribution methods. Banks, auction houses and hospitality businesses are introducing online tools at a fast-growing rate. As they do this, strategists are finding that they need to ask themselves a fundamental question: what blend of offline and online distribution activities is right for our particular industry in order to maintain a high degree of customer satisfaction while keeping our distribution costs low?

Pricing strategies

> In this new model, information or content is not merely transmitted from a sender to a receiver, but instead, mediated environments are created by participants and then experienced. (Hoffman and Novak, 1996)

In terms of pricing, this means that e-consumers are empowered by the very nature of online technologies. e-Tailing, by definition, necessitates unprecedented levels of transparency on the part of the vendor. Company information, product features, after-sales support and, of course, pricing/payment terms and conditions must all be presented clearly for easy access by a prospective buyer or his or her 'intelligent agent' (discussed earlier). Websites such as www.PriceScan.com, www.BotSpot.com and www.consumerreports.org provide excellent product/price comparison opportunities for e-consumers of all ages (Kardes, 2002). The key question one might ask at this point is this: if online customers really do 'want it all', will the average e-tailer be able to afford to offer such great price deals on an ongoing basis? As is the case for offline marketing, e-tailers must learn to develop very different strategies when attempting to commercialise highly price-sensitive products.

Communications mix

We have seen that ICTs facilitate 'many-to-many' communication exchanges (Hoffman and Novak, 1995). Interactive TV shopping channels, Internet banner ads and pop-up windows, SMS (Short Message Service) marketing and webcasting (or multicasting) are but some of the e-marketing tools recently developed to help e-tailers communicate with netizens. But how can e-tailers maximise the effectiveness of their Internet-based communications? Nicovich and Cornwell (in Richardson, 2001, p. 155) support the view that traditional mass marketing processes do not appear to fit neatly with Internet culture. The authors recommend that marketers should:

> contact users and elicit information without violating the norms exhibited about commercial speech. The way to accomplish this is for marketers to become members of the communities in which they wish to communicate. In this manner, marketers will learn the social values and attitudes exhibited by the community as well as garner a greater appreciation of the communications they present.

e-Tailing is changing rapidly and, in the process, changing the way consumers and marketers look at commerce itself. We are witnessing the rise of 'the experience economy'. In a book of the same name, Pine and Gilmore (cited in Kotler and Armstrong, 2001, p. 292) suggest that more and more companies are staging, marketing and delivering 'memorable experiences' rather that ordinary goods and services. From Niketown to Sony's Metreon (an interactive entertainment experience) the consumer is being exposed to brand/product-related feelings and sensations as never before. We are witnessing the rise of a new breed of retailer, and strategists who ignore this trend may experience tough challenges ahead.

BUSINESS-TO-BUSINESS e-MARKETING

In Chapter 4 we stressed the complexity of the B2B buying process and outlined the eight 'buyphases' that characterise it. We saw that once a need has been identified, an organisation then goes through a fairly extensive process in order to secure the right product, under the right terms from the most suitable supplier available. These decisions are rarely taken by a single individual and often involve significant sums of money over extended periods of time. With brand names and corporate reputations at stake, B2B purchasing matters are rarely taken lightly.

Unlike the world of consumer-targeted marketing, B2B marketing has relied quite heavily on technologically supported information systems over the years. Whiteley (2000, p. 129) has identified four different 'generations' of such systems: business applications came first, followed by integrated business systems, then by

- *Automatic teller machines* (ATMs)
- *e-Mail messaging* (using customer lists)
- *Mobile personal devices* such as PDAs and palm top computers
- *Mobile telephony* (mostly SMS and WAP applications)
- *Paperless trading* such as electronic data interchange (EDI) – the transfer of structured data, by agreed message standards, from one computer system to another, by electronic means (Whiteley, 2000, p. 79)
- *Personal computer access* (facilitated by an information service provider) to e-commerce websites on the WWW via home pages and linked Web documents in 'html' format
- *Point-of-Purchase* (POP) technologies – such as electronic cash registers, credit card readers and bar code scanners.
- *Portals/Vortals* maintained by information service providers (ISPs)
- *Scanning guns/pens* – also known as hand-held 'reorder' scanners
- *Value Chain Extranets* such as virtual private networks (VPNs) – networks that can operate over the Internet but only permit access to approved users (Chaston, 2001, p. 226)
- *Value Chain Intranets* such as enterprise resource planning systems (ERPs) – software that links together all databases from marketing, logistics, manufacturing, procurement, accounting and so on to permit real-time analysis of activities in progress across the organisation (Chaston, 2001, p. 225)

Figure 10.2 Popular B2B e-marketing ICTs

inter-organisational systems and finally we have the Internet-enabled systems of today.

As a result of this evolution, business-to-business and e-B2B organisations have come to rely upon a growing number of ICTs. A list of some of the more popular ICTs and related applications currently used in B2B e-marketing can be found in Figure 10.2

Who are the online customers in the B2B world? Research by Windham and Orton (2000) suggests that most business e-customers may be regrouped into three main categories: IT professionals, purchasing professionals and small business people. In order to serve these groups well, Windham and Orton recommend the following:

> For e-commerce to succeed in the business-to-business space, systems must adapt to the ways purchasing is done today, rather than attempting to totally reinvent well-established business practices. This points to:
>
> - Seamlessly interfacing Web procurement systems with legacy [established] enterprise purchasing systems.
> - Automating procurement policies, such as purchase authority, approved brands, and credit limits into the e-commerce solution.

- Acknowledging and allowing for the importance of human contact in the sales relationship, especially in high-involvement product and service categories.'

Chaston (2001, p. 248) goes further by suggesting that:

> The feature of the Internet that seems of critical interest to business-to-business marketers is its interactivity. This means that in addition to the execution of automated order entry tasks in the past implemented through EDI [electronic data interchange], the business-to-business marketer is able to offer a wider breadth of on-line support services, such as assisting in the design of specialist components, permitting automated customisation of product specifications, co-ordination of production schedules to avoid goods being out-of-stock, and offering online training in the application and exploitation of new technologies. Companies that were early entrants into business-to-business cyberspace marketing are now committed to the concept of eventually using the technology to manage all aspects of the customer transaction process, from initial enquiry to post-purchase product support.

Product and distribution

Even as interest in online shopping is growing rapidly, the fact remains that a large proportion of all online purchases is in business-to-business markets.

> One reason for this is that prior to the advent of the Internet many large manufacturing companies had already automated many of their procurement, production and distribution processes using a technology known as EDI (electronic data interchange). Hence it has been a relatively small conceptual jump to incorporate e-commerce platforms into existing operations. (Chaston, 2001, p. 38)

For B2B it is often difficult to disassociate production from distribution. Today, most business clients are keenly interested in effective supply chain (also known as *value* or *quality* chain) management. The trick behind this is for suppliers and their clients to adopt a cooperative electronic data exchange philosophy. For this approach to succeed, participants must:

- Be customer driven
- Have a long established commitment to just-in-time (JIT) and total quality management (TQM)
- Have expertise in IT-based supply chain management.

Pricing and communications

There are no big changes in strategy to report in this area except for the likely growth in the use of intelligent agents (discussed earlier) to help business customers get the best deals available, minute by minute, day by day. It is also safe to suggest that more and better online data should inevitably lead to more effective customer relationship management (CRM) systems.

PLANNING STRATEGY IN A DIGITAL AGE

Whether planning e-marketing strategies for consumer markets or business clients (or possibly both), today's marketing decision-makers must consider their options more carefully than before. The good news is that, although electronic trading is still a very young field, a number of useful approaches and techniques have already emerged to provide some form of guidance. We will discuss these briefly now.

e-Business models

Although a number of e-business models have already been tried (see Rayport and Jaworski, 2001; O'Connor and Galvin, 2001) and many new ones will no doubt come along soon, we believe that there are really only four truly strategic directions one can choose from, namely:

- Bricks and mortar only (strictly conventional trading, nothing digital)
- Bricks and some clicks (many online activities but no online transactions)
- True bricks and clicks (complete range of commercial activities both offline and online)
- Clicks only (trading is 100 per cent digital, no conventional or physical business).

Note: 'clicks' simply refers to the use of online technologies, more often than not through the click of a mouse.

e-Marketing planning

A good starting point usually involves e-customer marketing research. Although marketers are often quite skilled at this, many of the emerging technologies present new challenges to even the most seasoned researcher. For example, O'Connor and Galvin (2001, p. 39) have found varying degrees of IT applicability when conducting market research:

- Defining research objectives – low applicability
- Developing the research plan – low applicability
- Collecting data (primary and secondary) – high applicability
- Analysing data – high applicability
- Presenting findings – medium applicability.

In terms of the type of data to collect, researchers are uncovering fresh challenges as well. In terms of collecting *secondary* data (pre-published), the sheer amount of information now available may be a problem in itself. Researchers find many discrepancies between published studies, reports and off-the-peg analyses because their authors or sponsoring institutions may well have vested interests in their findings.

Happily, a growing number of responsible sources backed by self-regulated industry groups, government and scholarly institutions is growing rapidly all over the globe. Such sources include Cyber Atlas (http://cyberatlas.internet.com/), Forrester Research (http://www.forrester.com/), NOP Research Group (http://www.nopres.co.uk), NUA (http://www.nua.ie), the Internet Index (http://www.openmarket.com/intindex/index.cfm) and many others.

As for *primary* data collection, ICTs offer a number of potentially fresh and affordable approaches to this customarily tricky problem. Online questionnaires, e-mail surveys and iTV polls are just a few examples of such new tools. Of particular interest to researchers is the fact that even *qualitative* information is now being gathered online, thanks to a growing arsenal of innovative multimedia technologies and software applications enabling almost instantaneous images, sounds and words.

As if all this was not enough, online services such as SurveyMonkey (http://www.surveymonkey.com) and several others offer ready-to-use online questionnaire templates. Researchers can easily customise a survey by adding/removing questions and identifying the respondents of their choice. From there the process is fully automated.

It may be useful at this point to reflect upon the possible dangers of 'technological intoxication'. In a recent keynote address to the Marketing Research Society (MRS), Nicky Perrott, Head of e-MORI, listed four such dangers (Perrott, 2001):

- The commoditisation of research data (the issue of data relevance, and possible use of data out of context);
- The impact on the quality of survey research (respect for ICT limitations);
- The development of technology-led (rather than respondent-led) solutions;
- The de-personalisation of the interview process.

Clearly, tomorrow's e-researchers must grapple with ethical concerns not dissimilar to those related to traditional methods which have been an issue for many years now.

We can now turn our attention to 'e-strategy' which is inextricably tied to formal strategic planning and typically includes a marketing plan. Eisner Reding (2001) and Chaston (2001), like many other contemporary academics, seem to agree that 'in the context of e-commerce there are few differences between cyberspace and terrestrial marketing when it comes to the construction of a plan' (Chaston, 2001, p. 136). As discussed earlier, a fundamental direction must be selected in terms of the appropriate clicks and mortar balance. Most if not all 'e-plans' will include some form of website (or multiple website) strategy. This key aspect has been particularly well researched by Windham and Orton (2000). They propose a six-phase 'E-Business Road Map' to assist with the development of a potentially effective corporate website:

- Opportunity assessment
- Business strategy development
- Functional specifications development
- Prototyping
- Site building (form and content)
- Launch/ongoing refinement.

The authors caution existing bricks and mortar operations against developing their first website as an afterthought, instead of as a critical customer relationship business vehicle.

Effective webpage design

Readers may find it useful to use or adapt the website evaluation checklist (see Figure 10.3). It has been developed by the authors over a period of several years and allows researchers to compare e-business websites on qualities such as presence, interactivity, content and overall feel. This checklist could also be used by incorporating a rating scale such as 0 to 5 for each factor listed.

1. Presence

- Download time (with images and graphics)
- Use of cookies (purpose, frequency, etc.)
- Home page captures spirit of organisation or individual
- Home page provides essentials without having to 'scroll'
- Suitability of site architecture (layout, use of subsections, etc.)
- Aesthetic appeal:
  - Vividness (resolution, contrast, use of colour, motion, etc.)
  - Originality (compared with related or competitive sites)
  - Legibility (fonts, headings, etc.)
  - Clarity, use of white space
  - Consistency (or unity)
  - High impact graphics/images
- Degree of humour (if applicable)
- Entertainment value
- Educational value
- Degree of clutter

2. Interactivity/Convenience (leading to user *immersion/engagement*)

- Search facility (if applicable)
- Registration process (online form, e-mail requests, etc.)
- Trial option
- Payment options (methods, security issues, etc.)
- Feedback options (mailing lists, chat rooms, bulletin boards, etc.)
- Special program requirements (multimedia plug-ins, Java, JavaScript, etc.)
- Site navigation (logic, order, flow, degree of immersion, etc.)
- Sense of community (welcome message, contextual content, links, etc.)
- Number of clicks required to access relevant information
- Ease of saving/printing/forwarding relevant information

3. Information/Content

- Confidentiality
- Quality (complete, current, relevant, well rounded, accurate, etc.)
- Non-sexist and non-patronising
- Language options available (if appropriate)
- First time users' guide
- Site navigation instructions (site map, tool bars, navigational buttons, etc.)
- Organisation/product information (specs, delivery, warranties, return policy, etc.)
- Useful links (related sites, jobs, upcoming events, etc.)
- FAQs (frequently asked questions)
- Amount (too little, too much)
- Geographical parameters (local, national, international, global)
- Advertising (banners, frames, logos, etc.)

4. Overall Feel

- Appropriate level of formality/informality
- Degree of elegance/professionalism
- Ease, rhythm, tone
  - Is this 'bookmark' material?
  - Degree of personalisation
  - Language level
  - Degree of transparency

Figure 10.3 Website evaluation checklist

Once a website has been fully developed, tested and formally launched, it can be promoted/positioned quite effectively using the services of a Web positioning service such as NetBooster (http://www.netbooster.co.uk). Site performance is improved by:

- Registering the client's website address according to site content and search tool parameters. This process may be handled through automatic tools or manually, and may involve significant technical actions (click stream analysis, net linking and affiliation, e-branding and so on);
- Repeating this process on a regular basis in order to obtain a desirable position for the client's webpages, and maintain this position over time.

STRATEGIC CHALLENGES AND ISSUES

Emerging challenges

We have seen that e-marketing is generally more advanced for business markets than it is for e-tailing. 'For many [B2C] marketers, including fast-growing Internet superstars such as Amazon.com, the Web is still not a money-making proposition' (Kotler and Armstrong, 2001, p. 645). The authors suggest that some of the key challenges faced by these e-marketers include:

- Limited consumer exposure and buying (the issue of limited access)
- Skewed user demographics and psychographics (although this is changing rapidly)
- Chaos and clutter
- Online security
- Ethical concerns (privacy, disclosure and access limitation issues, for example).

Another point raised by O'Connor and Galvin (2001, p. 193) relates to what they call the 'marketing/IT gap'. They suggest that, for the moment, few marketing professionals can really claim to be fully IT literate. This state of affairs is acknowledged by inside observers such as Workz.com (http://www.workz.com), who have generated a useful list of nine common 'e-commerce mistakes':

- Making hasty (and costly) decisions
- Neglecting customer service (empty promises)
- Forgetting to use META and TITTLE tags (key words and descriptions routinely used by search engines)
- Forgetting to integrate e-business with traditional operations
- Neglecting to test (and retest) online tools
- Failing to prepare for success (growth rate is sometimes phenomenal)

- Underestimating marketing needs (the need for aggressive online and offline promotion, for example)
- Submitting customers to overlong download times
- Serving up aging and out-of-date content.

Competence factors

So what does it take to make it all work? Jobber (2001, p. 469) has developed a list of seven 'online competences' to help strategic planners implement potentially effective e-marketing plans:

- Strategic competence (market leadership)
- Financial competence (means to sustain e-position)
- Innovation (to offset imitators)
- Workforce (blend of skill and performance)
- Quality (total commitment)
- Productivity (focus on added value)
- Information systems (to support effective information management).

The Web and the other ICTs we have discussed in this chapter are seen as both media and markets. ICTs can free customers from the shackles of their traditional passive roles, and this in turn may challenge e-marketers to provide superior goods and services.

SUMMARY

Electronic marketing is currently the subject of a rapidly growing number of published articles, discussion papers, dissertations and books. Although it is not possible to include everything in a single chapter such as this one, we have attempted to provide readers with a useful overview of this fascinating field. Marketing strategists will do well to remember that e-marketing is still a young field of enquiry: 'The use of the Internet as a means of satisfying partner exchange needs is just starting to be explored and it will be sometime before we, as marketers, have exhausted all the possibilities' (Nicovich and Cornwell, in Richardson, 2001, p. 157).

Questions for discussion

1. How is the 'many-to-many' environment described in this chapter so different from the more traditional 'one-to-many' approach?
2. Why do you think the World Wide Web is currently more attractive to e-marketers than most other non-traditional tools?
3. 'ICTs have impacted B2B marketing mix strategies differently than B2C marketing mix strategies.' Discuss this statement.
4. When a researcher sets out to compare a number of similar websites using pre-selected criteria, is this considered *primary* or *secondary* data collection? Justify your answer.
5. Can e-marketing be useful to any sort of business? Why or why not?

References

Chaston, I (2001), *e-Marketing Strategy*, Maidenhead: McGraw-Hill

Eisner Reding, E (2001), *Building an eBusiness From the Ground Up*, New York: McGraw-Hill Irwin

Hoffman, D L and Novak, T P (1995), *Marketing in Hypermedia Computer-Mediated Environments: Conceptual Foundations*, working paper number one (revised 11 July) for 'Project 2000: Research Program on Marketing in Computer-mediated Environments', available through http://www2000.ogsm.vanderbilt.edu

Hoffman, D L and Novak, T P (1996), *A New Marketing Paradigm for Electronic Commerce*, paper published in the 19 February edition of *The Information Society*, available through http://www2000.ogsm.vanderbilt.edu

Jobber, D (2001), *Principles & Practice of Marketing*, 3rd edn, Maidenhead: McGraw-Hill

Kardes, F R (2002), *Consumer Behavior and Managerial Decision Making*, 2nd edn, Upper Saddle River, NJ: Prentice Hall

Kotler, P and Armstrong, G (2001), *Principles of Marketing*, 9th edn, Upper Saddle River, NJ: Prentice Hall International

Nicovich, S and Cornwell, T B (1998), 'An Internet Culture?: Implications for Marketing', *Journal of Interactive Marketing*, John Wiley & Sons, reprinted in *Internet Marketing* (2001), by Paul Richardson, New York: McGraw-Hill International, pp. 147–58

O'Connor, J and Galvin, E (2001), *Marketing in the Digital Age*, 2nd edn, Harlow: Financial Times/Prentice Hall

Perrott, N (2001), *The Dangers of Technological Intoxication*, MRS Conference Keynote Address, 23 March

Pine, B J and Gilmore, J H (1999), *The Experience Economy*, New York: Free Press, quoted in Kotler, P and Armstrong, G (2001), *Principles of Marketing*, 9th edn, Upper Saddle River, NJ: Prentice Hall International, pp. 292–3

Rayport, J F and Jaworski, B J (2001), *e-Commerce*, New York: McGraw-Hill Irwin, MarketspaceU

Richardson, P (2001), *Internet Marketing: Readings and Online Resources*, New York: McGraw-Hill International

Schneider, G and Perry, J (2001a), *Electronic Commerce*, 2nd annual edn, Boston: Course Technology – Thomson Learning

Whiteley, D (2000), *e-Commerce: Strategy, Technologies and Applications*, Maidenhead: McGraw-Hill

Windham, L and Orton, K (2000), *The Soul of the New Consumer*, Oxford: Windsor Books

Sources

Abramson, R (2001), 'Sniff-Company DigiScents is a Scratch', *The Industry Standard*, IDG.net, 11 April issue

Afuah, A and Tucci, C L (2001), *Internet Business Models and Strategies*, New York: McGraw-Hill International

Edictionary (current), http://edictionary.com

Haig, M (2001), *The e-Marketing Handbook*, London: Kogan Page

McLaren, C and McClaren, B (2000), *E-Commerce: Business on the Internet*, Cincinnati: South-Western Educational Publishing

O'Connor, J and Galvin, E (1998), *Creating Value Through e-Commerce*, London: Financial Times/Pearson Education – London

Postma, P (1999), *The New Marketing Era: Marketing to the Imagination in a Technlogy-Driven World*, New York: McGraw-Hill

Schneider, G and Perry, J (2001b), *New Perspectives on E-commerce*, New Perspectives Series, Boston: Course Technology – Thomson Learning

Sterne, J (1999), *World Wide Web Marketing*, New York: John Wiley & Sons

Whitworth, M (2001), 'The Joy of Text', *Caterer & Hotelkeeper*, 15 November, p. 28

Wiseth, K (1998), Corporate Intranets as Business Enablers, *Oramag*, 1 September, http://www.oracle.com/oramag/oracle/98-Sep/58corp.html

Glossary of e-Marketing Terms

ATM automatic teller machine, also known as 'bank machine' or 'cash point'

Chatroom an Internet site that facilitates online discussions for users with shared interests

Digital of or relating to a device that can read, write or store information that is represented in numerical form

e-Business an individual organisation conducting commerce electronically

e-Commerce short for electronic commerce. Involves conducting business electronically. Any form of business transactions or information exchange executed using information and communication technology, between companies, between companies and their customers, or between companies and public administrations

EDI electronic data interchange. Pre-Internet technology allowing linked corporate computers to exchange information electronically

e-Mail messages sent and received electronically via telecommunication links, such as between microcomputers or terminals.

e-Marketing stands for either electronic or online marketing

ERP systems enterprise resource planning systems

e-Sourcing using the Net to manage all procurement activities

e-Tail electronic retail. Online marketing specifically targeted to consumers

Extranet a corporate website with restricted access. Frequently used in value chain management

FAQs frequently asked questions

FTP file transfer protocol

Home page a website's welcome page

HTML hypertext mediated language

ICTs information and communication technologies (what used to be simply IT). The study of the technology used to handle information and aid communication

Intelligent agent a program that performs functions such as information gathering, information filtering, or mediation running in the background on behalf of a person or entity

Intranet a website for use strictly within an organisation

ISP Internet service provider

iTV interactive digital television

Link a segment of text or a graphical item that serves as a cross-reference between parts of a hypertext document or between files or hypertext documents. Also called hotlink, hyperlink

Marketspace(s) electronic markets in which sellers offer their products and services electronically, and buyers search for information, identify what they want and place orders using a credit card or other means of electronic payment

m-Commerce stands for mobile (wireless) e-commerce

Netizen a person who is a frequent or habitual user of the Internet

Pop-up ads also known as 'interstitials'. Ads that pop up as you wait for your webpage to load

Portals/Vortals these provide entry points to the WWW and usually feature instructions, search capabilities and menus of selected links

SMS short message service allows e-marketers to send brief commercial text messages to customers who have signed up to the service

URL universal resource locator. Every website has a domain name or URL that is equivalent to the site's address or telephone number

VPN virtual private network. The use of encryption in the lower protocol layers to provide a secure connection through an otherwise insecure network, typically the Internet. VPNs are generally cheaper than real private networks using private lines but rely on having the same encryption system at both ends. The encryption may be performed by firewall software or possibly by routers

WAP wireless application protocol

Webcasting from 'World Wide Web' and 'broadcast'. Webcasting implies real-time transmission of encoded video under the control of the server to multiple recipients who all receive the same content at the same time. This is in contrast to normal Web browsing which is controlled from the browser by individual users and may take arbitrarily long to deliver a complete document

Website a WWW file written in html containing text and often pictures, colour, sound and motion

chapter eleven

Marketing Strategy for Mass-mediated Services

Learning objectives

By reading this chapter you will learn:

- The importance of the media in certain consumer service sectors
- The publics that a consumer service organisation needs to target
- The factors that impact upon marketing strategy in mass consumer services
- The functions of the media for distribution or communication of the service
- The relative importance of customer acquisition and retention.

INTRODUCTION

Mass-mediated consumer services are defined as those where many tens of thousands of consumers are catered for, often with a strong component of the service distributed and/or communicated through the mass media. Examples of such contexts include football spectatorship and political campaigning. Both voters (see Newman, 1988; Baines and Egan, 2001) and football spectators (see Tomlinson et al., 1995) have been likened to consumers and the management of their experiences can essentially be regarded as being delivered by mass consumer services marketing activities. Similarly, in the more traditional consumer services sector, the financial services and airline industries (among others) also offer mass consumer services. To discuss football spectatorship and political campaigning as consumer services may sound somewhat trite, yet political parties and football clubs are beginning to adopt just such a market orientation as they fight to obtain a sustainable competitive advantage over their rivals in highly competitive markets. The broadening of the concept of marketing is based on the notion that where an offering of value to the other party is exchanged between two parties, marketing activity can be utilised. This has ensured that marketing has been applied to social causes, churches and political parties (see Kotler and Levy, 1969). Although sport has been 'big business' in the US for many years, it is only since the emergence of the Premier League in Britain, Serie A in Italy, Spain's Primera Liga and France's Division 1 that European football clubs have started to generate significant sources of sponsorship income. In the UK, the mainstream use of marketing by a political party is generally associated with the Conservative Party under Margaret Thatcher in the late 1970s and early 1980s (Scammell, 1994) and, more recently, with Tony Blair's New Labour Party.

Media markets throughout the Western world are increasingly fragmenting. In the UK, the British Broadcasting Corporation (BBC) and Independent Television franchises (ITV) have historically controlled the UK terrestrial television market. However, with the advent of two more commercial channels, Channel 4 in the early 1980s and Channel 5 in the late 1990s, competition is increasing even in this highly regulated sector. Cable (for example NTL) and satellite (for example BSkyB) companies provide the subscribing television viewer with an even greater choice of channels. This fragmenting media market has an important influence on the marketing of mass-mediated consumer services such as political parties and football clubs. Political parties in the UK rely on broadcast news channels and the print media to distribute political information to the general public. Football clubs have also become reliant on television to distribute full games and match highlights and rely on the print media to provide coverage of match results. However, there are significant differences between football and politics that alter the way in which marketing can be utilised. Each sector is considered individually in the following two sections.

MARKETING AND EUROPEAN FOOTBALL CLUBS

Football clubs in the UK are currently facing a significant challenge. A report on football financing, published by accountants Deloitte and Touche (2000), states that most English football clubs are operating at a loss. The report highlights the widening gap between football's rich and poor clubs. In 1992, Sunderland's chairman, Bob Murray (cited in Boulding, 1992, p. 22), predicted that 20 or 30 clubs from the lower three divisions would go bankrupt by the end of the decade as the gap between them and the elite Premier League clubs widened. This has not occurred, principally because the Football Association has organised generous loan packages for clubs in danger of receivership (Hillsdon, 2000). Many commentators discuss the commercialisation of football in negative terms, suggesting that business might bankrupt 'the beautiful game' (Clark, 1998) and has benefited only a small number of elite clubs. In Europe, such clubs include England's Manchester United, Holland's Ajax, Spain's Real Madrid and France's Paris St Germain. The growth of sports spectatorship has been driven by its symbiotic relationship with television (Meenaghan and O'Sullivan, 1999) and media companies are purchasing football clubs to widen their audiences (for example BSkyB's attempt to purchase Manchester United and Canal Plus' ownership of Paris St Germain). Wealthy, entrepreneurial owners (for example Elton John and Watford, Mohammed Fayed and Fulham and Alan Sugar and Tottenham Hotspur) have always directed clubs in the UK. However, it looks increasingly likely that spiralling wage costs, and the need for an efficient marketing and merchandising operation, will ensure that commercial, rather than entrepreneurial, ownership will become more commonplace in the future. Thus, football clubs are increasingly likely either to merge with media companies, or to be taken over by them. Clubs are likely to form joint ventures or strategic alliances to take advantage of their partners' skills in any or all of the following areas: IT; marketing; distribution; and merchandising.

Nevertheless, despite the increase in television spectatorship, live spectatorship at football stadiums has decreased generally over the decades. However, revenues are increasing due to product diversification, in that revenues derive not just from gate receipts, but from television rights, merchandising and sponsorship. For instance, Manchester United announced a £30m, two-year deal with Vodafone Airtouch in 2000 and a £300m deal over 15 years with Nike to distribute Manchester United sportswear in the same year. At the heart of the Vodafone partnership is the notion that Vodafone will benefit from customer acquisition through an increased European subscriber base and the increased voice and data traffic that will occur through watching matches on mobile Internet platforms. These matches could become available through WAP (wireless application protocol) or GPRS (general package radio service) mobile phones (so-called 3G and 21/2G). Manchester United benefits from the extra revenue gained with which it can buy players and from increased exposure to potential overseas supporters.

Sport itself is intangible, subjective, inconsistent and unpredictable (Shilbury, 1989, p. 22). The core product could be regarded as the reinforcement of a supporter's identity with the club and the game. The actual product could be regarded as the uncertainty of the outcome of a match, crowd behaviour and the current success of the team. The augmented product, the area where marketing can have the greatest influence, includes supporter sponsorship of seats, merchandising and the provision of identity-reinforcing labelled consumer goods and services. Figure 11.1 illustrates the football product in further detail.

The augmented, indirect revenues are frequently greater than the direct operating revenues obtained through gate receipts. Wolverhampton Wanderers Football Club, for example, derived more than half its estimated £10.7m turnover in 1996 from the sale of branded goods, sponsorship deals and hiring its Molineux stadium out for conferences and receptions (Dignam, 1996, p. 8). The stadium, because it is only used once or twice every two weeks, offers the club an opportunity to obtain further revenue. Wembley stadium, for instance, hosted pop concerts for many years.

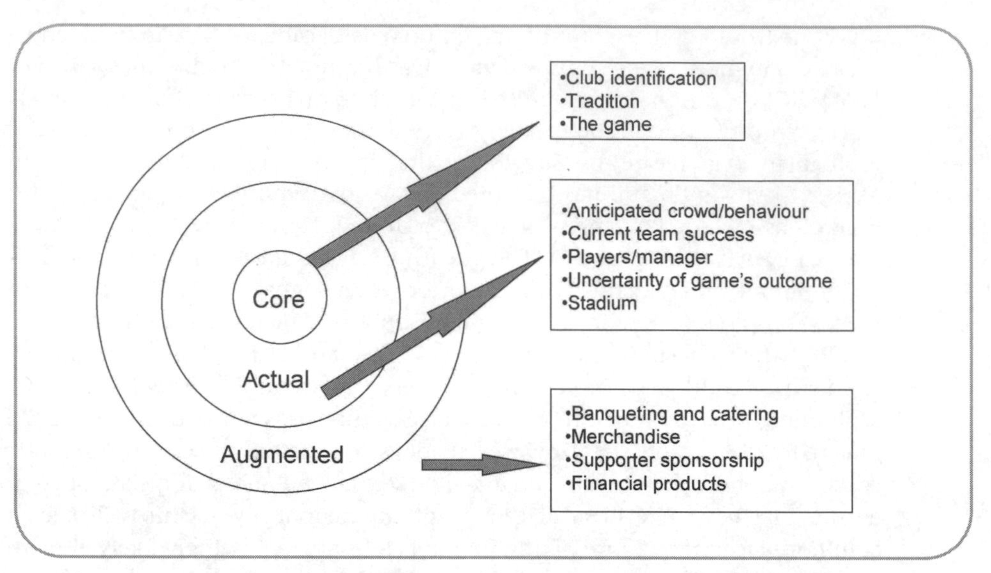

Figure 11.1 An anatomy of the football marketing product
Source: Barn and Baines (1998)

As football clubs are commercialising, marketing activity is becoming increasingly important to ensure that a club's return on investment is maximised. According to a survey of 447 UK sports associations by Evans et al. (1996), marketing activity encompasses a number of specific areas. These include, in order of decreasing importance:

- Obtaining revenue from sponsorship and advertising (usually perimeter fences and banners displayed around the stadium)
- Promotional awareness generation through public relations and the advertising of forthcoming matches and events through radio, billboard, press and magazine advertising
- Segmentation of customers and markets, merchandising, store and new product development
- Television and supplier contract negotiation
- Ticket sales (incorporating the general public and corporate clients)
- The commissioning of market research.

The application of the marketing mix to football clubs provides a useful understanding of some of the problems associated with the application of traditional marketing methodology (see Table 11.1). For instance, while a basic customer need is easily identifiable and the target market capable of being segmented (for example by loyalty), the product is more difficult to define. The nature of price as applied to football clubs is relatively straightforward. However, it is important for clubs to realise that in future, as media companies increase their viewing audiences, associated revenue streams will no longer fall under their direct control.

Table 11.1 The football club's marketing mix

Marketing aspect	Football club (EU)
Basic customer need	Pride, identification, escapism
Target market	Football supporting population (comprising television, radio and live audiences)
Product	Excitement, current team success, club identification, merchandise, supporter sponsorship, physical and intangible peripherals
Price	Cost of match attendance, cost of match subscriptions, merchandise and sponsorship costs, banqueting and catering charges
Principal promotional tools (in order of importance)	1. Sports new management 2. Direct mail 3. Press, radio and billboard advertising 4. The Internet
Distribution	Broadcast matches (pay-per-view, subscriber and terrestrial), news (press and broadcast) through conferences and releases, matchday programmes (on- and offline), websites, retail outlets for merchandise and peripheral services
Process	Not just during football seasons or particular competitions, further market orientation possible through supporter panels
Physical evidence	Merchandise, matchday programmes, food service products and supporter sponsorship programmes
People	Football players (sports clubs own their own celebrity endorsers), marketing department should be explicit rather than fragmented or subsumed within customer service, for example

Because of the considerable exposure gained by football clubs through broadcast distribution of live matches and match highlights and through articles in the local and national press, football clubs concentrate on news management. Therefore, the distribution of the football offering is also tied into its communication, although football clubs do also use direct mail, radio, billboard and press advertising. The process is regulated by competition authorities (for example the Football Association) and international football competition bodies (for example FIFA and UEFA). The competitive structure of the industry is akin to an oligopoly since clubs are effectively forced into playing in particular leagues.

The concept of making tangible the intangible through physical evidence provides football with a significant opportunity. However, football clubs should be careful not to be seen to be exploiting their supporters' loyalty. A number of clubs were investigated by the Office of Fair Trading in the UK in 2000 for overcharging their fans for football strips and introducing strip changes too many times during a season. Similarly, there has been some discussion in the media over costs of attendance to live matches and the considerable prices charged by the likes of BSkyB for pay-per-view services.

MARKETING AND UK POLITICAL PARTIES

A number of authors have proposed definitions of political marketing. Shama (1975) defined it as 'the process by which political candidates and their ideas are directed at voters in order to satisfy their potential needs and thus gain their support for the candidate and ideas in question'. Later definitions transform the meaning to incorporate: the process of lobbying (Lock and Harris, 1996); a long-term societal objective (Henneberg, 1997); and a focus on competition, opinion research and environmental analysis (Wring, 1997). More recently, Baines (2001) incorporates an international and organisational perspective, defining political marketing as:

> the process by which political organisations communicate their message, policies and/or objectives to other political organisations, or the electorate, in order to solicit their support within the constraints of the electoral and political system(s), laws and regulations and the general political environment in which they are operating, in order to further their organisation's interests, or the interests of a client.

In this definition, Baines acknowledges the significant obstacles faced by political parties in communicating their policies and messages to citizens because of the nature of electoral law. For instance, in the UK, political parties are not allowed to advertise on broadcast television, although all major parties receive a small number of two and a half minute broadcasts at election time and they are allowed to advertise in cinemas. Individual candidates are not allowed to appear on news programmes unless all other candidates contesting a constituency seat are available or give their consent (under section 93 of the Representation of the People Act 1983).

The political product, shown in Figure 11.2, demonstrates that the core product consists of constituency representation by an MP at the local level and a voice in government at the national level.

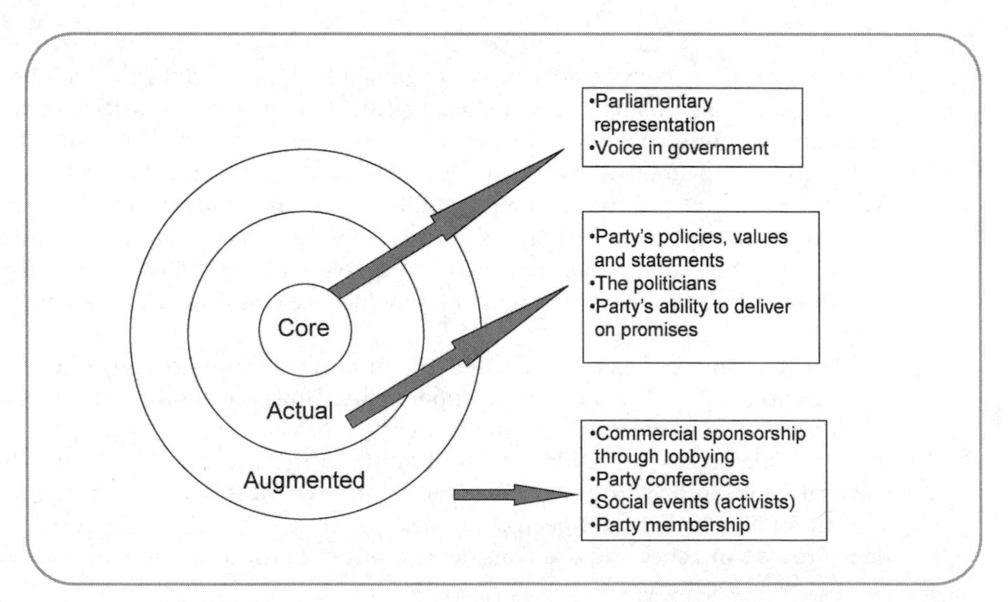

Figure 11.2 An anatomy of the political product

The actual product incorporates the policies, values and statements espoused by the party, the politicians themselves and the party's ability to deliver on its promises, or pledges as New Labour refers to them. Augmented aspects of the product include party membership (where members receive policy newsletters and social function information), regulatory information on forthcoming policy (for example purchased by companies to aid in lobbying efforts) and party conferences. Most citizens vote because they regard it as their civic duty. In the UK, in the latter part of the twentieth century, typically around 75 per cent of the electorate vote in a Westminster general election (the turnout in the 2001 British General Election was a post-war low at around 59 per cent). The choice of which party to vote for in England (rather than Wales, Scotland and Northern Ireland) is limited to three major parties (the Conservative Party, New Labour and the Liberal Democrats).

The application of the marketing mix to political campaigning provides a useful understanding of some of the problems associated with the application of traditional marketing methodology (see Table 11.2). For instance, while a basic customer need is easily identifiable and the target market capable of being segmented (for example by demography – age and sex – and geopartisan means – using regional canvass records), the product is more difficult to define. However, the real problem comes in under-

Table 11.2 The political party's marketing mix

Marketing aspect	Political party (UK)
Basic customer need	Voice in government, parliamentary representation
Target market	Electorate (comprising numerous segments)
Product	Party policies, personality and principle (O'Shaughnessy, 1999), and information on government and governance
Price	Could be policy implications for voter likelihood (Egan, 1999), effort of political participation, although no easily applicable direct equivalent
Principal promotional tools (in order of importance – floating voter persuasion)	1. Election broadcasts 2. Direct mail 3. News management 4. Poster campaigns 5. and 6. The Internet (partly derived from Worcester and Mortimore, 1999, p. 123)
Distribution	News (press and broadcast) through press conferences and releases, direct mail, party manifestos (on- and offline), websites and party conferences
Process	Not just during election, further market orientation achievable through citizen policy fora, most UK marketing activity conducted in-house except advertising and voter research
Physical evidence	Candidates and party, manifestos, provision of party spokespeople in and out of election cycle
People	Structured career paths in party politics with high degree of policy development and campaign training necessary

Source: Adapted from Baines (2001)

standing how the concept of price is applied to the process of voting. Egan (1999) has stated that the price could be regarded as the cost associated with specific proposals on voter livelihood (for example tax and educational implications). Because of electoral law, political parties in the UK tend to achieve the greatest exposure of their policies and messages through the broadcast and print news. However, while broadcast news has a duty to remain impartial (regulated by the BBC and the Independent Television Commission – ITC), the print press is under no such constraints. As a result, political parties have traditionally concentrated on advertising through press advertising and billboard campaigns. Distribution of the political service offering is intricately tied into its communication because the offering is ephemeral: a set of promises and an experience. The political process is highly regulated (the Representation of the People Act 1983, the Broadcasting Act 1990, the Elections, Parties and Referendums Act 2000 and so on). The nature of competition is akin to an oligopoly (Baines et al., 2001).

Because of the intangible nature of political campaigning, providing the voter with physical evidence of the service becomes paramount. Political parties have not yet been able systematically to provide this, although the Labour Party made its manifesto available in multiple retail grocery outlets such as Sainsbury's at the 1997 British General Election. Parties even made attempts to e-mail and send text messages to voters' mobile phones in the 2001 British General Election. The service nature of political campaigning and its interface with voters underlines the importance of the party's spokespersons, since they are the link with the voters.

IMPLICATIONS FOR MARKETING STRATEGY

There are a variety of similarities in the difficulties faced by political parties in the UK and football clubs operating in Europe. This section aims to provide the reader with an understanding of what these difficulties are, and how they relate to strategy. The brand management process is particularly affected by the following factors:

- The size of the marketing budget, since it determines the level of investment in the brand
- The length of promotional campaigns, since organisations need to maintain their image for as long as possible in order to generate awareness, encourage repeat purchase, retain old, and acquire new, consumers
- The level of competition, as competitive offerings can reduce brand potential and dilute market share
- The level of consumer loyalty, as increasing loyalty can encourage repeat business, further strengthening brand image
- The nature of the product, as this affects how the brand can be positioned and the marketing mix employed
- The degree of product or market orientation.

Table 11.3 provides further details of how each of the above factors impacts upon the brand management process for football clubs and political parties vis-à-vis traditional commercial mass consumer services. Let us look at each in turn. First, the size of the

Table 11.3 Impact of brand management factors on football clubs, political parties and commercial mass consumer services organisations

Brand management considerations	Commercial organisation	Political party	Football club
Size of marketing budget	■ Dependent on size of organisation but can be huge (for example BT)	■ £20m for each party per election cycle (Westminster general election) nationally ■ Approx. £15m for all constituencies locally	■ Depends on club but can be very small and/or non-existent
Length of promotional campaigns	■ Could be of any length ■ Usually 1–5 and 10-year plans	■ Formal election campaign – 4 weeks, informal – 1 year	■ Depends on status of club but usually relates to a season
Level of competition	■ Depends on industry but often fairly high	■ Winning an election likened to winning an exclusive franchise bid in industrial markets (Baines et al., 2001)	■ Competition fundamental to product (European Cup Winner's Cup, FA and so on)
Level of consumer loyalty	■ Depends on product and organisation ■ But loyalty generally only moderately high for FMCG	■ Polarised: high for party loyalists, low for young voters, negative for other party's supporters	■ High (for example season ticket holders)
Nature of product	■ Capable of being continually changed and repositioned	■ Repositioning difficult though possible (for example New Labour, American Democratic Party)	■ Repositioning of core product (game exceedingly difficult although repositioning of club less so)
Market orientation	■ Depends on organisation but usually quite high (Egg in financial services, easyJet in airline industry)	■ Often product oriented but becoming increasingly voter oriented	■ Non-existent except in larger, more commercially oriented (for example Manchester United)

marketing budget for football clubs and political parties can be quite small or even non-existent. This is because of their historical product orientation. Second, both types of organisation receive a high degree of publicity in the form of unpaid exposure. Indeed, football clubs are *paid* millions of pounds in broadcasting rights. Third, both types of organisation have relied on shorter periods of advertising, because of the short election campaign period and the fixed duration of the football season. Yet one could see advertising campaigns running over longer periods of time in both cases, providing they were allocated sufficient budget.

In both football and politics, competition is somewhat artificial and is not a free market (see Baines and Egan, 2001, for a discussion of this concept and its application to political campaigning). In the case of football, clubs form part of a league and so the nature of competition is fundamental to their product. Yet this also limits the brand potential, if the marketing strategist only views the football club as a provider of football entertainment within a specific league. Mason (1999) states that the league can be regarded as 'a joint venture, or cartel of independently operated franchises', while Egan (1999) has also likened local political campaigns in the UK to franchise operations.

The loyalty demonstrated by football supporters (fanatics or 'fans') is legendary. Often rival fans have been involved in violent clashes (for example Euro 2000 and the death of a Leeds United fan prior to a home game with Turkish rivals, Galatasaray). Despite this considerable degree of supporter loyalty, not usually demonstrated so negatively, clubs have often treated their fans poorly, providing 'dreadful facilities, poor customer care and little respect' (Parker and Stuart, 1997). Political parties are also able to motivate thousands of activists during election time to deliver election addresses, leaflets and to encourage other party supporters to go out and vote at election time through canvassing activity. This level of customer involvement is not typical in traditional mass consumer services.

In politics and football, the nature of the product is all tied up with image. The image of a football club is greatly dependent on the success of the team, and yet Wimbledon is relatively successful on the field but returns low gate receipts for a side in the British Premier League (see Deloitte and Touche, 2000). Thus, to some extent, the nature of the product negates a greater degree of market orientation as far as the core game is concerned. However, football fans have other needs related to their identification with the team where marketing activity can enhance the customer experience. Only through market research can a club endeavour to understand its fans. Again, political parties are also heavily dependent on their image. The 'red rose' of the Labour Party and the Conservative Party's 'blue torch' both serve as icons to convey images of patriotism, passion and fire, playing on the voters' emotions. Political parties generally have difficulty in repositioning their image when the image to which they aspire is radically different from that which they have adopted previously (see Baines et al., 1999). Yet, New Labour changed its policies substantially in order to win the 1997 British General Election, and many voters celebrated their win at the time. Reorienting a political party requires sophisticated use of market research, in order to determine how the segments of the electorate will view particular changes in policy.

Multiple Publics, Distribution and Communication

Political parties and candidates also need to transact with a variety of other publics. Kotler and Kotler (1981) have stated that the political strategist has six markets to communicate with. These are the voters, the party, the candidate, interest groups, campaign contributors (donors) and the media. The role of the media is central to communicating with the other five markets and the markets are all interlinked. Sweeney (1995) also states that political candidates have a number of audiences, referring to primary and secondary audiences, where the primary audience is the voter and the secondary audiences are campaign staff and volunteers, organisations, opinion leaders, political party, contributors, allies and friends, and the media. It is increasingly important, particularly in the UK where political advertising is illegal, to target messages and policies at the appropriate journalists in the broadcast media and press. This aspect of the political campaigning process is often referred to as 'spin-doctoring'. Figure 11.3 illustrates this interconnection between the various publics and the political party, highlighting, in addition, the importance of regulatory bodies such as the Electoral Commission, the BBC and ITC, although not the Advertising Standards Authority since non-broadcast political advertising is not subject to any regulation.

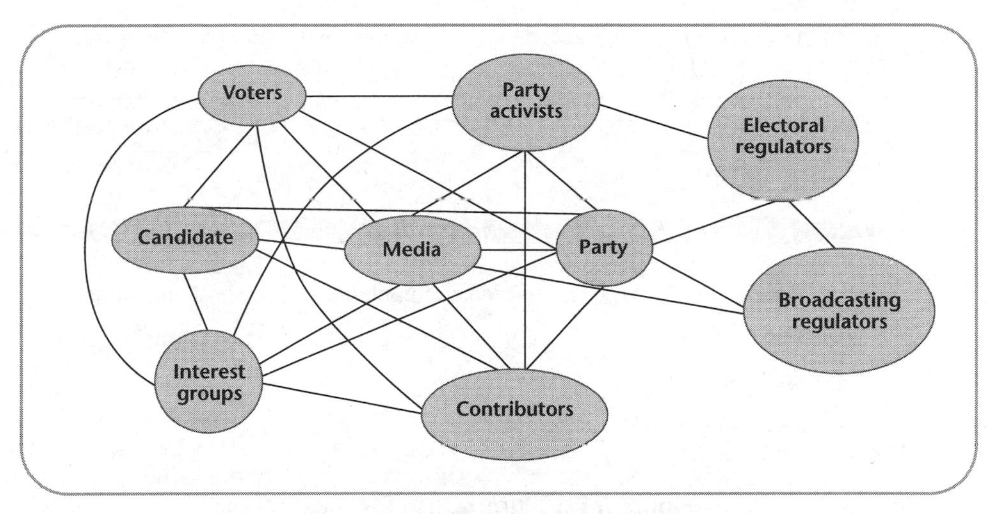

Figure 11.3 Publics of a political party
Source: Adapted from Kotler and Kotler (1981)

Football club publics (see Figure 11.4) include their players (with whom their supporters so clearly associate), sponsors (who provide substantial revenue), community groups (who can resist and block planning applications for stadium and site development), supporters, and competition and regulatory bodies (for example the Football Association, local authorities' planning departments, the police and so on). These publics are also interconnected by the media and to each other as they seek to purvey a favourable image to their own primary audiences.

The diverse nature of a political party's and a football club's publics ensure a complex process of distribution and communication (see Tables 11.1 and 11.2). For

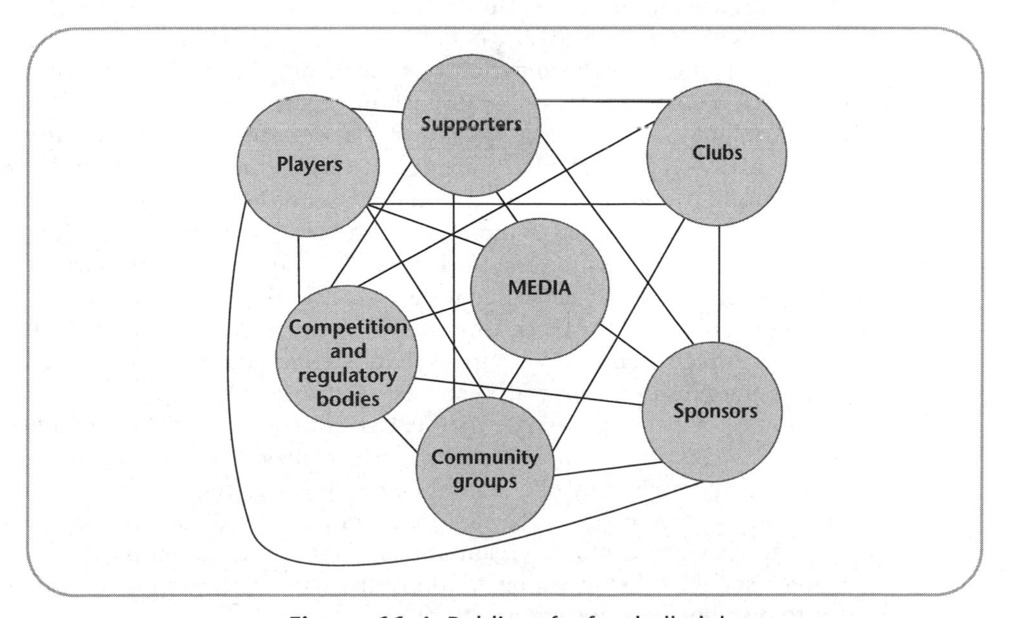

Figure 11.4 Publics of a football club

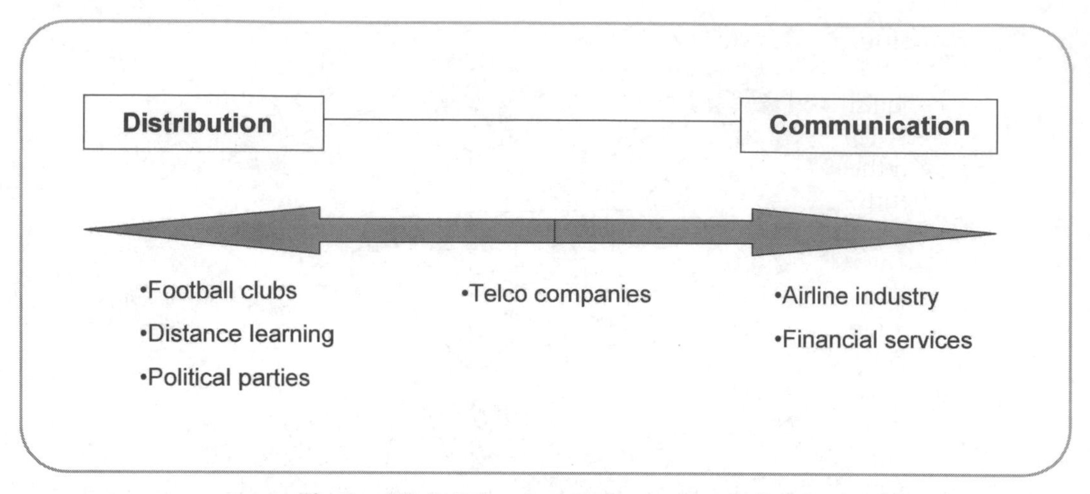

Figure 11.5 Primary use for mass media: distribution/communication continuum

instance, while opposition political parties actively need to court the media to ensure that their messages get across to the electorate, the governing party obtains much greater coverage because of its potential to affect the lives of voters. Similarly, broadcast media organisations actively court football clubs as they seek to drive up television ratings by purchasing broadcasting rights for matches. Newspaper and magazine organisations also provide readers with content on the teams that they support to increase readership figures and, therefore, the revenue that they can earn from advertisers. The difference lies in the distribution of power between the media and the football club or political party concerned. If one considers the television audience of a football club, the media are pivotal in the distribution of the product (in the same way they are with a political party). The football club might also use some of the same media organisations for advertising purposes (for example radio).

Figure 11.5 illustrates the importance of the media in communicating and distributing the mass consumer service product. Those organisations on the right-hand side of the continuum, such as the airline industry and financial services companies, use media organisations principally for communication of the benefits of using their core product mainly for advertising or information purposes. Thus, it is important for them to foster strong working relationships with advertising agencies, media planners and buyers. Those organisations on the left-hand side of the diagram, such as political parties, football clubs and educational distance learning programmes (for example such as those offered by the Open University) use the media principally for the distribution of their core product. By comparison, it is important for these organisations to strengthen their relationships with broadcast media organisations.

One mass consumer service that exists somewhere in the middle of the continuum is telecommunications services, since they have diversified into media organisations themselves by offering online content services. Nevertheless, they still use other media organisations through joint ventures for distribution of their products, while also using media organisations for advertising purposes. Thus, such companies should develop strong relationships with both groups of organisations related to distribution and communication.

Customer acquisition and retention

The acquisition of customers in mass consumer services is critical to their continuing success. This has been the reason for the mergers and alliances that have taken place in both the banking and airline industries as companies vie with their competitors for competitive advantage. Vodafone's acquisition of a variety of other mobile telecommunications operations including Mannesmann and BT's Japanese interests highlights this fact. Similarly, the mergers that took place in the banking industry in the 1990s (for example Lloyds and TSB, HSBC and Midland Bank) also took place so that these organisations could cross-sell financial services products to an enlarged customer base. Manchester United's ventures in the Far East, and their partnership with Vodafone, are both attempts to widen their customer base beyond the UK and Western Europe. In politics, the voter market is finite. It comprises the electorate, which was around 43 million people in the UK in 2001. Thus, acquisition activity focuses on obtaining other parties' voters rather than growing the market generally, although, targeting non-voters could be considered the exception.

Customer retention is also an important strategic activity in marketing mass consumer services. Research has demonstrated that when a company retains its loyal customers it is more likely to be profitable than its competitors who do not (see Reichheld, 1993 and the discussion in Chapter 9). Thus, much of BT's marketing activity in the past has been to persuade customers to stay with BT or come back to using their services after defection. Retention programmes typically focus marketing activity on enhancing customer service satisfaction, rewarding loyalty, database management and sales promotion activities in mass commercial consumer services such as telecommunications, the airline industry and financial services.

Unfortunately for democracy, consumer involvement in political campaigning is limited and declining due to the limited voter turnout at elections and the consistently declining membership of political parties in the UK (Ware, 1995). This makes the introduction of customer retention and acquisition techniques all the more important, since the levels of membership and activism have an effect on election results (Seyd and Whiteley, 1992). The implication is that the voter needs to be made to feel more involved in the political process. This may demonstrate a need for the use of relationship marketing methods in political campaigning. Similarly, football clubs should strive to maximise their brand equity as they rely disproportionately on season ticket holders who demonstrate the greatest loyalty.

The previous section demonstrated the diverse range of publics with which a political party and a football club must communicate in order to ensure the effective distribution of their services. However, in each case, both organisations have supporters that may be more or less inclined to participate in their activities. Tomlinson et al. (1995, p. 27) stated that sport spectators are far from homogeneous. For example, in football, one can distinguish between regular and less frequent spectators (Barn and Baines, 1998). In comparison, although political markets have frequently been segmented (for example using geopartisan, geodemographic, lifestyle bases), segmentation of the electorate is arguably an unethical activity since election procedures now provide for universal suffrage. That said, segmentation methods can reasonably be used for customer acquisition and retention purposes in determining which voters are most likely to receive, and be persuaded by, party policies and arguments.

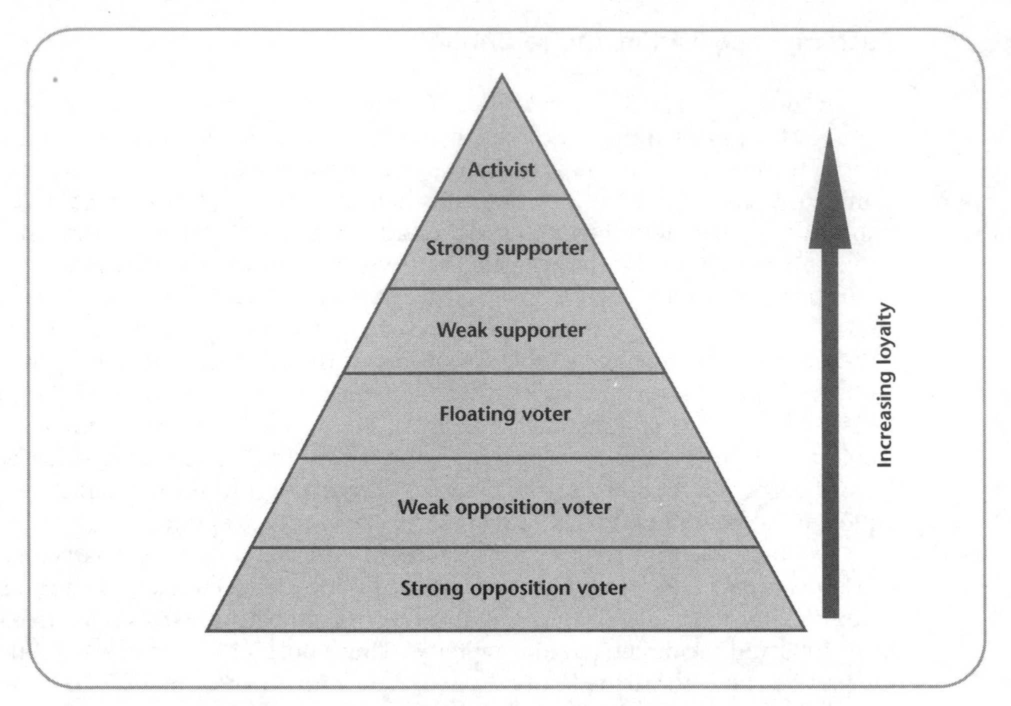

Figure 11.6 The political relationship pyramid

Targeting certain types of supporters offers several advantages. A football club, or a political party, is able to commit its limited resources more efficiently. It is also more able to spot opportunities if it defines segments of the market that are more likely to contribute greater revenue (in the case of the football club) or are more likely to vote (for a political party). In a highly competitive market, the inability to identify and develop market segments has been said to lead to a failure to achieve organisational objectives (Yorke, 1983, p. 100). Egan (1999) believes that paying too much attention to voters may actually heighten the disappointments they feel about a party's past performance. Football supporters can also become disillusioned if they think that football clubs are trying to exploit them. A large number of Manchester United fans voted against its takeover by BSkyB, part of the Murdoch media empire, because they felt that they would have to pay higher prices at the gate. Figures 11.6 and 11.7 illustrate the pyramidal nature of football and political party support. Figure 11.6 indicates the different stages of loyalty through which a voter may progress. For instance, activists delivering campaign material within constituencies demonstrate the greatest level of support and loyalty. They also make telemarketing calls (for research, fund-raising and get out the vote purposes) and canvass voters in local areas (usually for get out the vote efforts but also for voter identification for later targeting either by direct mail or telephone). Political parties generally target floating voters (who are unsure of which party they will vote for) and weak opposition voters in parts of the country where they need the support most.

In Figure 11.7, season ticket holders who attend home games and pay for their tickets upfront represent football supporters with the greatest loyalty. This provides the club with a significant cash flow. Thus, football clubs should make it their priority to encourage fans to become season ticket holders, perhaps through the provision of

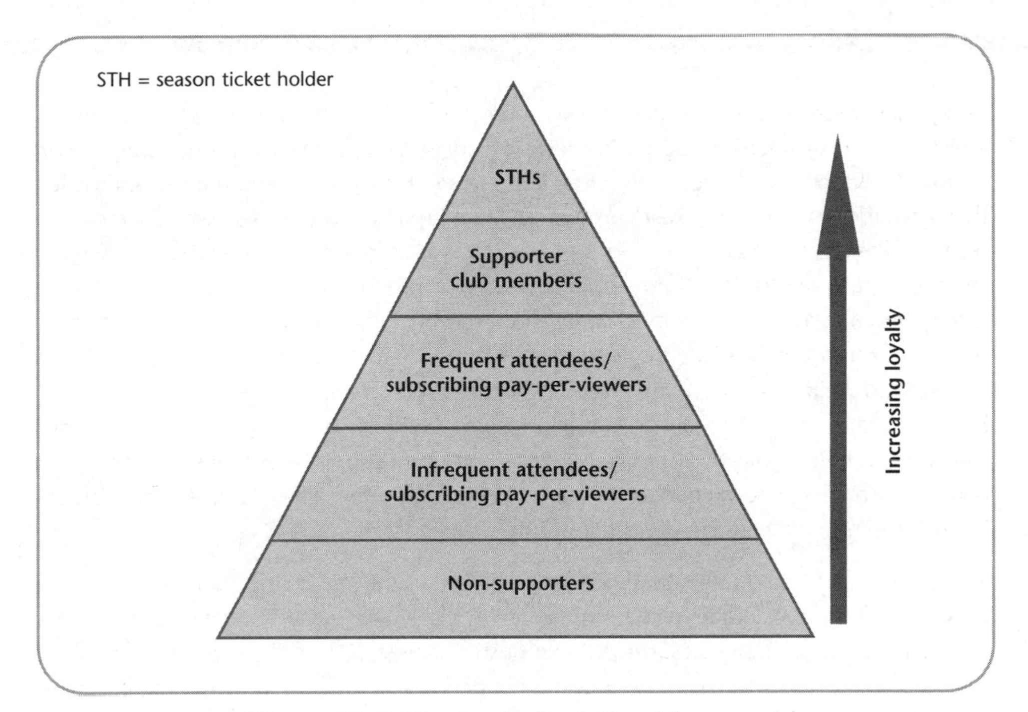

Figure 11.7 The football relationship pyramid

travel incentives, the ability to sell tickets for matches they cannot attend and through customer loyalty programmes generally. Less frequent attendees should be encouraged to become more frequent attendees and research undertaken to determine where and how this is possible.

The pyramidal diagrams illustrate how both football and political party's supporters can be segmented by their loyalty to their respective organisations. This process could be regarded as segmenting consumers on the basis of benefits sought, since season tickets holders and activists require different offerings from infrequent attendees and floating voters and demonstrate different levels of loyalty. In each case, the segmentation is both behavioural (in that supporters attend more matches and political activists distribute more leaflets) and attitudinal (in that they relate more to the party and the team).

SUMMARY

Football clubs and political parties essentially offer mass consumer services just as the airline and financial services industries do. However, they rely on the mass media to distribute their products rather than simply communicating the benefits of using or not using their products. Such organisations often have substantial numbers of customers, which can be considered to be a considerable asset in itself as it facilitates the cross-selling of other products and services. However, in the case of the politics and football industries, they are differentiated from their commercial counterparts in the sense that they are often reliant on relatively small marketing budgets, short promotional campaigns, highly regulated competitive structures, an ephemeral service product and, often, a resistance to developing a market orientation. Despite this, organisations that can easily distribute their service through the mass media need to recognise the importance of generating strong relationships with media organisations, either through strategic alliances or informal or formal partnership agreements. This allows organisations operating in mass-mediated markets to communicate with their consumers and supporters more effectively. In contrast, traditional consumer service organisations are more likely to use media organisations to communicate the benefits of using their services.

This chapter has attempted to highlight how important the distribution and communication components of the marketing mix are in these two relatively new mass consumer service contexts. In both cases, these two industries have traditionally been highly product oriented. A movement towards further market orientation will probably require emphasis in marketing activity on the service components of the marketing mix: people, process and physical evidence.

Questions for discussion

1. What is the function of the mass media in the financial services market? Is it used to distribute the product or communicate its benefits?
2. What are the major publics for a telecommunications company? What is the nature of the relationship with each of these publics?
3. Outline what the different elements of the marketing mix are for a public university in the UK.
4. Draw a relationship pyramid for a major national cancer charity. Explain the nature of the loyalty of these customers/consumers/supporters.

References

Baines, P R (2001), Marketing and Political Campaigning in the US and the UK: What Can the UK Political Parties Learn for the Development of a Campaign Management Process Model?, unpublished PhD thesis, Manchester School of Management, Manchester, UK

Baines, P R and Egan, J (2001), 'Marketing and Political Campaigning: Mutually Exclusive or Exclusively Mutual?', *Qualitative Market Research*, **4**(1): 25–34

Baines, P R Lewis, B and Ingham, B (1999), 'Exploring the Positioning Process in Political Campaigning', *Journal of Communication Management*, **3**(4): 325–36

Baines, P R, Brennan, R and Egan, J (2001), 'Structural Characteristics of Political Markets and their Strategic Implications', *Proceedings of the AMA Summer Educator's Conference*, August, Washington, DC

Barn, S S and Baines, P R (1998), 'Football Marketing: Towards an Hypothetical Paradigm', in *Proceedings of the Academy of Marketing Conference*, CD-ROM edition, July, Sheffield: Sheffield Hallam University

Boulding, C (1992), 'Pitch Pickings', *Marketing Week*, 3 July, pp. 22–5

Clark, G (1998), 'Will Business Bankrupt the Beautiful Game?', *Independent on Sunday*, 12 July, p. 3

Deloitte and Touche (2000), *Annual Review of Football Finance*, Manchester: Deloitte and Touche

Dignam, C (1996), 'Football Brands that Net Profit', *Marketing*, 4 January, p. 8

Egan, J (1999), 'Political Marketing: Lessons from the Mainstream', *Journal of Marketing Management*, **15**(6): 495–504

Evans, A, James, T and Tomes, A (1996), 'Marketing in UK Sports Organisations', *The Service Industries Journal*, **16**(2): 207–22

Henneberg, S C (1997), 'Research in Political Marketing – An Overview', in Henneberg, S C and O'Shaughnessy, N J (eds) *Readings in Political Marketing*, New York: Praegar, pp. 777–83

Hillsdon, M (2000), 'Own Goal?', *Business Life*, pp. 39–40, 42

Kotler, P and Kotler, N (1981), 'Business Marketing for Political Candidates', *Campaigns and Elections*, Summer, pp. 24–33

Kotler, P and Levy, S J (1969), 'Broadening the Concept of Marketing', *Journal of Marketing*, **33**(1): 10–15

Lock, A and Harris, P (1996), 'Political Marketing – Vive La Différence!', *European Journal of Marketing*, **30**(10/11): 21–31

Mason, D S (1999), 'What is the Sports Product and Who Buys It? The Marketing of Professional Sports Leagues', *European Journal of Marketing*, **33**(3/4): 402–18

Meenaghan, T and O'Sullivan, P (1999), 'Playpower – Sports Meets Marketing', *European Journal of Marketing*, **33**(3/4): 241–9

Newman, B I (1988), 'A Services Oriented Strategic Framework for Politicians', in *Proceedings of the 7th Annual Decision Science Institute Western Regional Conference*, Honolulu, HI: Decision Science Institute, pp. 192–5

O'Shaughnessy, N (1999), 'Political Marketing and Political Propaganda', in Newman, B I (ed.) *Handbook of Political Marketing*, Newbury Park, CA: Sage, pp. 725–40

Parker, K and Stuart, T (1997), 'The West Ham Syndrome', *Journal of the Market Research Society*, **39**(3): 509–17

Reichheld, F F (1993), 'Loyalty-based Management', *Harvard Business Review*, March–April

Scammell, M (1994), 'The Phenomenon of Political Marketing: the Thatcher Contribution', *Contemporary Record*, **8**(1): 23–44

Seyd, P and Whiteley, P F (1992), *Labour's Grass Roots: The Politics of Party Membership*, Oxford: Clarendon Press

Shama, A (1975), 'The Marketing of Political Candidates', *Journal of the Academy of Marketing Science*, **4**(4):766–7

Shilbury, D (1989), 'Characteristics of Sport Marketing: Developing Trends' *The ACHPER National Journal*, 123: 21–4

Sweeney, W R (1995), 'The Principles of Planning', in Thurber, J A and Nelson, C J (eds) *Campaigns and Elections American Style*, Oxford: Westview Press, pp. 14–29

Tomlinson, M, Buttle, F and Moores, B (1995), 'The Fan as Customer: Customer Service in Sports Marketing', *Journal of Hospitality and Leisure Management*, **3**(1): 19–36

Ware, A (1995), *Political Parties and Party Systems*, Oxford: Oxford University Press

Worcester, R and Mortimore, R (1999), *Explaining Labour's Landslide*, London: Politico's

Wring, D (1997), 'Reconciling Marketing with Political Science: Theories of Political Marketing', in *The Proceedings of the 1997 Academy of Marketing Conference*, Manchester: Manchester Metropolitan University, pp. 1131–44

Yorke, D (1983), 'The Definition of Market Segments for Leisure Centre Services: Theory and Practice', *European Journal of Marketing*, **18**(2): 100–13

chapter twelve

Analysing Strategic Marketing Case Studies

Learning objectives

By reading this chapter you will learn:

- The role of case studies in studying strategic marketing
- The importance of clear problem identification to successful case analysis
- A series of steps that can be adopted to make case analysis effective
- How to prepare successful oral presentations and written reports on case studies.

INTRODUCTION

Strategic marketing poses particular challenges to the student. Prominent among these is the fact that it is unlikely that you will have the opportunity, while studying the course, to explore the new concepts that you have learnt or try out your new skills in a real world organisation. There are certain aspects of management and marketing learning that can be put into practice as you learn them. For example, you can implement new ideas that you learn about self-management, such as the effective use of time and allocating priorities to tasks. If your course offers you the opportunity to work in small groups, then you can explore ideas about group dynamics and seek to improve your teamworking skills. However, most students are probably not in a position to take the ideas presented in the foregoing chapters and immediately apply them in practice. It is for this reason that we regard the strategic marketing case studies as an indispensable part of the book.

Through the case studies, you will gain an insight into the complexities of strategic marketing in practice, and you will have the opportunity to apply the tools of strategic marketing to real world situations, when you are presented with strategic dilemmas and are challenged to come up with workable solutions. You may find an analogy from medical education helpful in understanding the place of case studies in the learning process. Medical students, quite obviously, cannot be allowed to diagnose illnesses or prescribe medical interventions until they are far advanced in their studies and have gained clinical experience under the supervision of a medical professional. Extensive use is made of case studies to introduce medical students to the kind of problem that they will encounter in practice, to allow them to sharpen their diagnostic skills before trying 'the real thing'. In strategic marketing, we use case studies for very much the same reasons, to allow you to sharpen your analytical skills, to test out your 'diagnoses' and your 'prescriptions' for strategic marketing problems, before moving on to 'the real thing'.

In addition, case studies provide an excellent way to practise many of the communications skills associated with marketing management. Many careers in the field of marketing, such as field sales, public relations, brand and product management, marketing research and consultancy, require excellent skills in presenting information, both orally and in writing. Therefore, towards the end of this chapter, once we have discussed the process of case study analysis, we provide some guidance on the communications skills that can be developed by preparing formal reports and giving formal presentations, based on the cases.

STRATEGIC MARKETING CASE STUDIES

Case studies are descriptions of business situations that require the student to identify a business problem, usually with the aim of conducting relevant analysis and suggesting a solution. All of the cases in this book concern real marketing situations that were faced by real organisations, although in one or two cases some names have been changed to preserve the anonymity of the companies and individual managers involved.

The case study gives you an opportunity to develop skills in problem identification, market analysis and decision-making in a simulation of the strategic marketing process. Most people taking courses in business or management will encounter case studies in a variety of different areas, such as operations management, accounting and finance, and human resource management. This book is concerned with strategic marketing, so the main emphasis is on major decisions concerning the organisation's allocation of marketing resources in order to meet the challenges presented by the competitive and macroenvironments. However, when tackling such case studies, it is important to remember that marketing does not take place in a vacuum, but has to be integrated with other aspects of the management of organisations. You may find that your analysis of a case study throws up interesting issues relating to the management of operations, money, or people. In earlier chapters of the book, we have often remarked upon overlaps and links between strategic marketing decisions and other aspects of management. For example, in Chapter 9, Reichheld (1996) linked customer loyalty, employee loyalty and shareholder loyalty, while Grönroos (1991) emphasised the importance of part-time marketers in service industries. Although it may not be appropriate to analyse such issues in depth for a marketing class, it is important to demonstrate that you understand the wider business context within which marketing activity takes place. If you are already an experienced manager, you will recognise that, in reality, management problems tend not to come neatly packaged as 'finance', 'human resources', or 'marketing'!

The underlying problem in the case studies will not be defined. It is up to you to identify the problem. What you will find in the case study is a description of a marketing situation, with a certain amount of information about the problem situation. Just as in real life, you should expect the information to be incomplete in some areas, irrelevant in others, and perhaps excessive in still other areas. The information in the case study may well be ambiguous, capable of interpretation in two or more different ways. Case studies are usually written in narrative form. They are not organised analytically for your convenience, nor are they necessarily organised chronologically, with the various events described following each other in a logical pattern. In other words, it is your job to organise the facts in the case. Sometimes you will find that the problem situation is described in the terms of one of the actors in the case study, but it is up to you to separate fact from opinion. It is a fact of managerial life that you will encounter people with strong opinions, who may well contradict the opinions of others who appear equally well informed. For example, in the 'BriCol Engineering' case study, you will find three close colleagues, each with access to much the same information, all disagreeing with each other about the way forward for their company.

To analyse and learn successfully from case studies, requires you to involve yourself in them. In some cases, you are allocated a particular role, such as that of a consultant, or a marketing manager. Try to think about the case situation as though you actually filled that position, and apply the concepts and techniques of strategic marketing from the point of view of that role. You will find that while the nature of the problems underlying the case studies in the book is varied, there are common decision-making approaches that can be applied. Perhaps the most important lesson to learn is that the problem should be clearly defined, and the data carefully inspected, before more detailed analysis is carried out and proposals for action emerge.

LEARNING FROM CASE STUDIES

Much of the responsibility for learning from case studies rests with you. If you are studying this book as part of a formal course, then you will benefit from a tutor who can guide you by identifying appropriate cases to use at different stages and for different topics within your strategic marketing course. Where case studies are discussed in class, the tutor will encourage participation and the evaluation of alternative proposals, but will not usually provide an 'answer'. The tutor generally facilitates a case study class by encouraging people to summarise the discussion at appropriate points and leading the class through the following general process:

- What can we learn from this case study?
- What generalisations emerge from the case that can be carried forward to other cases?
- Was the approach we adopted to this case productive? Could it have been improved?
- What marketing concepts and techniques helped us to understand and analyse this case?

In the early stages of a strategic marketing course, when you have only limited experience of case analysis, you may feel a sense of frustration. Case discussions can seem disorganised and often fail to reach a clear conclusion. When dealing with strategic marketing case studies, the tutor will normally refrain from providing a 'solution', on the grounds that there is no single correct answer to a strategic marketing case study. This may be contrasted with the kinds of case study that are used, at an introductory level, in accounting and finance, for example. Such cases usually do have an answer, and you know whether you got it right or wrong. However, even in accounting and finance, as the cases become more complex and a better simulation of real world decision-making, it becomes ever-more difficult to provide a single right answer. In marketing you are unlikely ever to have the luxury of knowing that your proposed solution was clearly right. Even if you can follow up the case study company and establish that 'their' solution was very much what you had suggested yourself, this does not guarantee that it was 'right'.

As you progress through your strategic marketing course, you will find that the process of case analysis becomes easier and seems much better organised. You will learn to tolerate the fact that there is no single right answer, and will find that you can present your own conclusions with great conviction, while understanding that others may come to different conclusions on the basis of the same data. Indeed, these are some of the very skills that the case study method of instruction is designed to teach you. The skills of developing a feasible solution, presenting it to a professional audience and defending it against reasoned attack are some of the most important skills for a marketing manager to possess.

CASE STUDY ANALYSIS

Figure 12.1 provides an overview of a process that can be used to approach case study analysis. In fact, what we see in Figure 12.1 is a 'generic problem-solving process' that can be applied to almost any management problem. Many large organisations have their own internal version of this kind of process, often adapted to the particular circumstances of the business. Two important aspects of this kind of problem-solving process need to be explained before we consider the process in more detail.

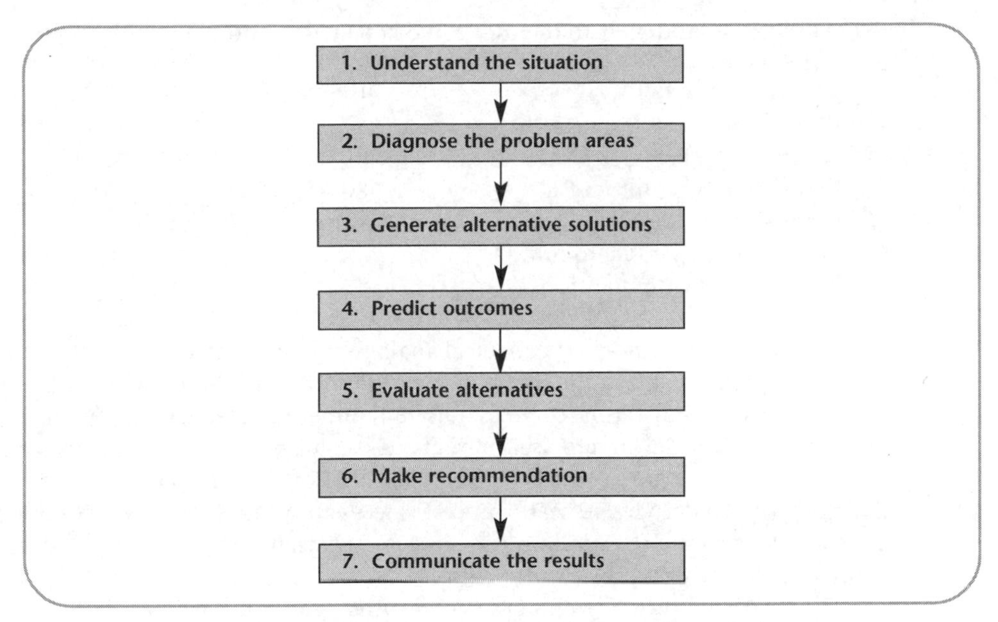

Figure 12.1 A process for case study analysis

Source: Adapted from Easton (1992)

First, careful problem diagnosis and analysis precedes any attempt to formulate a solution. This avoids wasted effort being spent on formulating solutions to the wrong problem. For example, suppose that we identify 'declining market share' as an important symptom. There may be many underlying causes for this symptom, such as an obsolescent product, poor promotional support or inadequate distribution channels, to name but three. Clearly, the appropriate solution will depend on the correct identification of the underlying problem. Careful problem diagnosis and analysis is a useful discipline both for students and practitioners of strategic marketing. It avoids the risk of jumping to a conclusion without taking into account all the facts.

Second, the process assumes that more than one alternative will be considered before a final recommendation is made. In most management situations, and certainly in most strategic marketing situations, there will be more than one plausible course of action. Suppose that the market share symptom in the paragraph above was found to be the result of poor distribution channels, then we might consider whether to terminate our existing distribution contracts and work with new distributors, or we might devise a training programme to improve distributor performance. There are pros and cons to these two options. They need to be weighed against each other before a decision is made. Once they have been weighed against each other, it should be possible to recommend one option as superior to the alternatives, and to justify why.

We now consider the case study analysis process in a little more detail.

Understand the situation and diagnose the problem areas

As a first step, read the case study as though it were simply 'a story'. This will enable you to get an overall impression of the marketing situation. At the second read through, you should start to identify some key factors and make notes. Consider the following issues:

- Who is the decision-maker?
- What are the key facts?
- What are the symptoms?
- What is the underlying problem that is causing the symptoms?
- What solutions come to mind?
- What are the case questions?

It may help to return to the medical analogy that we used earlier in the chapter in order to explain the key difference between symptoms and underlying problems. To a doctor, physical indicators such as raised temperature, aches and pains, fatigue, blurred vision and so on, are useful inputs to the diagnostic process. However, many different diseases share similar symptoms. The doctor's aim is to use the symptoms to diagnose the underlying disease process successfully, in order to recommend the appropriate treatment. Similarly, in case study analysis we should try to avoid confusing the 'symptoms' with the 'disease'.

The following process will assist in ensuring that you have uncovered an underlying problem rather than simply a list of symptoms. Once you have a preliminary view of the underlying problem, test it with these steps:

- *Relate to symptoms.* Does your problem as stated match the list of symptoms that you developed earlier? Does your problem statement explain all or most of the symptoms? If not, revise it until it does.
- *Determine what has changed.* A problem usually occurs because something in the organisation or in the environment has changed. List the changes. Could one of these be responsible for the symptoms observed? If so, revise your problem statement.
- *Relate to intuitive solution.* Compare your first 'off the top of your head' solution with the problem statement. Does the solution meet the problem that you defined? If not, does it help you towards redefining the problem statement?
- *Ask – what is the cause?* The problem definition must deal with the underlying problem rather than with the symptoms alone.
- *Relate to case questions.* Compare your problem definition with the case questions. Does your problem statement incorporate these questions?
- Write a final version of the problem and note the evidence that you found that will justify your problem definition.

Several of the analytical tools described earlier in the book will facilitate the process of problem definition. For example, SWOT analysis, sales variance analysis, portfolio analysis and environmental analysis may well help to clarify the exact nature of the problem to be addressed.

One further word of warning – beware of the highlighter pen! Reading through a case and marking the 'key sections' with a highlighter can give a sense of security that is almost always false. It is wrong to think that at a first, or even a second reading, you can identify the key facts, opinions or actions in a complex case study. Furthermore, once you have marked the case study with a highlighter you will find it difficult to read the case again with an open mind, even if you subsequently decide that your first thoughts were quite wrong. The same can apply to making marginal notes on the case study. Once you have written (possibly in red ink!) 'this is the key problem' at a point in the margin, you will probably be reluctant to change your mind, even though subsequent analysis may create new insight.

Generate alternative solutions and predict outcomes

Using the facts and data from the case study, identify the plausible solutions to the problem you have identified. This part of the process is designed to answer the question 'what could we do?' not 'what should we do?'.

There are a number of techniques that can be used to assist in the process of generating solutions. Probably the most important source of ideas, in dealing with strategic marketing case studies, will be the application of the analytical tools that we have discussed in the earlier chapters of the book. For example, SWOT analysis, product or customer portfolio analysis, Porter's generic competitive strategies, Ansoff's growth vector matrix, relationship building strategies or Internet-based strategies are some of the ideas that are likely to be valuable in creating solutions to the strategic marketing problems you will find in the case studies.

Going beyond strategic marketing techniques, one may draw upon relevant experience or knowledge to generate alternative solutions, or one can employ specially designed creative thinking techniques. Relevant experience or knowledge comes from having encountered similar business problems before, although not necessarily in the same industry. Prior experience and knowledge can, of course, be very valuable in assisting the process of identifying alternatives. For example, if the case study concerns doing business with China, then someone with prior knowledge of the Chinese business environment and culture will certainly be able to make a useful contribution. There is a risk, however, of relying too much upon prior experience, and failing to recognise the contextual differences in a particular situation. A simple example – if our expert on Chinese business practices gained that experience in Taiwan, how useful is that knowledge to us in dealing with a case study (or a real business problem) in China?

Finally, creative thinking techniques may assist the process of generating alternatives. Probably the oldest and best known is brainstorming. This is particularly useful for group case study analysis. The basic principles of brainstorming are:

- Postpone judgement
- Freewheel
- Hitchhike
- Quantity breeds quality.

The key focus at first is on the generation of a lot of ideas, and to build upon the ideas of other members of the group (hitchhiking). In the initial phase, criticism of ideas is prohibited. Only later, once a substantial list of ideas has been created, can some evaluation begin. Usually a number of the more ridiculous ideas will be discarded quickly, leaving a shorter list to which more thoughtful evaluative methods can be applied.

Evaluate alternatives

The preceding steps in the process have generated a number of possible solutions. The evaluation process is about selecting one or more solutions to be recommended for implementation. The essence of the process is to identify a set of criteria against which the alternatives will be assessed, and then to consider each alternative against all the criteria. The criteria to be used in the evaluation process will vary from case to case, but are likely to include a number of recurrent themes:

- To what extent will this alternative enable the firm to meet its goals?
- What are the direct and indirect costs of this alternative?
- How quickly will this solution take effect?
- How likely is it that this solution will work?
- How acceptable is the solution to the various stakeholders identified in the case study?

A number of the concepts discussed earlier in the book may assist in the process of evaluation. For example, gap analysis will assist in evaluating the extent to which a solution meets the firm's goals, and value-based marketing provides an evaluative approach that is suitable where the achievement of shareholder value is the overriding concern. Although discounted cash-flow analysis is unlikely to be used directly as an analytical method in a strategic marketing case study, the concept that underlies discounted cash-flow analysis – the time value of money – could be very valuable in assessing alternative solutions. If there is no other way of choosing between alternatives, then prefer the solution that generates positive cash flows quickest.

Make a final recommendation

Almost invariably, you are asked to conclude your analysis of a case study with a recommendation. It is not enough simply to outline the various alternatives, with their pros and cons, and leave it at that. You should select your preferred alternative and forecast the likely outcome of adopting this decision, in whatever terms seem appropriate, given your definition of the problem. In proposing a solution, take into account the problems which might be encountered in implementing it (for example resistance from consumers to a brand repositioning, or the likely response of a key competitor to a price change). One of the most common mistakes in the presentation of case study reports is failure to relate the recommendations to the analysis of the facts of the case. Take care to explain how your recommendations emerge logically from your analysis.

Communicating the results of case study analysis

One of the most important skills that the case study method allows you to practise and improve is the communication of your findings and recommendations through a written report or an oral presentation. One way of looking at this process is as an exercise in selling – selling yourself and selling your ideas. It is not enough simply to believe that you have the best analysis. Even if this is true, a poor sales job could spoil all your hard work. It is definitely worthwhile putting in the effort required to produce a well-written and convincing report, or to develop a coherent and persuasive presentation. In order to do this, aim to achieve the following:

1. Your recommended decision must be presented clearly and succinctly.
2. The logic by which you arrived at your recommendation must be made clear.
3. The recommendation should be supported by facts developed from the case. You must do more than simply list the case study facts after each element of the problem. The data must be intelligently manipulated. Calculations, tables, graphs and diagrams should be used to bring out the significance of the facts.

The above three points apply regardless of whether you are writing a report or making an oral presentation. The objectives of both methods of communication are the same, namely to gain acceptance for your arguments and recommendations. Where you have to give a formal oral presentation, there are a number of further points to bear in mind.

ORAL PRESENTATIONS

There are five key aspects of the oral presentation to be considered. These are:

- the use of visual aids
- effective presentation style
- question handling
- timekeeping
- presentation feedback.

We will consider each of these in turn.

Visual aids are a standard part of the armoury of business executives making presentations, and should also be employed in case study presentations to enliven proceedings and give a professional feel. Probably the most common medium in use for business presentations today is computer projection (often referred to as a 'Powerpoint presentation' because Microsoft Powerpoint is the leading commercial software package, but there are other similar packages such as Freelance Graphics from Lotus). Plastic transparencies for overhead projection are, of course, still in use, although increasingly replaced by computer projection. Flip charts and whiteboards can be useful for small-scale presentations, but they are more appropriately used for recording group meetings and brainstorming sessions than for actually making a presentation.

Computer-generated visual aids have many advantages:

- Computer-generated graphics and text can be printed directly on to transparencies, or transferred from paper via a photocopier.
- Good software for the production of overhead transparencies is readily available for all popular personal computer formats – modern word-processing packages have a wide variety of font sizes, graphics packages and desk-top publishing packages provide huge creative scope, and spreadsheet packages enable data to be easily converted into charts and diagrams.

- The medium is flexible enough to be used with a small audience for an informal presentation, or with an audience of hundreds.
- Many sales executives, consultants and marketing professionals carry their presentations on floppy disks and output their pre-prepared slides directly to the overhead projector on the client's premises. If you plan on doing this, just check that they have the right hardware and software before you arrive!

However, despite improvements in the supporting technology, the basic principles of designing good visual aids remain much the same. They should contain a limited amount of text, or an easily legible chart or diagram. The information should be well organised, to help the audience understand your argument. Well-designed, logical visual aids that are carefully handwritten will be much more effective than poorly designed visual aids produced on the latest technology.

Presentation style develops with practice. Those who are inexperienced at giving presentations, regardless of age, are almost always nervous. If you have not had much experience of giving presentations, then you will find that rehearsals really do help. When rehearsing your presentation, take care to simulate the real thing as closely as possible, with a friendly audience if one is available. Time your presentation, to make sure that it is of the right duration. You will probably find, for the first few presentations you give, that you need to refer to notes. A method which many people find effective is to put key words for each section of their presentation on to a postcard. Cards are easier to handle than paper when you are feeling nervous in front of an audience. At all costs resist the temptation that you may feel to read a pre-prepared presentation verbatim. This method is guaranteed to bore your audience. It prevents you from achieving any eye contact with the audience or conveying enthusiasm for the subject.

The ability to handle questions in front of an audience is another valuable managerial skill that can be developed through case study presentations. Just as it is your responsibility to convey enthusiasm, so it is your responsibility to encourage the audience to ask questions or make comments. It should be possible to predict at least some of these questions in advance – where it took you a long time to understand a particular issue in the case study, it is likely that other people may have the same problem. All presenters have the choice of whether or not to allow questions during the course of the presentation. Unless you are confident of your presentational abilities, only allow questions once you have completed your presentation. If you have carried out your case study analysis effectively, you will find that answering questions is stimulating and enjoyable. You should, as a minimum, expect and prepare for questions which challenge your understanding of the underlying marketing problem, which suggest alternative solutions to the one which you recommend, and which challenge the basis for your own recommended solution.

Good timekeeping is an important part of making a presentation. You should know how long you have available for your presentation, and whether or not this includes time for questions. Only with practice will you gain a feel for how long a presentation will take. Even experienced presenters often find that they are trying to pack too much presentation into too little time. Having too much to say, rather than too little, is the most common mistake to make. Whatever you do, make sure that you keep to the time allotted for the presentation!

The final aspect of making presentations that we consider is the giving and receiving of feedback. Once again, here is an important opportunity to practise real managerial skills in the simulated case study environment. The competent marketing manager should be capable of providing constructive feedback on a presentation, assisting the presenter to learn and improve, and should also be eager to receive constructive feedback in order to improve performance. In addition to comments on the quality of the ideas that you present, you may also receive feedback on the effectiveness of your presentation style. This feedback may come from a tutor, or other members of your class. Done well, this feedback is an invaluable method of improving your performance for the future. If you are already a manager, the benefits of this should be obvious. If you are a student intending to embark on a management career, bear in mind that an increasing number of employers value (and sometimes even test at interview) good communication ability. You should also be able to provide useful feedback to your colleagues in class. The elementary rule to bear in mind is 'do as you would be done by', in other words provide feedback to others in the same way that you expect them to treat you. Table 12.1 provides further guidance on how to assess and provide feedback on case study presentations.

Table 12.1 Providing constructive feedback on a case study presentation

Principles of providing feedback

1. Mention the good aspects of the presentation as well as the weaknesses.
2. Phrase criticisms positively, so do not just say that something was done badly, rather, explain how it could have been improved.
3. Use tact and common sense. For example, if the presenter was making the presentation in a language other than their mother tongue, or if they were clearly suffering from severe stage fright, then take these factors into consideration.
4. Apply the principle 'do as you would be done by' – treat the presenter with courtesy and respect.

Criteria for evaluating presentations

1. Has the presenter successfully conveyed a sense of enthusiasm for the subject?
2. Did the presenter speak clearly to the audience? (Weaknesses to look out for are talking while looking at the screen with back turned to the audience, and extensive reading from a prepared script.)
3. Was the audience interested in what the presenter was saying, or were there some signs of boredom?
4. Was the presentation clearly structured, so that you always knew how particular points related to the overall structure of the presentation?
5. Was the presentation delivered audibly and clearly, and at a speed that you found comfortable (allowing for language difficulties or physical impairments)?
6. If visual aids were used, did they conform to the standards of good design, and were they clearly relevant to the subject matter of the presentation?
7. If visual aids were not used, was there a clear reason why not? Might the presentation have been better if visual aids had been used?
8. Did the presentation run to time?
9. Were you invited to contribute by asking questions?
10. Were the answers to the questions clear and relevant?

WRITTEN REPORTS

Just as the delivery of a case study presentation can be, and perhaps should be, treated as preparation for giving management presentations, so writing a case study report can be treated as preparation for writing management reports. As with management report writing, it is important to be clear who is the intended audience for your work, and what the 'brief' is. Your brief is the set of instructions that you are responding to. It is an expression that is used extensively in marketing and more widely in management – for example a market research brief is the set of instructions from a client, to which the research company responds with a proposal. You need to establish whether you have a clear-cut brief or not. The questions that we have appended to the case studies in this book make it fairly clear what is expected. However, many instructors in the field of strategic marketing argue that it is not appropriate to present a clear-cut brief, since one of the aims behind engaging with strategic marketing case studies is to allow the student to work out for him or herself what the important issues are.

Clearly, if you are using this book as part of a structured course, then the immediate audience for your report is the course instructor. However, in order to provide a better simulation of the managerial process of report writing, you may be asked to write for another audience. This can make a difference to your approach. Here are some examples:

- You are writing as the marketing manager of the case study company and your report will be considered by all the directors of the firm
- You are writing as an external strategy consultant to the company and your report will be considered by the marketing director
- You are writing as an external consultant appointed by a major shareholder of the company, to provide an objective view of the current market position and marketing strategy.

In the first case you are a specialist, writing for an audience who know the business but who probably have limited knowledge of professional marketing. In the second case, you can assume that your audience has extensive marketing knowledge and experience. In the third case, your audience may have neither extensive knowledge of the company nor professional marketing knowledge. Before starting to write the report, be clear whom the intended audience is, and take this into account in the writing process.

The normal structure for a written analysis of a case study is 'report format'. Report format uses a system of headings and subheadings to indicate the purpose of the sections within the document, and it is not unusual to use 'bullet points' or numbered lists in the text of a report (this differentiates a report from an essay – headings and lists are not used in an essay). There is no single, right way to structure a case study report. However, it is almost always helpful to develop the structure and headings of the report first, before working on the detail of the text. Easton (1992) has suggested that there are two characteristic approaches to report structure. The first is the more 'academic' approach, which consists of a careful discussion of the evidence and analysis in the early sections, culminating in the presentation of the conclusion (and possibly recommendations). The second is the more 'managerial' approach, which begins with a clear statement of the conclusions from the analysis, and then moves on in the later sections to justify that conclusion. Easton proposes that the 'academic' approach is appropriate for complex, analytical case studies, and the 'managerial' approach for simpler case situations. To this advice we would add another reminder that the brief and the audience for the report will affect your choice of structure. If the audience is looking for an easily digested report to inform them of the key issues in the case situation, then the 'managerial' approach will be preferable. However, if the audience is looking for a closely argued report containing substantial analysis, as the basis for making key strategic decisions, then the 'academic' approach is more suitable.

SUMMARY

Since few students will have the chance to practise their strategic marketing skills on a real organisation, case studies provide a valuable opportunity to test what you have learned in a realistic marketing situation. Case study analysis can be tackled using a problem-solving approach. This begins with the careful formulation of the underlying problem, moves on to the generation and evaluation of alternative solutions and, concludes with the selection of a preferred solution. The underlying problem must be differentiated from the symptoms that are used to diagnose it. Similar symptoms (such as loss of market share or unprofitable sales) can be the result of different underlying problems. The concepts and models of strategic marketing can be used to assist at all stages of the case analysis process. Case study presentations and reports provide the opportunity to practise important management communications skills. Whatever the medium of communication used, there must be a clear link from the problem diagnosed to the analysis that is conducted, and conclusions must be demonstrably based on evidence and analysis.

References

Easton, G (1992), *Learning from Case Studies*, 2nd edn, Hemel Hempstead: Prentice Hall

Grönroos, C (1991), *Strategic Management and Marketing in the Service Sector*, Lund: Studentlitteratur & Chartwell-Bratt

Reichheld, F F (1996), *The Loyalty Effect: The Hidden Force Behind Growth, Profits, and Lasting Value*, Boston, MA: Harvard Business School Press

part two

Case Studies

OVERVIEW OF THEMES IN CASE STUDIES AND READINGS

	Principal themes addressed									
Case studies and readings	The nature of strategic marketing	Understanding consumer behaviour	Understanding organisational buying behaviour	The competitive environment	The macro-environment	Strategic marketing analysis	Marketing strategy formulation	Relationship marketing strategies	e-Marketing strategies	Mass-mediated consumer services
1. British Telecommunications plc 'A': the strategic dilemma	✓			✓	✓					
2. British Telecommunications plc 'B': tomorrow the world?	✓			✓	✓					
3. Competition in the UK ice cream market	✓			✓		✓				
4. Fulham FC: strategic marketing for football clubs								✓		✓
5. Regaining the international market for British beef			✓			✓	✓	✓		
6. GlaxoSmithKline in South Africa					✓		✓			
7. Should UPS purchase the shuttle?			✓						✓	
8. News corporation in the British newspaper market					✓	✓	✓	✓		✓
9. A tale of two wine brands		✓				✓	✓			
10. BriCol Engineering Ltd			✓			✓	✓	✓		
11. Crisis in the European airline industry				✓	✓					
12. Internationalising the Chartered Institute of Marketing				✓						
13. Golden Arch Hotels							✓		✓	
14. Marketing Australia to the world		✓			✓	✓				
15. Trouble with the CPC100						✓				
1. Turnbull et al. (1996)			✓				✓	✓		
2. Sheth and Sisodia (1999)		✓	✓	✓			✓		✓	
3. Grönroos (1995)								✓		
4. White and Griffith (1997)	✓					✓	✓			
5. Doyle (2000)	✓					✓				

case study one

British Telecommunications plc 'A': The Strategic Dilemma

In his chairman's message of May 2001, Sir Christopher Bland explained to shareholders the extraordinary challenges that faced BT. Few could disagree with him that 'the past year has been one that no one with any involvement in the communications industry will ever forget'. The company's net debt had risen to £27.9 billion, described by the chairman himself as 'unsustainable'. Arrangements were in hand to demerge – that is, to float off as a separate quoted company – a large part of the business. Only a few weeks before BT had announced a £5.9 billion rights issue, and the chairman explained that BT would not be paying a dividend to shareholders at the end of the 2000/2001 financial year. Furthermore, the chairman's message was presented by a man who had only been recruited to BT one month before. Sir Iain Vallance, the former, long-standing chairman, had only recently ended his association with BT. In a brief statement recorded in the 2001 annual report, Sir Iain observed that: 'Nearly all BT shareholders are BT customers. And nearly all BT employees are BT shareholders. That exceptional association between owners, employees and customers has been a core strength of the organisation since it moved into the private sector some 17 years ago.' Optimistic words from a man who had presided over an unprecedented decline in the company's share price; a company that was about to post its first ever operating loss.

To the casual observer, all this must have seemed quite strange. Everyone knew that BT was a money-making machine, with a phone in just about every British home, a stake in all the most exciting areas of the information technology revolution, and partnerships with several of the biggest players in the digital economy. Yet, for the first time, in 2001, the BT Group reported a loss – of £336 million. Compared to a profit of £3198 million in 2000, and £3474 million in 1999, this was more than a little shocking. To begin to understand the problems facing BT in 2001, we need to understand the origins of the company as a public sector organisation, and the way in which it has tried over nearly two decades to transform itself into a market-oriented commercial operation, capable of competing with the best in the world.

BT'S ORIGINS

Remarkable changes took place in the UK telecommunications industry in the 1980s. Prior to 1981 the monopoly supplier of all telephone services was the Post Office (Telecommunications Division). British Telecommunications plc was created in 1981 as a nationalised enterprise separate from the Post Office, and subsequently, in 1984, the first block of shares was sold to the public. Competition was introduced to the industry at about the same time. Although BT retained much the largest share of the UK market for telephone calls, competitors quickly made inroads in such areas as the sale of terminal apparatus (such as phones), the supply of value-added services (such as electronic mail), and the provision of in-company telephone networks for major corporate users. Even in the ordinary telephone call business, Mercury Communications Ltd (a subsidiary of Cable & Wireless) was beginning to represent a real threat by 1990.

In the 1980s, BT could live fairly comfortably with its new competitors because the economy as a whole was growing rapidly. Even though BT's market share declined steadily, the business grew at an impressive rate because the total market expanded even more rapidly than the economy at large. Accustomed to almost effortless growth in turnover and profits, BT suffered when the British economy went into a recession in the early 1990s. Just as competition was beginning to bite harder, so the rate of total market growth slowed down. The assumption, formerly made by customers, employees, shareholders and quite possibly managers of the company, that BT was invincible was thrown into doubt for the first time.

Throughout the 1980s, BT and Mercury enjoyed a duopoly in the supply of basic telecommunications services. Nobody else was allowed to compete, because the UK government decided not to issue any more licences for public telecommunications operation. While shareholders were unlikely to complain about the relatively effortless profits that flowed from a near-monopoly provider of an essential service, some wiser heads did wonder whether such a cosy arrangement was the best way to prepare the UK telecommunications industry, and its champion BT, for an era of global competition. Business and technology analysts talked about the concept of 'convergence'. Telephone exchanges increasingly resembled computers. Telecommunications traffic was increasingly digital. Computer system designers increasingly talked about distributed systems, with multiple processors connected by communications links. So the telecommunications and computing industries were expected to 'converge', with the information technology industry as the offspring. How would a former public phone company like BT, used to statutory protection and easy market domination, deal with competition in the global information technology industry?

BT'S EARLY STRATEGIC DEVELOPMENT

Business portfolio

As a public enterprise, BT's main international interests lay in the exchange of telephone and telex calls between the UK and foreign countries. A range of other international services was provided, such as international private circuits (telephone lines rented from telephone operators for the use of a single organisation), international data services and videoconferencing, but none of these generated anything like the revenue of international telephony. In virtually all cases international services were provided under a 'correspondent agreement' with BT's overseas partners. BT concentrated its marketing efforts on the UK, leaving the management of demand in other countries to the local national or international telecommunications carrier (described as 'cartel practices' by the *Financial Times*).

Although very large, BT was narrowly based in terms of the range of services it offered and its geographical markets. The first reflex of the company when freed from public ownership was to reduce the vulnerability that this seemed to entail. So it was that BT went in search of new business opportunities, extending the portfolio of services it offered to the UK market, and looking for opportunities in overseas markets. An early development was the agreement of a joint venture with Du Pont of the USA for the development and manufacture of optoelectronic components. Among the other early ventures entered into by BT were:

- acquisition in 1986 for C$322 million of a 51 per cent interest in Mitel Corporation of Canada, a manufacturer of telecommunications equipment
- the acquisition in 1989 for $355 million of Tymnet Inc., a US-based organisation operating an international data communications network
- acquisition in 1989 for $1.48 billion of a 20 per cent stake in McCaw Cellular Communications Inc., a US cellular telephone company.

In the UK, BT's activities were extended beyond the traditional telephony business to activities such as a share dealing service and an alarm company. An early attempt to dominate the UK value-added services market through a joint venture with IBM was shelved when it met resistance from the regulatory authorities concerned that these two giants would wield too much monopoly power.

This initial enthusiasm for business development outside the UK and in diverse business areas waned in the late 1980s, as it became clear that not all these ventures had proved successful. In 1990, BT decided to divest itself of the 51 per cent stake in Mitel, at which point the original investment of C$322 million was worth C$109 million. According to the *Financial Times* (23 January 1990) 'buying control of Mitel was a costly mistake'. On its stake in McCaw, bought as a strategic investment in the largest mobile communications market in the world, BT had suffered a paper loss of $560 million by the middle of 1990. McCaw's 1989 financial results showed a loss of $289 million on revenue of $504 million. Many analysts doubted the wisdom of BT's investment, estimating that it would be the mid-1990s before McCaw began to make a profit in such a highly competitive market.

There was clearly a risk that too much management attention was being spent on diverse overseas activities while the core business came under increasing pressure. In addition to home-grown competitors, there was a growing domestic threat from major international companies such as America's AT&T and MCI. The UK telecommunications market is one of the most open in the world. To ambitious overseas companies, the UK market itself is attractive, but there is the added attraction that the UK forms a bridgehead in Europe. Continental European markets were expected to become open to competition as the Single European Act of 1992 took effect. The strategic focus of attention within BT shifted back to the company's core business of operating telecommunications services.

Price rebalancing

Like the majority of public telecommunications operators worldwide in the 1970s, the British Post Office cross-subsidised services to residential customers from those to business customers. In practice this meant that the charges for telephone system rental and connection were below the fully allocated costs of provision, while large profits were made on long-distance and (in particular) international calls. This was a form of social policy, which encouraged wider ownership of the telephone even among fundamentally unprofitable customer segments, and was only economically viable as long as there was a monopoly provider. Entrants to the market in the 1980s found a soft target in the large business customer segment, where customers were paying prices far in excess of the costs of provision. Mercury and other competitors could undercut BT's prices and still make a substantial profit on their own costs. The obvious response from BT was to 'rebalance' its prices. This would have meant large rises (above general inflation) in rental and connection charges and local calls, and actual price cuts for long-distance and international calls. However, any ambitions BT had to rebalance prices rapidly were held in check by OFTEL, the regulatory authority for the UK telecommunications industry. For social reasons, it was considered undesirable for BT to increase rapidly the price of basic telephone services. For reasons of competition policy, BT had to be prevented from competing unfairly in competitive markets by raising prices excessively in uncompetitive ones. A pricing formula called 'RPI minus X' was introduced for BT's core telephone services; each year BT was not allowed to increase prices on these services by more than the increase in the retail price index (RPI) less an efficiency improvement (X). For example, in 2000, retail price inflation was 3.32 per cent, X in the price control formula was 4.5, so that BT was required to reduce prices on regulated services by at least 1.08 per cent. In return for this regulatory intervention, the level of competition in the basic phone business was restricted for some years. Looking back, it is easy to ask if such government policies contributed to BT's slowness in transforming itself into a truly commercial enterprise. Perhaps if BT had faced more aggressive competition sooner, it would have been better able to deal with the even greater challenges that were to follow. It was around 1990 that the company began to demonstrate a serious commitment to change, evidenced by major changes in human resource strategy.

Human resources policy

The ancestry of British Telecommunications plc can be traced back to the civil service, and many of the manpower practices in the organisation had clear roots in the 1970s civil service. The company was heavily unionised in both manual and managerial grades. In 1990, over 80 per cent of employees belonged to four main unions recognised by the company. In the 1980s, a sequence of changes was implemented to transform people management within the organisation. A long-standing system of management appraisal was augmented by the introduction of 'management by objectives'. The focus of formal management appraisal became performance against agreed objectives. In a later logical progression, performance-related pay was introduced for management grades, so that outstanding (or appalling) performance against objectives could be suitably rewarded (or penalised) through the annual pay review. A management bonus scheme was also introduced, to reward people who performed well in a one-off project. As part of the same process to increase the flexibility of managerial pay, 'personal contracts' were introduced progressively from senior management grades down to middle management. BT's position as a monopolistic provider generating large profits enabled it to make the offers to staff 'too good to refuse', so avoiding any real risk of industrial action. By 1992, it was estimated that, of 4000 middle managers who had been offered personal contracts, fewer than 200 remained on terms and conditions negotiated by the managers' union, the Society of Telecommunications Executives.

Managers who had, until the late 1980s, received only a salary, now found themselves with a remuneration package which might include a bonus, a car, a share option scheme, private health insurance and a free telephone call allowance. Many of them were in the same place doing the same job but with a much-enhanced package. If they questioned how BT could afford to do this without demanding some quid pro quo, the answer was to be found in Project Sovereign.

Project Sovereign

BT has often been accused of being insufficiently responsive to customers and overmanned. A response to these twin criticisms was precipitated by the environmental pressure of growing competition in a stagnating market. In order to sustain profit growth, and to satisfy shareholders, BT devised a strategy which combined restructuring with manpower reductions. This was launched in 1990 as 'Project Sovereign'. Sovereign was about cultural change, reorganisation and manpower reductions. The cultural change built further on a 'total quality management' (TQM) programme which BT had initiated in the mid-1980s. TQM in BT was summarised in the phrase 'meeting the customer's agreed requirements, first time, every time'. The idea of internal customers was introduced, and departments were encouraged to draw up 'supplier/customer agreements' with those departments that they directly served or which served them. These agreements would contain the performance standards expected by the customer of the supplier, and the corresponding responsibilities of the supplier to the customer (for example in providing a clear and realistic statement of requirements).

By 1990, it had become clear that, despite an extensive programme of training, TQM had only had partial success in transforming the culture of the organisation. Sovereign aimed to reinforce the cultural change by giving those jobs that directly affected customers greater prestige. As part of the Sovereign process, all management jobs were subject to job evaluation and, if necessary, regraded. Within this process, greater weight was placed on contact with the customer than had hitherto been the case.

Finally, in 1991, after years of failing to bite the bullet of staff reductions, the number of employees in BT declined substantially (by 19,000, or 7.7 per cent, between March 1990 and March 1991). Part of this was achieved through management redundancies (all voluntary) directly attributable to Sovereign. Additional manpower reductions were achieved through a reduction in directory enquiry work (charging for enquiries was introduced during this period), by contracting out certain services and through business disposals. This was only the start. During the 1990s, 'outsourcing' and 'downsizing' became the latest management fashion, and BT embraced them wholeheartedly. Employee numbers, 246,000 in 1990, were down to 125,000 by the end of 1999.

THE STRATEGIC POSITION IN 1992

In 1992, BT had had some success in improving its public image. Apart from the ritual baying of the tabloid newspapers whenever a further set of financial results was reported – since BT was making very large amounts of money in absolute terms – media coverage of the company had become more sympathetic. This was perhaps not surprising considering that tangible improvements had been made to services. The quality of the telephone service was undoubtedly improving – faults were cleared more rapidly, calls were failing less often and there had been an enormous improvement in the availability of public payphones. Even the introduction of charging for the directory enquiries service had been accomplished with little negative PR.

Indeed, as it looked towards the year 2000, BT could look back with some satisfaction on the previous decade. In the face of growing competition it had retained a large majority share of the UK telecommunications market. It had weathered a crisis of public confidence in the mid-1980s and was no longer high in the list of most disliked national institutions. A start had been made on the process of transforming the organisational culture and slimming down staff numbers, at very little cost in terms of industrial conflict.

However, the telecommunications market in the UK was only going to become more competitive. Local cable television companies, often part-owned and supported by major US telecommunications operators and therefore well resourced, were now allowed to carry telephone calls over their cables. BT remained – arguably – a one-product, one-market company. Admittedly this is taking a broad definition of product (telecommunications services) and πmarket (the UK). However, within those definitions of product and market, BT was certainly going to face increasing competition, in a core market that was likely to grow more slowly in the 1990s than in the 1980s. On the one hand, BT was a cash-rich company operating in the exciting information technology industry, with an enviable research and development department and some very powerful partners. On the other hand, BT was also an ex-public sector monopoly, still overmanned, and lacking an embedded culture of market and customer orientation.

Questions for discussion

You are a strategic marketing manager working for British Telecommunications plc in 1992. You are a member of the team that is preparing BT's long-term strategic plan. The questions that the team has asked you to address are as follows.

1. What are the principal factors in the macroenvironment affecting BT that should be taken into consideration in preparing the long-term strategic plan?
2. What are the principal factors in the competitive environment?
3. Prepare a SWOT analysis for BT as at 1992, and use this analysis to develop strategic options that you think the company should consider for its long-term strategic plan.

Selected web links

www.att.com	major American telecommunications operator
www.bt.com	BT site
www.cw.com	Cable & Wireless site
www.groupbt.com	BT Group site
www.mci.com	major American telecommunications operator
www.oftel.gov.uk	the UK telecommunications industry regulator

case study two

British Telecommunications plc 'B': Tomorrow the World?

> BT, instead of being a lumbering telecoms giant, is now a large telecoms conglomerate (*The Times* 15 April 2000).

Case Study One showed how Britain's premier telephone company had achieved some success in addressing the major challenges raised by privatisation and the introduction of competition in the 1980s. There had been substantial reductions in staffing, and marked improvements in certain areas of service such as public telephone provision. However, BT remained essentially a one-product, one-market company. Most of BT's revenue and profits were generated from the plain old telephone service offered to British telephone customers (see Tables C2.1 and C2.2). New competitors were beginning to make inroads into key markets, and new communications technologies were beginning to emerge in which BT had no obvious competitive advantage – the Internet being perhaps the most obvious example. A decade on, the challenges facing BT were different ones, but certainly no less fearsome.

BT's turnover continued to grow, and showed a further 4.7 per cent growth to £15.6 billion in 1998, and 8.4 per cent growth to £17.0 billion in 1999. However, in May 2000, it was announced that for the first time since it became a private company BT's profits had fallen. This was reported in characteristic style by the flamboyant British tabloid newspaper, the *Sun*: 'BT shareholders got a double dose of misery yesterday as the firm announced a dive in profits – and further problems to come. BT shares plunged 70p to 922p after the company announced a 32 per cent fall in profits to £2.942 billion. It means BT is now only making £5597 a minute.' Flamboyant reporting or not, the truth of the matter was that BT's share price had been in decline for several months from a high of nearly £15.00. Then, in 2001, BT reported its first ever loss. Compared with other high-technology stocks, BT was seen as a seriously underperforming invest-

Table C2.1 British Telecommunications plc key statistics 1993–97

£ Million	1997	1996	1995	1994	1993
Turnover	14935	14446	13983	13675	13242
Net profit	2101	1992	1736	1805	1248
Operating profit	3245	3100	2663	2982	2403
Total assets	25062	23536	21459	22565	21234
Long-term debt	2693	3322	3361	3199	3386
Capital expenditure	2719	2771	2671	2171	2155
R&D expenditure	291	282	271	265	233
Earnings per share (pence)	32.8	31.6	27.8	28.5	19.8
Total employees	127500	130700	137500	156000	170700
UK sales %	97	98	98	99	98
Overseas sales %	3	2	2	1	2

Source: Adapted from *The Directory of Multinationals* (1997, p. 263)

ment. With stakes in mobile telephony, the Internet and WAP (wireless application protocol), the question was – why was BT not the darling of the stock market? Perhaps it's the product mix?

Inland and international telephone calls are self-explanatory. They have represented a slightly declining share of revenue as increasing competition and regulatory action have combined to squeeze BT's prices. Telephone exchange line rental is the amount that customers pay to remain connected to the telephone network. Private circuits are dedicated communications circuits provided to business customers for their sole use. Often they are used by large companies to build their own internal communications networks, which, in the case of major multinationals and financial institutions, may be global in scope. In 1994, BT established a joint venture

Table C2.2 British Telecommunications plc product analysis 1993–97

%	1997	1996	1995	1994	1993
Inland telephone calls	33	34	36	38	38
International telephone calls	12	14	14	14	14
Telephone exchange line rentals	19	19	18	18	17
Private circuits	8	7	7	7	–
Mobile communications	6	6	5	4	–
Customer premises equipment supply	6	6	7	7	8
Yellow Pages and other directories	3	3	3	–	–
Other sales and services	13	11	10	12	23

Source: Adapted from *The Directory of Multinationals* (1997, p. 264)

Note that some product lines were not separately identified in 1993 and 1994, and are included in 'other'.

(Concert) with the US firm MCI (and later AT&T) to address the market for private network management.

BT has a big stake in mobile telephony through its Cellnet subsidiary, which is also at the forefront of mobile Internet (WAP) technology. Customer premises equipment supply is the rather dull business of renting or selling the machines that sit at the end of telephone lines, such as telephones, fax machines and answering machines. Yellow Pages is the strongest business directory brand in the UK.

BT'S STRATEGY

In broad terms, BT's corporate strategy has remained largely the same since it was first exposed to competition and privatised. At privatisation, BT was overmanned, running with excessively high costs, maintained a conservative product portfolio and employed a great many talented engineers but few talented marketers. Sixteen years later, BT had drastically reduced the number of people it employed, had invested heavily in new network technology to reduce costs and had made some progress in developing a more innovative product portfolio. Undoubtedly, BT employed fewer talented engineers and employed more talented marketers. In 1984, the culture of the company owed a great deal to the British civil service. By 2000, the culture of the company, if not truly customer-oriented, was certainly a lot more responsive to market and customer demands. So, again in broad terms, BT's strategic marketing objectives remain to diversify the product portfolio by developing innovative new products to meet customer requirements, to increase sales and profits generated outside the UK, and to reposition BT as an international information technology firm rather than a public utility.

In addition to the normal activities of any major private enterprise seeking to achieve its goals, BT has also to be mindful of the likely reaction of OFTEL, the UK telecommunications regulator. OFTEL has outlined its own key strategic factors for the UK telecommunications industry in its management plan for 2000/2001 (OFTEL, 2000). OFTEL's aim is the achievement of the best deal for the customer, and it has stated that where there is effective competition there needs to be less regulation. BT would certainly argue that the UK telecommunications market is becoming ever-more competitive. More importantly, BT would argue that its new business development ventures are in highly competitive markets where it does not enjoy any monopoly power – so that these new ventures should be free of regulatory intervention by OFTEL.

In the 1980s, the achievement of BT's objectives meant the development of a major position in the cellular telephony market, achieved in the UK through Cellnet, and in the USA temporarily and abortively through McCaw Cellular Communications. The McCaw adventure was fairly typical of BT's early attempts to internationalise. BT bought 20 per cent of McCaw in 1989, the maximum permitted foreign stake in a US wireless operator. Three years later, AT&T bought McCaw outright – BT was prevented from bidding itself because of US regulation. BT had no choice but to sell its stake to AT&T. Sure, BT made $250 million profit on the deal. But the strategic aim of gaining a major position in the US mobile market was foiled. Strategic ineptitude? Bad luck? It certainly didn't inspire confidence in the strategic capabilities of BT's management.

In the 1990s, BT again had to ride the waves of technological change to develop new products and new solutions for its customers, based on emerging mobile technologies and the Internet. Meanwhile, a fundamental question could not be ignored – was telecommunications capacity becoming a commodity product?

The 1970s and 80s had seen tremendous development of the telecommunications infrastructure. The BT network had been converted from analogue to digital technology, and much of the trunk network had been converted from copper coaxial cable to optical fibres. Increasingly large numbers of international calls were being handled by undersea optical fibre cables. The capacity and transmission quality of telecommunications networks across the industrialised world had been transformed. Even given the substantial expected growth rate of demand for services, there was a feeling by 2000 that supply might have run ahead of demand, with all-too-obvious consequences for prices. Allied with this feeling was the concern that the source of added value in the 'information age' would not lie in the hardware – the network itself – but in the information provided over that hardware. And, following this logic through, there was the feeling that BT might simply be in the wrong business. Could, and should, BT pursue a major initiative to develop itself as more a provider of information and less a manager of a network?

MERGERS AND ALLIANCES

Mergers and alliances are the principal tools that BT has used to pursue its global ambitions (see British Telecommunications plc 'A' for information on merger and alliance activity in the 1980s). The abortive acquisition of a stake in McCaw Cellular Communications has already been mentioned. In the same year that the stake in McCaw was sold, 1994, BT acquired a 20 per cent stake in the US firm MCI. Originally established as a rival to America's number one telecommunications firm, AT&T, by 1994 MCI was a large (sales turnover $13.3 billion), broadly based communications company. Together, BT and MCI launched Concert Communications, a joint venture designed specifically to manage the private telecommunications networks of multinational corporations. Large, international firms often maintain their own private networks in order to facilitate internal communication, including voice, data, fax and electronic mail transmissions. Following the corporate fashion of the 1990s, more and more large companies decided to focus on their 'core competencies' (Hamel and Prahalad, 1984) and to outsource the management of their telecommunications (outsourcing means buying in a product or service that was previously done in-house). Concert aimed to capitalise on this trend.

Just as with the McCaw deal, things did not end up quite as BT might have intended. Two years later, in 1996, BT proposed to buy the 80 per cent of MCI that it did not already own. After a protracted period of negotiation, during which BT's original bid of $24 billion was revised downwards to $19 billion, the BT bid eventually failed when US firm WorldCom made a successful higher bid for MCI in September 1997. For a while, Concert Communications became a wholly owned subsidiary of BT, who paid MCI $1 billion for their share of the joint venture. According to the *Independent* (2 October 1997), the merchant banker James Dodd of Dresdner Kleinwort Benson had these unflattering words to say when WorldCom outbid BT for MCI: 'This is a godsend. I can hear BT's shareholders cheering. An even bigger fool has saved BT from itself.'

In its restless search for a partner who can provide truly global reach, BT has also unsuccessfully courted the British firm Cable & Wireless. Cable & Wireless plc is a federal company which owns telephone operating companies in several Caribbean and Asian countries (including the particularly attractive Hong Kong Telecommunications Ltd), and has a controlling interest in BT's major UK rival Cable & Wireless Communications plc. Cable & Wireless Communications Ltd was formed in 1997 by the merger of Mercury Communications Ltd with three UK cable television companies. The aim was to create a company that was more capable of competing not only with BT, but with the other emerging competitors in the UK telecommunications market. Cable & Wireless plc owns 52.84 per cent of Cable & Wireless Communications. However, BT's 1996 bid of £35 billion to merge with Cable & Wireless plc was rejected by the Cable & Wireless board.

The saga of Concert Communications continued in 1999 when BT found another partner to play with. This time it was AT&T, the second largest telecommunications company in the world (after Japan's NTT), who agreed to enter into a joint venture with BT and acquired 50 per cent of the equity of Concert. The BT/AT&T Concert joint venture was officially launched in January 2000, and was expected to achieve sales turnover of $10 billion in 2000, mainly from major accounts transferred to Concert from the parent companies. Given the complex history of the Concert operation, it is perhaps not surprising that the 2001 BT annual report noted that discussions continued between BT and AT&T regarding the future of the joint venture. To quote: 'These discussions may or may not lead to any sale or other business combination and may or may not lead to any change in the existing alliance arrangements.' Perhaps not the clearest statement of vision for this major global venture.

CORPORATE REORGANISATION 2000–2001

In 2000, BT embarked on a major reorganisation programme. Getting the organisational structure right was seen as a key element in pursuing the company's strategy to become a truly international information technology company, rather than a dull, British phone utility. In the new structure, there are six businesses (strategic business units, or SBUs) operating as part of a federal company. The old core of the BT business, namely the supply of telephone service to British domestic and business customers, has been split into two. There is a retail telephony business (BT Retail), still selling calls and services to customers, and a wholesale business (BT Wholesale). The wholesale business is responsible for the telephone network and for selling capacity on the network to those companies delivering services to customers, including other parts of BT. One aim here is to ensure transparency in the supply of wholesale telecommunications capacity to those companies dealing with the general public. As simultaneously the major network operator and one of a number of competitors delivering services to end-users, BT has often been accused of offering more favourable terms to its own divisions than to competitive rivals. This has led to more than one confrontation with competitors and with OFTEL. BT hoped that by separating the network operation into wholesale and retail, and declaring that the in-house retail operation will have to buy capacity on the same terms as competitors, the regulatory heat could be turned down. The intention was that the regulator's attention would quite properly by focused on the wholesale business, leaving the retail business relatively unfettered to develop new products and compete aggressively for share in the UK market. OFTEL's response to the reorganisation was enough to cause a little optimism at BT: 'The proposals by BT are a significant step to create a structure where there will be greater transparency ... Transparency is a key component of effective competition. OFTEL's strategy is that where there is effective competition, there is less need for regulation' (OFTEL press release, 13 April 2000).

The more immediately exciting part of the 2000 reorganisation was the creation of four new international business units:

- *BT Ignite*, which comprises the group's international networks and data business
- *BTopenworld*, containing retail Internet-related operations, such as the Internet service provider BTInternet
- *Yell*, BT's international yellow pages business, aspiring to be an international directories business and information provider
- *BT Wireless*, grouping together Cellnet with mobile telephony assets elsewhere in the world.

Clearly, one of the strategic possibilities created by this restructuring was the disposal of some or all of the new international business units, perhaps in order to generate funds with which to reduce debts incurred as a result of large-scale spending on licences for third-generation mobile phone operations. Furthermore, by decoupling these exciting, growth business areas from the dull utility business, BT aims to benefit from investor enthusiasm for the Internet, information provider firms, and the mobile telecommunications market.

THE CHALLENGE REMAINS

According to the *Independent* (19 May 2000):

> It has taken a lot longer than it should have done, but at last deregulation of the telecommunications market is working in the way intended. For evidence of this, look no further than British Telecom's full-year figures. Ever since privatisation in the early 1980s, profits at BT have been on a rising, sometimes strongly rising, trend ... for the first time since privatisation, underlying profits are falling, despite the huge uplift in volume brought about by mobiles and the Internet.

Oddly, throughout those 17 or so years BT has seemed unable to please anyone. Customers and regulators have grumbled that prices stayed too high for too long. Investors have grumbled that the share price has performed below expectation. From time to time government ministers have grumbled, to the effect that BT has not made as much of a contribution to the UK's development as an information economy as it should. Competitors have grumbled loud and often that BT has used every trick in the book to avoid fair competition. Among many of these groups one senses *schadenfreude* – a sense of pleasure taken from BT's reversal in fortunes. But, after 16 years of profit growth, should the profit decline of 2000 and the operating loss of 2001 be seen as evidence that BT is in terminal decline? Or will this company, which still controls massive resources and holds a big stake in such exciting ventures as the Internet and third-generation mobile communications, confound its critics and return to profitable growth?

Questions for discussion

1. What are BT's key strengths and weaknesses? As bases for comparison in making judgements about BT, 1995 and 1996 data are provided in the Appendix on two other major telecommunications firms mentioned in the case study.
2. Why do you think BT has selected mergers and alliances as such an important component of its product/market development strategy?
3. What difficulties might BT experience if it tried to become more established as an information provider rather than just a network operator?
4. If BT wished to become a more established information provider, what entry methods might it try? What are the pros and cons of the different entry methods?

Selected web links

www.att.com – major American telecommunications operator
www.bt.com – BT site
www.cw.com – Cable & Wireless
www.groupbt.com – BT Group site
www.mci.com – major American telecommunications operator
www.oftel.gov.uk – the UK telecommunications industry regulator

References

Hamel, G and Prahalad, H K (1994), *Competing for the Future*, Boston: Harvard Business School Press
OFTEL (2000), Proposals for Implementing OFTEL's Strategy: 2000/2001 Management Plan, http://www.oftel.gov.uk/about/mapl0400.htm
The Directory of Multinationals (1997), Basingstoke: Macmillan – now Palgrave Macmillan

APPENDIX: 1995 AND 1996 DATA ON COMPARATIVE TELECOMMUNICATIONS COMPANIES

Table C2.3 MCI Communications Corporation

US$ million	**1996**	**1995**
Revenue	18494	15265
Net profit	1202	548
Operating profit	2313	1118
Total assets	22978	19301
Long-term debt	4798	3444
Capital expenditures for property and equipment	3347	2866
Earnings per share (US$)	1.73	0.80
Total full-time employees	**55285**	**50367**

Source: Adapted from *The Directory of Multinationals* (1997, p. 905)

Table C2.4 Cable & Wireless plc

	1996 £m	**1996 %**	**1995 £m**	**1995 %**
Turnover	5517		5133	
Hong Kong		44		44
UK		31		32
Caribbean		10		10
North America		8		8
Other		7		6
Net profit	607		252	
Operating profit	1311		1134	
Hong Kong		70		73
UK		17		13
Caribbean		14		15
North America		3		3
Other		(4)		(4)
Total assets	9020		7875	
Long-term debt	1839		1373	
Earnings per share (pence)	**27.5**		**11.5**	
Total employees	**39636**		**41124**	

Source: Adapted from *The Directory of Multinationals* (1997, p. 292)

case study three

Competition in the UK Ice Cream Market

Until the 1980s, certain aspects of the UK ice cream market were regarded as unchanging. Ice cream (including ice lollies) was predominantly sold to children. UK consumers preferred a product made largely from vegetable fat rather than dairy fat – thus confirming the national stereotype for rather unsophisticated tastes. Ice cream was a highly price-sensitive 'commodity' product, and the ice cream market was incorrigibly seasonal. Yet all these assumptions were challenged or overturned in the late 1980s, and the nature of competition in the 1990s turned out to be quite different.

Demographic factors played a large part in transforming competition in the UK ice cream market in the latter part of the twentieth century. For example, the 1980s saw a substantial decline in the number of children aged 5 to 14. In order to maintain and grow sales, an appeal had to be made to the adult market. This shift within the target market necessitated product development, since adult tastes differ from those of children. Adults prefer more sophisticated products, for which they are prepared to pay premium prices. So, in the 'impulse' ice cream market, competition became ever-more intense for the profitable, premium, adult market segment. Meanwhile, as UK households became wealthier they acquired more consumer durables, so household freezers became much more common. This enabled ice cream manufacturers to sell more multipacks, bulk packs and ice cream desserts (such as Wall's Viennetta).

Spying the opportunity offered by the UK market for ice cream products, Mars identified the adult ice cream market as a growth opportunity in the late 1980s and successfully entered the market in 1989 by exploiting its well-known confectionery brands (such as Mars and Bounty), supported by the renowned Mars marketing machine. Product launches in the market were directed explicitly at the fast-growing market for premium, adult ice cream products. Market entry was supported by large-scale mass media advertising. One of the most famous names in UK ice cream, Lyons

Maid, soon fell victim to this aggressive competitor. Competition in the market was getting tougher.

The factors that emerged in the marketing environment in the 1980s and early 1990s set the scene for later competitive battles. The ice cream market, which was considered to be mature and relatively dull, changed considerably. Consumer tastes had changed considerably, with rapidly growing demand for premium and super-premium products, which use high levels of dairy fat in the ice cream and other high-quality ingredients. This trend is closely associated with the development of the adult market, and the belief that the UK ice cream market is far from being saturated. The take-home sector of the market continued to grow rapidly, with the emphasis on premium ice cream sold in relatively small volume 'bulk' packs (around 1 litre). On the other hand, the market for complete ice cream desserts (such as Viennetta) was seen as relatively mature, with little prospect of rapid growth. The growth in premium dairy ice cream products meant that the value of the ice cream market would continue to grow faster than volume. The volume of sales of economy and standard quality bulk ice cream, typically sold in large containers of 2 litres or more, can be expected to decline. Advertising and promotional activity, stimulated by the entry of Mars, would continue at a high level. New product development, innovative packaging and design, and promotion by substantial mass media advertising expenditure were to become key features of the UK ice cream market.

By 1990, it was clear that the entry of Mars into the UK ice cream market had been initially successful, and that the rivalry between Mars and the older established ice cream companies would shape competition in the 1990s. What was not appreciated so well at the time was the important role that legal and regulatory action would play in the competitive battle. As expected, Mars brought all the respected strengths of a major American, fast-moving, consumer goods marketing operation to the formerly rather staid UK ice cream market. Rather less expected, Mars brought with it a peculiarly American form of competitive strategy, namely, trying to demonstrate that a rival's dominant place in the market is sustained through unfair anti-competitive practices. The scene was set for a lengthy war of attrition, which is described in a later section.

MARKET SIZE AND CONSUMER TASTE TRENDS

Consumer taste trends that emerged in the 1980s continued into the 1990s. Ice cream was no longer solely a kids' product. Ice cream could be a snack, a dessert, a treat or an indulgence. However it was presented, one fairly clear characteristic was that consumers were demanding better quality and better ingredients. This was equally clear in both the take-home and impulse sectors. Commenting on trends in the take-home market, *Market Research GB* (February 1997) said:

> A growing number of consumers are less interested in cheaper, everyday products, and more interested in higher quality ice cream as an indulgence. Consequently, use of four litre packs has decreased in favour of one litre or even smaller tubs, which allow consumers to buy different varieties in smaller amounts. Luxury products are sold on their real dairy ingredients, exotic flavours and the 'total indulgence' factor.

It is fair to say that if the 1980s was the decade during which British consumers discovered good ice cream, then the 1990s was the decade in which good ice cream

Table C3.1 UK ice cream market, volume and value trends 1994–98

	Impulse Volume per cent	Take home Volume per cent	Impulse Value £m	Take home Value £m	Total Value £m
1994	28.5	71.5	637.8	326.4	964.2
1995	30.2	69.8	696.5	342.7	1039.2
1996	29.6	70.4	645.7	332.4	978.1
1997	30.5	69.5	682.1	337.5	1019.6
1998	30.5	69.5	660.0	336.5	996.5

Source: Adapted from *Market Research GB* (January 2000, Tables 2 and 3, p. 28)

became an established part of the British lifestyle. As a result, many new opportunities had opened up for ice cream manufacturers, who had responded with new products, new brands and even new concepts. The killer ice cream concept of the decade was the ice cream chocolate bar, which started with the Mars ice cream and spread to just about every established brand of chocolate confectionery.

Overall, the UK ice cream market grew in volume terms by 5.6 per cent between 1994 and 1998, while sales value over the same period increased by only 3.3 per cent. The market is conventionally subdivided into the impulse sector and the take-home sector. Impulse ice creams are usually bought from kiosks and small grocery shops for immediate consumption, while take-home ice cream is bought from grocery shops for home consumption. Although the take-home sector is much the larger of the two in terms of volume (that is, litres of ice cream sold), the much higher unit value of impulse products means that the impulse market is worth roughly twice as much as the take-home market.

The impulse market is dominated by major brands, whereas the take-home market sees a much greater penetration by private retailer brands. One of the major

Table C3.2 Value sales of single impulse ice cream by type 1996 and 1998

% by value	1996	1998
Soft/Scoop	25.0	25.6
Adult indulgent	20.2	21.0
Children's	21.0	18.4
Adult refreshment	12.7	13.6
Filled cones	6.0	8.1
Confectionery	11.2	7.5
Other	3.9	5.8
Total	**100.0**	**100.0**

Source: Adapted from *Market Research GB* (January 2000, Table 6, p. 31)

Table C3.3 Value sales of take-home ice cream by type 1993 and 1995

% by value	1993	1995
Countline multipacks	33.8	39.7
Standard	34.5	28.8
Premium	20.2	18.4
Luxury	2.9	5.5
Ice cream desserts	8.6	7.6
Total	**100.0**	**100.0**

Source: Adapted from *Market Research GB* (February 1997, Table 6, p. 8)

objectives of manufacturers has been to reduce the seasonality of demand for ice cream, that is, to reduce reliance on summer sales. They have had some success by promoting ice cream as a year-round treat and dessert. However, ice cream sales still show marked seasonality and rise sharply when the sun shines.

COMPETITIVE ACTIVITY

In 1995, Birds Eye Wall's remained the market leader by a large margin. However, the decline (and eventual demise) of the Lyons Maid brand meant that Mars had risen from third to second in the market. Birds Eye Wall's retains its leadership position as a result of a fairly solid one-third share of the take-home market, and nearly two-thirds share of the impulse market. Mars is only a small player in the take-home ice cream market, but had seen its share of the impulse market grow to 15 per cent by the mid-1990s. It was in the impulse market that Lyons Maid/Nestlé had suffered most. Having lost market share to Birds Eye Wall's and Mars throughout the early 1990s, the Lyons Maid/Nestlé share of the impulse ice cream market had more or less halved from 20 per cent in 1990 to 11 per cent in 1995. Major rivals claimed that Birds Eye

Table C3.4 Manufacturers' shares of ice cream 1991, 1993 and 1995

% by value	1991	1993	1995
Birds Eye Wall's	43	45	46
Mars	8	9	10
Lyons Maid/Nestlé	10	7	8
Haagen-Dazs/Grand Metropolitan	1	3	4
Own-label	27	26	23
Others	11	10	10
Total	**100**	**100**	**100**

Source: Adapted from *Market Research GB* (February 1997)

Wall's had an important advantage – which they argued was an unfair advantage – in the key impulse sector of the market, owing to its privileged access to distribution channels. This was the 'freezer exclusivity debate', discussed in a later section.

The market leader

Birds Eye Wall's Ltd has been the market leader in the UK ice cream market for many years. A subsidiary of the international consumer goods giant Unilever, Birds Eye Wall's owns a large number of household ice cream brand names, among them Wall's Ice Cream, Carte D'Or, Cornetto, Magnum, Solero, Viennetta, plus a range of products targeted at children, such as Mini Juice, Twister and Sparkles. Magnum was the UK's biggest-selling ice cream brand in 1998, with a 7.5 per cent share of the market by value. Advertising, particularly TV advertising, has been the main medium for developing these brands. Birds Eye Wall's spent £31.8 million on advertising in 1998, up from £28.6 million in 1997, and it employs three advertising agencies to handle its ice cream brands. Three out of the top five ice cream brand names in the UK are owned by Birds Eye Wall's.

Parent company Unilever sees ice cream as a key growth product category, and is prepared to invest in the UK and elsewhere to defend its market position and grow the market. The marketing director of Birds Eye Wall's was quoted in *Campaign* magazine (19 May 2000) as saying: 'We will have to keep spending and supporting the products and focus on the big ones. New products can be used to create excitement. People want our ice-creams so it's important to get them to where people want them. We have to have a quick response distribution to make sure that the ice-creams are in the cabinets when the sun shines.' Throughout the 1990s, Birds Eye Wall's has recognised the importance of maintaining a grip on its distribution channels, and has worked hard to defend itself against the attack on freezer exclusivity by Mars. This key battleground is discussed further below.

One of the strategies that Unilever employs to build its position in key target markets is corporate acquisition. In April 2000, on the same day that it acquired Slim-Fast Foods, a manufacturer of slimming aids, Unilever also bought the luxury ice cream company Ben & Jerry's Homemade. The acquisition of Ben & Jerry's confirmed Unilever's determination to invest in the ice cream market globally. Ben & Jerry's is a super-premium ice cream brand with which Unilever will hope to challenge the Haagen-Dazs brand, owned by Grand Metropolitan (itself a part of the Diageo empire). One of the issues with most acquisitions is whether or not the buyer will find it possible to merge the acquired company into its own corporate culture. When Unilever, one of the world's largest and reputedly most aggressive consumer goods marketers, acquired Ben & Jerry's, this aspect of corporate integration was uppermost in the minds of commentators. Ben & Jerry's is famous for donating 7.5 per cent of profits to charity, banning synthetic hormones from its milk, and campaigning for environmental causes – in other words, for a rather offbeat approach to business. Just as it will be interesting to see what Unilever do with the Ben & Jerry's brand, so it will be interesting to watch it integrate such an unorthodox company into the ultimate establishment multinational. As the *Financial Times* put it (17 April 2000): 'Last week, when Unilever suggested that it would devote a larger part of Ben & Jerry's sales to charity, it was not acting out of the goodness of its heart. It was just part of the deal. If Unilever really believed in giving away such a large whack to charity, it would do just the same for its other businesses. The idea of a multinational with some parts more moral than others strikes me as a pragmatic and slightly cynical product of a complex world. And complexity, cynicism and pragmatism are as far from New Age as it is possible to get.'

The key rivals

The key branded rivals to Bird Eye Wall's in the UK ice cream market are Mars Confectionery and Nestlé Ice Cream. In addition, Pillsbury (UK) Ltd, a subsidiary of the multinational food and drinks company Diageo, is a niche player in the important super-premium market sector, through its Haagen-Dazs brand.

Mars Confectionery is part of Mars UK Ltd, a subsidiary of the privately owned US firm Mars Inc. Mars Inc. is a substantial world player in a range of product areas including snack foods, pet care products and main meal foods. Key Mars ice cream brands include Mars Ice Cream, Galaxy Dove Bars Ice Cream, Milky Way Ice Cream, Snickers Ice Cream and Twix Ice Cream. Mars Ice Cream is the biggest selling brand, taking 4.2 per cent of the UK market by value in 1998. The main focus of Mars's strategy has been the impulse ice cream market, where the company has sought to take maximum advantage of its well-established chocolate countline brands.

Nestlé lies in third place in the UK market behind Birds Eye Wall's and Mars. Nestlé established a substantial position in the UK confectionery market in 1988 when they acquired Rowntree Mackintosh plc. Later, Nestlé Ice Cream acquired a modest share of the UK ice cream market when it acquired Lyons Maid in 1992. Subsequently Nestlé decided to phase out the Lyons Maid brand name. Nestlé Ice Cream is part of Nestlé UK Ltd, but has no brands that can match Magnum or Mars Ice Cream. The best-selling Nestlé ice cream brand in 1998 was the Rowntree's Fruit Pastille Lolly, which took 0.8 per cent of the market by value. Other Nestlé ice cream brands are Fab, Mega Truffle and Rolo. Like Birds Eye Wall's and Mars, Nestlé UK is part of a multinational organisation, in this case Nestlé SA (*Société Anonyme*), which is incorporated in Switzerland.

FREEZER EXCLUSIVITY

Obvious though it is, channels of distribution are fundamentally important to consumer goods marketing. None more so than the ice cream market. Throughout the 1990s, controversy raged in the ice cream market over the control of space in freezer cabinets in confectionery, tobacconist and newsagent shops (CTNs). These shops are usually owned and managed as small businesses, and any assistance with investment in major appliances is welcomed by the hard-working businesspeople who run them. A freezer is a major appliance, and there is often only space in any one shop for one freezer. Birds Eye Wall's had been the traditional supplier of freezer cabinets to CTNs, offering to lend them the freezer free of charge, insisting in return that its products would be stocked but not those of its rivals. Existing competitive rivals, and the major new arrival of the 1980s, Mars, complained that this prevented them from competing effectively in the market for impulse ice cream sold through CTNs. While the competitive battle raged on through the more traditional mechanisms of new products, advertising and sales promotions, the control of space in freezer cabinets became a major focus of competitive effort.

This has by no means been solely a British controversy. On entering the ice cream market in 1989, Mars quickly discovered that Unilever (parent company of Birds Eye Wall's) had a stranglehold on distribution through CTNs in several European countries, as a result of freezer exclusivity arrangements. Mars took its case to the European Commission, arguing that the practice of freezer exclusivity was anti-competitive. If a CTN can only reasonably have one ice cream freezer, and the products that are sold through that freezer are restricted to a single manufacturer, then competitive rivals are effectively denied access to an important part of the market. Furthermore, as Mars argued vociferously, consumer choice is restricted. However, the case is by no means one sided. Obviously Birds Eye Wall's (and other European Unilever subsidiaries) wished to maintain freezer exclusivity. Their powerful argument was that they had invested very substantially in the freezer cabinets, and they should decide what was sold from them. If rivals wanted to sell ice cream through the same outlets, then let them incur the heavy fixed costs of establishing a network of freezers. The point is that ice cream manufacture and distribution is a business with high fixed costs and low variable costs. The ingredients that go into an ice cream bar cost a great deal less than the selling price, but simply to be in the ice cream business at all costs a great deal of money – in particular because of the need to maintain a 'cold chain' from factory to retailer to consumer. A competitive rival that could avoid investing in some fixed costs would have a lower breakeven point, creating the opportunity either to compete more keenly on price or to boost profits. A more detailed analysis of the argument about fixed costs and breakeven points is provided in the Appendix.

Table C3.5 Key moments in the freezer exclusivity controversy

Date	Event
1979	The British Monopolies and Mergers Commission (forerunner of the Competition Commission) rules that outlet exclusivity, the practice of tying retailers to a single manufacturer, is unlawful
1994	The Monopolies and Mergers Commission reports that freezer exclusivity does not pose a sufficient threat to the public interest for action to be necessary
March 1998	The European Commission rules that Unilever had abused its dominant position in the Irish ice cream market to exclude competitors – this ruling was expected to affect all European Union markets
July 1998	The Monopolies and Mergers Commission finds that Birds Eye Wall's wholesaling practices are anti-competitive and recommends a full review of competition in the UK ice cream industry
December 1998	Britain's Competition Commission begins an investigation into freezer exclusivity – the director general of fair trading says that there are 'continuing problems with competition in the supply of impulse ice cream'
May 1999	Preliminary findings from the Competition Commission are that monopolistic practices exist in the ice cream market
January 2000	Britain's Competition Commission rules that retailers supplied with a freezer cabinet by Birds Eye Wall's will be allowed to fill up to half the space with rivals' products

As far as Unilever and Birds Eye Wall's are concerned, they are simply striving to maintain the quality of their products by offering the best possible distribution channel. They would claim that the freezer exclusivity controversy has been stirred up by Mars, a privately owned US company, and is a typical example of the US practice of competing through legal and regulatory mechanisms. Mars, on the other hand, would argue that where its products face a level playing field they sell equally as well as those of Birds Eye Wall's. According to this argument, the market leader owes its position to an anti-competitive stranglehold on part of the distribution chain. Mars would say that all it wants is fair competition to demonstrate the merits of its products in the marketplace.

Table C3.5 shows some key moments in the freezer exclusivity controversy. The arguments of the key players, primarily but not solely Birds Eye Wall's and Mars, were directed at national and European institutions which have the role of ensuring fair competition. In the UK, this is the Competition Commission (formerly the Monopolies and Mergers Commission).

Questions for discussion

1. The case study contains examples of strategic marketing decisions. List as many examples as you can find of this type of decision.
2. Imagine that you are a strategic analyst working for Nestlé SA in Switzerland. You have been asked to prepare a brief summary of competitive conditions in the UK ice cream market for the next board meeting.
3. Suppose that one board director has argued that Nestlé should sell its ice cream interest in the UK and withdraw from the market. That's one strategic option. What other options does Nestlé have, and how do they compare with a strategic withdrawal?

Selected web links

www.benjerry.com – Ben & Jerry's site

www.mars.com – Mars Inc.

www.nestle.com – Nestlé SA

www.unilever.com – Unilever plc

References

Market Research GB (1997), 'Special Report: Ice Cream, Yoghurts and Chilled Desserts', volume XXXVIII, February, Euromonitor International

Market Research GB (2000), 'Market Report, Food: Ice Cream', volume XXXXI, January, Euromonitor International

APPENDIX: A NOTE ON BREAKEVEN ANALYSIS

The manufacture and marketing of ice cream is a business with high fixed costs and low variable costs. It costs a lot to invest in manufacturing equipment, and production facilities have to be maintained to high standards. More than this, a great deal of money has to be spent on building the brand before one can become a serious competitor in the ice cream market – particularly in the impulse sector of the market where well-known brands account for the vast majority of sales. All of these are fixed costs – they remain the same whether the company sells one ice cream bar or a million.

One particular aspect of the ice cream business that receives attention in the case study is access to freezer cabinets in small shops. Historically, these cabinets have been supplied by Birds Eye Wall's, which has denied its competitors the right to sell their products from Birds Eye Wall's supplied freezers. The competitors argue that this is unfair competition, since they cannot gain access to essential distribution channels. Birds Eye Wall's argues that the freezer cabinets represent a substantial fixed cost, and that it would give its rivals an unfair advantage if they could use the freezers without incurring the fixed costs involved.

Figure C3.1 illustrates what Birds Eye Wall's is saying. Both diagrams show (hypothetical) costs and revenues for manufacturing and marketing an impulse ice cream bar. In both diagrams, it is assumed that the ice cream bar sells for £0.75, that the unit variable costs of production are £0.10, and that the fixed costs of manufacture and marketing are £800,000. However, in the left-hand diagram, the manufacturer also has to pay for freezer cabinets at small shops, so incurring additional fixed costs of £200,000, making fixed costs of £1,000,000 in total. If these were two manufacturers

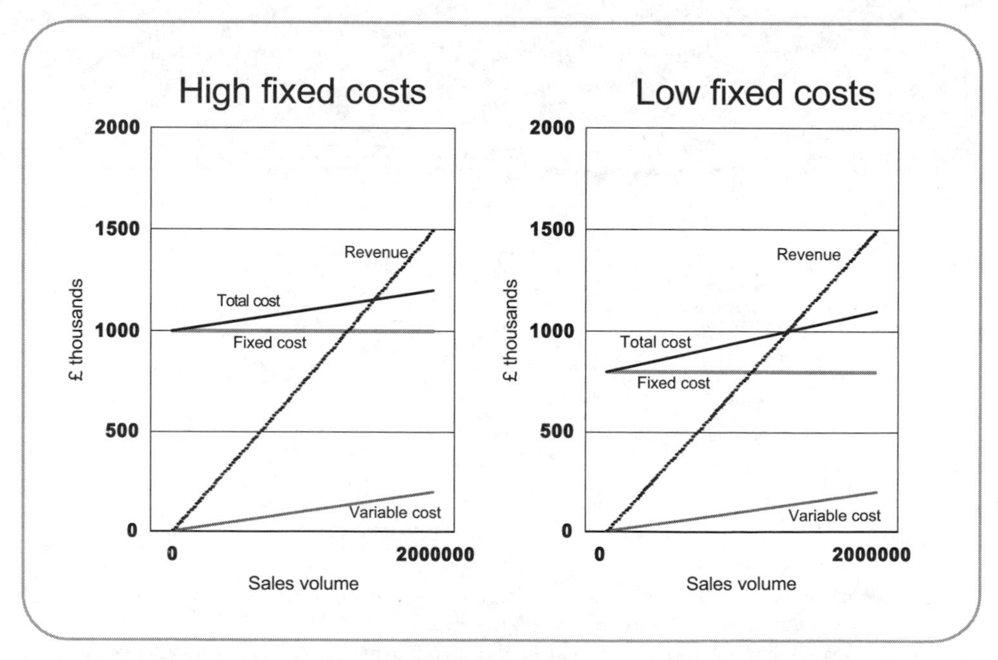

Figure C3.1 Breakeven analysis

competing against each other, then clearly the manufacturer in the right-hand diagram holds a big competitive advantage. In fact, this manufacturer's breakeven sales volume (the point at which sales revenue just covers total cost) is 1.23 million ice creams, whereas for the other manufacturer it is 1.53 million ice creams. If it sells the same number of ice creams, then the company on the right would make a lot more profit. If the company on the right wanted to compete aggressively on price, it could reduce its price to £0.62 per ice cream bar – and its breakeven point would be 1.53 million units, the same as its rival.

Of course, the other competitors in the ice cream market would argue that Birds Eye Wall's 'privileged access' to distribution channels more than outweighs the cost disadvantages illustrated above. These are the kinds of issue that the British and European competition authorities had to weigh in making their judgements.

case study four

Fulham FC: Strategic Marketing for Football Clubs

LOOKING BACKWARD

The English describe football (soccer) as their national game. At the pinnacle of the sport lies the Premier League, or 'Premiership', graced by iconic clubs such as Liverpool, Arsenal and, of course, Manchester United. Underneath the Premiership there are the four divisions of the Football League. The aspiration of any ambitious Football League club is one day to play in the Premiership.

In September 1997, Fulham Football Club languished in the middle of the Second Division. It had little money and did not own its own ground. Supporters at this point were relatively few and support was difficult to raise except during the local derbies against Brentford and Gillingham, which were hardly worthy of front-page news. Yet, ironically, Fulham FC was a club steeped in history, and was perhaps the original London glamour team.

Then, like a modern day fairy story, along came Mohammed Al Fayed, the fairy godmother (father). He purchased the ground from the Royal Bank of Scotland and promised the injection of millions of pounds to ensure Premiership status within five years. Supporters, while always ready to enjoy a good bedtime story, were sceptical. After all, Fulham FC has a location with 'desirable riverside views' which, therefore, represented a prime site for redevelopment. As a way of placating and quashing supporter fears, Al Fayed invited Kevin Keegan, a latter-day Prince Charming, to manage the team. The future of the club was more assured. It now had money, management expertise of the highest calibre and a five-year plan. The financial involvement of Al Fayed was important because cash at the bank was a necessary ingredient to ensure the club's success in the Premiership. Moreover, it ensured compliance with the Taylor Report and the necessity to build an all-seater stadium if it was to reach the Premiership.

MOVING FORWARD

Within a couple of years, the personnel had changed. Jean Tigana, the new football manager, had taken Fulham FC to mid-table Premiership status after winning promotion as champions of Division One in the 2000–01 season.

As football has developed a new reputation from being just a sport to one of being an industry, Fulham has demonstrated the importance of communicating with supporters. It undertook a number of independent surveys aimed at discovering supporters' opinions, views and perceptions. The promise of the Premiership had given the supporters a future to look forward to. In focus groups conducted in January 1999, fans reported that other Premiership clubs' supporters were finally beginning to respect their support for Fulham. Yet the perception of Fulham FC from the fans of less successful teams, such as Brentford, is that Fulham has gone from being 'healthy rivals to just a money team ... like Manchester United'.

The importance of perception cannot be understated, not only among supporters but also within the local community. Football teams are inextricably woven into the fabric of the locality from which they come. In Fulham, there has been an embourgeoisement of the football supporter base, as the locality itself has become wealthier. The necessary development of the ground, as the team has progressed through the divisions, has brought with it a need to keep the local community on-side. Increased car and pedestrian traffic during matchdays makes the non-football-supporting public particularly angry, as they are affected by noise, (flood) light pollution, litter and vandalism. The local community becomes an important stakeholder when one considers the ease with which they can hinder developments at the ground through planned resident opposition.

Harrod's retailing and business experience have added a new impetus and dimension to the club's business outlook. In spring 2000, Harrods added a Fulham FC concession to the fifth floor of its prestigious department store, selling football strips and other branded merchandise. Previously, the marketing function was much more fragmented with no dedicated marketing employees and a sole commercial manager. Marketing operations now exist with a separate budget and the team comprises a marketing director and marketing manager with a team of support staff. There now exists greater scope to understand the nature of the Fulham supporter

SPECTATORS AND THE FOOTBALL EXPERIENCE

Traditionalists may lament the loss of atmosphere at football grounds as a result of a conversion to all-seater stadia, but such developments have attracted a new breed of supporter who shows a greater predilection for the comfort that stadia now offer. The working-class roots of the game have been all but lost. The new supporter tends to be more fickle and may not demonstrate the same degree of loyalty as the die-hards of the past.

The nature of football club supporters extends beyond traditional marketing considerations. There is a need for clubs to have an understanding of what football *really* means to the football fan and to integrate this understanding into the products and services that they then make available. Thus, the core product would quite simply be the game itself. Some games may naturally be more important than others, that is, matches involving promotion, relegation and cup ties. However, the level of importance the supporter places upon the core product will vary according to those factors that affect attendance.

The uncertainty of the outcome of a game adds to the supporters' interest and desire to consume the football experience. There is an inconsistency in the consumption of the product from one occasion to the next because of the variability of performance of the two teams during the game. The marketer cannot influence the outcome of the game at this level and, therefore, emphasis should be placed upon those elements that can be influenced by the marketer. Supporters (consumers) should be provided with an offering that goes beyond the game itself and extends to an overall package built *around* the game. By enhancing the overall experience of the dedicated and casual supporter, marketers engender a desire on the part of the supporter to return and consume the experience again.

Through an understanding of the different reasons for attendance, marketers are able to provide a range of services that will meet the needs and wants of their supporter base. The cultural aspect of football emphasises the established tradition of the club, family, the socialising process of support and the enormous degree of identification that fans have with the symbolic and ritualised artefacts associated with a club.

SUPPORTERS AS CONSUMERS

Supporters display intense loyalty to the football brand. Brand switching as a phenomenon therefore occurs less frequently than with the typical commercial service consumer. For instance, high street bank customers are more likely to switch their current accounts from Natwest to HSBC if they are unhappy with the level of service that they receive than Fulham FC season ticket holders are likely to become Brentford FC fans, if the Fulham team perform poorly on the pitch. Football supporters may have been socialised into becoming season ticket holders (that is, the purchasing decision) by their family and friends over, say, a 10- or 20-year period.

It is not unreasonable for many football supporters to feel alienated from the clubs that they support and follow so fervently. Certainly the wealthier clubs of the Premiership have courted the attention of corporate clients and attracted large sums of money from television coverage and sponsorship. Manchester United fans were particularly vociferous in their opposition to the takeover of their club by the satellite broadcaster BSkyB in October 1998 for £2.40 a share. At that time, this would have valued Manchester United at around three-quarters of a billion pounds. The fans' opposition, in conjunction with the opposition of the then Monopolies and Merger Commission (now reorganised as the Competition Comission), ensured that the deal was prevented.

Supporters have been expected to follow their clubs, accept higher ticket prices and mid-season changes of strip without comment or criticism. Mothers of young football fans despair when continually pestered by their football-supporting children who wish to sport the latest club kit to impress their friends.

Many supporters pass the loyalty test by taking on these additional costs because the team that they follow plays an important role in their lives. An example of where this loyalty was tested to the limit was at Newcastle United. For many seasons, matches at St James's Park were sold out to season ticket holders, with 12,000 fans on a reserve waiting list. Indeed, such was the commitment of supporters that many queued for tickets at the nearby Odeon Cinema for live broadcasts of matches. Newcastle further tested the patience of its supporters once local resident opposition thwarted its stadium expansion plans. Supporters were asked to relocate from their traditional seats to other areas of the ground in order to make way for corporate entertainment areas.

UNDERSTANDING THE MARKET FOR SEGMENTATION PURPOSES

Undoubtedly, one of the greatest attractions that Fulham FC offers is its excellent setting overlooking the river Thames, together with its aura of romance and tradition. The club finds itself labelled as the 'quaint, friendly club' and, thus, has been very much overshadowed in recent years by its neighbour, Chelsea FC, which has a greater media profile because of its longer Premiership status.

Although the football product is diverse, opportunities do exist to offer and meet the differing needs of the various supporter groups. One such opportunity is attracting supporters from other teams such as Chelsea. The historic ties between the two clubs ensure that supporters from either team can watch the other on alternate weekends. The opportunity for Fulham lies in the promotion of the idea that the costs of attending Chelsea matches are prohibitive for the average London fan. Fulham FC regularly attracts crowds of around 12,000 supporters, although the current ground capacity is around 18,000. With approximately 3000 season ticket holders in January 1999, they represent a large section of the crowd attending on any one particular day.

The season ticket holder represents the most frequently attending supporter. However, there are other supporter types. For instance, while some supporters are frequent attendees, others are infrequent attendees and some supporters are non-attendees, preferring to watch the match at home on television or follow the results in the newspapers, on the radio or the club's premium rate results line. There are also supporters who attend, frequently or infrequently, who are also supporters of another major football club. Similarly, while some attendees are loyal, others may be less so and may defect to another club if an opportunity arises.

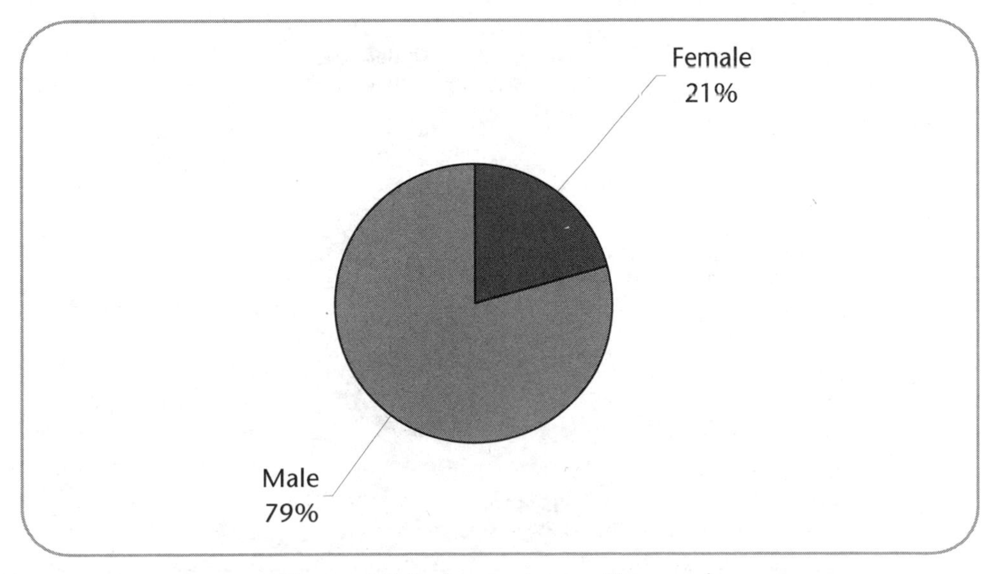

Figure C4.1 Supporter profile: gender

In March 1999, Fulham FC commissioned independent market research to determine the profile of its supporters. Approximately 800 questionnaires were distributed to matchday attenders at the game against Lincoln and collected using a freepost business reply service. Matchday attenders represent the largest proportion of fans at the ground at any one time, at approximately three-quarters of the entire audience. The proportion of respondents who were female was 21 per cent, which was broadly in line with expectations from previous surveys conducted independently at the club (see Figure C4.1). This relatively high figure indicates that Fulham is probably a more female-oriented club than many other Premiership clubs. Fulham has its own ladies soccer team too.

The age of respondents was bracketed into categories, and the results were: under 16 – 6%; 17–24 – 10%; 25–34 – 21%; 35–44 – 29%; 45–54 – 21%; and 55+ – 13%. This is represented in Figure C4.2. These results show a slightly different age distribution to a survey conducted two years previously. The main difference is that there are fewer younger fans (16% in the first two categories, as opposed to 32% aged 16–24 in the 1997 survey) and a greater number of older fans (34% aged 45+, as opposed to 16% in 1997). A further cause of the variation is the growth of this segment, and rising attendance generally, may be altering the age profile – older fans who may not have attended regularly may be being enticed back by the current success of the club.

The sample was predominantly composed of socioeconomic groups C1 and C2, which accounted for 30% and 29% of the sample respectively. Groups A and B were 5% and 20%, and groups D and E were 12% and 4%. Again, some small differences between these results and those seen previously are discernible – although direct comparison is not possible due to this research being new to the survey. However, it would appear that there is a higher proportion of group C2, mainly at the expense of group C1 (see Figure C4.3).

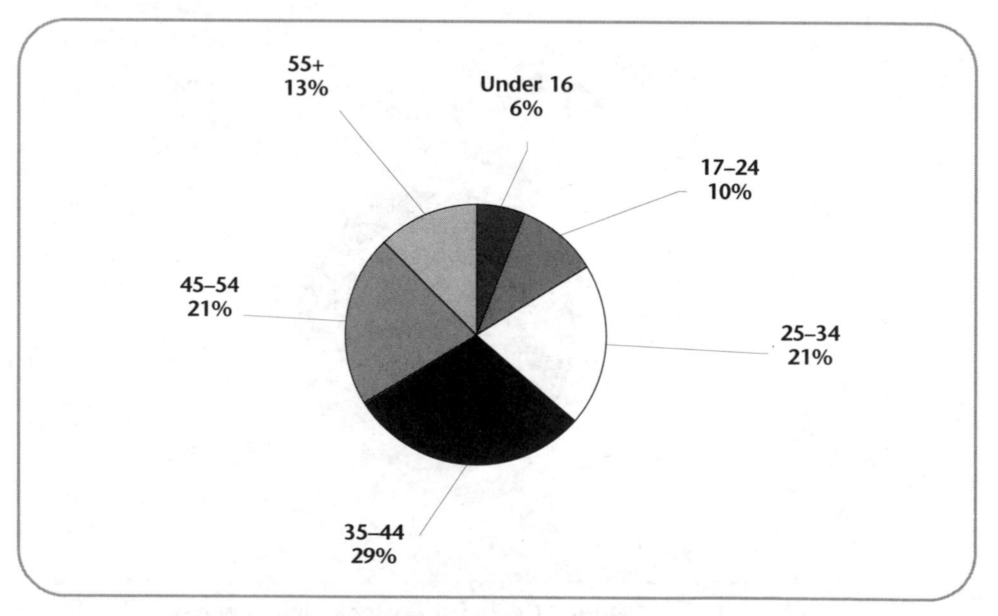

Figure C4.2 Supporter profile: age

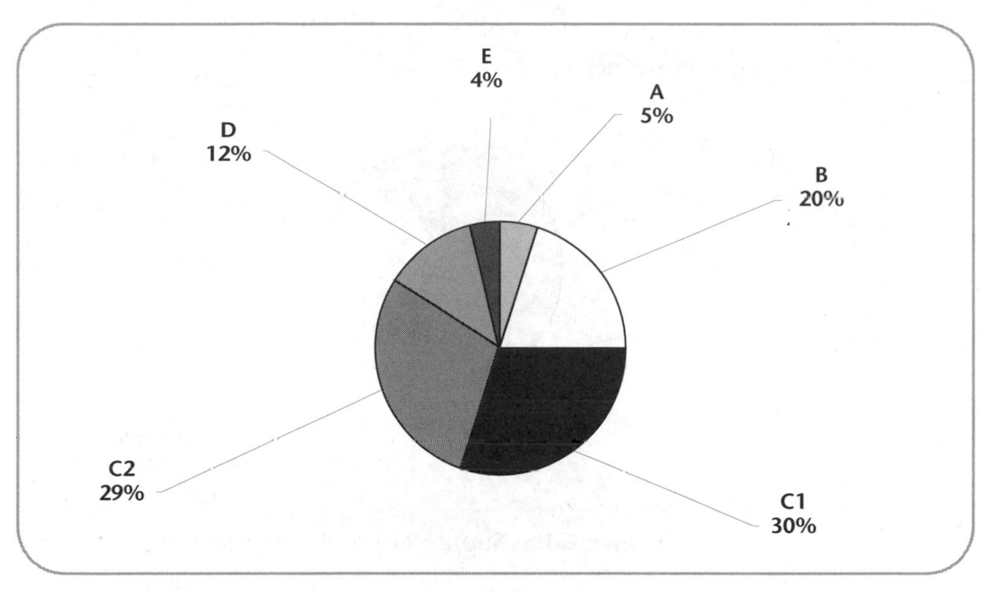

Figure C4.3 Supporter profile: socioeconomic group

Analysis of the postcodes provided by respondents indicates that there is a wide geographic spread of home addresses. A representation of this analysis is aided by only focusing on groupings of two or more respondents in a particular postcode area, as shown in Figure C4.4. It can be seen that of the 128 valid responses the largest grouping is SW6, followed by SW15 and TW16.

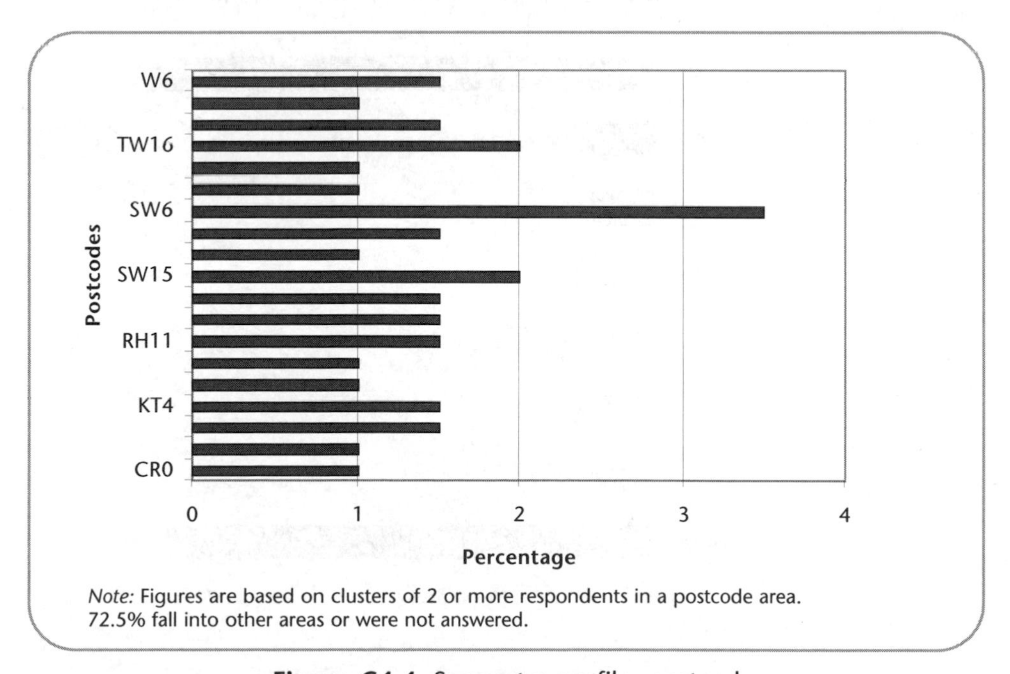

Figure C4.4 Supporter profile: postcode

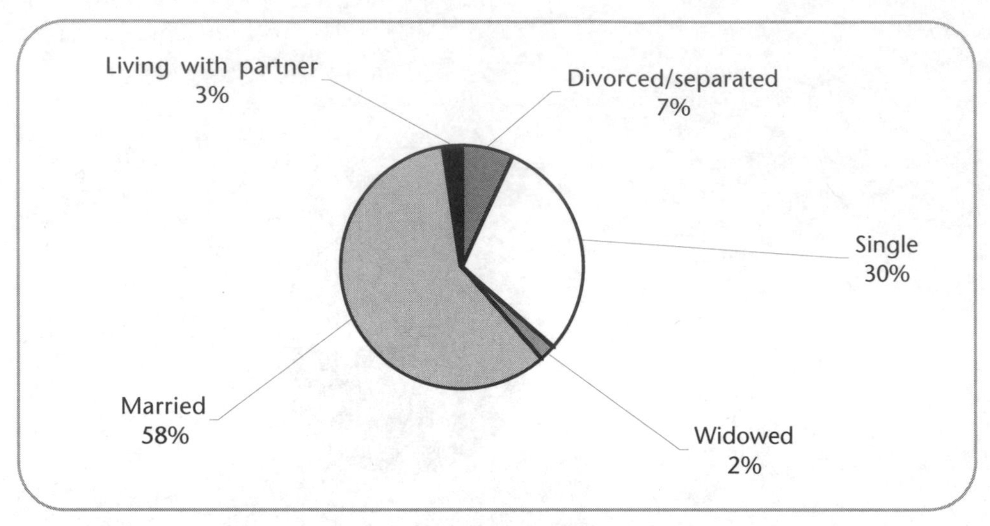

Figure C4.5 Supporter profile: marital status

The small size of these groups indicates the wide and even geographical spread. One possible reason may be that the nature of the segment means that a key reason for their not being either season ticket holders or privileges members is their distance from the ground, and this may in turn impact on their ability to attend games regularly.

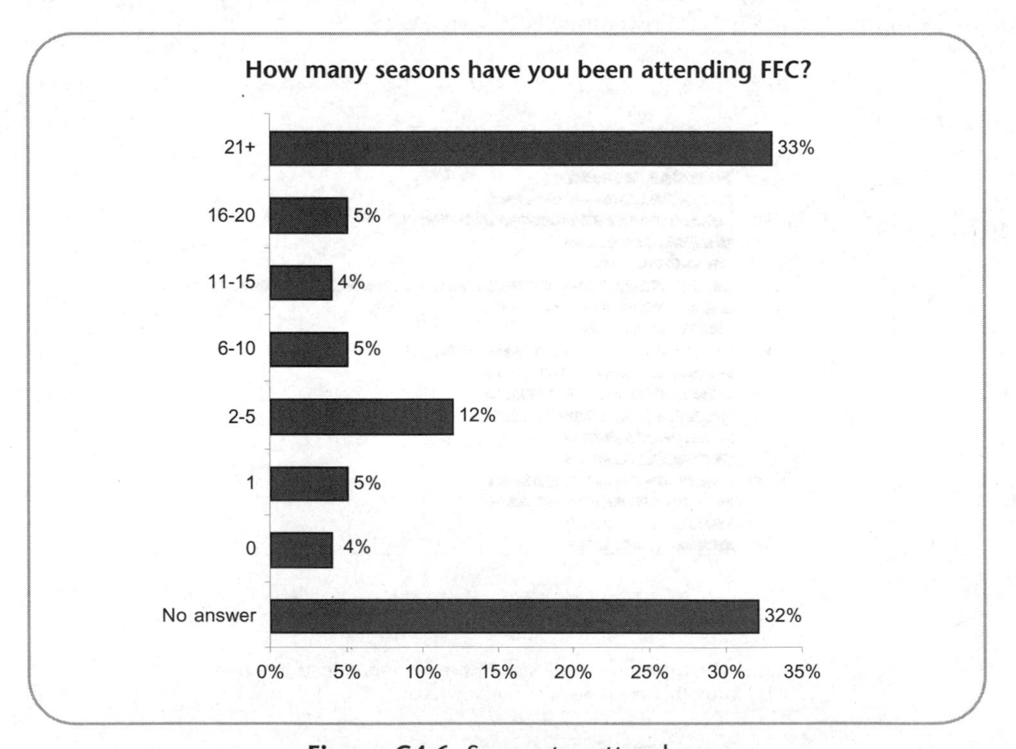

Figure C4.6 Supporter attendance

Lifecycle stages of respondents are indicated by the following analysis of marital status: 58% married; 30% single; 7% divorced/separated; 3% living with partner; and 2% widowed. This is illustrated in Figure C4.5.

Fans were questioned concerning the length of time that they had been attending FFC games (see Figure C4.6). The percentage attending for over 21 seasons appears surprisingly high at 33%, however, when it is remembered that 50% of the sample are aged between 25 and 44, and that many fans are taken to games from an early age, this is not so startling. It does illustrate the intensity of loyalty of some fans.

Many loyal supporters had attended the club's matches for over ten years. For whatever reason, they had not purchased a season ticket. Such fans had not had their loyalty recognised by the club and there is, perhaps, a danger that new fans purchasing season tickets in the last two years may get priority over these more loyal and regular supporters.

REVENUE GENERATION AND MARKET SEGMENTATION

If we accept that within football there is a direct correlation between success on the field and financial success, English football has a long way to go. Only a few of the top Premiership clubs have really grasped the concept of market orientation in comparison to their European counterparts. For English football clubs to compete successfully in major European competitions, players of greater calibre will need to be attracted. Herein lies the problem. Clubs in Germany and Italy are able to lure high-quality players since they are able to offer significantly higher wages because their sources of income have become more varied and greater (see Table C4.1).

English football shows a historic reliance upon revenue collected from gate receipts, merchandising and catering. Clubs need to actively source revenue from more lucrative and longer term deals with providers of new technologies rather than the seemingly antiquated industries of tobacco, alcohol and consumer goods (see Table C4.2).

Revenue can be earned from a variety of sources. Fundamentally, football clubs require a great deal of finance in order to attract suitably talented players to the club. However, history has shown that chairmen will not continually finance a venture if

Table C4.1 Shirt sponsorship revenue 1999–2000

	% (of total revenue)
Italy	27
Germany	25
England	16
Holland	14
France	12
Spain	6

Source: Wolstenholme (2000)

Table C4.2 Sources of revenue (Premier League) 1998/1999

	%
Matchday	37
Commercial (inc., merchandising, hospitality and sponsorship)	34
TV	29

Source: Deloitte and Touche (2000)

they do not see an element of return from their investment. Diversification of the club and its product becomes essential to generate these alternative sources of finance. There is a need for a greater understanding of the supporter base and the kind of services that they seek. Supporters are only part of the solution, however. Clubs need to be able to segment their market not only according to the needs of their supporters but also in order to satisfy their sponsors' needs.

Fulham needs to segment its fan base in the same way as a commercial organisation, such as a financial services company, segments its markets; assessing measurability, accessibility, substantiality, exclusivity and homogeneity of the various bases, be they psychographic or geodemographic. Segments change over time and what the supporter of today wants may differ substantially from tomorrow's. However, do supporters really want to be treated in this way, as part of a segment? Individualism is becoming increasingly important in society and paramount to one's sense of self. Classifying supporters on the basis of their supposedly homogeneous behaviour may not serve any real purpose. Similarly, the segmentation process is normally based on previous consumer behaviour. Where there have been large changes, such as in the supporter base for Fulham FC, future consumption may bear little resemblance.

Understanding the importance and limitations of the application of segmentation to a supporter base is one factor in the overall strategy of clubs in generating finance. Targeting alternative sources of finance is crucial to the overall success of clubs. Sponsorship and advertising revenue has traditionally been an underexploited source within the English leagues. However, as we go lower down the divisions, the opportunity for attracting lucrative sponsors becomes more limited as the levels of exposure and success such teams experience becomes more limited. Yet even within the Premier League there are clubs who, due to their location or generally unfashionable nature, do not attract the levels of attention from potential sponsors that their league status should command. Therefore, as well as a gap between rich and poor clubs between the divisions, there is a distinct wealth gap within the Premiership.

Clubs should develop strategies that exploit their relative strengths, rather than compete in areas where opportunity for success is more limited. In the case of Fulham FC, it has three major sponsors – Pizza Hut, Adidas and Carlsberg, the most visible of which is Pizza Hut, its shirt sponsors. European teams show a particular strength in this area, where they have sponsors for different parts of their business. While their core activity may be football, they have come to realise that sponsors have many clients who have no interest in the game beyond the kudos of attending and the corporate entertainment that they receive. Similarly, Manchester United has an integrated approach to its sponsorship strategy. By having different sponsors for different activities within the club, there is less conflict between sponsoring organisations and they are able to deliver a clear, consistent message to their targeted audience.

It is essential that Fulham develop expertise, knowledge and experience in this area in order to capitalise on sponsorship opportunities. Many clubs, as they are promoted from the First Division to the Premiership, are ill-prepared not only for the change in style of football but for the management and marketing demands placed on them as a Premiership team. This places a greater urgency on the need for good, continual, market(ing) research.

Figure C4.7 shows the importance of understanding the market, that is, the needs of supporters, but also the corporate entertainers who watch from the boxes. Clubs try to dovetail the interests of these diverse groups with the needs of their sponsors who understandably ask what they will get from such a relationship. For example, BT Cellnet became the sponsor of Middlesbrough FC because it saw that mobile phone penetration in the northeast of England was low in comparison to the rest of the country.

The length of the relationship between clubs and sponsors is also relevant in that it dictates the strategy that the club wishes to adopt. Some clubs choose shorter contracts because they have more powerful bargaining positions and negotiate more lucrative deals based upon a previous season's success. However, if the team is relegated, the potential for TV and media exposure is considerably reduced. The relationship often needs to be carefully managed over the longer term to ensure a constant revenue stream for the club. Cricket, as a sport, illustrates the importance of such relationships. Historically, it has relied upon financial institutions as sponsors to support

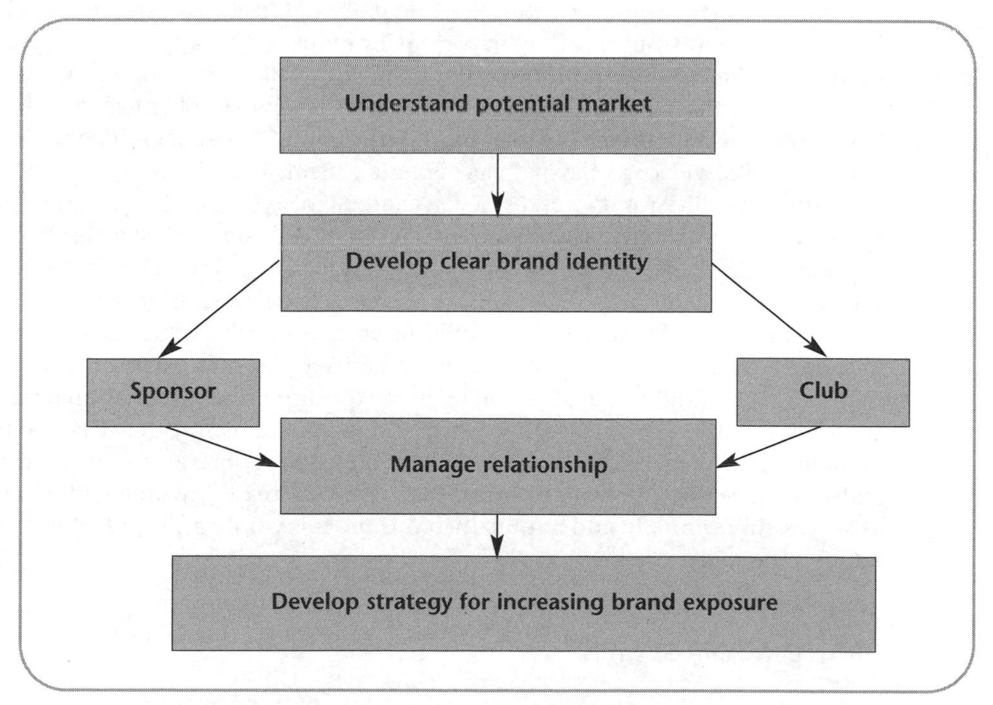

Figure C4.7 Critical success factors in football club sponsorship
Source: Adapted from Wolstenholme (2000)

Table C4.3 Matching club and sponsor needs

Type of club	International market	National market	Regional market
Successful	Manchester Utd	Arsenal	Wolverhampton Wanderers
Aspirational	Newcastle Utd	Leeds Utd	Fulham
Underexploited	Liverpool	Everton	Southampton

certain competitions for long periods of time. Cornhill, until recently the major sponsor of English test cricket, almost became synonymous with the event. Relationships can only be maintained, however, if both parties understand, know and obtain whatever they are trying to receive from the relationship.

One of the ways in which we can understand the relationship between clubs and sponsors is by matching the type of club and the nature of its supporter base with the market of the sponsor. Table C4.3 provides some examples of clubs and their nature in this regard. The table shows the types of market in which clubs seek to expose their brand. Thus, are sponsors looking for clubs with supporters from an international, national or regional marketplace? In recent years Fulham FC has developed its profile both within the immediate locality and within the southeast of England generally. It can still be seen to be aspirational in this aspect, insofar as the bulk of its support is geographically located within London.

During its First Division status, the Fulham brand received very limited exposure on a national basis, since it only had a small number of TV appearances throughout the season. Premiership status now allows the potential for developing joint ventures or alliances with media and technology companies who could enhance Fulham FC's Web presence and offer its fans, around the world, matches broadcast through streaming Web video, as pay-per-view entertainment. Manchester United has developed this capability for its worldwide fans and has also set up its own dedicated football channel with archive footage of previous matches using a media partner.

Sponsors are also seeking high levels of exposure. Given the size of their own organisations, some may be seeking to develop their reputation within a specific locality because that area is strategically important or where their main business is located. Similarly, there will be larger organisations, who may already have a national reputation, but are seeking to gain exposure on an international scale and, therefore, will seek association with clubs which can offer that potential. Manchester United has been successful in exposing its brand on an international scale, as indeed has Arsenal. Contrast this with Chelsea FC, who could be regarded as successful regionally and nationally but is probably only aspirational in the international field.

BRAND MANAGEMENT

Football clubs should not underestimate the value of their brand. How this brand is perceived by supporters and sponsors is important, since if there is a mutually congruent relationship, sponsorship is more likely to be successful. Fulham FC has developed six brand dimensions which it wishes to promote to its supporters and potential supporters. These are that the club is proactive, stylish, exciting, friendly, accessible and professional. The brand values tested by Fulham FC did not refer to activities on the football pitch, but were a reference to the perception that the supporters had of the club.

A brand must add a value to the supporter in their consumption of the product because the brand enhances the core and augmented levels of the product. Brand differentiation should not stress the core football product, since this is particularly difficult in football marketing due to the nature of the supporter loyalty and the structure of football competition. Dissatisfaction with the football product does not lead to defection to another product in the same way it does for a traditional commercial product or service. When choosing a club to support, individual decisions are based upon a myriad of reasons: family, friends, geographical proximity, success, players, underdog factor and so on, and the reasons for choice will vary from individual to individual.

Figure C4.8 illustrates the key marketing definitions of branding, and how football should move away from being product oriented and presenting the brand as product tangibles such as the logo or the club itself. The emphasis is a move towards intangible elements which take into account value, personality and relationships as a way of personifying image and identity, this then becomes of greater relevance to the consumer, that is supporter.

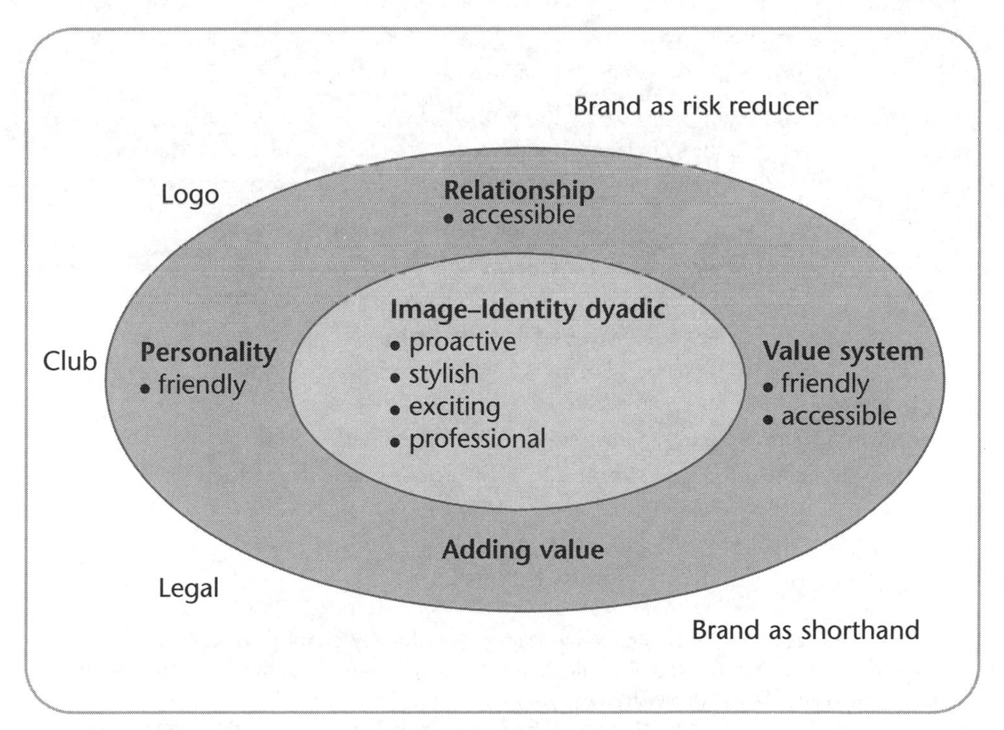

Figure C4.8 Football branding

Source: Barn and Baines (2000)

THE BRAND: A DEFINITION FOR FOOTBALL

> The football brand is more than the sum of its parts: name, logo, design, sponsorship. It should emphasise culture, personality, self-projection, reflection and relationship. A complex symbol representing a variety of ideas and attributes in which supporters find value beyond functional utility. (Barn and Baines, 2000)

The role of the brand is to act as an important link that brings the club, supporters and potential sponsors together. Building a brand that emphasises values is important to the supporter and other stakeholders alike, as clubs begin to operate in conjunction and with reference to their supporters and sponsors, rather than against them. Fulham understands the importance of its supporters and the relationship it has developed with them and, thus, the importance of fan equity. It has dovetailed its corporate activities with initiatives that take local opinion and supporter values into consideration.

Questions for discussion

1. Conduct a five forces analysis on Fulham FC. What are the major points for consideration for success in the football industry?
2. The cost of Premiership players is constantly increasing and yet Fulham must continue to purchase strong international players if it is to continually improve. Fulham's wage/turnover ratio is reputed to be around 120 per cent for the 2000 season. In what areas should Fulham Football Club focus its revenue generation activities so that it covers its costs in the longer term?
3. Fulham has a relatively low fan base and a ground capacity that is currently hindered by the need to obtain planning permission approval. How important are the fans in the generation of revenue? Why couldn't Fulham simply focus on television spectatorship?

Selected web links

www.fulham-fc.com – official club site

www.fulhamweb.com – another site for Fulham supporters

www.britishpremiersoccer.com – covers all UK premier league soccer teams

References

Barn, S S and Baines, P R (2000), 'Brand and Deliver, Your Money or Your Life: Helping Football Refocus on "Fan Equity" Through Building Brand Values', Proceedings of the Academy of Marketing Conference, July, Derby University, Derby

Deloitte and Touche, (2000), *Annual Review of Football Finance*, Manchester, Deloitte and Touche

Wolstenholme, N (2000), 'PL Sponsorship', *Soccer Analyst*, September 2000, **2**(3)

case study five

Regaining the International Market for British Beef

INTRODUCTION

In February 2002 the British agricultural industry heaved a collective sigh of relief as Britain was officially declared free of foot-and-mouth disease. Over the preceding 41 weeks, since the disease had first been discovered in British pigs, tens of thousands of animals had been destroyed and many British farmers had seen their businesses devastated. For the pig and sheep farming industries this was the signal to return to business as usual. For the beef industry, however, a longer term and arguably even more catastrophic animal health problem remained unsolved. This was the problem of bovine spongiform encephalopathy (BSE). This case study deals with the continuing problem facing the British beef industry in trying to regain its international markets following the discovery of BSE in the British beef herd.

The British beef industry has suffered considerably since the EU placed a worldwide export ban on British beef products in March 1996. This occurred after British scientists determined that UK citizens had died from Creutzfeldt-Jakob disease (CJD) that derived from infected (BSE) beef products. Although the ban was subsequently removed three years later in August 1999, an industry worth around £520 million (at 1995 prices) had been demolished. Less than 1 per cent of the British beef export trade had been won back a year later (BBC News Online, 2000). Even when the EU lifted the worldwide ban, the French national government and several German states refused to lift their own bans. The French ban still remains in place despite legal proceedings being instituted against it by the European Commission. However, other EU nations also suffered from their own BSE crises (for example France). According to the National Farmer's Union of Scotland:

> the only solution now for rebuilding the shattered confidence of European consumers is for EU Ministers en masse to stop trying to protect their own narrow national self-interest and take decisive action to bring this sorry mess to an end. That means rigorous enforcement of bans on meat and bonemeal and effective controls on specified risk materials. It also includes the introduction of a scheme, similar to the UK, one where in countries with rising incidences of BSE, beef from cattle over 30 months is removed from the food chain. This should remain in force until an effective live test for BSE can be introduced. Labelling and traceability must also be tightened up, and quickly, to the standards demanded here in the UK. (NFUS, 2000)

More recently, the UK meat and livestock industry has suffered further from an outbreak of foot-and-mouth disease, which has resulted in individual countries instituting short-term import bans on imported meat products. There has been a sharp drop in the consumption of beef throughout the EU because of BSE. In January 2001, the EU's Agriculture Commissioner, Franz Fischler, warned that the latest beef market indications were alarming. EU beef consumption is down by 27 per cent (RTE, 2001).

BSE IN BRITAIN

By September 2000, over 74 human deaths had been attributed to new variant CJD (v-CJD), the human equivalent of BSE, considered by scientists to have crossed the species barrier through the food chain (Philips, 2000). Jenkins (1998) argues that the root cause of the crisis was that a group of UK scientists changed the risk of contracting CJD through eating beef from 'an inconceivable risk' in 1995, to 'a very small one' in 1996. In actual fact, UK government scientists made the first official diagnosis of BSE in 1986 and the first human death from v-CJD was diagnosed in March 1993. It was not until March 1996, however, that the health secretary admitted the possible link between BSE-infected cattle and v-CJD. The EU imposed a worldwide trade ban in the same month. The following month, the Prime Minister, John Major, referred the ban to the European Court of Justice, although this action was ultimately unsuccessful. The UK government eventually succeeded in having the ban lifted in August 1999, although this was partly through its introduction of a scheme where all cattle over the age of 30 months (those most likely to have contracted BSE) were slaughtered. Despite these measures, the French national and some German state governments continued to enforce their own bans, although the German bans have since been lifted. The French ban, however, remains.

Politically, the crisis indicated the importance of the industry to the UK, since costs to the taxpayer were reported to have been between £3–£3.5 billion, with a considerable further cost to UK exporters of between £1–2 billion over the full three years of the ban. The cost to the government represents payments to farmers to destroy cattle over 30 months old, which had cost the UK government £1.2bn in payments up to the end of July 1999 (MAFF, 1999). A further scheme, the calf processing aid scheme was also introduced, which ended in July 1999, in order to provide farmers with support for their sudden loss of markets.

REGULATION IN THE EUROPEAN BEEF MARKET

The production of beef in the EU is largely governed by the political and administrative arrangements of the EU and by competition policy in both the UK and the EU. It is also affected considerably by the value of the pound within and outside the EU. Thus, when the pound is strong, UK beef exports become expensive to other European countries, making domestic supply more profitable. In the UK, the supermarket chains Sainsbury, Asda, Tesco and Safeway control more than 60 per cent of the food retailing industry (Wrigley, 1992) with considerable implications for the balance of power of supermarkets concerning their suppliers. Shaoul (1999) states that, under the Food Safety Act 1990, companies could avoid conviction for safety offences if they could demonstrate that all reasonable precautions had been taken to avoid infringing a requirement of the Act. This was the reasoning behind the introduction of the traceability of products by supermarkets; to ensure that the supply chain for products could be determined and that responsibility for faulty products could be apportioned.

The EU provides support to the beef industry through import levies, import quotas and export refunds on products traded outside the EU to ensure that European beef production stays at prices above world market prices. The Common Agricultural Policy (CAP) effectively governs this support regime and was designed to protect the EU farming sector from external competition. The CAP has long been criticised in Britain because of its apparent bias towards the French and German farming industries.

Prior to joining the EU, the UK beef sector operated as a fresh meat industry and had not traditionally exported to other countries. British meat suppliers were, at the time, generally not equipped to comply with the chilled meat regulations operated in many potential export markets. However, in order to join the CAP, Britain was obliged to upgrade its slaughterhouses, although Shaoul (1999) argues that not one UK slaughterhouse could meet the EEC's requirements as an approved slaughterhouse at the time of Britain's membership of the EEC. The Philips Report (2000, p. 166) highlights that when the Single European Act came into force, requiring compliance of UK slaughterhouse hygiene standards with existing EU law, 564 British slaughterhouses sought temporary derogation from compliance. When these establishments were subsequently surveyed by hygiene inspectors, 68.5 per cent of them were considered to be of concern or grave concern. This led to legislation, The Bovine Offal (Prohibition) (Amendment) Regulations 1995, which enforced greater restrictions on the removal of specified bovine offal (SBO) material; the very infected material which was said to have caused the BSE crisis in the first instance. Around this time, the government also set up the Meat Hygiene Service to monitor and oversee compliance with the regulations.

In order to export fresh beef to EU countries, exporting companies must comply with the Fresh Meat Export (Hygiene and Inspection) Regulations 1981, which ensure that meat is certified as risk free by veterinary inspectors. The Live Cattle Council Directive 64/432/EEC, which governs the export of live animals, states that the animals may be exported only if they have no signs of clinical disease. Animals must come from herds that have not been infected within a thirty-mile radius. 'Abattoirs that wish to supply the European market will have to be dedicated to that market, making the economics of the export business more problematic' (*Independent*, 1999).

The Date-based Beef Export Scheme (DBES) for the UK imposes restrictions on the preparation of beef products. Thus, from 1 August 1996, the meat must be de-boned and has to be aged between 6 and 30 months. This scheme also imposes traceability restrictions and requires DBES-approved slaughterhouses, although up until September 2000 only two slaughterhouses were DBES-approved (DEFRA, 2001a). Exporters are also expected to comply with Commission Decision 2001/172/EC, which states that veterinary certification is required for fresh or frozen beef and other beef preparations including hamburgers and sausages. In addition, cooked meats, meat sandwiches or pizzas and soups containing pieces of meat are also covered under the regulations.

Northern Ireland, which has a computer tracking system and has been able to demonstrate that its herd is BSE-free, is covered under the Export Certified Herds Scheme, which allowed export to recommence after the BSE crisis in September 1998. Export to third countries are generally covered through bilateral agreements between the two countries involved, although veterinary certification is a common requirement. The Department of the Environment, Food and Rural Affairs (DEFRA) assists in this certification provision.

THE UK BEEF EXPORT INDUSTRY SUPPLY CHAIN

In 1995, total domestic beef consumption in the UK was 901,000 tonnes, although a sharp drop took place as a result of the BSE crisis. By 1998, it had risen back up to 884,000 tonnes, partly because of advertising efforts and quality assurance schemes developed by the Meat and Livestock Commission (MLC). Safeway plc continued to sell its Heritage beef range, originally launched in 1994, with confidence because it had previously developed production protocol and traceability systems as a result of the Food Safety Act 1990.

The generally fragmented food industry is controlled by a few large vertically integrated companies (Shaoul, 1999). The beef supply chain comprises farmers (who raise and maintain beef herds), the meat processing industry and, within this, the slaughtering and rendering industries, and the knacker's yards. Farmers maintain herds of relatively small sizes over a wide range of locations (Shaw and Gibbs, 1995). They can either sell their cattle at a set dead-weight cost to meat processors or sell them via auction markets where prices fluctuate. This latter option can allow farmers to obtain significantly higher prices per head of cattle. Farmers have traditionally alternated between the different sources of income because of low switching costs. The meat processing industry has been characterised by defensive horizontal mergers between companies and vertical integration between the slaughtering and the wholesale meat market (Shaoul, 1999). The supermarket J. Sainsbury operates abattoirs to supply its own beef through one of its subsidiaries. Other supermarket groups have begun to follow this model.

The slaughtering industry in the UK comprised around 491 abattoirs in 1992, although this had declined to around 402 by 1996. Their role is to kill the animals and ensure that certain aspects of the carcass are removed prior to the despatch of cuts to the meat processor. The vast majority of these abattoirs had not altered their procedures and practices sufficiently to comply with existing EU directives. The Meat Hygiene Service (MHS), set up in 1996 to police the BSE controls and modifications to procedures in slaughterhouses, has the power to close abattoirs for non-compliance with the new regulations. The slaughter industry is responsible for the removal of

SBOs – the material most likely to contain BSE-infected tissue – and the MHS was set up to ensure that this is conducted satisfactorily.

The bovine carcass contributes by-products including material for pet food, gelatine, sausage skins, animal feed, and material for use in the production of glue, soap and fertilisers. Renderers remove the material required for the manufacture of these by-products. It is as a result of material sold to the animal feed industry that the BSE crisis is said to have originated, since infected tissue is thought to have been sold by the renderers to bonemeal manufacturers in the UK and throughout the EU. They, in turn, sold this to farmers who fed it to cattle. Knackers' yards are responsible for the disposal of diseased and dead animals from farms by incineration and burial. This role was also being played by officially approved rendering plants with the responsibility for the separation of pathogenic material.

STAKEHOLDER MAPPING IN THE BRITISH BEEF EXPORT MARKET

The export market for British beef inside and outside Europe rests on the cooperation, collaboration and competition between member organisations of the supply chain

Table C5.1 Stakeholder mapping for UK organisations involved in British beef export

INTEREST	POWER: High	POWER: Low
High	**KEY PLAYERS** Abbatoirs (EU approved) French national government British prime minister/EU president Secretary of State for Department of the Environment, Food and Rural Affairs The Meat and Livestock Commission (UK) EU beef processors Multiple retail grocers (UK, other EU)	**KEEP INFORMED** Farmers (UK)
Low	**KEEP SATISFIED NECESSARY** The UK Meat Hygiene Service Auctioneers (UK) The European Commission (UK) EU agriculture ministers (non-EU approved) EU domestic governments	**MINIMAL EFFORT** Cattle Knackers' yards Abbatoirs

Source: Adapted from Harris and Baines (2001)

within the domestic market. They in turn rely on relationships with organisations within the EU beef supply chain and relationships with foreign governments. In addition, the export market for British beef is influenced by organisations within the political sector such as non-governmental organisations within the sector (for example, the MHS and the MLC) and politicians associated with the competitiveness of what is a key British industry. Table C5.1 provides an analysis of the important stakeholders in the beef export market.

Different organisations within the supply chain contribute in different ways. For instance, beef processors prepare packaged products for export, multiple retail grocers supply European subsidiaries with pre-packaged beef products, and selected farmers are used to raise and develop herds. The MLC, which exists to raise British export revenues and domestic production, impacts upon production through the levy of export charges. EC-approved abattoirs are very important for the preparation of beef carcasses for export. Politically important stakeholders include the French national government, the British prime minister and other senior politicians involved in agricultural policy-making. The European Commission is also important since it negotiates with member governments the terms of the CAP and other relevant agriculturally related legislation and oversees the implementation and removal of trade bans.

THE EXPORT MARKET FOR BRITISH BEEF

British beef export became a global trade issue. Japan, which has not allowed imports of UK beef since 1951 out of fear of foot-and-mouth disease, announced plans for the banning of all UK beef products including pet food. Taiwan announced a ban on canned beef, sausage and ham to supplement its original ban placed on British and Irish beef in 1990. In the Middle East, Iran and Egypt both turned away Irish beef shipments (USMEF, 1999), although Irish meat processors have since re-established more friendly trade relations with the Middle East.

Prior to the BSE crisis, France and Italy represented substantial markets for British beef exports, representing almost 50 per cent of total exports in 1995. However, since 1990, significant growth had been achieved in exports to South Africa and Italy over the five years between 1990 and 1995. Table C5.2 illustrates UK beef exports. 'The proportion of UK beef and live cattle exported to the EU represented between 80% and over 90%, by value, of the total. Beef and live cattle exported to France made up about half of the value of all beef and live cattle exports' (Philips, 2000, p. 61).

One of the MLC's core objectives is to seek the removal of continuing trade bans around the world and, after removal, to re-establish government and consumer confidence in key export markets. The MLC's export objective is to assist the government in the lifting of the beef export ban and recover the markets for British beef. To achieve this objective, the MLC aims to influence opinion-formers' lobbying activities and, consequently, operates an office in Brussels and France. Along with DEFRA, it also has agents in other EU countries. MLC and DEFRA representatives have taken part in overseas trade missions, including visits to countries such as South Africa, China, the Philippines and Japan.

It is in the Pacific Rim and the Far East that beef imports are most likely to increase. The Japanese and South Korean markets are forecast to grow and import

Table C5.2 Revenue obtained from UK beef exports by country

Importer	1995 value (£m)	1999 value (£m)
France	179.0	0
Italy	126.0	0
Ireland	52.0	0
Netherlands	49.4	0
Spain	17.4	0
Denmark	12.0	0
Belgium	10.0	0
Portugal	7.0	0
Sweden	3.0	0
Greece	0.6	0
Germany	0.6	0
Finland	0.0	0
Austria	0.0	0
South Africa	23.8	0
Mauritius	4.0	0
Ghana	2.5	0
Angola	1.5	0
Malta	2.2	0
Saudi Arabia	1.7	0
Hungary	1.8	0
Philippines	1.5	0
Gabon	1.7	0
Hong Kong	1.8	0
Other non-EU	20.5	0
Total	**520.0**	**0**

Source: MLC (2000)

requirements are likely to increase substantially over the next five years. Growth is expected in South America but domestic production is set to overcome supply. China's liberalising market is increasingly likely to demand greater beef imports. However, UK beef exporters require better knowledge and attitudes of markets and consumers in order to take advantage of export opportunities (MLC, 2000). Table C5.3 provides a forecast of the likely trends in world beef import and export over the next ten years.

Table C5.3 clearly shows that exports are set to decline for the EU-15 as a group, although this could hide substantial intra-country trade deficits in beef import and export. The increasing capacity for production in South America looks set to provide sufficient beef products for the growing levels of consumption in this region, while New Zealand are also likely to increase their success in this field, building on their international reputation in the pork and lamb trades.

Table C5.3 Likely trends in world beef trade, 2000–10

Importers	Exporters
East Asia +++	South America +++
Middle East +	EU-15 –
	Australasia +
	New Zealand ++
	USA =/+

Key
+ gaining in importance; – declining in importance; = no change in importance
extent of change shown by number of indicators

Source: MLC (2000)

Table C5.4 provides an indication of the changes in beef consumption throughout the world between 1988 and 1998. It clearly indicates that consumption was highest in North America, Australasia and South America with Russia and the EU-15 trailing behind in terms of consumption levels. However, significant growth has taken place in consumption levels in China and, to a lesser extent, in the Asia Pacific Rim region. In view of the very large population that lives in this region, this represents a sizeable market. Clearly, though, such a market opportunity would require considerable negotiation, and collaboration, with Far Eastern trade partners in order to ensure that the cold chain, necessary for distribution and storage of the beef product, was maintained from carcass to customer.

Table C5.4 World per capita consumption levels

	Beef	
	Kg	**% change 98/88**
Africa	5.3	–15
Australasia	31.6	–12
China	3.8	+375
Asia Pacific Rim	5.4	+35
Other Asia	3.9	+30
Eastern Europe	10.3	–29
EU-15	19.2	–15
North America	42.8	–7
Russia	19.9	N/A
South America	29.5	+13
World	9.8	–6

Source: MLC (2000)

Questions for discussion

1. Conduct an industry analysis for the British beef export industry, explaining the major influences on the export and marketing processes.
2. What are the British beef industry's strategic options? Outline credible alternatives using Ansoff's matrix.
3. Assuming you are the Meat and Livestock Commission, outline a strategy for the British beef industry to restore distribution in non-domestic markets, indicating which markets it should concentrate on and why.

Selected web links

www.meatmatters.com – Meat and Livestock Commission consumer site

www.mlc.org.uk – Meat and Livestock Commission site

References

BBC News Online (2000),'Europe Snubs British Beef', Tuesday, 1 August, http://news2.thdo.bbc.co.uk/low/english/uk/newsid_860000/860422.stm

DEFRA (2001a), 'Date Based Export Scheme', Department of the Environment, Food and Rural Affairs, http://www.maff.gov.uk/animalh/int-trde/prod-ex/dbes/dbes.htm

Harris, P and Baines, P (2001), 'Lobbying for Survival: The UK BSE Crisis and the Role of the Meat and Livestock Commission in Lifting The EC Export Ban', in Moss, D and DeSanto, B (eds) *Public Relations Cases: International Perspectives*, Routledge: London, pp.130–43

Independent, the (1999), 'UK Farmers Can Export Beef Again', 10 July 1999, http://www.millenium debate.org/ind10july.html

Jenkins, S (1998), 'Scientific Terrorism', *The Times*, p.18

MAFF (1999), 'MAFF BSE Information: Support to the Beef Industry', Ministry of Agriculture, Fisheries and Food, http://www. Maff.gov.uk/animalh/bse/market-support/market-support-index.html

MLC (2000), 'New Horizons – The Global Meat Industry to 2010', MLC Planning and Forecasting Group, MLC: Milton Keynes

NFUS (2000), Press Release 222/00, National Farmer's Union of Scotland, accessed at www.nfus.org.uk

Philips, Lord (2000), 'BSE Enquiry: Findings and Conclusions', 1: 34, HMSO: London

RTE (2001), 'Sharp drop in EU beef consumption', RTE news online report, Monday 29 January, http://www.network2.ie/news/2001/0129/bse.html

Shaoul, J (1999), 'Rendering: An Account for BSE?', paper presented at the Interdisciplinary Perspective on Accounting Conference, July 1997, University of Manchester, Manchester

Shaw, S A and Gibbs, J (1995), 'Retailer–Supplier Relationships and the Evolution of Marketing: Two Food Industry Case Studies', *International Journal of Retail and Distribution Management*, **23**(7): 7–16

USMF (1999), 'BSE Scare Becomes Global Beef Issue', United States Meat Export Federation Export Newsline, http://ifse.tamu.edu/cknowledge/usmefexport.html

Wrigley, N (1992), 'Anti-trust Regulation and the Restructuring of Grocery Retailing in Britain and the USA', *Environment and Planning*, **24**: 727–49

case study six

GlaxoSmithKline in South Africa

BACKGROUND

There can be no doubt that modern drugs have had an enormously beneficial effect on the welfare of a great many people around the world. Perhaps the most obvious example was the development of the antibiotic (antibacterial) family of drugs, such as penicillin and oxytetracycline. These are drugs that act against bacterial infections. They make it possible to cure, at very little cost, diseases that in comparatively recent history were deeply feared and often fatal. For example, in mid-nineteenth-century Europe, it is estimated that around a quarter of deaths were caused by tuberculosis. The use of vaccination has very much reduced the incidence of the disease, and sufferers today have a high chance of survival if they are treated with the appropriate antibiotics.

However, the mention of tuberculosis raises two awkward current issues for the health industry. First, although tuberculosis is little feared in the developed world – where vaccination levels are high, hygiene and nutrition standards are generally good, and the necessary drugs are available – it remains a feared disease in many developing countries that do not benefit from the same conditions. Second, tuberculosis is a much more dangerous disease if it is contracted by people who have an impaired immune system. The immune system is the body's defence mechanism against disease. In recent years a virus has emerged that can significantly reduce the ability of the human body to fight disease – the human immunodeficiency virus (HIV). Tuberculosis, and many other infections, are much more dangerous to those infected with HIV than to healthy adults.

The global pharmaceutical industry has been responsible for the development and marketing of a wide range of products that have cured disease, extended life and improved the quality of life for many human beings. However, the combination of the global pharmaceutical industry with the developing world and with HIV has proved to be an explosive political and commercial mixture. Drug firms have found themselves under heavy fire from respected international charities such as Oxfam and Médicins sans Frontières. Whether just or unjust, these attacks have certainly focused the attention of the world on the marketing practices of the pharmaceutical companies in developing countries. This case study explores the issues raised by looking at one major drug firm, GlaxoSmithKline, and how it has dealt with the controversy surrounding the pricing of drug therapies for HIV infection in South Africa.

A BRIEF HISTORY OF GSK

GlaxoSmithKline plc was created in 2000 through the merger of Glaxo Wellcome and SmithKline Beecham (SKB). The compound names of these firms give some impression of the complexity of their history, and illustrate the way in which corporate mergers and acquisitions have played a large part in creating the structure of the global pharmaceutical industry.

GlaxoSmithKline can trace its history as far back as 1715 when the Old Plough Court pharmacy was set up in London. This was later renamed Allen and Hanbury's and subsequently merged with Glaxo in 1958. The Beecham organisation began in 1842. In 1875, Smith, Kline and Company was formed. Burroughs Wellcome was formed in 1880. Glaxo, a corruption of the name of the company's principal dried milk product, Lacto, was formed in 1906. In 1976, SmithKline French (SKF), as it had become, produced the world's first multi-billion dollar drug, Tagamet. An anti-ulcer drug, it effectively rescued the parent company from serious financial pressures, ensuring SKF's continuing future as a world leader in the manufacture and distribution of medicinal treatments. However, its major competitor, Glaxo, launched its own premium-priced version, Zantac, backward engineered from the original Tagamet compound in 1981. In 1982, SmithKline French acquired Beckman Instruments and formed SmithKline Beckman. By 1986, Zantac had become the world's best-selling medicine. A year later, Wellcome registered the AIDS (acquired immune deficiency syndrome) treatment, Retrovir, a ground-breaking treatment for HIV/AIDS. In 1989, SmithKline Beckman and Beechams Group plc merged to form SmithKline Beecham, providing SmithKline with a major capability in the over-the-counter non-prescription medicine market. In 2000, SmithKline Beecham and Glaxo Wellcome merged to form GlaxoSmithKline (GSK), the world's largest pharmaceutical company.

GSK products in context

GlaxoSmithKline describes itself as a major global healthcare business operating in two segments:

- prescription medicines and vaccines
- consumer healthcare. These are further divided into 10 major therapeutic areas, outlined in Table C6.1.

Table C6.1 Sales by therapeutic area

Therapeutic area	2000 (£m)	1999 (£m)	1998 (£m)
Central Nervous System Disorders	3,279	2,720	2,400
Respiratory	2,789	2,382	2,096
Anti-bacterials	2,472	2,383	2,278
Anti-virals	1,899	1,610	1,347
Metabolic and gastro-intestinal	1,232	886	908
Vaccines	842	776	726
Oncology and emesis	710	613	549
Cardio-vascular	463	449	390
Dermatologicals	249	254	243
Arthritis	210	275	301
Others	837	842	949
Divested products	447	428	376
Total	**15,429**	**13,618**	**12,563**

Source: GlaxoSmithKline (2000a). Reproduced by kind permission of GlaxoSmithKline plc

Table C6.1 clearly indicates the scope of GSK's activity in the global healthcare market. The acquisition of Wellcome and the merger with SKB ensured that Glaxo moved from being overreliant on the anti-ulcer market (and then suffering when the product ceased to have patent protection) to a position of strength. Strength was first achieved in the antiviral and vaccines sector (through Wellcome), then in the central nervous system and respiratory sectors (through SKB). In the HIV/AIDS sector, GSK has a number of HIV/AIDS products including Retrovir and Epivir (combined as Combivir), Ziagen and Agenerase. GSK now has sustainable leadership in this market.

The development of these drugs is crucial in curtailing the HIV/AIDS pandemic, particularly in sub-Saharan Africa, where the virus is most prevalent. The pharmaceutical industrial has a critical role to play in making the relevant drugs available at reduced prices. The difficulty for the multinational pharmaceutical company, however, is in ensuring that patents continue to be recognised throughout the world. If patents cease to hold their legal power, huge R&D expenditures will be wasted as smaller pharmaceutical companies, operating challenger positioning strategies, produce generic 'me-too' versions of the product.

The scale of geographic distribution of GSK products is outlined in Table C6.2, which clearly illustrates the focus of its operations. GSK principally sells its products to wholesale drug distributors, independent and multiple retail pharmacies, physicians, hospitals, clinics and government purchasing entities in the US and Europe. The Middle Eastern and African market, by comparison with other geographic markets, is relatively small. GSK and other drug firms such as Merck and Co., Boehringer Ingelheim, Hoffman LaRoche, and Bristol Myers Squib all began offering low-price HIV/AIDS drugs under the UN scheme, Accelerating Access Initiative (AAI). By 10 February 2001, only Rwanda, Senegal and Uganda had signed up to the initiative. This scheme is likely to be furthered hampered by the offer from an Indian

Table C6.2 Sales by geographic region

Geographic region	2000 (£m)	1999 (£m)	1998 (£m)
USA	7,705	6,276	5,635
Europe	4,268	4,288	4,059
Rest of the world:			
Asia Pacific	1,049	929	876
Japan	832	704	592
Latin America	682	636	662
Middle East, Africa	511	461	468
Canada	382	324	271
Total	**15,429**	**13,618**	**12,563**

Source: GlaxoSmithKline (2000a). Reproduced by kind permission of GlaxoSmithKline plc

company, Cipla, to sub-Saharan governments to supply the necessary drugs for approximately one-fifth of that charged under the AAI scheme (Mutume, 2001). Sub-Saharan African governments wanted to import drugs from other countries where drugs have already gone ex-patent (for example Brazil). This is known as parallel importing. In other countries, such as India, governments have passed laws that allow competing pharmaceutical companies to produce generic versions but they must pay royalties to the existing patent-holder (this is known as compulsory licensing).

The solution to the problem of ensuring distribution of HIV/AIDS drugs in the developing world requires a multiple stakeholder approach. Figure C6.1 provides a graphic illustration of the relevant stakeholders and their areas of responsibility.

Multilateral agencies work to coordinate international responses, define health-care priorities and support intellectual property rights. The governments of developing countries mobilise their own national resources to this problem. Equally, they should enforce drug safety and quality standards. The pharmaceutical industry has a role to play in offering drugs at preferential prices, and in researching and producing the relevant vaccines and medicines. The media can help to raise awareness of the problems among Western citizenry. Non-governmental organisations (NGOs) provide support and develop local community partnerships. The distribution and development difficulties required to ensure mass treatment in the developing world of the HIV/AIDS pandemic requires greater financing than the global healthcare industry can afford by itself; particularly with drugs offered at preferential prices. Funding is required both for capacity-building and R&D, from funding agencies (for example the World Bank) within a framework of support designed and maintained by the governments of the developed countries.

The solution to the problem of making life-saving drugs available in poor, developing countries has to be set in the context of a world trade system that aims to offer legal protection against patent infringement. Depending on your perspective, the regulatory regime governing international trade is either an essential protection for legal rights, or a barrier to the distribution of life-saving products to very poor, very ill people.

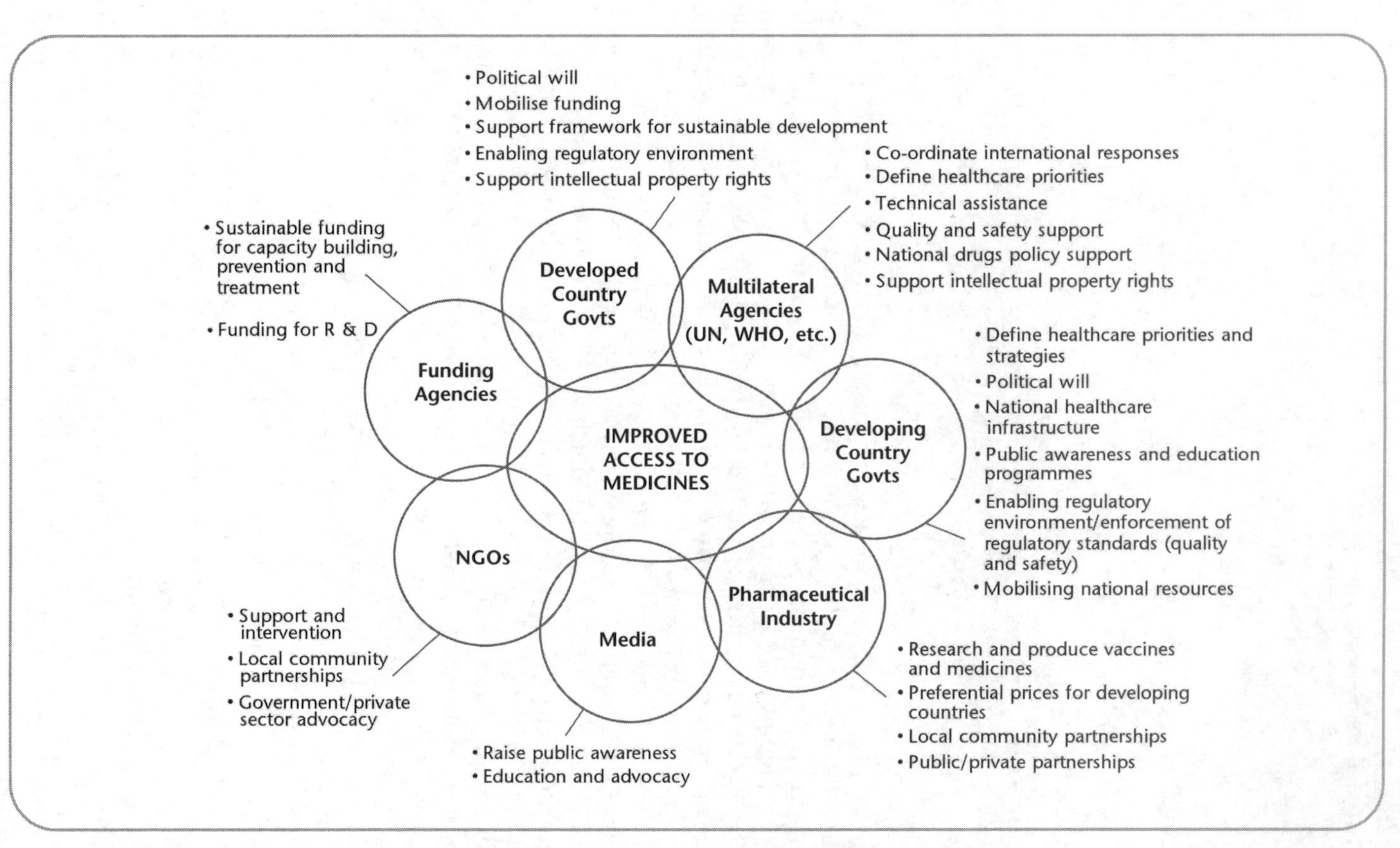

Figure C6.1 Shared responsibilities – healthcare in the developing world

Source: GlaxoSmithKline (2000b). Reproduced by kind permission of GlaxoSmithKline plc

THE INTERNATIONAL TRADE CONTEXT

The rules governing world trade are negotiated by governments within the framework of the World Trade Organization (WTO). The WTO has more than 140 members, accounting for over 90 per cent of world trade. The top decision-making body in the WTO is the Ministerial Conference, which meets at least once every two years. Generally, it is the most senior political leaders from member countries that attend the Ministerial Conference. Underneath the Ministerial Conference, the General Council meets several times a year at the WTO Geneva headquarters. Three further councils – for goods, services and intellectual property – report to the General Council. In addition, there are numerous committees, working groups and working parties that deal with individual trade agreements and other issues such as the environment and membership applications. The WTO has a permanent secretariat of around 500 staff, based in Geneva, Switzerland, which supplies technical support to the various councils and committees and the Ministerial Conference.

The WTO's stated overriding objective is 'to help trade flow smoothly, freely, fairly and predictably'. At the heart of the WTO system is a set of trade agreements to which member countries are signatories. Generally, the member governments will have enacted domestic legislation to ensure that their citizens must comply with WTO agreements. The WTO framework of agreements includes the Trade Related Intellectual Property Rights (TRIPs) agreement. TRIPs requires all countries to enforce 20-year patent protection for new drugs, or face trade sanctions. This requirement has led to bitter disputes over the availability of expensive patented, life-saving drug treatments to patients in poor, developing countries. The dispute has been at its most bitter in the case of treatments for HIV/AIDS, where South Africa was the focus of a key legal battle.

HIV/AIDS

Around 40 million people are infected with HIV/AIDS in the world; two-thirds of them live in Africa. In some of the poorest countries, about one in every five adults is infected with HIV. As yet there is no cure for HIV/AIDS, but the life of a victim can be improved and prolonged through the use of anti-retroviral drugs. Since there is no cure, anti-retroviral drugs must be taken for the duration of the sufferer's life. Many people living with HIV/AIDS in the developed world (for example in the USA, the UK and Australia) benefit from these drugs. However, comparatively few people with HIV/AIDS in developing countries have access to them.

HIV damages the body's ability to combat certain infections. People infected with HIV are known as 'HIV positive'. It is possible to be HIV positive for up to 10 or 12 years, before developing AIDS. The body's natural defences contain millions of TD-4 cells that fight the virus. The human body continually produces millions of new TD-4 cells but the virus is continually replicating. The ratio of TD-4 cells to the number of replicated viruses is known as viral load. Someone without HIV might also carry the same organisms inside their body but without the risk of becoming ill (National AIDS Trust, 2000). A patient is said to have AIDS when particular infections are diagnosed because of their weakened immune system. Ultimately, AIDS leads to death. However, in developed countries, the rate of HIV infection has been reduced through the promotion of safer sexual practices, and the death rate from HIV/AIDS has declined through the use of combination drug therapies ('drug cocktails').

Avert (2001) cited a recent UNAIDS (United Nations HIV/AIDS programme) report, outlining that there were 3 million AIDS-related deaths in 2001. There were 5 million new HIV infections and the number of people living with HIV/AIDS reached the 40 million mark. Of the 5 million new infections, 3.4 million were from the sub-Saharan Africa region. In 2001, there were on average 14,000 new infections a day, with over 95 per cent of these occurring in developing countries. Of those 14,000 people, 2000 are children under 15 (Avert, 2001).

Médicins sans Frontières argues that lower drug prices are crucial to the fight against HIV/AIDS in the developing countries. The Pharmaceutical Research and Manufacturers of America (PhRMA – a trade association for pharmaceutical companies) argues that medicines are only one part of the solution to the AIDS crisis. PhRMA points out that many developing nations lack the infrastructure to deliver quality healthcare, and that governments have often failed to acknowledge the seriousness of HIV/AIDS or have preferred to give priority to other spending areas (such as defence). So, while AIDS lobby groups and major international charities such as Médicins sans Frontières and Oxfam argue that the priority must be to make drugs more affordable, the pharmaceutical companies argue that drugs are only one part of the solution. For example, better sex education might reduce the spread of the disease, and governments could change their policies to increase the priority allocated to HIV/AIDS treatment.

THE BROADER ARGUMENT ABOUT DRUG PRICES

'Bluntly stated, minor sexual problems in rich countries make serious money, while life threatening diseases among poor people do not' (Watkins, 2001, p. 104). Watkins points out that total spending on drugs in sub-Saharan Africa is less than $1 billion a year, while the Pfizer corporation alone has eight drugs with sales of over $1 billion. One of these drugs is Viagra, used to treat 'erectile dysfunction' in men. On the other hand – so the argument goes – the worldwide patent protection offered to certain drug products by the TRIPs agreement will prevent millions of poor people from receiving life-saving treatment because prices will simply be too high.

Many drug prices bear little relation to their costs of manufacture. Frequently, the cost of manufacturing drugs is but a small fraction of their retail price. However, the fixed costs associated with discovering and developing a new drug can be very high indeed. The global pharmaceutical companies claim that high prices are necessary to recoup the costs of R&D, and to reinvest in research into new drugs. A typical new patented drug will cost around $800 million in R&D costs, and take 12 years from invention through to commercial launch. Without patent protection, the drug companies argue, it would be possible for competing manufacturers to copy the drug and offer it for sale at a much lower price. This would remove the incentive to develop new drugs and would ultimately harm patients. Cheap copies of patented drugs are known as 'generics'. The difference between the price of a patented drug and a generic copy can be staggering. A typical claim is that to treat one person for a year with the basic 'cocktail' of anti-retroviral drugs necessary to control HIV/AIDS costs between $10,000 and $15,000 using patented drugs, while manufacturers of generic copies claim that they could offer the same treatment for around $250. These claims need to be treated with some care. For example, it is easy to create a dramatic but inaccurate comparison by comparing the treatment cost using the very latest patented medicines with the treatment cost using older drugs that are ex-patent.

The drug fluconazole provides an excellent illustration of the way in which drug prices can vary dramatically in different geographical markets, depending on the extent to which there is competition from generics. Fluconazole is an antifungal drug with a wide range of applications – for example in the UK it is marketed under the brand name Diflucan as an over-the-counter remedy for the common, minor fungal infection thrush. However, fluconazole can also be a life-saving drug. A significant proportion of people (over 10 per cent in some countries) living with HIV/AIDS are affected by cryptococcal meningitis, which will normally kill them in less than a month unless treated. Cryptococcal meningitis is a fungal infection, and fluconazole is an invaluable part of the treatment – this involves first bringing the condition under control and then taking a maintenance treatment for life. According to Médicins sans Frontières, the June 2000 wholesale price of Diflucan varied from US$ 6.20 per 200 mg capsule in Thailand to $27.60 in Guatemala. In countries where the patent is not recognised, generic versions of fluconazole are available. The wholesale price of generic fluconazole in June 2000 was US$ 0.29 per capsule in Thailand and $0.64 in India. Clearly, such variations in drug prices make a substantial difference to the ability of health services to afford life-long treatment for HIV/AIDS patients affected by cryptococcal meningitis. A study by Médicins sans Frontières showed that the cost of maintenance treatment would be US$9 per patient per month using generic fluconazole in Thailand and $828 per patient per month using the patented product in Guatemala.

One of the world's most significant manufacturers of generic drugs, and India's leading drug firm, is Cipla – parent company to South African firm Cipla-Medpro. In February 2001, Cipla offered to sell a generic version of the basic anti-retroviral 'triple therapy' for $600 (per patient per year) to governments and for $350 to Médicins sans Frontières. The patented equivalents sell for $10,000 to $15,000 in Western countries. Of course, as a manufacturer of generics, Cipla spends almost nothing on research and development. Representatives of the major drug companies argue that high drug prices are not the only reason that HIV/AIDS sufferers in developing countries were not receiving treatment. They point to a lack of political will among governments to spend enough money on medicines, poorly developed physical and medical infrastructures, and an inability among poorly educated people to use such drugs properly.

For a few weeks in late 2001, the complex issues of the TRIPs agreement, drug patents and generic drug competition became big news in Western countries. The reason? In the wake of the catastrophic terrorist attacks of 11 September (including the destruction of the World Trade Center in New York), several envelopes containing anthrax spores were received at US media and governmental offices. The antibiotic Ciprofloxican (Cipro) is the standard treatment for anthrax infection. Cipro is a patented drug in the USA, and a 30-day course of treatment with the patented product costs around $350. However, in some other countries, Cipro does not have patent protection and generic versions of the drug sell for about $30 for a course of treatment. Lobby groups in the USA asked their government to set aside the patent for Cipro so that an equivalent generic product could be manufactured to counter the public concern over anthrax. In the end the US government struck a deal with the patent-holder to buy branded Cipro at a discounted price.

THE CASE OF SOUTH AFRICA

According to the *Guardian* (19 August 2001), there are 4.7 million people living with HIV/AIDS in South Africa. More than 120,000 people have died from HIV/AIDS-related illnesses, and around half a million children have been orphaned by the disease. By 2010, AIDS is expected to have reduced life expectancy in South Africa by 20 years. In South Africa, HIV/AIDS has had a noticeable impact upon the demographics of the country (ING Barings, 1999). According to one source, one-tenth of the population were infected in 2000 (Stephenson, 2000), and some unofficial estimates place the degree of infection even higher. The provision of treatment for HIV/AIDS is, therefore, a high-profile issue in South Africa. For example, in July 2000, the South African *Sunday Times* published an exchange of letters between President Thabo Mbeki and the leader of the official opposition Tony Leon. Both leaders demonstrated a detailed understanding of HIV/AIDS treatments, and the pros and cons of using AZT (a GlaxoSmithKline product) to prevent HIV infection in rape victims. Nevertheless, President Mbeki has been criticised by many commentators for refusing to accept that HIV is responsible for AIDS, and his government has come under criticism for refusing to buy anti-retroviral drugs.

In 1997, the South African government passed a law (the Medicines and Related Substances Amendment Act) that authorised the government to allow the importation of lower priced drugs where patented medicines were 'unaffordable' or in the case of a national health emergency. The government hoped to take advantage of a clause in the TRIPs agreement (section 5 article 31) permitting WTO members to set aside a patent 'in the case of a national emergency'.

In response, 39 drug companies – including GlaxoSmithKline – initiated legal action against the South African government. In their view, the Act gave too much freedom of action to the health minister, and went beyond the legitimate interpretation of the TRIPs opt-out clause. The Pharmaceutical Manufacturers Association won a court injunction blocking the implementation of the Medicines Act on the grounds that it breached the TRIPs agreement. The case came to court in 2001, although a number of interesting developments had occurred before then.

- *May 2000:* It was announced that five major pharmaceutical companies, including Glaxo Wellcome (as it then was) had offered 75 per cent price reductions on the prices of anti-AIDS drugs. The international medical charity Médicins sans Frontières claimed that even at a 75 per cent discount the patented drugs would still be a great deal more expensive than equivalent generic copies.
- *November 2000:* The government of the Western Cape province struck a deal with Glaxo Wellcome to get supplies of AZT at one-fifth of the prevailing market price.
- *March/April 2001:* The case brought by 39 pharmaceutical companies against the South African government finally came to the Pretoria High Court. A submission of evidence by a small AIDS rights group, the Treatment Action Campaign (TAC), brought proceedings to a halt for a six-week adjournment. TAC claimed that the R&D costs for all five of the main anti-AIDS drugs had been met by US universities or the United States National Institute for Health, and provided expert opinion to support this argument. By now the pharmaceutical companies were receiving particularly adverse publicity over the issue, and at this point it perhaps

also dawned on them that they might lose the case. So in April 2001 the companies abandoned their case against the South African government.

- *June 2001:* GlaxoSmithKline offered a comprehensive package of discounts on the medicines most needed by poor countries. As a result of the various offers made by both multinationals and generic manufacturers, the average price of anti-AIDS drugs, available to the governments of countries in sub-Saharan Africa, had fallen by roughly 80 per cent in one year.
- *October 2001:* The South African Competition Commission began an investigation into the price of anti-AIDS drugs. In a case initiated by generic drug manufacturer Cipla, GSK and Boehringer Ingelheim were accused of charging 'exorbitant' prices for anti-AIDS drugs in South Africa. GSK gave South African drug manufacturer Aspen Pharmacare a voluntary licence on its anti-HIV/AIDS products AZT, 3CT and Combivir. Reportedly, Aspen Pharmacare planned to sell AZT for the equivalent of £1 per patient per day, 3TC for 40p and Combivir (which combines AZT and 3TC) for £1.20.

GSK found itself in the curious position of having offered huge discounts on some of its most important, patented products, yet still facing criticism from international charities and the threat of legal action from the South African government. One can almost hear the scratching of heads among GSK top management.

Questions for discussion

1. What is the purpose of patents in the pharmaceutical industry?
2. How would you characterise patents using Porter's industry analysis framework?
3. What strategic options does GlaxoSmithKline have for the South African market?
4. Prepare an outline analysis of the world market for anti-AIDS drugs in terms of the underlying logic of the market economy.

Selected web links

www.gsk.com – GlaxoSmithKline site

www.msf.org – Médicins sans Frontières, international charity

www.oxfam.org – Oxfam, international charity

www.phrma.org – industry association site for pharmaceutical manufacturers

References

Avert (2001), 'Number of people living with HIV/AIDS reaches 40 million', http://www.avert.org.uk/news.htm, accessed 28 November

GlaxoSmithKline (2000a), Annual Report, http://corp.gsk.com/about/downloads.htm, accessed 2 December 2001

GlaxoSmithKline (2000b), Facing the Challenge, http://corp.gsk.com/about/downloads.htm, accessed 2 December 2001

ING Barings (1999), 'The demographic impact of AIDS on the South African Economy', December, Johannesburg

Médecins sans Frontières, www.msf.org

Mutume, G (2001), 'Pressure Against AIDS Drug Companies Blackmailing Africa', Misanet.com/IPS 10 February 2001, http://www.afrol.com/Categories/Health/health051_aidsdrug_price.htm, accessed 2 December 2001

National AIDS Trust (2000), 'Find out about AIDS', http://www.worldaidsday.org/difference/findout.cfm, accessed 4 December 2001

Stephenson, J (2000), 'AIDS in South Africa Takes Centre Stage', *Journal of the American Medical Association*, **284**(2), http://jama.ama-assn.org/issues/v284n2/jmn0712-1.html, accessed 2 December 2001

Watkins, I (2001), 'Pharmaceutical Patents', in Bircham, E and Charlton, J (eds), *Anti-capitalism: A Guide to the Movement*, London: Bookmark Publications, pp. 93–109

case study seven

Should UPS Purchase the Shuttle?

This case concerns logistics – that is, comprehensive (often global) supply chain solutions that reduce costs, improve customer service, reduce inventory investments and speed up product delivery, resulting in enhanced organisational performance for business-to-business clients.

NINE DECADES ON WHEELS

United Parcel Service (UPS), now one of the most recognised brands in the world, actually got started on two wheels. Founded in Seattle back in 1907, UPS was established as a foot and bicycle-based messenger and package delivery service. The company grew rapidly by emphasising service and teamwork, constantly developing effective managerial practices and applying new technologies to improve overall efficiency. In 1929, the progressive firm launched the world's first air express service. The next four decades allowed UPS to expand aggressively across the entire country. By 1975, the company had become the first package delivery service capable of serving every address in the USA with its famous fleet of shiny brown delivery vans. In the 1980s the firm proceeded to build its own airline. This led to a global expansion programme in the 1990s to more than 200 countries and territories, providing the logistics enterprise with access to two-thirds of the world's population. As growth accelerated, the company changed in late 1999 from one of the world's largest private corporations – owned by its employees – to a public company with its stock traded on the New York Stock Exchange. Equipped with a new corporate charter and fresh funds, UPS could now greatly expand the company's view of its role in the world. Over the next 18 months, the corporation launched an e-logistics division (specifically for e-commerce clients) and a service parts logistics division, purchased the leading Latin American air cargo fleet, expanded UPS Capital into Asia, secured the right to fly cargo directly to and from China, consolidated its global customs brokerage operations with freight forwarding services and acquired First International Bancorp (commercial lenders).

UPS TODAY

UPS is now the largest express carrier, the largest package delivery company and one of the world's largest employers, with 370,000 people working around the globe. Reporting assets totalling US$24 billion and annual revenues in excess of US$30 billion for 2001 (see Table C7.1), the company has come to see itself as a pre-eminent 'enabler of commerce', building leading-edge supply chain capabilities for clients everywhere. Its list of services has grown extensively over the years and now encompasses a broad range of categories such as finance, logistics, customs brokerage, freight movement, electronic commerce and even venture capital.

From its corporate headquarters in Atlanta, its high powered managerial team headed by Chairman and CEO Michael Eskew keeps an ever-watchful eye on the corporation's global sprawl. UPS currently serves almost eight million customers each day using a delivery fleet of 149,000 package cars, vans, lorries and motorcycles (no more bicycles!). Add to this an impressive fleet of 253 company-owned and another 344 chartered aircraft (597 planes in all) and you start to get an idea of the massive scale of UPS's global operations. The logistics giant manages to handle and deliver approximately 13.6 million packages and documents daily, covering more than 200 countries and territories (providing access to eight billion people).

One key player on the management team is Gary Mastro – Vice President of Brand and Product Marketing – who is responsible for marketing communications, event marketing, customer relationship marketing and ongoing management of UPS's product portfolio. In a recent *Marketing Management Magazine* editorial, Mastro (2002) affirmed that 'brands that last are firmly anchored in core cultural beliefs'. He suggested that his corporation owes much of its popularity and strength to the core values that the company has consistently associated with the UPS brand over the years, namely: integrity, diligence, innovation, courtesy, promptness, reliability and appearance.

Table C7.1 UPS annual revenues (in billions of US dollars)

Year	1997	1998	1999	2000	2001
Revenue	22.5	24.8	27.1	29.8	30.7

Source: Adapted from 'United Parcel Service Inc. – Quote/Financial Snapshot/Chart', The Wall Street Journal *Online*, 27 April 2002, http://online.wsj.com

Purpose and mission

As its name implies, United Parcel Service Inc. does not manufacture anything. It is a 100 per cent service operation, concentrating mainly on the business-to-business sector. 'We enable global commerce' is the line they most often provide in answer to the famous question *what business are you really in?*

When it comes to its mission statement, UPS does not take matters lightly:

We fulfill our promise to our constituents throughout the world in the following ways:

- We serve the evolving distribution, logistics, and commerce needs of our customers worldwide, offering excellence and value in all we do.
- We sustain a financially strong company that provides a long-term competitive return to our shareowners.
- We strive to be a responsible and well-regarded employer by providing our people with an impartial, rewarding, and cooperative environment with the opportunity for advancement.
- We build on our legacy as a caring and responsible corporate citizen through the conduct of our people and company in the communities we serve. (UPS at a Glance, 1994–2001)

Structure

Over time, UPS has become the recognised industry expert in global distribution. It is important to note that this domain has evolved significantly from relatively straight forward transportation management and shipment processing, to include not only the physical movement of goods, but also the flow of information and the flow of finance as these elements move with the products being shipped. As industry demands grew, clients began to ask UPS to manage inventory for them, so that they could take advantage of late night cutoffs at company air hubs for next day delivery to their customers. The same clients began to value UPS's tracking-and-tracing technology not only for shipping effectiveness, but also in terms of using this information for customer invoicing purposes. The company's work programme gradually expanded to include same-day deliveries, order fulfillment, returns management, multi-modal shipping, service parts logistics (parts used for critical technical repairs), freight forwarding, customs brokerage, and logistical financial solutions. Table C7.2 provides a useful summary of what UPS refer to as 'the three flows of global commerce: goods, information, funds'.

Table C7.2 UPS's three flows of commerce

Goods flow	Facilities	1000 distribution centres worldwide for inventory/order management, product configuration, kitting/packaging, critical parts storage, transborder shipment/processing, simple subassembly, fulfillment and returns management
	Transportation	Via air, water, rail and road
	International trade support	Customs brokerage, freight forwarding, import/export document processing and mail services

cont'd

Information flow	Network design and optimisation	'Solutions teams' use modelling software to re-engineer client supply chains
	Supply chain management	Information systems are used to monitor the performance of entire supply chains
	Supplier and vendor monitoring	IT systems track and record vendor and supplier performance indicators
Flow of funds	Financial services	Asset-based lending, long-term financing, government-guaranteed lending programmes, working capital, inventory financing, export/import financing, international trade financing, business credit cards, equipment leasing, and parcel/credit insurance

Source: Based on information from ww.ups.com

UPS AND IT

UPS has invested US$17 billion in technology since the late 1980s, more than it spent on delivery vehicles. Its main website – www.ups.com – went live in December 1994 and is now accessible in 19 languages and handles a staggering 73 million hits each day. The company employs a small army of 5000 technology specialists to oversee a network featuring a 74-terabyte database accessed 24 hours a day by 15 mainframes, 911 mid-range computers, 226,000 PCs and 4500 servers. In addition, UPS clients wishing to tap into this logistical information 'on the road' (that is, China, Australia, Japan, Singapore, Hong Kong, Taiwan and South Korea) may do so by reaching the company's digital wireless service using one- or two-way text messaging or Web-enabled mobile phones, personal digital assistants (PDAs), pagers or other pervasive computing devices.

It is clear that UPS is working to integrate its technology solutions into customers' and partners' (that is, Oracle, SAP, eBay) business processes by:

- Developing products and services to facilitate easy collection of and quick access to package information.
- Creating seamless interfaces between buyer and seller by integrating UPS functionality into the business processes of customers regardless of geographic location.
- Partnering with leading innovators in the electronic commerce arena to offer greater access to UPS technology.
- Expanding channels to access UPS, making it easier to bring UPS functionality to its customers – and for its customers to bring UPS functionality to their customers.

Most, if not all, of UPS's growth opportunities seem to revolve around *information*. It is safe to say that information and communication technologies (ICTs) act as the centrepiece of the enterprise's worldwide logistics strategy. This becomes abundantly clear when we consider the impressive array of UPS interactive e-commerce tools in use today. UPS OnLine™ tools can best be described as a suite of seven application

Table C7.3 Seven UPS Online™ tools

Internet shipping	*Simple* Net-based shipping interface that does not require installation of any software or a UPS account for use by a large number of distributed users
WorldShip™	Next-generation global shipping software with real-time information access in over 30 countries and in six languages
Envoy™	Software interface that provides direct access between UPS and a participating client's computing system
Professional	Complete, highly customisable system (UPS installed and supported software and hardware) designed for shipping from the USA to anywhere in the world
Office	UPS's most widely used software. Relatively simple package that is installed on a PC and is LAN (local area network) compatible. It validates information, prints professional labels and includes powerful tracking capabilities
Host access	Provides shipping information directly from the UPS network into a client's service and/or accounting system
World link	Software that allows free 'fenced' Internet access to www.ups.com functionality. The accompanying CD provides access while protecting against productivity concerns caused by employees surfing the Web

Source: Based on information from www.ups.com

programming interface modules (APIs) offering users advanced Web-based functionality. These tools provide enhanced flexibility and speed for such key tasks as package tracking, calculating and comparing shipping costs, determining UPS package drop-off locations, rates and service selection, estimating package time-in-transit, requesting supplies, confirming shipping and handling arrangements, address validation, service mapping and electronic manifesting. The seven UPS OnLine™ tools are listed and briefly described in Table C7.3.

STRATEGIC MARKETING ISSUES AND CONCERNS

UPS can be described as a truly future-focused enterprise. Their overall strategy statement refers to their commitment to ongoing investment and growth, the need to develop fresh initiatives and innovative products, and the need for responsible sustainability. Table C7.4 provides a further breakdown of these strategic directions.

The customer base these strategies are reliant upon is unsurprisingly quite broad, including:

- Global corporations
- Limited companies, partnerships and sole traders
- Professionals
- Government departments and agencies
- Non-profit organisations

Table C7.4 UPS strategy statement

Cautious pro-activity	'Sustain the core. Create the future'
Continued focus	'We will invest in and continue to grow our core business of worldwide distribution and logistics'
Three flows of commerce	'We will build additional competencies in the integration of goods, funds, and information flows around the globe'
Centrality of IT	'We will harness the appropriate technology to create new services and to strengthen our operations and networks'
Human resource assets	'We will attract and develop the most talented people whose initiative, good judgement, and loyalty will help realise our company's mission'
Customer orientation	'We will continually study customers' behaviour, anticipate their needs, and design our products and services to exceed their expectations'
Continued growth	'We will create a practice of innovation that leads to sustainable growth'
Complacency avoidance	'We will develop an environment that enables us to treat each customer and delivery as if it is our only one'

Source: Based on information from www.ups.com

- Public/private health organisations
- Public/private educational institutions
- e-Businesses
- Entrepreneurs working from home
- Consumers (accessing UPS directly through their network of high street shops and counters).

All the potential UPS customers on the above list – except consumers – have one thing in common: they may, sooner or later, require 'third-party logistics', also known as 3PL. This simply means that organisations and/or individuals need to outsource their logistical requirements from time to time. Some commercial ventures choose to simply 'UPS' a package or envelope while others may well hire a logistics specialist such as UPS to manage their entire supply chain. A 3PL firm utilises its own assets (that is, warehouses, vehicle fleets and ICTs) for this purpose, while a 4PL (fourth-party logistics) provider also subcontracts others and manages those contractors on behalf of its client. It is important to note that although UPS is the world's largest 3PL, the corporation is also a global leader in 4PL. As a 4PL facilitator, UPS uses ICTs on the client's supply chain to add greater value and to help maximise supply chain efficiencies. The process is highly information-based and non-asset focused, and coordinates several players on behalf of its customers.

Competition

Although well ahead of the competition in what is widely regarded as a highly fragmented industry, UPS cannot afford any degree of complacency. Hot on the industry leader's heels is the sharp, fast-growing 'number two' Federal Express Corporation or simply FedEx. With 215,000 people on its payroll and revenues exceeding US$20 billion for 2001, this company is decidedly set on victory. The company also sees itself as 'a global provider of transportation, e-commerce and supply chain management services'. It too offers:

- Worldwide express delivery
- Ground small-parcel delivery
- Less-than-truckload freight delivery
- Supply chain management
- Customs brokerage
- Trade facilitation
- Electronic commerce solutions.

FedEx currently operates in 211 countries which the company groups into four regions: Asia-Pacific, Canada, Europe/Middle East/Africa, and Latin America/Caribbean. Table C7.5 details the five branches of the FedEx family and the regions they currently serve.

Return services

Many companies (especially e-tailers) now realise the return process is just as important as fulfilling the initial order. Proper handling of returns has become a significant issue for companies striving to create tight, efficient supply chains as a competitive tool. UPS has developed an array of services to manage both business-to-business and consumer-to-business returns. These ICT-based services facilitate the tracking of inbound packages (providing useful information to the consumer as well as to the original suppler), assist with package routing, and enable timely e-mail messaging.

Table C7.5 The FedEx family

FedEx ground	Provides small-package ground delivery to every business address in the US, Canada and Puerto Rico
FedEx freight	Provides less-than-truckload freight service to Canada, Mexico, Central and South America, and the Caribbean
FedEx custom critical	Offers surface- and air-expedited solutions for door-to-door delivery of time-specific shipments in the US, Canada and Europe
FedEx trade networks	Provides global e-customs clearance in the US and Canada, also offers freight forwarding services that connect the US and Canada with Asia, Europe, Latin America and other major international regions
FedEx supply chain services	Leverages the global transportation and information networks of the FedEx companies and their affiliates to provide international supply chain management solutions to customers in North America, South America, Europe and Asia

Source: Based on information from www.ups.com

Sports marketing

UPS has been the official express delivery company of NASCAR Winston Cup Racing since 2000, and continues as primary sponsor of the number 88 UPS Ford Taurus driven by Dale Jarrett. The company has successfully leveraged the motor sport's growing popularity and fan loyalty by creating an array of marketing, business development, employee and community programmes that link its services to the speed, precision and reliability of NASCAR racing.

UPS Foundation

In keeping with the ideology enshrined in its corporate mission, UPS boasts a culture of community involvement. In 2001, the UPS Foundation continued its 50-year tradition of providing support through grant programmes and initiatives that help improve the quality of life in communities where UPS employees live and work. The Foundation donated more than US$40 million to charitable organisations worldwide, including funding through the Volunteer Impact Initiative, the Prepared and Perishable Food Rescue Programme, and initiatives to support workplace and family literacy.

The environment

Initiatives in the area of environmental preservation and protection at UPS have included:

- Adoption of more environmentally friendly packaging
- Creation and adoption of reusable envelopes
- Increasing use of alternative fuels
- Development of hybrid electric vehicles
- Efficiency gains thanks to improved route planning and better fleet maintenance.

THE FUTURE: GLOBALISATION, TECHNOLOGY AND ... SPEED!

According to UPS CEO Michael Eskew (2002), 'globalization is about the universal need to be connected, to have opportunities and to be individually empowered'. Joe Pyne, Senior Vice-President of Marketing and Corporate Development at UPS, goes somewhat further by suggesting that there are currently two strong forces creating a revolution in commerce – globalisation and technology – and that, in tandem, these forces are set to accelerate the speed of business. He also believes that speed should not be feared, but rather it should be leveraged to reinvent business. In a recent address to a group of business executives in San Diego, Pyne (2002) confidently declared that 'the victors in business will be those with the fastest and most integrated supply chains'. Perhaps the best way forward for UPS, at least for now, is to purchase the shuttle before any of their competitors think of it.

Questions for discussion

1. What would an annual strategic marketing plan look like for a global player such as United Parcel Service?
2. UPS has positioned itself as the leading third-party/fourth-part logistics facilitator on the planet. Discuss the advantages and disadvantages of this position.
3. UPS is gambling that globalisation will continue to spread unabated. Discuss other growth strategies the company might adopt, just in case!

References

Eskew, M (2002), 'The -I- in the Middle: Finding Common Ground in the Global Divide', speech to business leaders at the Los Angeles Town Hall, 10 April, website: http://pressroom.ups.com/execforum/spe...eech/1,1681,247,00.html

Mastro, G (2002), 'Marketing Management – Enduring Brands Start with Basic Values' *Marketing Management Magazine*, March/April

Pyne, J (2002) 'Speed ... is Good', speech given at the IMR Forum e-Business Summit in San Diego

Sources

Abdinnour-Helm, S (1999), 'Network Design in Supply Chain Management', International *Journal of Agile Management Systems*, **1**(2): 99

'About FedEx – The FedEx Family', 1995–2002, website: http//www.fedex.com/us/about/overview/fedexfamily.html

'About FedEx – Worldwide', 1995–2002, website: http//www.fedex.com/us/about/ overview/worldwide.html

Bhatnagar, S and Viswanathan, S (2000),'Re-engineering Global Supply Chains', *International Journal of Physical Distribution & Logistics Management*, **30**(1): 13–34

'Enabling Commerce in the 21st Century', UPS Pressroom Release, 2000–02, website: http://pressroom.ups.com/about/facts/view/1,1706,406,00.html

'Listed Company Briefing – FedEx Corporation', New York Stock Exchange, 2002, website: http://www.nyse.com/listed/fdx.html

'Listed Company Briefing – UPS Corporation', New York Stock Exchange, 2002, website: http://www.nyse.com/listed/ups.html

'Managing the Three Flows of Global Commerce: Goods, Information, Funds', 2000–2002, website: http://pressroom.ups.com/about/facts/view/1,1706,391,00.html

Remko, I and Chong, I (2001), 'Epilogue: UPS Logistics – Practical Approaches To The E-Supply Chain', *International Journal of Physical Distribution & Logistics Management*, **31**(6): 463–8

'The UPS Charter', 2000–2002, website: http://pressroom.ups.com/about/facts/view/1,1706,128,00.html

'United Parcel Service Inc. Lists on the NYSE', New York Stock Exchange, 2002, website: http://www.nyse.com/events/NT0002580E.html

'UPS Facts', UPS Pressroom Release, 2000–2002, website: http://pressroom.ups.com/ about/facts/ view/1,1706,165,00.html

'UPS Info', 1994–2001, website: http://www.ups.com/about/contact.html

'UPS at a Glance', 1994–2001, website: http://www.ups.com/about/glance.html

'UPS Technology Fact Sheet', 2000–2002, website: http://pressroom.ups.com/about/facts/view/ 1,1706,268,00.html

'UPS Wireless Fact Sheet', 2000–2002, website: http://pressroom.ups.com/about/facts/ view/1,1706, 276,00.html

'UPS Services', 2000–2002, website: http://pressroom.ups.com/about/facts/view/ 1,1706, 166,00.html

'UPS Electronic Commerce Strategy', 2000–2002, website: http://pressroom.ups.com/ about/facts/ view/1,1706,373,00.html

'UPS Return Service: The Supply Chain in Reverse', 2000–2002, website: http://pressroom.ups.com/ about/facts/view/1,1706,277,00.html

'UPS Motorsports Marketing Partnerships Backgrounder', 2000–2002, website: http://pressroom.ups. com/about/facts/view/1,1706,186,00.html

'UPS Foundation Backgrounder', 2000–2002, website: http://pressroom.ups.com/about/ facts/view/ 1,1706,301,00.html

'UPS – Environment', 2000–2002, website: http://pressroom.ups.com/mediakits/new/environment/ 0,1779,,00.html

case study eight

News Corporation in the British Newspaper Market

The British newspaper market is one of the battlegrounds on which global media warfare is waged. In July 2001, the *Guardian* newspaper voted Rupert Murdoch, Chairman of News Corporation Limited, number one in its list of the UK's most powerful 100 media personalities. In recent years the UK newspaper market has experienced volatile and complex changes. Some of these, such as the development of new technologies, have affected newspapers throughout the world. Others have been local to the UK, often instigated by the players in the newspaper market themselves. It is fair to say that News International, the UK newspaper publishing subsidiary of News Corporation, has contributed generously to the rate of change within the market. Rival organisations have had to face up to broader environmental changes, such as the development of the Internet and a broadly declining taste for newspapers, while still trying to cope with a competitive environment made all the more exciting by the activities of the News International titles.

RUPERT MURDOCH AND THE NEWS CORPORATION

Born in 1931 in Melbourne, Australia, Rupert Murdoch inherited his first newspaper (the *Adelaide News*) from his father in 1952. From these relatively small beginnings has grown one of the largest media empires in the world. Rupert Murdoch is a man who inspires strong feelings: 'Rupert the Barbarian, laying waste established orders, debasing the currency of journalism, bending politicians to his right-wing agenda, marching ever on towards international domination' as the *Observer* put it (rather tongue in cheek) in their 70th birthday tribute to Murdoch on 4 March 2001. One British MP is alleged to have said: 'Compared to Murdoch, William Randolph Hearst and "Citizen Kane" were men of modest ambition ... Murdoch's influence has been a malevolent one with job losses and anti-union activity being the norm, and the production of appalling "popular" newspapers and tabloid television.'

The News Corporation has interests in newspaper publishing, television broadcasting and Internet publishing. These are concentrated in three geographical markets, the USA ($10,507 million turnover in 2000), the UK ($2270 million turnover in 2000) and Australasia ($1374 million turnover in 2000). News Corporation is the world's leading publisher of English-language newspapers, publishing more than 175 different newspapers, printing more than 40 million papers a week. *The Australian*, the *Sunday Tasmanian*, the *Gold Coast Bulletin* and the *New York Post* are all part of the News Corporation's portfolio of newspapers. In the UK, News Corporation publishes the *Sun*, the *News of the World*, *The Times*, the *Sunday Times*, and a range of specialist newspapers under the 'Times supplements' brand, such as *The Times Educational Supplement* and *The Times Literary Supplement*. Murdoch first entered the UK newspaper market in 1969 when he acquired the *Sun* and the *News of the World*. He transformed these ailing titles into the two most popular newspapers in Britain. The *Sun* sells more copies than any other British daily newspaper, the *News of the World* is the biggest selling Sunday newspaper. A historical perspective on the involvement of News International in the UK newspaper market is provided at Appendix A.

THE UK NEWSPAPER MARKET

In contrast to the USA and Australia, the UK is a relatively small and densely populated country with a good travel infrastructure. For these reasons, the national newspaper industry has thrived in the UK. National newspapers are grouped into three categories by the Audit Bureau of Circulations (ABC), the organisation that provides an independent monitoring service for the newspaper and magazine industry. The 'popular' category, also known as the 'mass market tabloids', includes the *Mirror*, the *Daily Record*, the *Daily Star* and the *Sun*. These newspapers appeal primarily to readers in socioeconomic categories C2, D, E, and present a diet of sport, television (particularly popular soap operas) and celebrity gossip. The 'mid market' category includes the *Daily Express* and the *Daily Mail*. These newspapers target primarily C1, C2 readers, and have considerably more serious reporting of national and international events than the popular tabloids. The 'quality' category includes the *Daily Telegraph*, the *Guardian*, the *Independent*, *The Times*, and the *Financial Times* (which has nothing to do with *The Times*, and is owned by a completely different publisher). Clearly, these newspapers are aimed primarily at socioeconomic categories A, B, and they tend to differentiate their target audience on the basis of their political affiliation and views on social matters. For example, the *Daily Telegraph* attracts supporters of the Conservative Party, who also tend to have socially conservative views (in favour of 'traditional family values'). On the other hand, the *Guardian* attracts supporters of the left-of-centre political parties, who are more socially liberal. Table C8.1 shows the circulation figures for these newspapers for the period January 2001 to June 2001.

Newspaper publishing in the UK underwent a revolution in the 1980s. Entrepreneur Eddy Shah launched a completely new newspaper, *Today*, using the latest technology to produce the UK's first colour newspaper, and bypassing the print unions

Table C8.1 UK newspaper circulation, January 2001 to June 2001

Newspaper title	Daily or Sunday	Publisher	Average daily net circulation
Popular			
The Sun	Daily	News International	3,499,882
The Mirror	Daily	Trinity Mirror	2,193,791
Daily Record	Daily	Trinity Mirror	599,574
Daily Star	Daily	Express Newspapers	579,584
News of the World	Sunday	News International	3,974,458
Sunday Mirror	Sunday	Trinity Mirror	1,849,346
Sunday People	Sunday	Trinity Mirror	1,415,555
Mid market			
The Daily Mail	Daily	Daily Mail & General Trust	2,428,260
Daily Express	Daily	Express Newspapers	963,147
The Mail on Sunday	Sunday	Daily Mail & General Trust	2,362,011
Sunday Express	Sunday	Express Newspapers	912,996
Quality			
The Daily Telegraph	Daily	Telegraph Group	1,017,797
The Times	Daily	News International	715,310
Financial Times	Daily	Pearson	487,263
The Guardian	Daily	Guardian Media Group	403,306
The Independent	Daily	Independent News & Media	225,639
The Sunday Times	Sunday	News International	1,385,637
The Sunday Telegraph	Sunday	Telegraph Group	804,039
The Observer	Sunday	Guardian Media Group	451,144
Independent on Sunday	Sunday	Independent News & Media	250,164

who had until then successfully prevented the effective computerisation of the newspaper industry. *Today* was the first newspaper to use fully computerised typesetting, eliminating the laborious manual typesetting process, so increasing the efficiency with which newspapers were printed by reducing fixed costs enormously. In this way, the breakeven volume of newspaper sales was substantially cut (for a discussion of the implications of fixed costs in breakeven analysis, see Case Study 3 'Competition in the UK Ice Cream Market').

Today was not a great success. The title, launched in 1986, was acquired by the Murdoch empire in 1987, and eventually ceased publication in 1995. However, the revolution started by Eddy Shah and joined enthusiastically by other newspaper proprietors brought about fundamental changes in the industry. News International had played a full part in this revolution, through its pioneering move out of Fleet Street, traditional home of the UK newspaper industry, to a new plant at Wapping in London's dockland area.

NEWS INTERNATIONAL'S RIVALS

News Corporation is a very large and powerful international media group. There is a tendency to imagine that, therefore, it must sweep all before it in the competitive battle. However, rival publishers in the UK newspaper market are by no means all weaklings. Table C8.1 identifies the principal rivals as:

- Pearson (*Financial Times*)
- Trinity Mirror (*Mirror, Daily Record, Sunday Mirror, Sunday People*)
- Express Newspapers (*Daily Star, Daily Express, Sunday Express*)
- Daily Mail and General Trust (*Daily Mail, Mail on Sunday*)
- Telegraph Group (*Daily Telegraph, Sunday Telegraph*)
- Guardian Media Group (*Guardian, Observer*)
- Independent News & Media (*Independent, Independent on Sunday*).

Pearson, publisher of the *Financial Times,* is a substantial media group (sales turnover £3874 million in 2000) organised into three business units. Pearson Education publishes textbooks, online learning tools and associated educational products. The Penguin Group publishes a wide range of books, including fiction, non-fiction, classic works, children's books and reference works, in over 100 countries. The *Financial Times* is the leading British financial newspaper, the brand name behind a network of financial publications and information services that is used by business people around the world, and behind a successful business information Internet site (ft.com).

Trinity Mirror is a national newspaper company, formed in 1999 by a merger between Trinity plc and Mirror Group plc. In addition to the portfolio of national titles, the group owns a wide range of UK regional newspapers (for example the *Western Mail* in Cardiff, the *Daily Post* in Liverpool, the *Evening Mail* in Birmingham). Annual sales turnover was £1080 million in 2000. Like all newspaper groups, Trinity Mirror depends heavily upon advertising revenue. The early part of 2001 saw a slowdown in advertising revenue for Trinity Mirror, less marked among its portfolio of regional newspaper titles, but quite severe at the national titles.

Express Newspapers, was until November 2000, a part of the United MAI group, but was then sold to Richard Desmond, Chief Executive of Northern & Shell. Northern & Shell is a privately owned publishing company that publishes the popular celebrity gossip magazine *OK!*, and has interests in soft-core pornography. Following the acquisition (for £125 million), there was speculation that, while the *Daily Star* might flourish under the new ownership (it carries a lot of salacious material), the *Daily Express* might struggle (it is a notably conservative newspaper). Early in 2001, it was announced that substantial job cuts were to be made at Express Newspapers, following a complete review of the business by its new owner. Richard Desmond was expected to adopt a more centralised management approach, sharing resources across the three titles rather than employing dedicated teams of journalists for each newspaper. Since Richard Desmond's businesses are privately owned, there is rather less public domain information than on the publicly quoted media groups. In November 2000, plans to float Northern & Shell were shelved following the purchase of Express Newspapers. Northern & Shell was expected to have a stock market value of around £500 million, had the flotation proceeded.

Daily Mail and General Trust (DMGT) is a public company (sales turnover £863.1 million in 2000), predominantly focused within the UK. It has interests in national and regional newspapers, television, radio, exhibitions and information publishing. Like all of the other media groups discussed here, DMGT is investing heavily in new media developments associated with the Internet.

The Telegraph Group is the British newspaper publishing subsidiary of Hollinger International Inc. Hollinger also publishes English-language newspapers and magazines in the USA, Canada and Israel (for example the *Chicago Sun-Times*, the *Vancouver Sun*, the *Jerusalem Post*). Hollinger has a strong reputation as a company that buys newspapers to improve management, editorial, circulation and profitability, with the aim of generating shareholder value by later selling at a profit. For example, in 2000, Hollinger sold 13 metropolitan newspapers and 126 community newspapers, generating cash with which Hollinger was expected to seek new acquisition targets. According to the *Financial Times*, Hollinger had three items on its 'wish list' in 2001: a European newspaper business, a UK regional newspaper group and a large US city newspaper. There was some speculation that Trinity Mirror might be an acquisition target.

Guardian Media Group is a national operation of considerable historical significance. The origins of the group can be traced to the founding of the *Manchester Guardian* in 1821 (this became the *Guardian* in 1959, and moved to London in 1976). Group sales turnover in 2000 was £444 million. The group is primarily focused on British newspaper publishing, although it has some magazine (*Auto Trader*) and radio (*Jazz FM*) interests.

Independent News and Media is an organisation of modest size by the standards of the global media industry: sales turnover was €1342.5 million in 2000 – the group reports its results in euros – which is approximately £850 million. The group is based in Ireland, and regards the *Irish Independent* as its flagship publication. It has publishing interests in Ireland, New Zealand (Wilson & Horton), Australia (APN News & Media) and South Africa (Independent Newspapers Holdings Ltd) as well as the UK. During 2000, Independent News and Media launched iTouch, an Internet site offering information and entertainment services to both business and private mobile phone users.

The UK newspaper industry has been called the most competitive in the world. Clearly, News International faces a diverse range of competitors in this market. The competitors vary considerably in terms of their geographic scope, breadth of product portfolio, financial muscle, target market strategy and strategic objectives. Some of these corporations engage in rivalry with News Corporation in several markets across the globe, while others are much smaller organisations with more limited ambitions. These are factors that must be taken into consideration when News Corporation and News International frame their corporate and marketing strategies for the UK.

PRICE WAR AMONG THE 'QUALITIES'

Rupert Murdoch is renowned as an aggressive businessman, who thrives on competition and continually seeks to develop new competitive strategies. Even so, the strategy that *The Times* embarked upon in the mid-1990s was a considerable surprise. By 1992 it was clear that UK demand for newspapers was in long-term decline. National newspaper sales had declined by over 10 per cent in just five years, and the circulation of *The Times* had declined to 379,000 by 1992, a decline of over 15 per cent over a five-year period. In other words, *The Times* was capturing a declining share of a declining market. News International took the virtually unprecedented step of cutting the cover price of the newspaper to try to boost sales. Before embarking on the price-cutting strategy at *The Times*, News International had already cut the price of the *Sun* and had been rewarded with a sharp increase in market share (circulation increased by 400,000 between July and December 1993). Emboldened by this success, the strategy employed at *The Times* was even more aggressive. In September 1993, the price of *The Times* was cut from 45p to 30p.

There is considerable controversy surrounding the underlying objective behind this price cut. News International contended that the purpose was to attack the market leader, the *Daily Telegraph*, and so to boost sales of *The Times* and recapture lost market share. Managers at the *Independent*, however, argued that the real purpose of the News International strategy was to win market share from their newspaper, with the aim of rendering it uneconomic and driving it out of business. Certainly, the *Independent* was much the weakest quality newspaper in financial terms. While the *Daily Telegraph* was in a sufficiently strong financial position to respond in kind to price cuts at *The Times*, the *Independent* could offer no more than token resistance. The cover price of the *Daily Telegraph* was cut from 48p to 30p in June 1994, once the newspaper saw market share decline as readers migrated to *The Times*. The *Independent* tried a one-day cut in its cover price from 50p to 20p, with some success, but simply could not afford to enter into a long-term price war. Spurred on by its success, and in response to the actions of the *Daily Telegraph* and the *Independent*, the cover price of *The Times* was cut from 30p to 20p on 24 June 1994. By this stage, it is estimated that News International was only receiving 2.5p for every copy of *The Times* sold, since the amount paid to newspaper vendors had not been cut and they still received 17.5p on every copy sold. Clearly, News International spent a great deal of money implementing their price-cutting strategy. It was a strategy that came in for a great deal of attention for a number of reasons.

1. In the first place, the conventional wisdom in the newspaper industry had always been that readers were very loyal to 'their' paper, and that they did not buy newspapers on price. It now seems clear that this is a myth, and that newspaper buyers, like buyers of most other products, are influenced by price.
2. The conventional economic theory of oligopolistic markets implies that price competition is something that will be avoided virtually at all costs. The demand for newspapers is inelastic with respect to price, which means that a given percentage price cut will call forth a smaller percentage increase in sales volume. In the case of newspapers, price elasticity of demand is estimated to be about –0.25. The only way that a firm in such a market can profit from a price-cutting strategy is if competitors allow it to establish a sustained price advantage. Since this would mean losing market share, it is expected that if one firm cuts its price others will follow, so that all firms in the industry end up selling at a lower price and making less money.
3. If a price-cutting strategy in a market (such as the UK newspaper market) with inelastic demand leads only to lower profits for all competitors, then, so the argument goes, the strategy pursued by *The Times* must have been directed at the elimination of the *Independent* from the market. By doing this, *The Times* would have succeeded in creating enduring additional sales for itself (and other quality newspapers). It is for this reason that News International attracted so much attention from the UK government's Office of Fair Trading (OFT) during the latter part of the 1990s.

NEWS INTERNATIONAL AND THE 'PREDATORY PRICING' ALLEGATIONS

To many business people, the very possibility that a government agency might prevent them from cutting their prices must seem strange, if not perverse. Surely, to cut prices to consumers can only ever be beneficial? What on earth business is it of any government agency? But, strange or not, for an extended period in the latter part of the 1990s, the OFT spent a great deal of time and effort investigating the price-cutting strategies implemented by News International (NI) at the *Sun* and, more particularly, *The Times*. At the conclusion of this process, on 21 May 1999, the Director General of the OFT, John Bridgeman, said the following in a press release:

> I have concluded that NI deliberately made a loss on *The Times* during the period between June 1996 and January 1998 when the Monday edition was sold for 10p, and that this affected competition in the national daily newspaper market. Competitors alleged that they had been forced to cut prices or lose sales and that investment had been reduced accordingly.
>
> This behaviour ended 16 months ago and so it seems to me that informal assurances are the most appropriate remedy in this case. We have been told by Leslie Hinton, NI's chief executive, that there are no intentions to cut the price of *The Times* in the current trading conditions. If those conditions change and NI believes it necessary to cut the cover price, it will have to provide us with a detailed explanation and financial information.

Thus ended the fourth investigation in six years by the OFT into the price-cutting strategy of NI. This was the first occasion on which it was suggested that the strategy was 'anti-competitive'. Price cutting is, of course, a legitimate competitive strategy, but in certain circumstances it can fall within the scrutiny of competition law (this will vary from country to country). 'Predatory pricing' is not permitted under UK competition law, and is defined by the OFT (www.oft.gov.uk) as 'the deliberate acceptance of losses in a particular market in order to eliminate a specific competitor, so that supra-normal profits can be earned in the future, either in the same market or in other markets'. Clearly, the simple act of cutting prices, or undercutting the competition, cannot be construed as 'predatory pricing'. Even prices that are set below cost for a short period do not infringe this regulation, and such short-term strategies (selling 'loss leaders') are an accepted part of the marketing mix. But where prices are consistently set below cost, and the clear intention is to drive a rival out of business in order to create a more monopolistic market, then that constitutes predatory pricing and is prohibited. This regulation is of particular relevance in markets where complex global businesses operating in multiple markets (such as News Corporation) compete against local rivals who operate in a single market (such as the *Independent*). The global business may be able to afford losses in any one of its multiple markets, since it still has a healthy cash flow from the others (technically, this is described as cross-subsidisation). The local business relies entirely on its cash flow from a single market, and so cannot sustain losses other than in the very short term. The result of the investigations by the OFT was that conditions were imposed on NI relating to future price cuts on *The Times* (see Appendix B).

Rather ironically, only one UK newspaper group has actually been found guilty of predatory pricing, and it was not NI. In July 2001, it was announced that DMGT had been the first media company to be fined under the 1998 Competition Act for predatory pricing – an 'honour' that many people thought should have gone to NI, of course. Aberdeen Journals, owned by DMGT, was found to have deliberately incurred losses on advertising space in its *Herald* and *Post* titles in order to undermine local, rival free newspapers. A fine of £1.33 million was imposed on DMGT, although they disputed the decision.

THE FUTURE OF THE BRITISH NEWSPAPER INDUSTRY

Writing in the Hollinger International Inc. Annual Report for 2000, Chairman Conrad Black said:

> We were and remain confident that newspapers of information more than entertainment are solid franchises with proven brand loyalty for which the means of delivery is secondary ... the newspaper industry is not a declining industry ... there is plenty of room for new products intelligently conceived, carefully targeted and competently launched.

While it is clearly in the interest of a newspaper group chairman to talk up the future of newspapers as a medium, it does seem unlikely that the newspaper is going to disappear as an information medium in the near future. Conrad Black does suggest that the newspaper as a medium of entertainment has a more limited future.

The *Daily Telegraph*, part of the Hollinger portfolio, was the first British national newspaper to publish an Internet edition (the *Electronic Telegraph* was launched in November 1994). Since then all the national newspapers have launched their own electronic versions. For the moment, at least, giving the customer the ability to access essentially the same content over the Internet without paying the cover price is not seen as a threat. The electronic version is regarded as complementary to the newspaper itself. The companies that own the national newspaper titles would generally describe themselves as 'media groups' rather than 'newspaper companies'. This is clearly more accurate in some cases than in others. For example, News Corporation has extensive broadcasting and new media interests (including the famous *page3.com*, a 'glamour photography' Internet spin-off from the original topless photos of young women shown on page 3 of the *Sun*). Guardian Media Group is primarily a newspaper company, which aspires to broaden its portfolio of wider media interests. All these companies have to tread a fine strategic line between their historic 'core business' of newspaper publishing, and the unpredictable but potentially enormous new media markets. The former generates solid cash flows based on some of the best-known brand names in Britain (arguably, in the case of *The Times*, in the world). The dotcom bust of 1999–2000 undermined the latter, at least temporarily. The British newspaper industry has a long, distinguished and turbulent history. The future is likely to be no less turbulent.

Questions for discussion

You are a marketing consultant engaged by News Corporation to conduct an independent analysis of their newspaper publishing interests in the UK.

1. Prepare a summary analysis of the competitive environment in the UK newspaper market.
2. Focusing on direct competitive rivalry, assess the strengths and weaknesses of the principal players (including News International).
3. Propose alternative strategic options open to News International, and briefly evaluate each option.
4. Select your preferred strategic option, and develop an outline action plan for implementation.

Sources

Financial Times – www.ft.com
The *Guardian* – www.guardian.com
Hollinger International Incorporated – www.hollinger.com
News Corporation – www.newscorp.com
OFT (The Office of Fair Trading) – www.oft.gov.uk
The *Sun* – www.the-sun.co.uk
The Times – www.the-times.co.uk

APPENDIX A: A BRIEF HISTORY OF THE NEWS INTERNATIONAL PORTFOLIO OF BRITISH NATIONAL NEWSPAPERS

It is something of a paradox that while, to the business person, a newspaper is just another product to be bought and sold, for the wider community this 'product' can carry considerable cultural significance. To the politician, national newspapers are regarded as tools of enormous importance in the battle to win elections, particularly newspapers with the circulation and influence of *The Times* and the *Sun*. The newspaper portfolio of News International may simply look like a coherent group of products, targeting complementary markets and promising good future cash flows. However, these newspapers, and particularly *The Times*, have an almost iconic status in British culture. It is widely accepted that the support of News International titles was a major reason why the government of Margaret Thatcher was elected in 1981, leading to fundamental political and social change that has moulded contemporary British society. *The Times* is deeply embedded in British history – the first ever illustration to appear in *The Times* was on 10 January 1806, and was of Lord Nelson's funeral! A brief chronology will demonstrate the depth of history embodied in the News International portfolio of British newspapers.

- *1785* The *Daily Universal Register* was founded, which became *The Times* on 1 January 1788. It is Britain's oldest surviving newspaper with continuous daily publication.
- *1814* *The Times* was the first newspaper to be printed on a power press.
- *1821* The *New Observer* was launched, which became the *Sunday Times* on 20 October 1822.
- *1843* The *News of the World* was founded and sold at 3d (old pence). Newsagents at first refused to handle it at such a low price. Clearly controversy over cheap newspapers is not just a phenomenon of the 1990s!
- *1911* The *Daily Herald* was launched, the first newspaper to sell two million copies.
- *1962* The *Sunday Times* magazine was launched as the Sunday Times Colour Section.
- *1964* The *Daily Herald* became the *Sun*.
- *1966* *The Times* began printing news on the front page (previously reserved for advertising).
- *1969* Rupert Murdoch bought the *News of the World* and the *Sun*, and relaunched the *Sun* as a tabloid.
- *1981* Rupert Murdoch bought *The Times* and *Sunday Times*.
- *1986* News International moved production of all national titles to its new plant at Wapping in London's Docklands.

It would be disingenuous, therefore, to argue that these are 'products' like any other. While Rupert Murdoch has been associated with *The Times* for over 20 years, which seems like a long time, this amounts to less than 10 per cent of the life of the newspaper. Of course, it is a product, and, if the managers at News Corporation considered it good strategy, they could sell *The Times*, or even liquidate the entire News International portfolio and exit the UK market. But until that happens, the intelligent strategic marketing of the portfolio demands that attention be paid to the historical, cultural and political significance of these venerable titles.

APPENDIX B: CONDITIONS IMPOSED BY THE OFT ON FUTURE PRICE REDUCTIONS OF *THE TIMES*

Where a cover price reduction on *The Times* is to be implemented for more than one month, or forms part of a series of price changes lasting more than one month, News International (NI) must do the following:

(a) Within ten working days after the price cut takes effect, NI must submit certain documentation to the Director General of Fair Trading. These are a detailed explanation of the rationale for the price cut, details of targets for the price cut, a statement of the length of time the reduced price will be in effect, and financial forecasts (revenue, costs, profits) associated with the price-cutting strategy.

(b) If the price cut is for a specified period, the forecasts must cover a period of not less than 12 months after the planned end date for the cut, with an additional long-term forecast of the impact of the cut.

(c) If the price cut is not for a specified period, the forecasts must cover the financial year in which the price cut takes effect, the following financial year, and all succeeding financial years until the time when NI believes the full long-term effect of the price cut will have materialised.

(d) NI has to state the assumptions underlying the forecasts, particularly expected changes in circulation, advertising revenue and costs. These assumptions have to include expected competitor response.

case study nine

A Tale of Two Wine Brands

INTRODUCTION

The global wine industry has been transformed over the last two decades. New production methods have ensured consistent product quality. Brands that were popular in the latter part of the twentieth century have struggled and in some cases died. The traditional wine producing regions of Europe have been challenged by New World producers from countries such as the USA, Australia, New Zealand, Chile and South Africa. Wine consumption has grown rapidly, and wine consumers have become increasingly sophisticated, showing a willingness to pay more for a bottle of wine and to experiment with new products. The UK market has been an interesting microcosm of the global market. The UK is a relatively high consumer of wine, but produces wine in negligible quantities – it is almost entirely an import market. Wine producers in the exporting countries prize the UK market because there is virtually no indigenous competition. While, for example, French consumers have a natural loyalty towards French wines and Australian consumers towards Australian wines, the British have no such loyalty and will respond to quality and value for money, whatever the source. The UK wine market has been the scene of intense marketing warfare.

Each year *Marketing* magazine publishes lists of 'Britain's biggest brands'. In 2000, a wine brand appeared in the top 50 for the first time. The Ernest & Julio Gallo wine brand entered the top 50 at number 49, registering 22 per cent sales growth for the year and brand sales of around £90 million. Wine brands figured prominently in another of *Marketing* magazine's 2000 league tables – the 'top 20 fastest growing brands' list put Banrock Station at number two (sales growth 164.8 per cent), Blossom Hill at number three (143.3 per cent) and Rosemount at number six (69.1 per cent).

The evidence that the wine sector is a very dynamic part of the UK consumer economy was reinforced in 2001 when *Marketing* magazine's league tables showed that wine brands had made even more progress. The Ernest & Julio Gallo brand rose ten places to 39th position, having registered sales growth of 12 per cent. Another wine brand entered the UK's top 50 brands – Jacob's Creek. This Australian wine brand became Britain's 46th biggest brand during 2001, having achieved 17.3 per cent sales growth. Both of these wine brands were now rubbing shoulders with famous consumer brands such as Mr Kipling and Sunny Delight (respectively 41st and 42nd in the 2001 list of top brands). The wine sector was acknowledged to be the fastest growing consumer brand sector in the UK. Jacob's Creek was ranked fifth in the sector in terms of sales growth, Ernest & Julio Gallo was eight on the same basis.

THE UK WINE MARKET

A sustained increase in consumption of still light wine (also known as table wine) ranks as the most important shift in UK drinking habits over the past 25 years. No other major alcoholic drinks sector has fared so well. Wine volume more than doubled in the 1970s and did so again in the 1980s. Growth rates have moderated in the 1990s but progress has been encouraging when compared with most drink categories.

Table wine is sold to the public through both the retail channel and the catering channel (such as restaurants and hotels). The retail channel is much the more important of the two. Real disposable household income has increased, British consumers have become better educated about wine, and have even been persuaded that wine (particularly red wine) might have some beneficial health effects. Meanwhile, the British have been taking more and more holidays overseas, where they are often exposed to cultures in which wine drinking is a part of everyday life. These influences have contributed to the dynamism of the UK table wine market. It is also fair to say that the UK market has been regarded as a particular prize by many international wine producers. A relatively wealthy nation, with a tiny indigenous wine producing industry, peopled by consumers with an evident taste for alcoholic drink but with low consumption of table wine in comparison with its near neighbours. To exploit this opportunity wine producers have engaged in aggressive new product launches and repackaging.

Market research companies estimated that the UK wine market increased in volume terms from 940 million litres in 1997 to 970 million litres in 1998. This indicated growth of over a third in the UK market over a ten-year period. Mintel (2001) reported that the UK market for wine was growing at 7 per cent per year, while sales of wines originating in the New World were growing at nearly 30 per cent. To put this in the wider context of the drinks market, beer sales (measured in terms of liquid volume) fell by close to 10 per cent between 1988 and 1998, while spirits declined by 23 per cent. Ordinary table wine grew in volume by 36 per cent over the decade from 1988 to 1998. Over the same period, it is estimated that UK consumption per head of wine increased from 15.6 litres per year to 21.7 litres per year. This represents an impressive 39.1 per cent growth, but still leaves the UK lagging far behind the traditional wine drinking countries of Europe – 60 litres in France, 59 litres in Portugal, and 53.5 litres in Italy. However, it is noteworthy that in France and Italy, traditionally the heaviest wine consuming countries, per capita consumption of wine has been in decline for several years. This is probably for two reasons. First, consumers have become better educated about the adverse effects of high alcohol consumption. Second, wine is the drink of choice for the middle-aged, while younger drinkers have begun to turn away from wine in favour of 'modern' branded alcoholic products.

Table C9.1 provides further data on trends in the UK market for alcoholic drinks. The data shown in Table C9.1 confirm trends that were evident throughout the 1990s. Beer remains the favourite alcoholic drink but holds a consistently declining share of the market. There has been a steady decline in the share of the market attributable to spirits. The principal growth sector has been wine and, within the wine sector, red wine. The 'other' category has remained fairly constant, with a balance between the declining popularity of fortified wines (mostly sherry and port) and increasing popularity of cider.

Among other reasons cited for the growing popularity of wine has been the supposed beneficial health effects of regular wine drinking. Of course, like all alcoholic drinks, excessive consumption of wine is very detrimental to the health. Unlike other alcoholic drinks, there is considerable scientific evidence that moderate wine consumption offers health advantages. Most notably, there is substantial evidence that wine consumption reduces the risk of cardiovascular disease (reducing the risk of a heart attack). Wine consumption may also reduce the risk of ulcers. There is even evidence that red wine, which contains high concentrations of anti-oxidant bioflavonoids, may reduce the risk of contracting cancer. Overall, moderate wine consumption seems to be associated with lower mortality rates. While the evidence is unlikely to be enough to persuade non-drinkers to take to the bottle, it certainly provides wine consumers with a self-righteous justification for enjoying their tipple!

In the mid-1990s, the arrival of high-quality, inexpensive own-label, Eastern European and so-called New World wines on the market undermined the dominance of traditional Western European wine growing nations. It has also made wine more accessible to a wider range of consumers. As a result, there has been a dramatic change in the country of origin of table wines consumed in Britain over the last decade.

Table C9.1 British consumption of alcoholic drinks

	1995	1999
Market subdivided by type of drink	**% by value at current retail selling prices**	**% by value at current retail selling prices**
Beer	54.7	50.1
Still light wine	16.7	19.2
– of which red wine	7.9	11.1
– of which white wine	8.8	8.1
Spirits	17.9	19.0
Other (for example cider, fortified wine)	10.7	11.7
	100.0	100.0

Sources: Market Research GB (2000a); *Market Research GB* (2000b); *Mintel* (2001)

Broadly, this change can be characterised as a shift away from the traditional wine producing countries in Western Europe and towards the New World and Eastern European producers. But, at a closer look, the losses suffered by the traditional producers have been by no means equally shared. Clearly, the most dramatic winner has been Australian wine, which took a 1.2 per cent share of the UK market in 1990 and an 11.1 per cent share in 1998. Equally clearly, the most dramatic loser has been German wine, which declined from 28.8 per cent (in clear second place behind France) in 1990, to 10.0 per cent (in fourth place behind France, Italy and Australia) in 1998. The dramatic rise of New World wines is exemplified not only by the increasing Australian share, but by rapid growth in wine imports from the USA (from 1.0 per cent to 6.1 per cent), Chile (0.2 per cent to 4.4 per cent) and South Africa (0.2 per cent to 5.0 per cent). While the progress made by Australian wine producers in the UK market has, indeed, been spectacular, that of the Chilean and South African producers has been at least as good, and arguably better.

As British consumers have grown increasingly sophisticated, so they have been prepared to be more adventurous in their wine buying. In the 1960s and 70s, white wines predominated, typically of medium-sweet character. Tastes have changed markedly since. Red wine became more popular than white wine in the 1990s, and many consumers made the switch from beer drinking to wine. Although white wines are still purchased in large quantities, the medium-sweet products characteristic of Germany and Eastern Europe have been largely replaced by drier New World wine varieties. It seems to be a characteristic of the British market that red wine is perceived, broadly, to be a more sophisticated drink than white wine.

One peculiarity of the British wine market is that the rate of excise duty per litre of wine in the UK exceeds the rate of duty on wine in France by some margin. At the rate of excise duty effective in April 2000, UK consumers were paying 33.8 pence duty per pint of beer and 115.8 pence per standard wine bottle, whereas French consumers were paying 4.5 pence on a pint of beer and 1.5 pence on a bottle of wine. Britain and France are separated by the relatively narrow English Channel, across which many ferries plough their way every day, and under which trains now pass (the Channel Tunnel). Journey times are short, and retailers of tobacco and alcohol have exploited the opportunity by siting outlets conveniently close to the embarkation points. A surprisingly large number of alcohol consumers (and tobacco consumers for the same reason) are prepared to make the not-too-arduous return journey from England to France to buy a large stock of wine (and beer, spirits, cigarettes and so on). Within the EU, private shoppers can, in principle, buy as much as they want in another country for their own use, paying duty at the local rate, with no further duty payable on returning home. In practice, and to try to stop widespread smuggling (tobacco and alcohol were being carried by the van load across the English Channel for illegal resale), there are limits on what a consumer can claim as 'private use'. But these limits are generous. In 1998, it was estimated that 7.5 per cent of the UK wine market was made up of legitimate personal imports from other EU countries (and a further 3 per cent was smuggled goods).

Wine branding has developed considerably over the last two decades. Before the New World wine boom of the 1990s, there was a small number of classic wine brands, such as Hirondelle, Blue Nun, Black Tower, Bull's Blood and Le Piat D'Or. Such names had the characteristic appeal of a good brand. They offered a consistent and easily recognised product in a market where the average consumer felt rather out of his depth, since British consumers were poorly educated about wine. The appeal of such brands faded with the rapid growth of the wine market, increased levels of consumer product awareness, and the emergence of trustworthy supermarket own-label products. In recent years, brands have made something of a comeback, but in a rather different form. The biggest wine brands are now associated with the name of the producer – Ernest & Julio Gallo, Hardys, and Jacob's Creek. These brands do not offer a single, homogeneous product, as earlier brands did. Rather, they provide an umbrella brand for wines made from individual grape varieties. Increasingly, the brands are used as a vehicle for the development of new, upmarket products, to encourage consumers to trade up from the drinkable, value-for-money wines that made these producers famous, to fine wines.

Certain trends seem set to continue in the UK market for table wine. Continued growth is very likely, with the red wine sector growing faster than white wines. Competition is certainly not going to become any less intense. In all likelihood, the next few years will see aggressive strategic action from the Old World producers to try to regain some of the ground they have lost during the last decade. Many of the innovations to which the success of Australian wine, in particular, has been attributed, can be reasonably easily copied. New World producers employing innovative wine production and marketing techniques have manifestly outmanoeuvred the Old World producers in many markets across the world. One might characterise the attitude of the Old World producers as being 'product oriented' rather than 'market oriented'. Australian producers have captured the consumer with consistent quality and fruity, easy drinking wines. They have then offered the consumer the opportunity to trade up to more complex and more expensive wines. For a while the Old World producers seemed to be stuck in a time warp, marketing their product (if at all) on the basis of tradition, esoteric production methods and exclusivity. They can now be expected to mount a serious fightback. Mintel (2001, p. 70) suggested as much:

> The Old World wine producers, such as France, are waking up to the threat posed by the New World upstarts to their traditional markets. They are changing their production methods and marketing strategies to meet the challenge. The next five years are likely to bear witness to an intense battle between Old World and New World wines for domination of the UK market.

The Internet will certainly play a role in the future of wine retailing, although how big a role it is difficult to tell. Some experts argue that it will be a key role and that the Internet will be crucial to the future role of the wine trade. One forecast has put global online wine sales at 1 million bottles in 1999, growing to 15 million bottles by 2005. The multiple retailer Waitrose has been eager to break new ground in online wine sales, and sold over 24,000 bottles of wine in the first ten weeks of the launch of Waitrose Direct, its online shopping arm. This has led the company to estimate that 10 per cent of its wine sales will be made online by Christmas 2005. For the moment, the wine producers seem to be content to use their Internet sites largely for promotional purposes, and there is no sign that they intend to use the Internet to gain direct access to the customer and bypass conventional channels.

A TALE OF TWO WINE BRANDS – JACOB'S CREEK AND BLUE NUN

The Jacob's Creek brand entered the list of 'Britain's biggest brands' in 2001 at number 46. The brand is owned by Orlando Wyndham Pty Ltd of Australia, which is itself a subsidiary of the large French group Pernod Ricard. Jacob's Creek is distributed in the UK by Pernod Ricard UK. According to Mintel (2001, p. 48):

> Jacob's Creek is firmly established as one of the UK's favourite wine brands. The brand's growth in some ways mirrors the dynamic growth of all New World wines, and Australian wines in particular.

The history of the Jacob's Creek brand can be traced back 150 years. Johann Gramp, a Bavrarian settler in Australia, first planted vines beside Jacob's Creek in South Australia in 1847. The brand name Jacob's Creek was first used in 1976. It has been the most popular wine brand in Australia for more than a decade (marketed under the catchy slogan 'Australia's top drop'), and has played a key role in Australia's wine export boom. More than 80 per cent of Jacob's Creek wine is exported, to a total of over 60 countries, including Ireland, New Zealand, the USA and the Scandinavian countries as well as the UK.

The basic formula behind the Jacob's Creek brand is deceptively simple – a good quality product at value-for-money prices. This is based on an excellent wine growing climate in South Australia, adoption of modern wine production techniques, and the application of sound marketing principles. The success of the Jacob's Creek brand did not 'just happen', but is built on carefully planned strategy. Stephen Couche, now Marketing and International Director, was Brand Manager for Jacob's Creek when it was launched in 1976. According to Stephen Couche:

> This has been a very careful brand building exercise and we have been single-minded in our approach. Quality of product, credibility and value for money have always been key priorities. Only after the brand had gained stature and acceptance in Australia did we venture overseas. To create a long-term brand internationally you need the right price, packaging and product positioning, and that is what we have established. Jacob's Creek is proving to be the ultimate wine brand. Our long-term strategy is for Jacob's Creek to be the ultimate quality benchmark for Australian wines across all major price categories. (www.jacobscreek.com.au)

The Jacob's Creek brand stands for everything that has been successful in the wine market in recent years. It is produced in Australia, is a 'producer brand', includes a number of good quality red wines in the brand portfolio, and has been successfully positioned as a sophisticated yet value-for-money product. Blue Nun, on the other hand, is a German brand, was until recently exclusively a white wine brand, and had become – to the British consumer – the epitome of poor taste and the butt of jokes.

Until comparatively recently, Blue Nun was a well-loved brand in the UK and elsewhere. A single-product brand, it was a common sight on supermarket shelves and restaurant tables. The product, a German Liebfraumilch, was a medium-sweet white wine very popular with British consumers in the 1970s and 1980s. Just about every trend in the UK wine market has been against Blue Nun. White wines came to be perceived as less sophisticated than red wines. German wines became deeply unfashionable. Tastes changed, with a rapidly growing preference for drier flavours and a widespread disdain for sweetish wines.

In June 2001, the Blue Nun brand was relaunched in the UK. No longer only a Liebfraumilch, the range includes a red wine (using the Merlot grape) and two additional white wines (a Riesling and an Eiswein). The brand owner is F. W. Langguth Erben Gmbh, Germany's leading wine producer. Working with UK agency Spirit Advertising, they planned a substantial campaign to rejuvenate the brand, capitalising on the high levels of brand awareness while side-stepping the 'unsophisticated' image. Langguth claim that Blue Nun is the world's oldest wine brand. There were some early signs of success as sales of Blue Nun grew by 15 per cent between 2000 and 2001. Some commentators saw the relaunch of Blue Nun as simply part of a fashion for everything 'retro'. In the *Guardian* newspaper (18 June 2001) a comparison was drawn between Blue Nun and other brand icons of the past, such as the Wimpy chain of hamburger restaurants, the Brut male fragrance range, and Babycham (recently relaunched) the sparkling alcoholic drink. Commentators were divided on the likely success of the Blue Nun strategy. How could something that had gained such an unfashionable and unsophisticated image make a comeback? And yet, at around the same time that the Blue Nun relaunch was taking place, sales of Skoda cars (once the butt of a great many more jokes than Blue Nun) were booming in the UK, on the back of an improved product range and a successful repositioning campaign. If Skoda could do it, why not Blue Nun?

Questions for discussion

1. 'Australian wine producers have seen sales increase by three-quarters in Britain. Two million cases (roughly 18 million litres) of Australian wine were sold in the year ended June 1992, a far cry from the situation in 1980 when only 100,000 cases were sold annually. However, there is doubt being cast over the continuation of this trend as most of the activity has been restricted to the cheapest end of the market, and low prices will be hard to sustain' (*Market Research GB,* 1994, p. 9). These words of warning seemed perfectly reasonable in 1994 but turned out to be misguided. Why?
2. Jacob's Creek has built a very strong position in the UK market. Could anything threaten the brand's success?
3. Will Blue Nun succeed in the UK market? Weigh up the arguments for and against.

Selected web links

www.jacobscreek.com.au – Jacob's Creek site

www.winetitles.com.au – Australian Wine Online

References

Consumer Goods Europe (2000), 'Wine in the UK', 446 (January), Retail Intelligence
Market Research GB (1994), 'Light Wine', April, Euromonitor
Market Research GB (2000a), 'Wine: Part 1', February, Euromonitor
Market Research GB (2000b), 'Wine: Part 2', March, Euromonitor
Mintel (2001), 'Wine', January, Mintel International Ltd
Marketing (2000), 'Biggest Brands', 9 August, p. 23

case study ten

BriCol Engineering Ltd

THE GLOBAL MOTOR INDUSTRY

Over 80 per cent of world car production is accounted for by six corporations. Recent years have seen considerable new consolidation within the industry, as formerly independent companies have been acquired by the most powerful groups. General Motors (GM), the largest automotive group in the world, owns stakes in other well-known motor manufacturers such as Subaru, Suzuki and Fiat. Ford, the world's second largest automotive group, owns brands such as Volvo, Mazda and Jaguar. The leading brand in Europe is VW, with an 11.0 per cent market share. GMs' Vauxhall/Opel brand lies in second place with 10.6 per cent, Renault is third with 10.4 per cent, and the Ford brand is in fourth place with 9.0 per cent European market share.

The prospect, in 2002, of a global economic slowdown was bad news for the motor industry. Sales of new cars are very susceptible to general economic conditions. Private customers may postpone a purchase, or trade down to a cheaper model, if they are worried about their job security. Corporate buyers make their vehicle fleets last just a little bit longer if there are concerns about profitability or even survival. Reductions in new car sales increase unit costs of vehicle production, just at the time that customers are becoming more price sensitive because of general economic conditions. The result is a severe squeeze on profit margins. Not surprisingly, therefore, 2001 and 2002 saw the major motor groups announcing profit reductions in all their major markets – North America, South America, Western Europe and Asia Pacific. Both Ford and GM posted losses on their European business in 2001.

One 'problem' for the motor manufacturers can be attributed to their success in revolutionising manufacturing quality during the 1980s and 1990s. 'Total quality' campaigns have been implemented throughout the motor industry, with the major manufacturers insisting that their suppliers should also demonstrate their commitment to quality by the achievement of recognised quality standards. The resulting improvements in product design and manufacturing processes meant that by 2001 all new cars were of good quality. As a consequence, quality could no longer be relied upon in the market as a product differentiator. The car had become less differentiable and a little more of a commodity item. The price premiums that traditionally high-quality brands could command was accordingly reduced, with companies like Mercedes and BMW having to reduce their price premium over their more mainstream opposition.

In a market with overcapacity, in which products are increasingly difficult to differentiate, the only sure way to achieve profit improvements is through unit cost reductions. The consolidation of the industry into fewer corporate groups, each seeking to benefit from massive scale economies, was the first part of the solution to this problem. The second part of the solution lay in seeking cost improvements among the networks of companies that supply the components that the car manufacturers use to build their vehicles. Within that network of supply companies was BriCol Engineering Ltd.

BRICOL ENGINEERING LTD

BriCol Engineering was created in 1975 by Brian Deans and Colin Platt, who named their company after themselves (Brian + Colin = BriCol). By 2000, BriCol was employing over 50 staff at its factory in Bedfordshire, England. The company is a manufacturer of metal parts primarily for the car industry, with annual turnover of £7.0 million, and is based near one of the GM manufacturing plants in the UK. The components supplied by BriCol Engineering are largely high-volume, low-unit value parts which could be readily supplied by many other companies. Approximately 60 per cent of BriCol Engineering's turnover is from the GM group, shared among four GM divisions. The company has been selling components to GM, or to its predecessor companies, for 20 years. BriCol Engineering's second largest customer is itself a supplier to the motor industry, but on a much larger scale. This customer generates 20 per cent of BriCol's annual turnover. It is in the business of purchasing sub-components from companies like BriCol, and then assembling them into integrated units (such as a complete front panel incorporating driver instrumentation, wiring and ventilation ducting) for sale primarily to Ford and Nissan. Other than its two major customers, BriCol supplies a wide range of basic metal components to whoever will buy them – no other customer takes more than two per cent of BriCol's sales.

Today Brian Deans is the Managing Director and Colin Platt is the Production Director of BriCol, which is a private limited company. Sales is the responsibility of Marie Dougan (Sales Manager), who joined the company in 1982 as an administrator, and has now worked her way up through the ranks to the point where she reports directly to Brian. There is no marketing department, and the only support that Marie has in her role as sales manager is a sales administrator, who deals with customers on the phone and chases orders with the production department when a customer complains.

At one of their regular monthly meetings with Marie, Brian and Colin share their concerns about the future of the business. As he has explained several times before, Brian repeats that he is uncomfortable with the high degree of dependence on GM and believes the company needs to develop new revenue streams. This would be a matter for concern in any case, given that the loss of the GM business would effectively put the company out of business. Recently, however, it has become clear that the local car plant is high on the list of facilities that GM would like to close down. There is excess capacity in the car industry, and the least efficient factories are at grave risk. The fact that the UK is outside the European single currency area (the 'Eurozone') has also been cited as a problem, both for British GM plants, and for British suppliers of automotive components.

'So, as I see it', explained Brian, 'we would be very foolish indeed to rely on a future revenue stream from GM on anything like the scale of the last few years. I really think that we – all three of us – ought to concentrate our efforts on finding new sources of business for the company. Obviously we need to stick to what we're good at, and that's making quality automotive components. There are two very obvious ways to go, basically south or north! Not far north we've got MG Rover's Longbridge plant, and we can look for business up there. Either direct with MG Rover, or we can try to win some business making sub-components for their major suppliers. Alternatively, not far south we've got Ford's Dagenham plant. We've been making auto components for over 25 years, we're fully quality accredited, and I say we make a pitch to MG Rover or Ford, maybe even both of them.'

Colin, as on many occasions before, was not entirely in agreement with Brian. 'Look, Brian, we've been doing business with GM for 20 years. I've sat down with their engineers more times than I care to remember. We've helped them out with rush jobs more than once. They know our quality – in fact, we designed our entire quality control system around GM procedures. I've been on nearly a dozen GM quality control training courses! I can't see that they are just going to drop us in it. There is such a thing as loyalty in business, you know. If they can't give us any more business from the local plant, then they'll add us to their list of suppliers for their overseas plants. We might not get quite as much business for a while, but we'll pull through like we always have. Don't you agree, Marie?'

No, Marie did not agree. 'GM like to talk about supplier partnerships, but when it comes to the crunch cost is everything. If we don't quote the lowest price, then we don't get the business. It seems to me that no favours are asked for or given. There may be such a thing as loyalty in business, Colin, but I think it comes a poor second to price. Frankly, I don't think either of you is really getting to the heart of the problem. The global car industry is facing a recession, and we could get squashed flat without GM even noticing we were gone. Brian's ideas for developing business with MG Rover or Ford might work, but needs a lot more thought. Failing that, we are going to have to look for new business outside the automotive sector.'

Brian decided it was time to wind up the meeting. 'Thanks for your thoughts on this. Marie, you said that we needed to take a closer look at MG Rover and Ford, and Brian wants to stick with our GM relationship and reinforce that. Obviously we do need more information on those options before we press the panic button and look elsewhere. So I've asked a friend of mine to take a look at the GM, MG Rover and Ford options for us and provide some objective input. He's a marketing consultant, but we shouldn't hold that against him! I'm expecting to receive his report in the next couple of days. If I get it copied to you, then let's meet again to discuss it a week today.'

Two days later the consultant's report arrived on Brian's desk.

Report on automotive industry buying behaviour for BriCol Engineering Ltd

Introduction

Responding to a brief from Brian Deans, Managing Director of BriCol Engineering, this report presents an analysis of the buying practices of three companies – General Motors, Ford Motor Company and MG Rover – identified as target customers by BriCol. This is a preliminary report based largely on secondary data, augmented by the author's previous experience as a marketing manager in the car industry. The report addresses each of the three target customers in turn, and then ends with a brief conclusion summarising some of the key issues that have emerged.

General Motors

GM is the world's largest automotive corporation. Total net sales and revenues for the GM group were $184,632 million in 2000, on which net income was $4452 million (2.4 per cent net profit margin). GM sold about 8.6 million cars and trucks in 2000. The firm's major markets are North America, Europe, Asia Pacific, Africa and the Middle East. GM cars and truck are sold under the following brand names: Chevrolet, Pontiac, Buick, Cadillac, GMC, Saturn, Hummer, Saab, Opel, Vauxhall and Holden.

All purchasing for GM is done through the Worldwide Purchasing Division. The UK is one of several purchasing centres around the world. The function of the UK purchasing operation is to develop and maintain the UK supply base and to negotiate with UK suppliers. There are two component procurement processes, 'advance purchasing' and 'global sourcing'.

Advance purchasing is the procurement of components for new vehicles. Suppliers are often required to undertake substantial design engineering work in collaboration with GM. A supplier that wins an advance purchasing order will be given a 12-month sole contractor guarantee, before a competitive tender may be announced.

Some favoured GM suppliers are offered long-term (multi-year) contracts, but annual cost improvements are written into such deals. Typically, the supplier has to deliver between 3 and 5 per cent annual cost savings if the long-term contract is to be maintained.

Global sourcing is the process of procuring components for the manufacture of the current range of GM vehicles. GM regularly reviews its supplier contracts. Reviews are a normal part of the supplier management process and occur at predetermined time intervals, although a review will be brought forward if GM managers feel that a supplier is underperforming. In evaluating suppliers GM uses a 'vendor rating system', where each supplier is scored against a set of criteria based on GM's purchasing objectives. Details of the vendor rating system are not available, but the underlying principles are clear – the company is looking for the best available combination of price, product performance and manufacturing quality. In principle, a new supplier always has a chance of winning business from GM if it can demonstrate a better price/performance/quality mix than the current supplier.

Overall, GM does not seem to lay great store by the development of supplier relationships. Years of doing business with GM do not count for nothing. However, a competitor offering equivalent product performance and manufacturing quality at a lower price will always have a chance of stealing away business from a long-term supplier. The GM purchasing function is respected within the automotive industry for its ability to deliver good quality components at very keen prices.

GM, like other major car manufacturers, is increasingly asking suppliers to provide pre-assembled systems rather than simple components. These pre-assembled systems (a complete exhaust system would be an example) incorporate components from multiple suppliers. In effect, therefore, a first-tier supplier to GM carries out project management work and assembly work which once would have been done by GM employees. Many smaller suppliers to GM will increasingly play the role of second-tier suppliers, selling their components directly to the first-tier suppliers rather than to the car company itself.

Ford Motor Company

Ford is a similar organisation to GM, which is to say an American-owned global automobile manufacturing company. Sales and revenues amounted to $141,230 million in 2000, with operating earnings at $6668 million (4.7 per cent margin on total revenue). Ford sold about 7.4 million vehicles in 2000. The Ford family of brands includes Volvo, Mazda, Lincoln, Mercury, Aston Martin, Jaguar and Land Rover.

All Ford purchasing is carried out by the Automotive Components Division, which operates on a global basis. Ford has a clear policy to move towards 'partnership sourcing', and makes a feature of emphasising 'relationships' with stakeholders as a core company value. The six key stakeholder groups with whom Ford aims to develop improved relationships are customers, suppliers, dealers, society, investors and employees. There have been formal plans to reduce the number of suppliers with which Ford does business for some years now. For example, a target of 30 per cent reduction in supplier numbers was set for 1990–93, and a target of an additional 50 per cent reduction for 1993–96. As a result of the progressive implementation of this policy, nearly 90 per cent of the materials and components used in Ford production are procured from only 200 suppliers worldwide.

Suppliers are divided into three groups:

- preferred suppliers
- potential suppliers
- short-term suppliers.

The aim is to source 100 per cent of materials and components from preferred suppliers, and to cut out short-term suppliers entirely.

Ford engages in extensive information sharing with suppliers at regular supplier performance review meetings. One important item of information that Ford does share with its suppliers is their current performance against the company's comprehensive vendor rating system. As with GM, the details of the vendor rating system are not available, but the broad criteria on which it is based are quality, technical performance, delivery and commercial soundness.

There seems to be little doubting the sincerity with which Ford has adopted the policy of building supplier relationships. However, two major hurdles to implementing a partnership approach have not yet been overcome. These hurdles are, first, the attitudes of the Ford buyers, many of whom have worked for Ford through an extensive period of confrontational purchasing, and, second, the mistrust of suppliers, who need to be persuaded that Ford has genuinely adopted the partnership approach. There is some concern that the company may be missing out on the opportunity to buy components at the very lowest prices, since it is tied into supplier relationships, while not yet achieving the full benefits of supplier partnerships enjoyed by leading Japanese firms such as Toyota.

MG Rover

MG Rover is a privately owned UK-based car manufacturing company. Formerly owned by British Aerospace, Rover Group was acquired by the German car firm BMW in March 1994. BMW was unable to turn Rover into a profitable business unit, and decided to dispose of the company after it reported massive losses in 1999. Rover was once an important national symbol for the UK, and there was great press and public interest in the circumstances surrounding the disposal by BMW. Eventually, Rover was acquired by Phoenix, a consortium of Midlands business people. They launched the new company, MG Rover, in May 2000. For the period from May to December 2000, MG Rover achieved sales turnover of £961 million, on which it made a loss of £254 million. Reportedly, Rover made a loss of £780 million in 1999. The target for the company is to eliminate these losses and break even within another two years.

Although MG Rover is a very much smaller firm than either GM or Ford, it is a big player as far as the UK automotive components industry is concerned. MG Rover manufactures more cars in the UK than any other company. In terms of sheer volume of purchasing, therefore, it is a key organisation in the UK industry. MG Rover's purchasing function, which is co-located with the Longbridge manufacturing site in Birmingham, is divided into 'production purchasing' and 'facilities and general services purchasing'. Facilities and general services purchasing is largely concerned with one-off contracts, and there is little or no attempt to use a partnering approach. For its production purchasing activities (where the amount spent is much greater), MG Rover aims to apply a partnership sourcing philosophy. Single sourcing – that is, buying a particular component from one supplier alone – is the norm for production items, and there is very little dual or multiple sourcing.

MG Rover has established a reputation for sound purchasing methods and good purchasing training, and experienced MG Rover buyers are sought after by other companies, both within and outside the automotive industry. Staff turnover is an acknowledged problem when it comes to the management of supplier partnerships, even though MG Rover tries to use systems which are sufficiently robust to allow for the loss of specific people.

In the early 1980s, MG Rover dealt with approximately 2000 production suppliers. By 1990/91 this had been reduced to around 1200, and by 1996 there were 670 suppliers, of whom 250 were 'strategic suppliers' providing approximately 85 per cent of the components bought by MG Rover. It would be possible to reduce this supplier base even further were it not for the substantial number of elderly products which MG Rover still manufactures. It follows that MG Rover is using fewer suppliers, but spending considerably more with each of them. On average, £5.4 million per annum is spent with each supplier, and £12.2 million per annum with each of the strategic suppliers.

Until comparatively recently, MG Rover's approach to purchasing was essentially confrontational. However, MG Rover has been attempting to adopt a relationship approach to supplier management for the last decade. The first efforts at actually intervening with suppliers to help bring about beneficial change were relatively unsuccessful. Recently a team has been put together to implement supplier development effectively. A substantial team of supplier development specialists has been created with the specific task of acting as highly qualified practitioners to improve supplier systems and processes. I have not been able to obtain any information on the effectiveness of this process from the suppliers involved.

Company size is regarded by MG Rover as an important issue in the automotive components supply industry. In general terms, MG Rover is buying from fewer, bigger companies. In part, this can be attributed to MG Rover's strategic purchasing policy. However, it also reflects the trend towards component integration. In electronics products, for example, advances in technology often enable the work which was once done by several components to be done by only one. There is a preference for single, pre-assembled components over the procurement of multiple subcomponents. Such an approach can make the components easier to work with on the production line, improve quality, and result in reductions in total cost. Increasing emphasis is being placed on design for ease of manufacture and assembly.

Conclusion

As you know, the automotive supply industry is commonly subdivided into first- and second-tier suppliers. First-tier suppliers sell directly to the automobile manufacturers. Second-tier suppliers sell to the first-tier suppliers. BriCol has been a first-tier supplier to GM for a considerable time. However, the car manufacturers are increasingly looking to their first-tier suppliers to carry out a substantial amount of systems integration work. The way the industry is moving, firms that supply components alone will become second-tier suppliers, while first tier suppliers will have to be able to offer substantial product development, project management and systems integration capability. BriCol has to decide whether it is capable of becoming a systems integrator, and dealing at a strategic level with the global automotive firms. If this is not thought realistic, then BriCol will have great difficulty succeeding as a first-tier supplier. In this case, it would make sense to pursue a second-tier marketing strategy. As things stand, if the local GM plant is closed, then BriCol is unlikely to have the logistic or marketing resources to continue to supply GM at its overseas plants. However, by becoming a preferred supplier to a small number of sound first-tier suppliers – businesses that already have international reach, and have export marketing and logistics skills – BriCol would have access to the global automotive market without making any major new investments.

One week later

One week later Brian, Colin and Marie got together again in Brian's office to review the consultant's report. Brian's opinion was clear: 'I think you'll agree that it's pretty evident from the report that we should pursue my idea of winning business from Ford and Rover. Probably we should target Ford first, because I like the sound of their supplier relationship strategy. I'm not sure that we ever got that much assistance from GM. But it looks as though Ford really offer their suppliers some support. Obviously all three of us need to get involved in this, but to start off with I'd like Marie to work on identifying a way into Ford. Do we know anyone at the Dagenham plant? Let's get the ball rolling on this.'

Colin looked dubious. 'Doesn't the report say that Ford are trying to cut back on the number of suppliers they use, Brian? And I think it's far too pessimistic about GM. What the report is missing out is our depth of knowledge of the company, our contacts, the fact that we already meet all of their quality standards. If we target another manufacturer, then we have to start building all of that over again from the start. Let's not throw out the baby with the bath water. Stick to what we're good at, but develop some new skills. Obviously we will need to deal internationally if we want to keep GM business. So let's start researching international logistics contractors who will be able to meet GM just-in-time delivery requirements at their other European plants. That's the way we should go.'

Marie was not so clear as the other two that there was an easy answer to BriCol's problems. 'Look, there are a lot of options here, and choosing the wrong one could mean the end for this company. I really don't think we should make a snap decision. In fact I'd like us to get together with this marketing consultant and talk things over. There are some interesting ideas in the report, but I'd like to see if he has a clear idea of what our next steps should be.'

Questions for discussion

1. How would you characterise the purchasing strategies of the three car manufacturing companies?
2. How attractive would you say that the three car companies were, compared with each other, as target customers for BriCol Engineering?
3. Should BriCol Engineering aim to remain a first-tier supplier – that is, should it aim to continue to sell directly to one or more of the car manufacturers – or should it aim to become a successful second-tier supplier?
4. If you were the marketing consultant, what would you advise Brian Deans and Colin Platt to do next?

Selected web links

www.ford.com – Ford site

www.gm.com – General Motors site

www.mg-rover.com – MG Rover site

www.smmt.co.uk – The Society of Motor Manufacturers and Traders

case study eleven

Crisis in the European Airline Industry

COMPETITION AND DEREGULATION

According to a recent House of Lords inquiry into airline competition (House of Lords, 1998), there are now more than 500 airline alliances involving around 200 airlines. Many of these alliances involve code sharing, where a particular airline books passengers onto another airline's plane that is operating on the same route. This allows airlines to maintain capacity on particular routes without the considerable fixed costs that operating a route on their own would bring. Since deregulation in the European airline market, in 1987, a wave of cooperative arrangements or alliances has occurred. These alliances have been designed to achieve fleet rationalisation, expansion and rationalisation of the structure of the flight path network, and purchasing and marketing economies of scale (Stragier, 1999).

The largest of the major global strategic alliances include the 'Star Alliance' and 'Oneworld'. The 'Star' alliance major partners include Lufthansa, SAS (Scandinavian Airline System), United Airlines, Air Canada, Thai Airways, Singapore Airlines, Ansett International and Varig. This is currently the most established of the alliances, beginning as it did with a ten-year agreement between Lufthansa and SAS ratified by the EU, to set up 'an operationally and commercially integrated transport system' in 1996 (Stragier, 1999). 'Oneworld' includes American Airlines, British Airways, Canadian Airlines, Cathay Pacific, Qantas (Queensland and Northern Territories Aerial Service), Finnair and Iberia. As the industry consolidates and passenger volumes decline, there appears to be increasing importance placed on the role of strategic alliances within the airline industry. Jean-Cyril Spinetta, the Air France Chairman, believes that a shake-out in the European airline industry will eventually leave only Air France, British Airways and Lufthansa, as they currently lead the major strategic alliances within the European airline industry (Airline Industry Information, 2001). Recently, British Airways and KLM have announced a 'cooperation pact' which will see them selling tickets on each other's flights as well as their own. There is speculation that this development is the first stage in a full merger plan, although the two companies apparently abandoned merger plans in September 2000 (Done and Odell, 2002).

Airline alliances usually fall short of equity sharing agreements. They are designed more to evade national government restrictions on ownership and control of 'slots'. Slots are essentially take-off and landing times. They do not relate specifically to a particular route. However, slots are frequently pre-allocated to particular airlines from particular countries. An airline can keep a slot assigned to it as long as it is used regularly in a previous year ('grandfather rights'). With recent growth in airline transport, the slots available to the airline companies frequently do not match the increasing demand.

However, slots have often generally been assigned to a country's national carrier. Where a country was not able to meet demand for slots, bilateral air services agreements have been established between individual states by exchanging air traffic rights. The USA has pioneered such an approach to airline liberalisation having concluded bilateral agreements with around 30 countries (House of Lords, 1998) including Germany and the Netherlands. However, such 'open skies' agreements are hugely weighted in favour of the USA, since US carriers can fly on within Europe but European airlines cannot fly on within the domestic USA. Further, European airlines cannot hold more than a quarter of the voting rights of US airlines and must recognise the law that forbids US public sector employees from flying on non-US airliners (*The Economist*, 2002).

Currently, multilateral agreements incorporating rights for airline companies to operate between the EU, USA and Asia Pacific are not in existence, although multilateral agreements do exist between EU member states. It is for this reason that the European Commission wants the right to negotiate airline agreements on their member states behalf (Tomlinson, 2002).

THE ENTRANCE OF LOW-COST AIRLINES

As a result of the deregulation of the European airline industry, major national carriers have seen a downturn in their economic outlook. The experience has been somewhat similar to the US experience of deregulation in the late 1970s, in that the new competitive environment has allowed the entry of low-cost carriers. These include Go (set up, but since sold off, by British Airways), buzz (owned by KLM Royal Dutch Airlines), easyJet and Ryanair (both newly formed independent operators). This mirrored the process of the development of low-cost airline companies in the USA, for example Southwest Airlines and other, initially small, provincial carriers. In the UK, it would seem that low-cost airlines are actually thriving while their larger, more established counterparts are struggling. For instance, passengers volumes on Ryanair have increased considerably since they were set up, while easyJet currently has another 23 Boeing 737-700s on order for May 2004 (Done, 2002) to cope with a projected rise in demand for its no-frills airline service. Meanwhile, Ryanair has placed an industry advert for expressions of interest to sell it 50 second-hand Boeing 737s with a preference for aeroplanes between 7 and 14 years old (Done, 2002). Not all low-cost operators have prospered though. One low-cost operator, Debonair, collapsed almost immediately after set-up. Meanwhile, national carriers such as Iberia and Aer Lingus continue to struggle to maintain profitability.

Low-cost airlines seem to possess the competitive advantage of operating at significantly lower costs than their larger national counterparts. They have achieved this partly by operating with lower wage costs, more flexible employment and quicker airport turnaround times. In addition, they have tended to cut the costs of landing charges by flying to and from provincial, regional airports rather than major hubs such as Heathrow in London, although easyJet is making Schipol its Continental European base. Furthermore, they have reduced channel marketing costs by reducing their reliance on travel agents and other middlemen. The low-cost airline services tend to operate their own virtual customer service networks offering their customers quick book and search facilities through the Internet with minimum fuss and cost. Both easyJet and Ryanair are growing rapidly, with turnover of £356.9m and £487.7m respectively and pre-tax profits of £40.1m and £123.4m respectively.

Despite this deregulation, significant monopoly power still exists in domestic markets, as certain carriers continue to dominate particular hubs (for example British Airways, Virgin Atlantic and American Airlines for Heathrow–JFK transatlantic traffic). National governments continue to protect national carriers.

AIR TRANSPORT DEMAND AND THE WORLD TRADE CENTER BOMBING

When the first plane flew into the World Trade Center in New York City at around 9 am local time on 11 September 2001, and a second plane crashed within the hour, the world and the aviation industry changed considerably. News about the incident was patchy, initially suggesting a freak accident but when a further plane smashed into the Pentagon, the US defence command centre, and another plane went down apparently en route to Camp David, the president's military retreat, it became clear that something very sinister was happening. The final tally of casualties, those inside the buildings and in the planes, is thought to have been around 3000 people, although the authorities are still trying to determine the true figure for loss of life. Slowly, it emerged that the planes had been hijacked by suicide bombers believed to be members of the Islamic fundamentalist Al Qa'ida network, reputedly financed by Osama bin Mohammed bin Laden.

Airline passenger confidence took a considerable knock. Passenger volumes dropped considerably as people, fearing possible further terrorist attacks, decided to stay at home. Governments around the world began to pass legislation to alter existing flight paths over cities and enforce extra security measures on airline companies as a consequence. In the wake of the attacks, Swissair (the Swiss national carrier) and Sabena (the Belgian national carrier) collapsed because of the considerable downturn in demand. Most other national carriers had operating losses for the 2001/2002 financial year. Passenger volumes declined within Europe by over 10 per cent, by 35 per cent from Europe to the US and by 17 per cent from Europe to Asia, in September and October 2001. In the UK, British Airways is likely to report losses of around £750m for the 2002 financial year. As a result of the terrorist attacks, 100,000 jobs have been lost in the UK aviation industry alone. In the USA, airline companies are set to lose around $5bn this financial year. Thus, British Airways is now reviewing its overall structure. A 'size and shape' team has been organised to assess every route operated on its short-haul services (those most in competition with low-cost carriers) on whether the route makes a profit, whether it makes a 'network contribution' by feeding passengers onto more profitable routes or whether the route is important to BA's large corporate clients (Harrison, 2001).

Questions for discussion

1. What can major national carriers such as British Airways do to stimulate consumer demand for their long-haul services, particularly to the USA and the Far East?
2. How can major national carriers check the competitive threat of the low-cost carriers such as easyJet and Ryanair?

Selected web links

www.british-airways.com – British Airways site
www.easyjet.com – easyJet site
www.qantas.com – Qantas site
www.ryanair.com – Ryanair site

References

Airline Industry Information (2001), 'Air France Chairman Sees Consolidation of European Airline Industry', 14 March

Done, K (2002), 'No Frills yet Plenty of Soaring Ambitions', *Financial Times*, Monday 7 January, p.18

Done, K and Odell, M (2002), 'BA and KLM Ready for "Co-operation Pact"', *Financial Times*, Monday 7 January, p. 18

Harrison, M (2001), 'BA to Trim Back European Routes that do not Pay', *Independent*, 20 January, http://news.independent.co.uk/

House of Lords (1998), 'European Communities: Thirty Second Report – Airline Competition', Select Committee on European Communities, November 1998, http://www.publications.parliament.uk/pa/ld199798/ldselect/ldeucom/156/15602.htm

Stragier, J (1999), 'Current issues arising with airline alliances', 11th Annual Conference, Recent Developments in European Air Transport Law and Policy, Lisbon, 5 November, http://europa.eu.int/comm/competition/speeches/text/sp1999678_en.html

The Economist (2002), 'No more Squalid Deals', 26 January **362**(8257): pp. 10–11

Tomlinson, H (2002), 'Talks on 'Open Skies' to Take off', *Independent*, 20 January, http://news.independent.co.uk/

case study twelve

Internationalising the Chartered Institute of Marketing

Arguably the world's leading professional marketing body, it would be difficult to accuse the Chartered Institute of Marketing (CIM) of setting overly modest aspirations for itself. With an annual turnover in excess of £15 million, coupled with a strong record of continuous innovation, the CIM appears well poised to tackle the challenges of the new millennium. As the only organisation of its kind to hold a Royal Charter, it feels entirely justified to refer to itself as an acknowledged 'world authority' on marketing.

A CENTURY OF INCUBATION

Around nine decades ago (1911, to be exact) when the roots of what was to become today's CIM first took hold, such an ideal was almost unthinkable. This was largely due to the fact that the field of 'marketing' was not to become recognised as a proper business discipline until the inter-war period (1920s and 30s). Early associations only focused on 'specialised' functions such as sales management or advertising. Market research was still in early development as were areas such as consumer behaviour, distribution management and new product development. Yet from its earliest days as the Incorporate Sales Managers' Association (ISMA), the organisation grew steadily despite two world wars and by 1968 had become the Institute of Marketing (IM). Three years later, the IM managed to acquire a superb facility with plenty of development potential at Moor Hall in Berkshire, England (where it has remained to this day). Another two decades of attentive growth led to the granting of a Royal Charter in 1989. Now a fully accredited college, the CIM wasted little time, expanding rapidly and proactively to meet the marketing profession's growing needs. Today, the CIM attracts over 60,000 participants and members from 40 different countries through approximately 400 centres worldwide.

A similar organisation – the American Marketing Association (AMA) – claims to have around 45,000 members in 92 countries. There is some agreement, however, that what gives the CIM its dominant position is the impressive breadth and depth of programmes and services it offers. At this point you may want to ask a fundamental question – why?

A sense of purpose

Simply put, the CIM is about communicating and innovating. More specifically, the body has striven to:

1. Raise the levels of awareness and understanding of marketing throughout industry and commerce;
2. Enhance the standards of professionalism in the education, training and practice of marketing.

In addition to these ongoing aspirations, the CIM's Council recently decided to include another priority to its list, namely to promote and increase membership internationally. During 2000, the Council approved a number of fresh strategies to ensure the attainment of the organisation's aims. Key among these were 'international membership development' and the creation of 'a canon of knowledge' (to include e-commerce, educational curriculum development and professional standards).

How has the CIM gone about achieving these ideals?

The CIM serves members who must pay an annual membership fee. These members are organised into formal groups. Currently some 35,000 members are students, while another 28,000 or so are either full members known as MCIM or FCIM, affiliated professionals (a new status) or top-of-the-range 'chartered marketers'. To qualify as a chartered marketer, a member must hold a CIM Postgraduate Diploma (see below), complete at least 35 hours of continuing professional development (CPD) each year for two consecutive years and hold relevant full-time employment.

Whatever the membership group, the basic idea is to welcome members, provide them with plenty of training opportunities and encourage them eventually to reach the top of their marketing profession. Accessible either by qualification or experience, an assortment of nine awards (and growing) is currently on offer at different levels:

- Foundation Certificate – 45 hours of training
- e-Marketing Award – 45 hours of training
- Certificate in Marketing – five modules
- Certificate in Selling – five modules
- Advanced Certificate in Marketing – five modules

- Advanced Certificate in Sales Management – five modules
- Advanced Diploma in Communication Studies – offered in conjunction with CAM*
- Higher Diploma in Integrated Marketing Communications – also through CAM*
  (*CAM = Communication, Advertising and Marketing Education Foundation, now also located at Moor Hall in Berkshire)
- Postgraduate Diploma in Marketing – four advanced modules.

How do you keep these people coming back for more?

In order to get it right, the CIM relies heavily on a permanent industry steering group (the Council) composed of top business leaders, plus a growing number of alliances with highly influential marketing bodies such as the Academy of Marketing (AM), the Communication, Advertising and Marketing Education Foundation (CAM) and the European Marketing Confederation (EMC). On top of these 'external' contributions, the organisation also develops and maintains an impressive range of services and goods targeted to its membership:

- *Training;* Formal, Internet-based, and continuing professional development (CPD) offered through the CIM as well as through CIM-accredited associate learning centres
- *Learner support:* Course materials, student newsletters, comprehensive student/tutor websites, library support, testing/examinations
- *Publications: Marketing Business* magazine, *Journal of Marketing Management* (in tandem with the Academy of Marketing), *The Marketing Series* and module workbooks (in association with Butterworth Heinemann)
- *CIM Direct:* Mail-order books and materials
- *Member support:* State-of-the-art conference centre (including a hotel, restaurants, meeting rooms and IT support), extensive online support (several websites, e-mail)
- *Professional activities and support including:*
  - Exhibitions and conferences
  - Industry effectiveness awards (in conjunction with *Marketing Week* magazine)
  - Annual marketing lecture
  - Annual sales and marketing reward survey (re: remunerations)
  - Teaching quality awards
  - Exploration of e-marketing issues
  - Research reports
  - Case studies
  - Trend analyses
- *There are more 'collaborative' products in the pipeline as well:*
  - Pay-per-view research (from Lexis Nexis)
  - Marketing jobs website (by TotalJobs.com)
  - e-Library (in conjunction with Butterworth Heinemann).

THE 21ST CENTURY – AN OPPORTUNITY TO BE THE BEST?

The CIM promises to offer prospective members an opportunity to enhance their relationship with the field of marketing. Also, the organisation is striving to do this better and in more countries than anyone else. By joining an 'elite group of professionals', members can expect improved competence, greater job satisfaction and enhanced career development – internationally. Marketing is all about serving the market well. The market (especially an international/global one) for an organisation such as the CIM is growing and shifting rapidly. It now seems clear that their strategists feel ready, willing and able to take on the world. Will their vision and determination be enough to keep them in the lead?

Note

This case was developed by Paul Garneau and is based on information gathered from a variety of sources. Please note that CIM, CAM, AM, AMA and other organisations discussed above are not in a position to provide any additional information at this time. Learners are therefore asked to refrain from contacting them directly concerning this case study.

Questions for discussion

1. The case clearly indicates the CIM's new commitment to 'promote and increase membership internationally'. Discuss the main strategic options currently available to the CIM and make an informed recommendation to the Council.
2. In its most recent publications, the CIM claims to have become a 'global' organisation. When can a service organisation such as this safely make such a claim? Is the CIM actually ready to 'go global'? Discuss.

Selected web links

www.cim.co.uk – the Chartered Institute of Marketing

www.marketingpower.com – the American Marketing Association

Sources

Constitutional Review 2001, published by The Chartered Institute of Marketing, Moor Hall, Cookham, Berkshire SL6 9QH , United Kingdom

CIM (Annual) Report and Accounts, published by The Chartered Institute of Marketing, Moor Hall, Cookham, Berkshire SL6 9QH, United Kingdom

CIM Student Manual: The Pathway to Career Success in Marketing
Becoming a Chartered Marketer
CIM Qualifications
Your Guide to Study
As well as numerous leaflets and updates
All published by The Chartered Institute of Marketing – Moor Hall, Berkshire, UK
Marketing Business, official CIM magazine published 10 times a year by CIM – Moor Hall, Berkshire, UK
Journal of Marketing Management, official journal of the Academy of Marketing published in association with the CIM by Westburn Publishers Ltd

case study thirteen

Golden Arch Hotels

Hungry for a good night's sleep? That's exactly what the folks at McDonald's are hoping. Not long ago, Jack Greenberg, Chairman and CEO, stated that 'innovation is always on the menu at McDonald's'. Speaking by video link at a conference in Switzerland on 9 November 2000, he added, 'we are not just in the business of serving food – we are serving people'. The purpose of the conference was to introduce the company's latest brand extension – the new Golden Arch Hotels (GAH).

For many, *not* thinking of McDonald's simply in terms of burgers, fries and shakes does not come easily. Interestingly, this has not been so in Switzerland. Over the past quarter century, the company's Swiss partners, inspired by their innovative Chairman and CEO, Urs Hammer, have frequently stretched the boundaries of what people normally expect from the number one fast-food giant. Examples include:

- *1976–2001* Launch of no fewer than 116 successful fast-food restaurants in a tiny mountainous country, enjoying a high standard of living
- *1992* Launch of the McTrain – a restaurant car running on Swiss Intercity Services
- *1996* Launch of the McPlane – a 162-seat charter aircraft employing special McDonald's hostesses to aid the regular cabin crew
- *1997* Launch of mobile restaurants transported by large lorries to various sports events
- *2001* Launch of the world's first two Golden Arch Hotels.

Hammer, a former hotelier himself, always thought that developing a chain of hotels seemed like a natural idea for McDonald's in Switzerland. He had studied hotel management in Lausanne, worked for several international hotel chains in Europe and South East Asia, and his father had been Dean of the Zurich Hotel School. He was convinced that lucrative synergies with the restaurant side of the business could be realised.

FOOD AND HOSPITALITY

Having pretty well saturated its home market (the USA) with restaurants, McDonald's developed its menu selections extensively (breakfasts, pizza, salads and so forth) and expanded into 119 foreign markets, the stage was set for the global giant to seize the challenges of diversification. The hotel concept is being put forward by management as a natural extension of the 'McFamily'. Greenberg insists that the McDonald's name is now a global 'brand' strongly associated with the now famous quality, service, cleanliness and value (QSC&V) formula. Each new hotel is to serve up a combination of food and shelter à la McDonald's. This means that these 'McGuests' can expect to be treated in a manner that has become the organisation's QSC&V signature.

According to the company's own media release (9/11/00), the Golden Arch chain represents a new line of hotels 'targeted at business travellers during the week and at families and young adults on the weekends'. It took the company four years to complete the first two, and third hotel is planned for the Geneva-Cointrin airport district. The first GAH opened amid considerable excitement on 19 March 2001. Built on a site in Rümlang, just minutes from Zurich Airport, it offers guests the choice of 211 well-furnished rooms. The second, offering 80 rooms, opened a mere two weeks later in Lully (Estavayer-le-Lac) on highway A1 in the canton of Fribourg. Each facility boasts a four-star rating from the Swiss Hotel Association, perhaps reflecting a desire to move McDonald's somewhat upmarket while continuing to offer good value for money.

To experience some of the quite unique features on offer, feel free to take a look around one of these new hotels.

ARRIVAL

You will probably arrive by taxi, airport limousine, private automobile or rented car, having spotted the distinctive 'h' logo from a distance of several city blocks. The company simply and cleverly cut the famous 'm' (original golden arches) in half (hence Golden Arch Hotel) to ensure instant association with the McDonald's brand. The newly constructed structure appears welcoming and affordable. The front entrance that features a not-so-customary fountain strikes you. You look at it attentively and realise that this fountain has only two jets. One of these shoots straight up while the other arcs gently across. The resulting effect is an unmistakable aquatic 'h'. You are now ready for the experience.

CHECKING IN

As you walk into the lobby, you immediately sense that the entire complex is highly contemporary in design with an obvious focus on convivial functionality throughout.

You observe that public spaces such as the lobby/reception area, the bar and the lounge have been decorated with soft furnishings, neutral colours and natural textures such as wood, leather, glass and stone. You may book a room right then and there by using one of the automated self-check-in stations in the lobby, or you could have pre-booked by phone, fax, e-mail or on the Web – www.goldenarchhotel.com – for slightly less money. All rates are fixed. On weekdays all travellers pay SFr189/Rümlang (US$114) or SFr169/Lully (US$102) for single occupancy and an extra SFr25 (US$15) for each additional person. If booked online, the rates fall to SFr174 (US$105) and SFr154 (US$93) respectively. On weekends, there is a family room rate of SFr174/Rümlang (US$105) or SFr154/Lully (US$93) for up to two adults and two children occupying the same room. Attractive 'family adventure weekend' and 'summer' rates are also available. Parking for your car is available underground. Once checked in, you are provided with an easy-to-use luggage trolley that will double as a clothes organiser once you get it up to your room. For added safety, the electronic lift is designed to operate only once your room key has been verified for identification purposes. Once on the right floor, you trolley down the hall and note that all room doors are fitted with spy holes.

YOUR ROOM

You open the door and discover that, in keeping with the rest of the building, your room has soft curving walls, maple parquet flooring and most (but not all) of the creature comforts you would expect. Designer Corinna Kretschmar managed to create a distinctive yet practical living space while respecting the principles of feng shui – so dear to Urs Hammer. Each room has one red wall, an unmistakable 'm' headboard, and distinctive custom-built wooden furniture with no sharp edges. Chairs are of course shaped like the letter 'h'. The bathroom is modern, well equipped and features a circular, free-standing glass shower. There are also a number of high-tech features in the room. The Bico – sit'n'sleep – unit, for example, can be converted from a couch to a fully adjustable bed in seconds. Each one costs about US$4000 and offers top-of-the-range comfort with features such as electronic positioning and remote-controlled operation. The all-important mattress has a two-year expiry date (unheard of in the hotel trade). Finishing touches include bedside remote controls and snowy white linen. Next on the list is the state-of-the-art 'infotainment' system. More than simply a TV, this unit can provide a range of speciality channels (some more spicy than others), lets you send and receive e-mail messages, and will even allow you to surf the Net when you feel like it. On the down side, you need to remember that most of this is self-serve. You will not find a 'minibar' or be able to ring for room service. Hallway vending machines, however, may be found on all floors.

MEALTIMES

Feeling peckish? There is of course a full McDonald's restaurant on the ground floor serving meals and snacks all day long. If you fancy a more traditional breakfast, the hotel also provides a Swiss continental breakfast in an upstairs dining room. You might prefer something light from the Aroma Café, also situated on the ground floor. If you are here on business, Hammer believes that food will not be a problem: 'Quite frankly, business people who are here the whole day want to see something else at the end of the day. The majority of business travellers don't tend to eat in their hotel anyway.' Another key point is that outside catering is available for business meetings and conferences.

OTHER AMENITIES

When not resting or eating, you may well want to workout in the well-equipped fitness room. If you have kids with you, be sure to check out the great deals on offer at the hotel's 'family adventure partners' in the vicinity. For business clients, well-appointed meeting rooms are available for groups of 10 to 100. After all that you may well be ready to reward yourself in the public bar, a cosy space with leather chairs and a modernist waterfall cascade. By the way, their main bartender at Rümlang, Hans Sivikaya, recently won the European Bartender Championship in Holland. Cheers!

Enjoyed your walkabout? Let's now get back to the case. 'The main reason for the launch is the incredible potential that lies in the McDonald's brand', says Hammer. 'The interest we received from other countries wanting to set up their own franchises, even before the hotel was finished, showed me that people believe McDonald's can extend their hospitality.'

Time will tell if enough people in Switzerland and elsewhere are hungry for a good night's sleep under the new arches.

Questions for discussion

1. It is stated in the case that other countries have expressed a desire to set up Golden Arch Hotels at home. Develop a balanced and realistic 'roll-out' strategy for the GAH concept.
2. The case also suggests that McDonald's Corporation feels ready to 'seize the challenges of diversification'. Discuss this with the help of the 'Ansoff matrix' model discussed in this textbook.

Sources

Adkins, H (2001), 'Golden Opportunity', *Caterer & Hotelkeeper*, 29 March, pp. 26–7

Chisholm, J (2002), 'Companies and Finance UK: Coffee Republic', *Financial Times*, 23 February, http://globalarchive.ft.com/globalarchive/article.html?id=020223001763&query=aroma (23/02/02)

Golden Arch Media Relations (2000), 'Golden Arch Hotels – A World Premiere of McDonald's Switzerland', *Media Release*, 9 November

McDonald's Company Facts Home Page, Biz/ed home, http://www.bized.ac.uk/compfact/mcdonalds/mcindex.htm (16/07/01)

McDonald's Suisse Holding SA (2000), 'Video Welcome Greetings Jack Greenberg, Chairman and CEO McDonald's Corporation', Media Conference, 9 November

McDonald's Suisse Holding SA, 'Be with us … again, au Golden Arch – le deuxième hôtel McDonald's du monde ouvre ses portes', http://gah.fconnection.com/en/background/ press.html (27/11/01)

McDonald's Suisse Holding SA, 'About Golden Arch Hotels', http://gah.fconnection.com/en/ background/index.php (21/02/02)

McDonald's Suisse Holding SA, 'Zurich Airport', http://gah.fconnection.com/en/ locations/index.html (20/02/02)

McDonald's Suisse Holding SA (2001), 'Grand Opening: It's the final countdown …', e-Mail Newsletter No. 1, March, http://gah.fconnection.com/en/home/news1.html (23/02/02)

McDonald's Suisse Holding SA (2001), 'Zurich Airport and Lully/Estavayer-le-Lac: Welcome!', e-Mail Newsletter No. 2, May, http://gah.fconnection.com/en/home/news2.html (23/02/02)

McDonald's Suisse Holding SA (2001), 'Golden Arch Locomotive: Trainspotting!', e-Mail Newsletter No. 3, July , http://gah.fconnection.com/en/home/news3.html (23/02/02)

McDonald's Suisse Holding SA (2001), 'Golden Arch Hotel Zurich Airport: Adventure, Here we come!', e-Mail Newsletter No. 4, September, http://gah.fconnection.com/en/ home/news4.html (23/02/02)

McDonald's Suisse Holding SA (2001), 'New Golden Arch Lounge: Relax and Enjoy', e-Mail Newsletter No. 5, October, http://gah.fconnection.com/en/home/news5.html (23/02/02)

McDonald's Suisse Holding SA (2001), 'Golden Arch Bartender the Best in Europe: Juggling with bottles', e-Mail Newsletter No. 6, December, http://gah.fconnection.com/en/ home/news6.html (23/02/02)

Turner, S (2001), 'In bed with McDonald's', *The Times* (travel section), 24 March, pp. 1–2

case study fourteen

Marketing Australia to the World

> Australia had struck me, on my first visit a few years before, as a sensible America. It was a nation with the same wild range of landscape, from beach to desert to throbbing metropolis, but discreetly peopled – 5 per cent of the US population in a nearly equal acreage – and these included considerably fewer psychopaths and neurotics. Australia was an America in which the populace was not possessed of the belief that it was specially blessed and directed by God, with a particular vocation to bully smaller nations. An America in which they played cricket instead of baseball. (Lawson, 1993, p. 47)

In common with many people across the world, journalist Mark Lawson clearly has a soft spot for Australia. Australia is regarded as a desirable and perhaps slightly exotic travel destination by tourists from many parts of the world. This country, populated by around 19 million people, offers the attractions of the sea and the beach, the wilderness, and cosmopolitan cities. Sydney, Melbourne, Brisbane, Perth and Adelaide all have more than a million inhabitants. Australia is a prosperous nation that is becoming more prosperous. At the end of 2000, Australia had benefited from nine years of uninterrupted economic growth. The Australian economy had grown considerably faster than the average for developed countries (members of the Organisation for Economic Co-operation and Development – OECD) over this period. Despite a temporary slowdown in the economy towards the end of 2000, it was expected that strong growth would soon begin again (OECD, 2001).

The Australian government is striving to sustain growth in the economy without damaging the natural environment. Australia is rich in biodiversity, with many unique species of plants and animals. Many are threatened with extinction due to habitat alteration and loss, or competition and predation from introduced species. The farming methods in use in Australia have also had substantial negative effects on both biological diversity and ecosystems. In trying to achieve economic growth without excessive damage to the environment, two key issues have arisen in Australia – dryland salinity and water scarcity. Australia is a relatively dry continent, in which water scarcity is worsened by climate variability, including periodic drought. The extensive use of irrigation in the farming industry contributes to high levels of water use in Australia (roughly four times as much water is used per person in Australia as in the UK), and to gradually increasing levels of salt in the land, which eventually damages agricultural productivity (dryland salinity).

The issues of economic growth and environmental protection provide a background to the future development of the Australian tourist industry. Tourism has been – and is expected to continue to be – a major contributor to Australian economic growth. The growth of tourism has brought clear economic benefits, but has increased the pressure on the environment and Australia's water resources.

THE AUSTRALIAN INTERNATIONAL TOURIST INDUSTRY IN 2002

Table C14.1 shows that international tourism is a growth business for Australia. By 2003 it was expected that international visitor arrivals would be 87 per cent higher

Table C14.1 Australian international tourism

	1993	1995	1997	1999	*2001* (estimate)	**2003** (forecast)
International visitor nights (millions) by originating country						
New Zealand	8.4	9.2	10.0	10.6	*10.4*	**10.8**
Japan	4.9	6.7	8.6	9.6	*8.9*	**7.8**
China	1.0	1.3	3.6	4.9	*7.6*	**10.7**
Singapore	2.4	3.4	3.6	5.5	*5.2*	**5.3**
South Korea	1.8	3.0	5.2	3.5	*5.2*	**5.9**
Other Asia	11.2	17.4	21.5	21.7	*21.1*	**22.5**
United Kingdom	12.6	14.6	14.3	18.8	*20.9*	**22.6**
Other Europe	13.2	15.4	16.1	19.4	*19.9*	**22.2**
North America	9.3	10.0	9.6	12.5	*13.3*	**14.5**
Rest of world	4.7	5.2	6.3	7.2	*7.5*	**8.0**
Total	**69.7**	**86.2**	**98.6**	**113.7**	***119.9***	**130.3**
International visitor arrivals (percentages) by purpose of visit						
Business	10.3	11.8	12.4	12.1	*12.3*	**12.6**
Holiday	64.4	61.9	59.9	57.4	*56.8*	**56.3**
Visiting friends and relatives	17.1	18.7	18.8	19.3	*19.2*	**19.2**
Other	8.3	7.6	8.9	11.2	*11.7*	**11.9**

Source: Based on data from http://www.industry.gov.au

than they were in 1993. As a proportion of this growing total, the number of people visiting Australia purely for a holiday is slowly declining, with business travel and travel to visit friends and relatives growing more quickly. Of course this does not mean that the number of international holiday visits to Australia is declining, just that it is growing more slowly than the other reasons for travel. In fact, the number of international holiday arrivals into Australia in 2003 was expected to be 57.6 per cent higher than the 1993 figure.

As 2002 dawned, the international tourist industry was still suffering from the after-effects of the terrorist attacks on the World Trade Center and the Pentagon in the USA on 11 September 2001. However, it looked as though the worst effects of those events were abating, and there were signs that inbound tourism to Australia was returning to its previous long-term growth trend. November 2001 had seen the worst decline in international visitor arrivals (20.5 per cent lower than the previous November). The impact was, however, clearly declining, so that by January 2002 international visitor arrivals were only 9.6 per cent lower than the previous January. February 2002 actually showed an increase in visitors over February 2001, although this was thought to be because Chinese New Year fell in February of that year, compared with January the previous year. The traditional tourism markets of the UK and USA were beginning to show renewed growth, and China was showing strong growth. New Zealand and Japan gave cause for concern, with indications that demand growth had stagnated in these markets. Overall, the Australian international tourist industry was looking forward with reasonable optimism to the next decade, expecting growth from most international markets. On the other hand, domestic Australian tourism seemed to have stagnated, and one suggestion was that in the increasingly competitive battle for consumers' leisure time tourism was losing out to alternative leisure pursuits.

Tourism, both national and international, is a discretionary item of expenditure for the consumer. As a result, tourism spending tends to be quite heavily influenced by general economic prosperity. Although Australia has been booming, the world economy has been in recession for some time. It seemed to be emerging from a recession during 2002, with potentially beneficial results for the tourist industry worldwide, and for Australia specifically. Economic forecasters have recently increased their projections for world economic growth for the next decade. Japan seems likely to have the most sluggish recovery, but the USA will probably lead the world into more prosperous economic circumstances. While the EU is unlikely to see economic growth rates on the same scale as the Americans, growth seems certain to improve over the next few years. Within Europe, the UK and Ireland look likely to be the leaders in growth terms.

This generally optimistic economic picture has to be amended to take into account a number of other influences affecting Australian tourism in the early years of the decade, and in the wake of the 11 September 2001 events. First, there is the question of the stability of the international air carriers (see also Case Study 11, 'Crisis in the European airline industry'). For obvious reasons – Australia is an island – virtually all the international tourists who visit Australia arrive by air. Several international airlines suffered serious financial problems after September 2001. Another concern was that travellers from Europe to Australia would be deterred since their flight path would take them through Middle Eastern air space. On the other hand, it was thought that Asian travellers might tend to switch their travel plans from northern hemisphere destinations in favour of Australia.

OVERSEEING THE AUSTRALIAN TOURISM INDUSTRY

> The aspect of tourism that has arguably generated most attention in recent times is that of its impact for good or ill on the natural environment, with most commentators suggesting that its effects are more often for ill than for good. (Brown, 1998, p. 45)

Tourism is a serious business in Australia. It is estimated that tourists spent $58.2 billion on goods and services in 1997–98. Of this total, 22 per cent was spent by international tourists. Another way of looking at this is that spending by international tourists in Australia amounted to 11.2 per cent of total exports in 1997–98. Tourism's contribution to the national income (gross domestic product), at 4.5 per cent, exceeded that of several traditional industry sectors such as communication services (3.2 per cent), and agriculture, forestry and fishing (3.3 per cent). In 1997–98, 513,000 people were directly employed in the Australian tourism industry (this is equivalent to 389,000 full-time jobs, since many people work part time in the tourist industry).

Tourism falls within the responsibilities of the Sport and Tourism Division of Australia's Department of Industry, Science and Resources. The stated mission of the Sport and Tourism Division is 'to contribute to Australia's economic and social well-being through the development of sustainable, internationally competitive and innovative sport and recreation and tourism industries' (www.isr.gov.au). In 2001–02, the top priority identified in the Sport and Tourism Division Business Plan was to improve the quality of the tourism experience provided by the inbound tourism sector, especially to visitors from North Asia. A range of other priorities was also specified, including:

- Facilitate the development of select tourism niche markets: indigenous, sports and ecotourism
- Develop a strategy for better acceptance and implementation of 'sustainable tourism'
- Ensure that tourism interests are considered in the management of Australia's protected natural areas
- Improve sport and tourism information and research
- Improve access to and use of online and emerging technologies in the tourism sector.

There is considerable emphasis on sustainable tourism and ecotourism. Once upon a time the natural resources of such a large and sparsely populated country as Australia would have been regarded as practically infinite. However, even in Australia, the pressure from tourists on popular tourist areas is having a detrimental effect on the local environment. Eventually, the damage caused by tourists to fragile ecosystems can result in the loss of the very things that originally attracted visitors in the first place. There are plenty of examples from other tourist destinations to warn Australia of the potential environmental dangers of tourism. In the UK, the popularity of long-distance footpaths, such as the Pennine Way, has resulted in severe erosion and scarred landscapes. Parts of the Himalayas, including Everest Base Camp, suffer serious litter problems. The influx of tourists to certain Mediterranean coastal areas often generates more sewage and other waste than local infrastructures can handle. The promotion of diving has contributed to the destruction of coral reefs in Belize, and is now believed to be having the same effect in Australia.

There are no simple answers to the issues associated with tourism and the environment. It is almost inevitable that tourism development will bring with it some undesirable environmental impacts. On the other hand, it will also create jobs. The management of environmental impacts is an issue that is closely related to that of positioning Australia in the global tourism market. If Australia's wilderness areas are to retain the sense of mystery and awe that they undoubtedly still hold in the minds of many international tourists, then mechanisms must be found to combine further tourist development with proper concern for the environment.

THE FUTURE FOR AUSTRALIAN TOURISM

> Thirty years ago the phrase 'Australian cuisine' rated with 'holy war' as one of the English language's great oxymorons. Aussie tucker conjured up visions of Vegemite sandwiches, gristly meat pies, and a stodgy dinner of lamb chops, three watery vegetables, and a bowl of ice cream for dessert ... These days Australia's top chefs enjoy celebrity status, and the vibrant restaurant and café scene is one of the highlights of a visit down under. (Smith, 1999, p. 22)

The Australian tourist industry has come a long way in 30 years. Over the next 30 years it will face several key challenges. At home the pressure is on to ensure that tourism development is consistent with national policy on environmental protection. Meanwhile, as established overseas tourist destinations continue to compete with Australia for the lucrative markets of Europe, North America and Asia, so new tourist destinations will emerge to offer the international traveller greater choice.

Tourism is important to Australia, and Australia has many natural and social advantages in sustaining a thriving international tourist industry. Australia's natural advantages are manifest. For example, it has beaches, wilderness and wildlife in profusion. Sensible management of these resources should ensure that they continue to attract international visitors indefinitely. Socially, Australia benefits from the wide range of peoples who have made it their home. This builds social links to many countries across the world, and contributes to the cosmopolitan character of Australia's major cities, which makes them attractive to tourists seeking the bright lights.

Nevertheless, complacency is certainly not an option for the Australian tourist industry. Because Australia is a long-haul flight for affluent tourists from Europe and North America, it is particularly badly affected by major international events. Even before the events of 11 September 2001 in the USA, Australian international tourism had been adversely affected by the Gulf War, and by the crisis experienced in the Asian economies in the mid-1990s. International tourism to Australia thrives on a stable international political situation and economic prosperity. When times get tough, Americans can choose to holiday at home or in the nearby Caribbean, and Europeans can enjoy the high life in Mediterranean resorts or the wildlife of Africa.

The market for affluent international tourists is becoming ever-more competitive, and Australian tourist providers – with the support of the Department of Industry, Tourism and Resources – have to compete with increasingly sophisticated rivals. It remains to be seen whether Australia can recover from recent international political and economic shocks and maintain or increase its share of the global tourism business.

Questions for discussion

You have been asked to provide the Australian Department of Industry, Science and Resources with an objective assessment of the key strategic marketing issues facing the Australian tourist industry.

1. Using a suitable analytical framework, summarise the key macroenvironmental issues affecting Australian tourism.
2. Put the issues that you have identified in question 1 into a rank order, based on their impact, probability and urgency.

Selected web links

www.afta.com.au – Australian Federation of Travel Agents
www.atec.net.au – Australian Tourism Export Council
www.industry.gov.au – Australian government site with tourism resources
www.isr.gov.au – Department of Industry, Science and Resources
www.ecotourism.org.au – Ecotourism Association of Australia
www.pata.org – Pacific Asia Travel Association
www.ttf.org.au – Tourism Task Force (of Australia)

References

Brown, F (1998), *Tourism Reassessed: Blight or Blessing?*, Oxford: Butterworth Heinemann
Lawson, M (1993), *The Battle for Room Service: Journeys to all the Safe Places*, London: Pan
OECD (2001), *OECD Economic Surveys: Australia*, August, Paris: OECD
Smith, R M (1999), *The National Geographic Traveller: Australia*, Washington DC: National Geographic Society

case study fifteen

Trouble with the CPC100

INTRODUCTION

This short case study, which deals with the issues of strategic marketing implementation and control (and sales variance analysis in particular), is written in the form of a play. We hope you find it an amusing change from the more conventional case studies. You will find that the characters in the play suggest their own diagnoses of the 'trouble with the CPC100', but that they do not always agree. The supporting table is very important to help you to diagnose what is going on, and to make sense of some of the characters' statements. You can assume that the CPC100 is only one of this company's product lines, although quite an important one. You can also assume that this company is not the market leader in the photocopier market (since it has to compete with firms such as Xerox and Canon).

Characters

Liz McSwain: Managing Director
Geoff Burrage: Sales Director
Marc Perrin: Marketing Director
Fred Elliot: Product Manager
Brad MacDonald: Sales Manager, North American Region

Dress

Liz is immaculately turned out, the impeccable businesswoman. Efficient and in charge. Geoff is smart if a little rumpled, tie is not entirely straight. University of life type.

Table C15.1 Model CPC100 compact office photocopier: UK market

		January	February	March	April	May	June	Year to date	July	August	September	October	November	December	
SALES REVENUE															
Market volume	Forecast	50000	45000	30000	35000	35000	45000	**240000**	60000	75000	75000	80000	70000	65000	665000
	Actual	45000	47500	33000	37000	34000	45500	**242000**							
	Variance	–5000	2500	3000	2000	–1000	500	**2000**							
	Variance %	–10	5.6	10.0	5.7	–2.9	1.1	**0.8**							
Sales volume (units)	Forecast	7500	6750	4500	5250	5250	6750	**36000**	9000	11250	11250	12000	10500	9750	99750
	Actual	6500	7250	5150	4900	5300	6250	**35350**							
	Variance	–1000	500	650	–350	50	–500	**–650**							
	Variance %	–13.3	7.4	14.4	–6.7	1.0	–7.4	**–1.8**							
Market share %	Forecast	15	15	15	15	15	15	**15**	15	15	15	15	15	15	
	Actual	14.4	15.3	15.6	13.2	15.6	13.7	**14.6**							
	Variance	–0.6	0.3	0.6	–1.8	0.6	–1.3	**–0.4**							
List price £		250	250	250	250	250	250	**250**	250	250	250	250	250	250	
Net price £	Forecast	225	225	225	225	225	225	**225**	225	225	225	225	225	225	
	Actual	215	223	213	210	218	220	**216.5**							
	Variance	–10	–2	–12	–15	–7	–5	**–8.5**							
	Variance %	–4.4	–0.9	–5.3	–6.7	–3.1	–2.2	**–3.8**							
Sales revenue £	Forecast	1687500	1518750	1012500	1181250	1181250	1518750	**8100000**	2025000	2531250	2531250	2700000	2362500	2193750	22443750
	Actual	1397500	1616750	1096950	1029000	1155400	1375000	**7653275**							
	Variance	–290000	98000	84450	–152250	–25850	–143750	**–446725**							
	Variance %	–17.2	6.5	8.3	–12.9	–2.2	–9.5	**–5.5**							
MARKETING EXPENDITURE															
Advertising	Forecast	25000	25000	25000	25000	25000	25000	**150000**	25000	25000	25000	25000	25000	25000	
	Actual	18000	24000	30000	25500	24000	23000	**144500**							
	Variance	–7000	–1000	5000	500	–1000	–2000	**–5500**							
	Variance %	–28.0	–4.0	20.0	2.0	–4.0	–8.0	**–3.7**							
Exhibitions	Forecast	0	0	10000	0	0	5000	**15000**							
	Actual	0	0	11000	0	0	0	**11000**							
	Variance	0	0	1000	0	0	–5000	**–4000**							
	Variance %	0	0	10.0	0	0	–100.0	**–26.7**							
PR & Events	Forecast	5000	5000	5000	10000	5000	5000	**35000**	5000	5000	5000	5000	5000	5000	
	Actual	5000	5000	5000	11500	5000	5000	**36500**							
	Variance	0	0	0	1500	0	0	**1500**							
	Variance %	0.0	0.0	0.0	15.0	0.0	0.0	**4.3**							
Market research	Forecast	5000	5000	10000	5000	5000	5000	**35000**	5000	5000	5000	5000	5000	5000	
	Actual	5000	5000	5000	5000	5000	5000	**30000**							
	Variance	0	0	–5000	0	0	0	**–5000**							
	Variance %	0.0	0.0	–50.0	0.0	0.0	0.0	**–14.3**							
Sales force															
Commission forecast		150000	135000	90000	105000	105000	135000	**720000**	180000	225000	225000	240000	210000	195000	
Commission actual		130000	145000	103000	98000	106000	125000	**707000**							
Sales expense forecast		75000	67500	45000	52500	52500	67500	**360000**	90000	112500	112500	120000	105000	97500	
Sales expenses actual		58500	65250	46350	44100	47700	56250	**318150**							
	Variance	–36500	7750	14350	–15400	–3800	–21250	**–54850**							
	Variance %	–16.2	3.8	10.6	–9.8	–2.4	–10.5	**–5.1**							
Total expenditure	Forecast	260000	237500	185000	197500	192500	242500	**1315000**	305000	372500	372500	395000	350000	327500	
	Actual	216500	244250	200350	184100	187700	214250	**1247150**							
	Variance	–43500	6750	15350	–13400	–4800	–28250	**–67850**							
	Variance %	–16.7	2.8	8.3	–6.8	–2.5	–11.6	**–5.2**							

Marc is smartly casual in a Californian style. Suave, relaxed, cool.
Fred is dressed in conventional British office attire. Nervous, geeky, uncool.
Brad is fairly relaxed in slacks and an open-necked shirt.

THE PLAY

[Liz walks briskly into a meeting room and sits down at the head of the table. The other characters are already seated and studying the data on the CPC100 (Table C15.1).]

Liz: Good afternoon, gentlemen. This is our six-month review meeting for the CPC100, right?

Geoff: Hi Liz. Yeah, that's right. And none too soon if you ask me, we're clearly in a big mess with ...

Liz: Thank you Geoff. Don't worry, I'll make sure you have your chance. But first you'll notice we've got a visitor with us today. This is Brad MacDonald, over in the UK for a few days from the Canadian office to see how we do things. OK Brad, you know I'm Liz McSwain, Managing Director, but I don't think you know the others. Gentlemen, if you could introduce yourselves.

Geoff: Geoff Burrage, Sales Director, nice to meet you Brad.

Marc: Marc Perrin, Marketing Director, nice to see you again Brad ... it's been a long time!

Fred: Oh! Yes. Hello. I'm Fred Elliott. Erm ... product manager for the CPC100. I work for Mr Perrin.

Brad: Thanks for the introductions. I should explain that I'm actually over in the UK on vacation right now, but I know that you've got some issues with the CPC100 and Liz thought it might be useful to have my input.

Liz: Right. Yes, I really appreciate you coming along today Brad. If you could cast your eye over the figures and listen to what these guys have to say maybe you can help us with this. Now, I've reviewed the six-monthly year-to-date figures on the CPC100 and there are a few things that are bothering me ...

Geoff: More than a few things if you ask me, it's a dog and we should never have launched it in the UK market ...

Liz: Yes, thank you Geoff. For the moment, if you'll allow me to outline my concerns? OK. Obviously the main priority is the sales variance. The way I see it, we started off the year way over our revenue target and it's been downhill all the way from there. Fred?

Fred: Huh? Sorry. Oh, yes. Well it's not quite that simple Liz ...

Geoff: Well it looks that simple to me. Year-to-date revenue is nearly 10 per cent below target, and it's pretty clear that with the kind of marketing support we've been getting, you're lucky to be off by that little. My team have been working bloody hard to shift, what is it, 35,000 units – look, just 650 off target. Bloody heroic, I'd call it, with that dog of a product. Especially when the market has been stone cold ...

Marc: *(interrupts)* So let me get this straight Geoff. The market is about 1 per cent over forecast, and that makes it stone cold? Actually, I'd say that was remarkably good forecasting by Fred. Overall, market volume variance is clearly not the problem. For that matter, we only have a 0.4 per cent negative market share variance. Now obviously, we want to do something about that, but, frankly, it's better than most product lines are doing at the moment. I'd like Fred to take us through what's going on here, if that's OK Liz? The market's up, our share is close to target, but our revenues are significantly off.

Liz: Yes, that's a good idea Marc. Fred, what's going on here?

Fred: Sorry. Yes, well, like Mr Perrin said, the year to date shows strong market figures, and our share is OK. The main problem is that we've just not been able to maintain our net selling price. So, nominally we set the list price at £250, and we allow for an average 10 per cent discount. But if you look at the year-to-date figures, the average discount so far this year has been £33.50, which is 13.4 per cent against list price. So, basically, what we've got is an unexpected adverse price variance.

Liz: Am I right that we agreed 10 per cent was the maximum discount that an individual sales executive could give, and anything more than that needs sales manager approval?

Geoff: Well, if what you're telling me is that it's a dog of a product and that we're getting bloody useless marketing support, so that the only option my blokes have got left is to offer the customer a bit of an incentive, then ... well, yes. Look at the marketing support we've had this year. Advertising spend is down, exhibitions spend is down. Even market research spend is down. And you'll not be surprised to learn that the sales team are pretty unhappy about the commission situation – I sent you a memo about that last week, Liz, have you had a chance to read it yet?

Liz: Get real Geoff. Commission payments are tied to sales volume. Volume is off by 1.8 per cent, so commission is off by 1.8 per cent.

Marc: Yes, actually I think it would be more realistic to tie commission payments to sales revenue. The way I see it, our sales execs are getting rewarded for giving away our profit margins in big discount deals.

Liz: What about the marketing expenditure variances, Marc?

Marc: Advertising's the main one. Actually, if you took out January we'd be slightly over budget. *Office Equipment World* were planning a special edition in January, and we had booked a full page, but in the end they decided not to go ahead. Other than that we're more or less on target. Exhibitions is down, because we agreed with Geoff not to go to the Brighton Office Equipment Expo this year – basically we got very few good leads out of it last year. And market research is down because we decided against that survey of CPC100 customers that we were going to run in March. Remember, Liz, I think your words were 'why should I waste £5000 finding out what I already know?'.

Liz: Thanks for reminding me. Can we summarise now, please? Revenue on the CPC100 is off 5.5 per cent. We have a positive market volume variance, share is off just a little so volume's slightly off. The adverse price variance magnifies that. Where do we go from here? Fred?

Fred: Sorry. Yes. On current trends we'll be £1.2 million down on sales revenue by the end of the year …

Geoff: Whoops! There goes your bonus Freddy-boy!

Liz: What's your recommendation Geoff?

Geoff: In the words of the immortal Boston Consulting Group, if it's a dog, terminate it with extreme prejudice.

Liz: I'm not sure that's exactly what it says in the manual, but I get your drift. Marc?

Fred: We can recover the situation. The product is still making a decent contribution over variable costs. I think we should ask Fred to come up with a get-well plan for next month's meeting.

Liz: Well, since we've got an expert with us from the Canadian office, we should use his expertise. What do you think, Brad?

THE END

Questions for discussion

Imagine that you are Brad MacDonald. Liz has asked you to comment on the CPC100 situation. Frame your response to her in the following terms.

1. What is the immediate problem that the CPC100 product manager should focus his attention on?
2. What might be the underlying causes of the 'trouble with the CPC100'?

part three

Readings

Interaction, Relationships and Networks in Business Markets: An Evolving Perspective

Turnbull, P, Ford, D and Cunningham, M (1996)

Extract from *Journal of Business and Industrial Marketing*, **11**(3/4): 44–62v

Interaction approach

The interaction approach takes the relationship as its unit of analysis rather than the individual transaction. It involves simultaneous analysis of the attitudes and actions of both parties and emphasizes the essential similarity between the purchasing and marketing tasks in relationships. It sees relationships both as important in themselves and as predictors of individual transaction behavior and is reviewed in detail in Hakansson (1982). Among the individual research tasks which have been addressed has been to find the variables which can best be used to describe relationships; how these relationships evolve over time; the variation in the nature of relationships in different circumstances; the atmosphere within which interaction takes place; the contact patterns between the two parties and the bonding which occurs between the companies.

The research has highlighted the importance of separating the short-term management of individual relationships from the longer-term development of a strategy for the company's portfolio of supplier and customer relationships (Turnbull and Valla, 1986). The research has also shown the inter-relationship between the resources possessed by companies and how these are used in and affected by their relationship activities. A review of this work is found in Ford (1990). This research has led to the view that it is the co-ordination and mobilization of the company's portfolio of relationships and the use and enhancement of the resources of both companies through interaction in those relationships that is the basis of enhancing a company's network position and hence its competitive advantage (Ford et al., 1996) This conceptual link between networks and competitiveness leads us to consider several contemporary research thrusts in the area of market competitiveness.

Competitiveness and competitive performance

An interaction approach view of competitiveness

Research studies in the field of competitiveness and competitive performance have assumed increasing importance in recent years and were originally stimulated by the contribution of Porter (1981) and Peters and Waterman (1982). Obviously achieving a competitive position in a market depends on many inter-related factors. Gains in productivity, market share dominance, high R&D investment, achieving economies of scale and concentration on knowledge-intensive, high value-added products have been the subject of study (for a brief summary see Cunningham, 1986).

Several researchers have linked competitiveness with a company's ability to develop and manage its array of network relationships. For example, Easton and Araujo (1985) and Araujo and Easton (1986) categorize the competition between suppliers in terms of the indirect and direct relationships which occur in selected industrial markets. Competition is viewed as being based on either conflict, competitive advantage, co-existence, cooperation or collusion. They use three theoretical frameworks for their analysis, first the traditional marketing strategy paradigms; second, the interaction approach and, third, the network approach. Their methodology is based on mapping, comparing and contrasting the perceptions and behavior of suppliers and customers in terms of identifying and characterizing competitors, examining competitive strategies and analysing inter-competitor communications through technical and marketing networks. This leads to a view of competitiveness as a dynamic process over time. Active rivalry between firms within a product market occurs simultaneously with competition coming from other product markets. This "competitive field" transcends the narrowly defined industry or product market. Hence, the industrial economist's paradigm of the market structure–conduct–performance relationship is clearly an inadequate representation of the competitive forces and real determinants of competitiveness.

Interaction and relationship strategy

The importance of inter-company relationships as a way of exploiting and enhancing resources requires that a strategic approach is made to their analysis and management. But it is important to base ideas on the development of relationship strategy on an understanding of those wider factors which strategy must bear in mind and seek to change. Without a wider network view, any approach to relationship strategy runs the risk of degenerating into short-termism. It can also mean that the company may be unaware of the potential effects on itself and its relationships arising from the actions of other companies elsewhere in the network or of the opportunities for improving its overall position in the wider network which can be achieved through its interaction in its relationships. This means that development of relationship strategy depends on analysis of the company, its individual relationships and its overall relationship portfolio and network position.

Interdependence of companies

The starting point for the development of relationship strategy is the interdependence of companies. This interdependence takes many forms. Perhaps the most obvious is the need to generate revenue from other companies for the continuing existence and development of the company. Interdependence is also based on the need to use the knowledge and abilities of others, delivered in the form of products or services. Perhaps even more importantly, a company may also need to acquire some of the knowledge of other companies for itself, or wish to develop its own knowledge through interaction with the other company.

The basis for the interdependence of companies in business relationships is the resources which they possess. Companies interact with each other and develop relationships in order to exploit and develop their resources (Turnbull and Wilson, 1989). In order to do this they seek those companies which have matching resources. Resources can be discussed in at least three categories:

Network position

The first is financial resources; these obviously affect the company's ability to acquire new resources, or to use the resources of others. The second category of resource is a company's network position. Network position consists of the company's relationships and the rights and obligations which go with them. For example, one aspect of a company's position which is a valuable resource is its access to a major consumer market as would be the case with a retail store chain, another would be its brand as a measure of reputation in the network. This reputation may be important as it can make a company an important reference customer and its "seal of approval" can lead to the company being able to develop further relationships elsewhere in the network. On the other hand, preservation of this relationship may inhibit a company from taking short-term advantage of a situation. For example, it may feel inhibited in raising its prices to make short-term profits in a situation of a product shortage. Many aspects of a company's network position are a function of the development of its resources through its interaction with others in its network relationships. In this way, network position is a dynamic and evolving characteristic.

A set of technologies

The third category of resources are the skills which companies possess and these skills can be understood as a set of technologies. For our purposes, technologies can be separated into three areas:

(1) product technology, which consists of the ability to design products or services;

(2) process technologies which comprise the ability to manufacture or produce these products or services;

(3) marketing technologies which consist of the abilities to analyze the requirements of others and to assemble the means to influence these others and deliver them to a recipient – this includes relationship competence; skills in managing relationships themselves.

A number of points need to be made about these technologies. First, they are all learned abilities which can be applied in a variety of ways. They can be used to provide an offering of a product or service, or they can be transferred "whole" to others for their use. Technologies are the basis of all companies' existence, but, in themselves, the technologies have no value. They exist only as potential and are only valuable if they are worth something to another company. This value to others is transmitted through the process of interaction between the companies.

Interaction in business methods

A company's pattern of interaction with others, based on the technologies of all parties, effectively defines the nature of the company and its position in the network. Interaction in business markets involves the technologies of both companies. For example, company A may buy components from B. The components may be to A's design (based on its product technology) but manufactured by B (based on its process technologies). In turn, A may use the components in its production (based on its process skills) and use its marketing technology to sell them to a number of resellers who will, in turn, use their marketing skills to reach a wider market. In the case of conventional product or service exchange, interaction between companies can take place on the basis of one or, more usually, a number of technologies of the supplier. For that technology to be effective it will have to be combined with one or more technologies of the buyer to transfer and/or transform an offering for a buyer elsewhere in the network.

Any one company in a network will have a variety of relationships each with different characteristics. These characteristics will depend on the respective motivations of the two parties but also on the technologies which are involved. For example, a relationship which is based on the purchase of a component to the buyer's design – "make to order" – is likely to be different to that for a component based on a supplier's proprietary technology. Similarly, the relationship between a franchisee and a franchiser (where product, process and marketing technologies are provided by the franchiser) is likely to be different to that between a major retailer and a manufacturer which supplies garments to its specification. It will also be different to that between joint-venture partners in a new technology development relationship. A company's relationship with its main bank is likely to be different to that which it has with a financial or other professional advisor. Finally, of course, relationships with large suppliers or customers will differ from those with small ones.

Relationship strategy

Relationship strategy comprises the tasks of managing each of these relationships both individually and as part of an inter-related portfolio, each element of which has a different function for both of the parties involved (Turnbull and Valla, 1986). It involves the process of exploiting the company's technologies in its relationships so as to maximize the return on the company's technological investment. It involves the task of acquiring technology directly, such as through a licensing relationship. It also involves acquiring technology indirectly through interaction. Examples of this include developing a product for a specific customer, which may then be sold to others; when a customer learns to "reverse engineer" a product from a supplier so that it can then make it for itself. Finally, relationship strategy can also be used to maintain or alter the company's network position. For example, by extending its access to the resources of other companies, a company may be able to use these resources elsewhere in the network.

Relationship development and investment

Ford (1980) suggests that supplier–customer relationships in business-to-business markets evolve over time, and considering the process of relationship development, careful management can obtain the best possible value from these relationships. Consequently, Ford analyzes the process of establishment and development of supplier–customer relationships over time according to the variables of experience, uncertainty, distance (including aspects of social, geographical, cultural, technical and time distance), commitment and adaptation. By considering the extent to which each of these variables is present in a supplier–customer relationship, it is suggested that such relationships follow a five-stage evolution process – pre-relationship, early, development, long term and final stage. Thus the development of supplier–customer relationships can be seen as an evolutionary process in terms of:

- the increasing experience of both partners;
- the reduction in their uncertainty and all kinds of distance in the relationship;
- the growth of both actual and perceived commitment;
- the formal and informal adaptations, and investment and savings involved in both sides' organizations (Ford, 1980).

Suppliers and customers

In order that supplier–customer relationships develop over time, it is necessary for both suppliers and customers to make some degree of investment in relationships. Consequently, business-to-business marketing can be seen as:

> A process of investments in market positions at the micro- and macro level. (Turnbull and Wilson, 1989)

Investment is of particular interest as investments in the relationship can be made by both the buyer and the seller. Johanson and Mattson (1985, p. 187) suggest that marketing expenditures can be viewed as investments in market networks. They point out that most of the literature on investment in marketing deals with methods of calculating investments and not with the conceptualisation of investments within marketing theory, although they quote two Swedish studies on the topic. Hammarkvist et al. (1982) position marketing problems as investments, organization and cooperation with other firms. Hagg and Johanson (1982) classify marketing investments as general, market-specific and relationship-specific.

Investment in relationships

Although there have been a number of studies focusing on investments in relationships (Hagg and Johanson, 1982; Hammarkvist et al., 1982; Johanson and Mattson, 1985), it is worthwhile to consider one of these studies, the framework developed by Wilson and Mummalaneni (1986), in more detail (Figure 1).

The framework begins with the assumption of need complementarily leading to exchanges through interactions, as does the Johanson and Mattson (1985) model. It suggests that "relationships develop through incremental investments of resources", which have to be made by both supplier and customer organizations. Such invest-

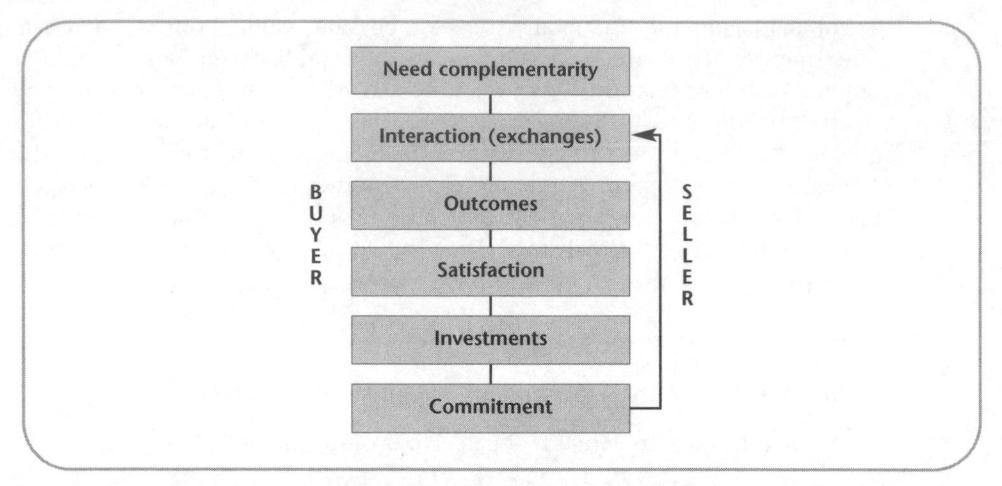

Figure 1 A framework of relationship development
Source: Wilson and Mummalaneni (1986)

ments tend to be made only if the outcomes of these interactions within the relationship are perceived to be satisfactory, either now or potentially in the future. These investments may take the form of adaptations to the areas of product, process and organization (Hakansson, 1982). However, such investments are made not only to intensify the relationship and to demonstrate the interest that the partner has in developing a strong relationship, but also with the faith that the other partner will reciprocate (Turnbull and Wilson, 1989).

In addition to furthering the development of supplier–customer relationships, according to Hammarkvist et al. (1982), these investment and adaptation activities may create social and structural (economic) bonds. These lead to mutual commitment as a measure of true source loyalty (Jarvis and Wilcox, 1977) and thus to long-term strong and profitable relationships which are cemented with social and structural bonds and which become difficult to break (Wilson and Mummalaneni, 1986).

Supplier–customer relationships

It follows then that most cost factors and marketing expenses involved in supplier–customer relationships can be regarded as investments in relationship development (Johanson and Mattson, 1985). Such investments are classified as "general", "market-specific", and "relationship-specific", by Hagg and Johanson (1982). These investments "made by one party in a relationship with another party have an important impact on the costs of that party's current or future transactions with the other" (Williamson, 1979, 1981).

It might be expected then that supplier–customer relationships will be very costly, perhaps making a negative contribution to supplier profitability, in their early stages. However, the costs of managing supplier–customer relationships might also be expected to decrease over time as a result of decreasing levels of investment and other marketing expenses in the following stages of the relationship (Fiocca, 1982; Turnbull and Wilson, 1989). Thus, the analysis of customer profitability is a key tool of strategic marketing management.

Customer portfolios

Throughout this paper it has been explicitly recognized that the successful management of supplier–customer relationships depends on the company's relationship management skills, the investments in initiating, developing and maintaining relationships and the allocation of resources between different relationships according to their likely return (Ford, 1980). To achieve this both sides of a dyadic relationship need to analyze the current and projected benefits resulting from the relationship. Ultimately, and specifically taking the supply side perspective, current and projected profits of customers (existing and potential) need to be analyzed and forecast, ideally on an individual basis but at least at market segment level. Such analysis, if combined with an identification of the stage of each customer relationship allows a better understanding of the potential of the customer base and helps in the strategic and tactical planning and allocation of resources between customers of all types.

Portfolio theory

In the development of customer relationship strategy, portfolio theory applied to the customer base can help maximize long-term profitability. As Turnbull points out, portfolio types of analysis can be:

> A useful management tool for enforcing a discipline in the allocation of suppliers' limited resources to an optimal combination of customers. (Turnbull,1990)

Portfolio analysis has its theoretical origins in financial theory but has been applied extensively in business strategy, product planning and supply chain management (Cunningham, 1986; Turnbull, 1990). The application of portfolio theory to customer relationships is more recent. Two of the earlier and influential attempts have been those of Fiocca (1982) and Campbell and Cunningham (1984a). In both papers, the analysis is derived from the theoretical view of business-to-business marketing embedded in the interaction approach and are intended to provide guidelines for marketing strategy formulation and resource allocation. These ideas were further developed by Yorke (1986).

Shapiro et al. (1987) also developed the concept when investigating customer behavior and produced a matrix to classify customer types on "cost to serve and net price dimensions". They identify four types of customers – passive, carriage trade, bargain basement and aggressive – and argue that profitability will vary between the groups. They further suggest managerial actions to manage this profit dispersion.

Relationship management process

Krapfel et al. (1991) have further developed the strategic approach to managing buyer/seller relationships. They suggest a model in which relationship types and relationship management modes are mapped together to assess the optimal relationship portfolio. This mapping takes into account the transaction costs involved. As part of the relationship management process they also recognize the importance of matching the relationships and signalling intentions to partners. They see signalling as an important aspect in the adaptation process. The relationship types they identify (partner, friend, acquaintance and rival) are determined by two factors: relationship value and interest commonality (commonality of a firm's economic goals with its perception of its potential partner's economic goals), while the relationship management modes, again identified two-dimensionally by perceived power position and interest commonality, suggested are collaboration, negotiation, administration, domination, accommodation and submission.

Turnbull and Zolkiewski (1995) test both the Shapiro et al. and Krapfel et al. portfolio models through an empirical analysis of a large UK computer supplier. While they found the Shapiro et al. customer classification the most appropriate for the researched company, they suggest a three-dimensional grid, with cost to serve, net price and relationship value as more generally valuable as a marketing analysis and planning tool.

Despite these rather normative outputs regarding customer-base management, our research indicates that resource allocation decisions are often taken without full assessment of the potential of and threats to each relationship. There are at least two reasons for this.

First, relationship analysis at either the individual or group level is an essential preliminary to investment and management decisions. For those companies with a few major relationships then individual analysis is likely to be both achievable and worthwhile. For companies with large numbers of relationships then such an individual analysis is unlikely to be feasible. Because of this it is important, although rare for companies to develop a system of categorization of relationship types as an aid to analysis.

Choice is the most difficult aspect

Second, relationship portfolio management inevitably involves choice. It is this choice which is perhaps the most difficult aspect for managers to handle. An interesting example of this issue is found in relationships between UK grocery manufacturers and the major retail store groups. These manufacturers are very concerned to develop their relationship with individual stores and in many cases have extended the relationship as the unit of analysis from the sales area into their marketing decision making. However, the development of a closer relationship with one store group, perhaps involving product modification, exclusivity, joint advertising etc., will, beyond a certain point, inevitably involve a level of commitment which will mean that the company has to accept a more distant relationship with others. The extent of this commitment and its associated costs in other relationships is difficult for some managers to accept. Their reluctance may be based on a realistic appraisal of the potential benefits of further commitment.

Two common self-delusions

However, if the supplier is unwilling to incur the costs of a closer relationship with one customer (partially expressed in terms of a more distant relationship with others) then the limitations of that relationship in terms of customer commitment to stock levels, information, etc. must be accepted by the supplier. If it is not accepted then the managers involved are also likely to be subject to two common self-delusions. The first is that their relationships are actually "closer" than they are in reality. The second delusion is the equally common view of relationship management as simply "being nice to customers". This view is false for at least three reasons. First, "niceness" involves resources and companies are unlikely to have sufficient resources to be "nice" to everyone. Second, the level of niceness given to each customer is unlikely to be significant if applied to all. Third, relationships are unlikely to be successful in the long term if based solely on one party's subservience to the other – as any marriage guidance counsel will relate!

Organizational evolution and bonding

The notion that industrial marketing is essentially an organization problem (Hakansson and Ostberg, 1975) has precipitated many research studies. The internationalization process of Swedish firms (Johanson and Vahlne, 1977; Johanson and Wiedersheim-Paul, 1975) postulated an approach to organization development linked to the sequential entry into countries according to the perceived psychic distance. The various levels of organizational commitment and resources allocation in companies were modelled with progressive evolution from direct selling to the ultimate establishment of subsidiaries in foreign countries. This work has been extended by Turnbull and Ellwood (1984) in their studies of UK companies involved in the IT industry as they penetrate French, German and Spanish markets. Turnbull (1986) also investigated organizations and interactions involving sales subsidiaries.

References and further reading

Araujo, L. and Easton, G. (1986), "Competition in industrial markets: perceptions and frameworks", *3rd International IMP Research Seminar on International Marketing*, IRE, Lyon, September.

Axelsson, B. and Easton, G. (Eds) (1993), *Industrial Network,: A New View of Reality*, Routledge, London.

Campbell, N.C.G. (1984), "The structure and stability of industrial market networks: developing a research methodology", *First IMP Conference on Research Developments in International Marketing*, UMIST, Manchester, September.

Campbell, N.C.G. and Cunningham, M.T. (I984a), "Customer analysis for strategy development in industrial markets", *Strategic Management Journal*, Vol. 4, pp. 369–80.

Campbell, N.C.G. and Cunningham, M.T. (1984b), "Managing customer relationships: the challenge of deploying scarce managerial resources", *Research Seminar on Industrial Marketing*, Stockholm School of Economics, September.

Clark, K., Ford, D., Saren, M. and Thomas, R. (1995), "Technology Strategy in UK firms", *Technology Analysis & Strategic Management*, Vol. 7 No. 2, pp. 169–90.

Cunningham, M.T. (1986), "The British approach to Europe", in Turnbull, P.W. and Valla J.R (Eds), *Strategies for International Industrial Marketing*, Croom Helm, London, pp. 165–203.

Cunningham, M.T. and Homse, E. (1986), "Controlling the marketing–purchasing interface: resource deployment and organizational issues", *Industrial Marketing and Purchasing*, Vol. 1 No. 2, pp. 3–25.

Cunningham, M.T. and Turnbull, P.W. (1982), "Inter-organizational personal contact patterns", in Hakansson, H. (Ed.), *International Marketing and Purchasing of Industrial Goods: An Interaction Approach*, John Wiley, New York, NY, pp. 304–15.

Easton, G. and Araujo, L. (1985), "The network approach: an articulation", *2nd Open IMP International Research Seminar*, University of Uppsala, September.

Fiocca, R. (1982), "Account portfolio analysis for strategy development", *Industrial Marketing Management*, April.

Ford, I.D. (1980), "The development of buyer–seller relationships in industrial markets", *European Journal of Marketing*, Vol. 14 Nos 5/6, pp. 339–54.

Ford, I.D. (1982), "The development of buyer–seller relationships in industrial marketings", in Hakansson, H (Ed.), *International Marketing and Purchasing of Industrial Goods: An Interaction Approach*, John Wiley, New York, NY, pp. 288–304.

Ford, I.D. (1984), "Buyer/seller relationships in international industrial markets", *Industrial Marketing Management*, Vol. 13 No. 2, pp 101–13.

Ford, I.D. (Ed.) (1990), *Understanding Business Markets*, Academic Press, London.

Ford, D., McDowell, R. and Tomkins, C. (1996), "Relationship strategy, investments and decision making" in Iacobucci, D. (Ed.), *Networks in Marketing*, Sage, New York, NY, (forthcoming).

Gilbert, X. and Strebel, R. (1988), "Developing competitive advantage", in Quinn, J.B., Mintzberg, H. and James, R. (Eds), *The Strategy process: Concepts, Contexts and Cases*, Prentice-Hall, Englewood Cliffs, NJ.

Hagg, I. and Johanson, J. (Eds) (1982), *Foretag i natverk*, SNS, Stockholm, Sweden.

Hakansson, H. (Ed.) (1982), *International Marketing and Purchasing of Industrial Goods: An Interaction Approach*, John Wiley, Chichester.

Hakansson, H. (1986a), "Relationships marketing strategies and competitive strength", in Turnbull, P.W. and Valla, J.R (Eds), *Strategies for International Industrial Marketing*, Croom Helm, London.

Hakansson H. (1986b), "The Swedish approach to Europe", in Turnbull, P and Valla, J.P. (Eds), *Strategies for International Industrial Marketing*, Croom Helm, London, pp.149–157.

Hakansson, H. (1986c), "The export markets and Swedish companies", in Turnbull, R and Valla, J.R (Eds), *Strategies for International Industrial Marketing*, Croom Helm, London.

Hakansson, H. and Ostberg, C. (1975). "Industrial marketing: an organizational problem?", *Industrial Marketing Management*. Vol. 4, pp. 113–23.

Hakansson, H. and Wootz, B. (1979), "A framework of industrial buying and selling", *Industrial Marketing Management*, Vol. 8, pp 28–39.

Hakansson, H., Johanson, J. and Wootz, B. (1977), "Influence tactics in buyer–seller relationships", *Industrial Marketing Management*, Vol. 5, pp. 319–32.

Hallen, L. (1986), "Marketing organizations: a comparison of strategic marketing approaches", in Turnbull, P.W. and Valla, J.R (Eds), *Strategies for International Industrial Marketing*, Croom Helm, London.

Hamfelt, C. and Lindberg, A.K. (1987), "Technological development and the individual's contact network", in Hakansson, H. (Ed.), *Industrial Technical Development: A Network Approach*, Croom Helm, London, pp. 177–200.

Hammarkvist, K.O., Hakansson, H. and Mattson L.-G. (1982), *Marknadsforing for konkurrenskraft*, Liber, Malmo.

Henders, B. (1992), "Positions in industrial networks: marketing newsprint in the UK", unpublished PhD thesis, University of Uppsala.

Jarvis, L.R and Wilcox, J.B. (1977), "True vendor loyalty or simply repeat purchase behavior?", *Industrial Marketing Management*, Vol. 6, pp. 9–16.

Johanson, J. and Mattson, L.G. (1985), "Marketing investments and market investments in industrial networks", *International Journal of Research in Marketing*, Vol. 2, pp. 185–95.

Johanson, J. and Vahlne, J.E. (1977), "The internationalisation process of the firm – a model of knowledge development and increasing foreign market commitments", *Journal of International Business*, Vol. 8 No. 1, pp. 23–32.

Johanson, J. and Wiedersheim-Paul, F. (1975), "The internationalisation of the firm – four Swedish case studies", *Journal of Management Studies*, Vol. 2 No.3, pp. 305–22.

Johanson, J. and Wootz, B. (1984), "A framework for the study of marketing investment processes", in Turnbull, P.W. and Palinoda, S. (Eds), *Proceedings of the IMP Conference: Research Developments in International Marketing*, UMIST, Manchester, pp. 301–17.

Johanson, J. and Wootz, B. (1986), "The German approach to Europe", in Turnbull, P.W. and Valla, J.R (Eds), *Strategies for International Industrial Marketing*, Croom Helm, London.

Kaplan, R.S. and Cooper, R. (1991), "Profit priorities from activity-based costing", *Harvard Business Review*, May–June, pp. 130–6.

Krapfel, R.E., Salmond, D. and Spekman, R. (1991), "A strategic approach to managing buyer–seller relationships", *European Journal of Marketing*, Vol. 25 No. 9, pp. 22–37.

McCall, G.J. (1970), "The social organization of relationships", in McCall, G.J. et al. (Eds), *Social Relationships*, Aldine Publishing Company, Chicago, pp. 3–14.

Mintzberg, H. (1988), "Opening up the definition of strategy", in Quinn, J.B., Mintzberg, H. and James, R.M. (Eds), *The Strategy Process, Concepts, Contexts and Cases*, Prentice-Hall, Englewood Cliffs, NJ.

Peters, T.J. and Waterman, R.H. (1982), *In Search of Excellence: Lessons from America's Best Run Companies*, Harper & Row, New York, NY.

Porter, M.E. (1981), *Competitive Strategy: Techniques for Analysing Industries and Competitors*, Macmillan, The Free Press, New York, NY.

Rusbult, C.E. (1980), "Commitment and satisfaction in romantic associations: a test of the investment model", *Journal of Experimental Social Psychology*, Vol. 16, pp. 172–86.

Shapiro, B.P, Rangan, V.K., Moriarty, R.T. and Ross, E.B. (1987), "Manage customers for profits", *Harvard Business Review*, September–October, pp. 101–8.

Smith, R and Easton, G. (1986), "Network relationships: a longitudinal study", *3rd International IMP Research Seminar on International Marketing*, IRE, Lyon, September.

Turnbull, P.W. (1974), "The allocation of resources to marketing communications in industrial markets", *Industrial Marketing Management*, Vol. 3 No. 5, pp. 2975–3018.

Turnbull, P.W. (1986), "Tri-partite interaction: the role of sales subsidiaries in international marketing", in Turnbull, P.W. and Paliwoda, S.J. (Eds), *Research in International Marketing*, Croom Helm, London, pp. 162–92.

Turnbull, P.W. (1990), "A review of portfolio planning models for industrial marketing and purchasing management", *European Journal of Marketing*, Vol. 24 No. 3, pp. 7–22.

Turnbull, P.W. and Cunningham, M.T. (1981), "The quality of relationships", in Turnbull, P.W. and Cunningham, M.T. (Eds), *International Marketing and Purchasing: A Survey among Marketing and Purchasing Executives in Five European Countries*, Macmillan, New York, NY, pp. 42–50 and pp. 81–9.

Turnbull, P.W. and Ellwood, S. (1984), "Internationalisation in the information technology industry", *Proceedings of International Research Seminar in Industrial Marketing*, Stockholm School of Economics, August.

Turnbull, P.W. and Holding, A. (1992), "Psychic distance in international markets", in Salle, R., Spencer, R. and Valla, J.R (Eds), *Proceedings of the 8th IMP Conference*, Lyon.

Turnbull, P.W. and Valla, J.R (1986) (Eds), *Strategies for International Industrial Marketing*, Croom Helm, London.

Turnbull, P.W. and Wilson, D. (1989), "Developing and protecting profitable customer relationships", *Industrial Marketing Management*, Vol. 18 No. 1, pp. 1–6.

Turnbull, P.W. and Zolkiewski, J. (1995), "Customer portfolios: sales costs and profitability", presented to the *11th IMP International Conference*, UMIST, Manchester.

Turner, R.H. (1970), *Family Interaction*, John Wiley, New York, NY.

Valla, J.R (1985), "The development of marketing networks and the internationalisation process", *2nd International IMP Research Seminar*, University of Uppsala, September.

Valla, J.R (1986), "Industrial marketing strategies: looking for new ways", in Turnbull, P.W. and Valla, J.R (Eds), *Strategies for International Industrial Marketing*, Croom Helm, London.

Valla, J.R and Turnbull, P.W. (1986), "The dimensions of industrial marketing strategy", in Turnbull, P.W. and Valla, J.R (Eds), *Strategies for International Industrial Marketing*, Croom Helm, London.

Williamson, O.E. (1979), "Transaction-cost economics: the governance of contractual relations", *Journal of Law and Economics*, Vol. 22 No. 2, pp. 233–61.

Williamson, O.E. (1981), "The economics of organization: the transaction cost approach", *Journal of Sociology*, Vol. 87, pp. 548–77.

Wilson, D.T. and Mummalaneni, V. (1986), "Bonding and commitment in buyer–seller relationships: a preliminary conceptualisation", *Journal of Industrial Marketing and Purchasing*, Vol. 1 No. 3, pp. 44–58.

Yorke, D.A. (1986), "Customer perceptions as a basis for the development of an international supplier's portfolio of market segments", *Industrial Marketing and Purchasing*, Vol. 1 No. 2, pp. 27–47.

Revisiting Marketing's Lawlike Generalizations

Sheth, J and Sisodia, R (1999)

Extracts from *Journal of the Academy of Marketing Science*, **27**(1): 71–87

Beyond location-centric lawlike generalizations

In the world of marketing, location has always been central. Marketing assets and activities are physically distributed over the relevant geography, products are entrusted (on consignment or credit) to intermediaries that are proximate to customers, sales forces are deployed over a market terrain in the manner of an army, and media-based communications are targeted to reach those locations where the product has been made available. Entry barriers are high (retailers serve as gatekeepers), deployment is slow (the process of building up or building down a channel can take years), and large players have a big advantage (sales forces and media advertising represent large fixed costs). The defining characteristic of location-centric marketing concepts is the use of specialized intermediaries: for transacting (retailers), communicating (an internal or external sales force), and disseminating information (advertising agencies). These location-centric concepts are now being affected by a major external force: the Internet.

The Internet and marketing

The number of Internet users worldwide was estimated at about 130 million as of July 1998 and has doubled in each of the past 6 years. The United States is adding about 52,000 Internet users every day, or about 18 million a year. If current trends persist, there will be 377 million users by January 2000 and 707 million by January 2001 (Nua Internet Surveys 1998).

The Internet's three primary capabilities are content (information), communication, and commerce (transactions), each of which has a significant impact on marketing's location-centric lawlike generalizations.

- *Content:* The Internet enables the direct on-demand provision of multimedia information from providers anywhere to customers anywhere. This has direct implications not only for the advertising function but also for retailing and sales.
- *Communication:* The Internet permits immediate and virtually free (to the user) two-way communication with as many or as few others as needed. In addition to

text information (e-mail), it now permits audio (voice-mail) and video (video-mail) communication as well. This capability most directly affects the sales function but also has an impact on retailing and advertising.

- *Commerce:* The Internet readily enables transactions for many types of goods and services, especially (but not restricted to) those that can be delivered electronically. The commercial potential of the Internet is widely seen as huge; for example, according to a Forrester Research report released in July 1998, trade over the Internet in the year 2001 will be $560 billion in the United States and $360 billion in Europe. Its impact on business-to-business marketing is enormous; it is estimated that at least $100 billion of transactions are already done on the Internet. The Internet has especially major implications for the financial, information, and entertainment markets, all of which deal with products that can be also delivered electronically.

The primary impact of the Internet revolution on marketing is to break the time- and location-bound aspects of traditional "gravitational" commerce. Customers can place orders, gather information, and communicate with the company from any place at any time; this has profound implications for all location-centric lawlike generalizations. It can also have a large impact on costs as customers do much of the work that would normally be handled by back-office operations; for example, the costs of Internet banking transactions are much lower than those associated with automatic teller machines (ATMs) or human tellers.

Intermediation or direct marketing?

Reilly's (1931) book *Law of Retail Gravitation* mathematically modeled the relative attractiveness of shopping areas to consumers who lived some distance away. Converse (1949) proposed additional laws of retail gravitation, including a formula to determine the boundaries of a retail center's trade area. This helped retailers to concentrate their merchandising efforts and newspapers to determine which territories they needed to emphasize the most. Work in this stream has continued over the years, refining the techniques and adding new variables (Ghosh and Craig 1983; Huff 1964; Reynolds 1953).

With the Internet's ability to fundamentally change the reach (time and place) of companies, retail gravitation laws have become less relevant. Companies small and large are able to achieve a high level of accessibility and establish a two-way information flow directly with end users almost immediately and at low cost. Serving huge numbers of customers efficiently and effectively is made possible by the automation of numerous administrative tasks. Every company is potentially a global player from the first day of its existence (subject to supply availability and fulfillment capabilities).

The Internet enables more and more companies to deal directly with more and more of their customers. In the process, they are putting enormous pressures on their intermediary (e.g., wholesaling and retailing) partners. For example, Alba et al. (1997) suggest that manufacturers with strong brand names and the ability to produce complementary merchandise are likely to disintermediate. The trend toward disintermediation is still in its early phases, and massive dislocations of traditional intermediaries will occur as a result of it.

In summary, the default assumption used to be that most companies needed to use intermediaries to create time and place utility, although there were conditions under which they could bypass middlemen and serve customers directly. The default assumption in the future is likely to be that companies will be able to go direct in most cases, although conditions can be identified under which it would be beneficial to use specialized intermediaries.

Electronic ordering or personal selling?

Along with retailing and wholesaling, marketers have also used location-centric approaches to organizing the sales function. This includes the geographical design of sales territories (wherein territory size and shape are determined based on factors such as sales potential within the territory), the amount of effort needed to service a territory, and the ease of transportation to and within the territory. Location-centric thinking has also been reflected in the organization of distributors and franchisees by geography, as well as in the organizational forms traditionally adopted by multinational companies.

With the Internet, companies can more readily engage in direct communication (or what could be called "selling without the sales force"), order taking, and technical support. Fundamentally, the same shift that occurred with customer service is now happening with personal selling; for example, operator services and bank teller services have both been dramatically affected by technology that allows most customers to serve themselves most of the time.

Direct or media-based advertising?

Much of advertising is location specific; media are local (such as local newspapers, local radio, and local television), national (most magazines, national radio, and television), and, to some extent, international (satellite television, the Internet). Advertising expenditures vary significantly by location and are tracked accordingly.

Advertising information has typically been created by intermediaries such as advertising agencies and then carried on information outlets such as television, magazines, and newspapers. With the Internet, we are entering an era of direct information; companies are creating Web pages and placing small advertisements on other Web pages to encourage customers to visit their sites. Traditional advertising agencies are getting disintermediated in the process, as are media such as the Yellow Pages and newspapers.

Just as with selling, advertising and sales promotions have also tended to be initiated and driven by marketers at targeted (and often untargeted) customers. Increasingly, we expect that customers will take a more active role in acquiring information. Web-based advertising is ideally suited to this since it instantaneously permits customers to get as much detailed information as they desire.

Reintermediation

A likely consequence of the trend toward electronic commerce is what we call reintermediation: the emergence of new types of intermediaries that will try to capture new value, creating opportunities arising from the new ways of interacting between consumers and producers.

The marketing function was primarily organized as going forward from the producer to the customer. Increasingly, the whole process is becoming reversed; as often as not, customers take the initiative in electronic commerce. This is true in consumer as well as business-to-business marketing; for example, Cisco Systems sells more than $5 billion a year of high-end networking equipment over the Internet.

For example, priceline.com has emerged as a new type of market intermediary, using a reverse auction method to bring buyers and sellers together. The company refers to its recently patented business model as buyer-driven commerce; potential buyers submit bids known as conditional purchase offers to buy products such as airline tickets at a certain price. Sellers can either accept, reject, or counter-offer. In essence, priceline.com enables individual consumers to function in a manner akin to a government agency that seeks a supplier that will provide a particular product for a stated price. The method is the opposite of that used by Internet auction companies such as Onsale.com, which has one seller and multiple buyers (Lewis 1998).

Intermediaries will play a key role in providing assurance to customers or vendors. When suppliers lack well-known brand names (and the reputations that accompany them), intermediaries that customers can trust will be important. Likewise, suppliers need to ensure that they are getting trustworthy customers, a task that intermediaries can perform well. Intermediaries can thus facilitate product trust as well as people trust.

Sarkar, Butler, and Steinfeld (1998) argue that intermediaries will play a key role in electronic markets. They refer to these new entities as cybermediaries, defined as "organizations that operate in electronic markets to facilitate exchanges between producers and consumers by meeting the needs of both producers and consumers" (p. 216). Cybermediaries "increase the efficiency of electronic markets . . . by aggregating transactions to create economies of scale and scope" (p. 218). The authors offer a number of propositions based on transaction cost analysis, some of which are counterintuitive and thus especially in need of empirical testing. For example, they propose that "the number of organizations involved in a complete producer-consumer exchange will be greater than in a comparable exchange in a traditional market" (p. 220). This is based on the reasoning that lower coordination and transaction costs will lead to greater unbundling of channel services with increased specialization.

Beyond market-centric lawlike generalizations

The origins of market-centric thinking in marketing can be traced to the advent of the marketing concept in the post-World War II period. This was a time when the United States and other developed economies shifted from a seller's economy to a buyer's economy (Sheth et al. 1988). With excess manufacturing capacity in most industries, the focus shifted from production to marketing. This required a much deeper understanding of customer needs, motivations, and the drivers of satisfaction than had previously existed.

The fundamental change in context here is that greater market diversity is leading to more market fragmentation. In the consumer market, market diversity is driven primarily by increased demographic diversity. In the business market, market diversity results from the derived demand implications of greater diversity in the consumer market, as well as greater diversity in terms of business size, scope, ownership, and structure.

Consumer market diversity

Market-centric concepts are clearly essential and have been fundamental to marketing for a long time. However, many of them were created in an era of relative demographic homogeneity (the proverbial 18- to 34-year-old household with two kids and a dog) and in the context of a mass-production, mass-consumption society. The market could readily be divided into large segments by demographics, socioeconomic class, and other variables. Today, the marketplace is characterized by higher levels of diversity by income, age, ethnicity, and lifestyle (Sheth, Mittal, and Newman 1999).

Income diversity. In the 1960s, about 60 percent of the households in the United States were considered middle class. By the year 2000, the middle class will only comprise 35 percent; the upper class will expand to about 30 percent, with the balance represented by lower economic classes. The implications of this are a much greater degree of divergence in consumption patterns; rather than mid-priced products representing the bulk of the market, we will see many more upscale and rock-bottom products. The ratio of the most expensive to least expensive products has been increasing in virtually every product category, from cars to food items to services.

Age diversity. The birth rate in the United States has been falling for more than two decades, while life expectancy has been rising. During the 1990s, the number of adults younger than age 35 will decline by 8.3 million. This transition is having a major impact on consumption patterns. The loss of population in developed countries over the next two decades will occur primarily in 30 to 39 age cohort – a net decline of approximately 7.5 percent for a group of 21 developed countries. The fastest growing segments of the population are centenarians and those age 80 and older. One of the impacts of changing age patterns is greater polarization; no one age dominates the population, which is more evenly divided than before. While there is a gradually rising influence of the mature market segment, we also see the coexistence of multiple generations to a greater extent than before. Each generation has different values, priorities, and concerns. Their response to marketing actions clearly reflects this.

Ethnic diversity. The ranks of minorities are growing; approximately 80 percent of all population growth for the next 20 years is expected to come from the African American, Hispanic, and Asian communities. Minorities comprised about 25 percent of the population in 1990; by 2010, they will represent about a third (Carmody 1991). Around 2005, Hispanics will become the nation's largest minority group.

Lifestyle diversity. The majority of households a generation ago consisted of a married couple with children; that group now represents 27 percent of all households. Another 25 percent are people who live alone, while married couples with no children represent 29 percent of all households (Carmody 1991). There are thus three very different household types of roughly equal size in the population. Alternative lifestyles (such as gay singles and couples and single-parent families) are also becoming more significant.

As the marketplace fragments into much smaller groupings, the concept of a mass-consumption society is becoming increasingly obsolete. If all the relevant variables that affect buyer behavior are taken into account, the result is an untenably large number of market segments; creating separate marketing programs for each becomes more difficult and less profitable. A segmentation mind-set is well suited to a context in which there are a handful of major segments. When segments proliferate, a mass customization mind-set is more useful.

Business market diversity

Along with consumer markets, business markets are also getting more diverse. Several factors are driving this.

Derived demand. As the consumer market gets more diverse, the business market also becomes more diverse due to the concept of derived demand. For example, as consumers demand greater variety in houses and cars, the "upstream" suppliers face greater diversity of demand.

Size and scope diversity. Businesses today are more polarized in size as well as scope. Some are global players, while others are local. Some are full-line players, while others are boutiques focused on particular portions of the market. New business formation has boomed in recent years as downsized executives have started their own ventures and emerging technologies have afforded new opportunities to entrepreneurs.

Ownership diversity. Ownership forms and shareholder expectations are quite different across businesses. Employee stock ownership plans (through the heavy use of stock options), employee-owned enterprises, and leveraged buyouts have added to the diversity. Private companies, owner-managed limited partnerships, and publicly traded companies tend to behave differently. Investors tend to evaluate companies listed on NASDAQ heavily on the basis of future growth, while those on the New York Stock Exchange are evaluated more on current and anticipated earnings.

Structural diversity. Even within an industry, some companies are structured as highly integrated entities (such as General Motors), while others (such as Dell and Amazon.com) operate more as virtual corporations, farming out most functions except, for example, design and marketing.

This context change will require changes in the marketing function, as discussed below.

Market segmentation or mass customization?

As one of the foundation concepts of the modern marketing discipline, market segmentation has attracted a great deal of research effort. Haley (1968) advocated the use of benefit segmentation, while Plummer (1974) proposed the concept of lifestyle segmentation. Assael and Roscoe (1976) presented a number of different approaches to market segmentation analysis; Winter (1979) applied cost-benefit analysis; Blattberg, Buesing, and Sen (1980) suggested segmentation strategies for new brands; and Doyle and Saunders (1985) applied segmentation concepts to industrial markets.

Greater market diversity makes it increasingly difficult to create meaningful segments. Therefore, we need to replace market segmentation with mass customization, a concept first proposed by Stan Davis in his 1987 book *Future Perfect*. Mass customization refers to the notion that by leveraging certain technologies, companies can provide customers with customized products while retaining the economic advantages of mass production. Although some companies have started to attempt to implement elements of mass customization, it has remained an understudied concept from a marketing standpoint.

Customer satisfaction or managing customer expectations?

With competitive intensity increasing in recent years, the concept of customer satisfaction has become more prominent. Customer satisfaction results from a comparison of perceived performance to expectations. It is presumed that higher customer satisfaction increases customer loyalty, reduces price elasticities, insulates market share from competitors, lowers transaction costs, reduces failure costs and the costs of attracting new customers, and improves a firm's reputation in the marketplace (Anderson, Fornell, and Lehmann 1994). Customer satisfaction has also been shown to be positively associated with return on investment (ROI) and market value.

While customer satisfaction is clearly a very important marketing concept, greater market diversity suggests that it is impossible to provide high levels of customer satisfaction across the board without clearly understanding the individual factors that drive it. We need more theories of managing customer expectations. Sheth and Mittal (1996) provide a detailed framework for managing customer expectations. As a determinant of customer satisfaction, the role of customer expectations has been underappreciated and underused. A study of 348 "critical incidents" in the hotel, restaurant, and airline industries found that 75 percent of incidents in which customers were unhappy were attributable to unrealistic expectations by customers about the ability of the service system to perform, and only 25 percent were due to service that could objectively be described as shoddy (Nyquist, Bitner, and Booms 1985). Companies spend the bulk of their resources on attempting to meet frequently unattainable customer expectations, failing to understand that they can have a greater impact on satisfaction by altering those expectations.

Market-driven or market-driving orientation?

A significant contribution to the marketing literature in recent years has come from researchers studying the concept of market orientation (Kohli and Jaworski 1990; Narver and Slater 1990), defined as "the organization-wide generation of market intelligence, dissemination of the intelligence across departments, and organization-wide responsiveness to it" (Kohli and Jaworski 1990:4). These scholars have studied the antecedents and consequences of market orientation (Jaworski and Kohli 1993), its relationship to innovation (Hurley and Hult 1998), derived its managerial implications, and shown that companies that are market oriented exhibit superior financial performance.

Kumar and Scheer (1998) summarize the market orientation literature's core message as "be close to your customers – listen to your customers" and point out that one of the innovation literature's core messages is "being too close to the customer can stifle innovation." This dichotomy needs to be resolved by studying the applicability of the market-driven and market-driving mind-sets.

According to Day (1998), market-driven firms reinforce existing frameworks that define the boundaries of the market, how it is segmented, who the competitors are, and what benefits customers are seeking. On the other hand, market-driving firms seek to uncover the latent undiscovered needs of current and potential customers; they also make explicit the shared assumptions and compromises made in their industry and break those rules (Slater and Narver 1995). Hamel and Prahalad (1991) have offered the related concept of "leading the customer:' and Hamel (1996) distinguished between firms that are rule makers, rule takers, and rule breakers in their industry.

Carpenter, Glazer, and Nakamoto (1998) point out that the common view of the customer as offering marketers a fixed target is systematically violated. Rather, buyer perceptions, preferences, and decision making evolve over time, along with the category, and competition is, in part, a battle over that evolution. Competitive advantage, therefore, results from the ability to shape buyer perceptions, preferences, and decision making. This market-driving view suggests an iterative process in which marketing strategy shapes as well as responds to buyer behavior, doing so in a manner that gives the firm a competitive advantage, which in turn shapes the evolution of the marketing strategy. An intriguing notion here is that of teaching organizations (akin to learning organizations), which are able to shape customer behavior through education and persuasion (Sheth and Mittal 1996).

This is clearly an important area, and marketing scholars have taken some important conceptual steps in this direction. We would like to point to a few additional concepts that may be useful. First, Kodama (1992) introduced the concept of demand articulation, which is an important competency of market-driving firms. Most firms are more comfortable in a world of prearticulated demand, wherein customers know exactly what they want, and the firm's challenge is to unearth that information. Second, Tushman and O'Reilly (1996, 1997) have offered the concept of ambidextrous organizations, which are simultaneously capable of incremental and fundamental innovation (architectural and revolutionary, respectively, in the authors' terms). Firms that are able to sustain success over a long period of time therefore need to be market driven and market driving simultaneously; most corporate cultures, however, are attuned to one or the other orientations.

Beyond competitor-centric lawlike generalizations

> Nature is not always red in fang and claw. Cooperation and competition provide alternative or simultaneous paths to success. (Contractor and Lorange 1988: 1)

Starting in the mid-1970s and accelerating in the 1980s, the marketing discipline added a number of competitor-centric perspectives to its toolkit. With globalization accelerating and competitive intensities rising, marketers began to emphasize the importance of explicitly considering competitive position and developing strategies that could deliver sustainable competitive advantage.

The fundamental shift is toward coopetition – simultaneous competition and collaboration. In addition, one of the fundamental premises of public policy is coming into question – namely, that the public interest is best served by a zero-sum game in which competitors engage in vigorous market share rivalry. We are now recognizing that it is possible to have positive-sum games in which a degree of cooperation results in greater value creation and enlarging the market pie for all participants.

Coopetition

Brandenburger and Nalebuff (1996) coined the term *coopetition* to suggest that cooperation is often as important as competition. Even before the term coopetition was coined, alliances, partnerships, joint ventures, joint R&D, minority investments, cross-licensing, sourcing relationships, cobranding, comarketing, and other cooperative arrangements between companies were becoming key requirements for successfully competing in the global marketplace. Such interfirm linkages are deeper than arm's-length market exchanges but stop short of outright merger; they involve mutual dependence and a degree of shared decision making between separate firms (Sheth and Parvatiyar 1992).

Prahalad (1995:vi) raises important questions about competition and cooperation:

> The current view of competition is that in a given industry structure, the relative roles of suppliers, customers, and competitors can be well defined; therefore, the focus of competitive analysis is on current competitors.... However, in the evolving industries, the lines between customers, suppliers, and competitors are extremely blurred. Are Sony and Philips competitors? Yes; but they work together in developing optical media standards and supply components for each other. They are, therefore, suppliers, customers, collaborators, and competitors – all at the same time. This complex interplay of roles, often within the same industry or in evolving industries and often based on a common set of skills, creates a new challenge. What are the rules of engagement when competitors are also suppliers and customers? What is the balance between dependence and competition?

The Internet vividly illustrates the trend toward coopetition and working with complementors. For example, Excite, a leading search engine company, has cooperative agreements in place with Netscape Communications, America Online, and Intuit, even though it competes with all of those companies in trying to become a "portal" or first stop on the Internet. The agreements involve sharing technology, customers, and advertising revenue. Yahoo has deals with Microsoft as well as Netscape – companies that are rivals of one another and of Yahoo itself. Infoseek, Lycos, and others have similar arrangements. These companies see the value in forming partnerships to add essential elements to their service (Miller 1998).

Porter's (1980) "five forces" of competition can also be viewed through the prism of cooperation (Sheth 1992). In terms of dealing with suppliers and customers, there has been a clear shift away from the adversarial mind-set implied by the bargaining power perspective and toward a cooperative stance focused on mutual gain. With regard to new entrants, cooperation is possible as well; for example, in the telecommunications industry, new entrants into long-distance telephony (such as local phone companies) become resellers of the excess capacity of incumbents such as Sprint rather than becoming facilities-based carriers. The threat of substitutes is muted by incumbents aggressively investing in substitute technologies; in the pharmaceutical industry, for example, every major company has invested in biotech. Cooperation in these circumstances is highlighted when the substitute technology offers substantial benefits in terms of lower production costs and higher quality. For example, Kodak, Fuji, and many other competitors in the photography business cooperated to facilitate the creation of a new hybrid photography system known as the Advanced Photo System. Incumbents within an industry cooperate, for example, in the standards creation process, the cross-licensing of technologies, campaigns to stimulate primary demand, and the development of shared infrastructures.

Market share or market growth?

The profit impact of marketing strategies (PIMS) studies have shown a strong relationship between a company's ROI and its relative market share of its served market (Buzzell and Gale 1987). Given the strong empirical base for the study, these results had a significant impact on competitive strategy, making the pursuit of market share a paramount concern of senior executives and strategic planners. Although some have cautioned companies about the dangers of pursuing market share too aggressively (e.g., Anterasian, Graham, and Money 1996), there has been continued evidence in support of the fundamental premise (Szymanski, Bharadwaj, and Varadarajan 1993).

Market share is an important concept and will continue to be so. However, it is inherently a zero-sum or win-lose proposition and is subject to the definitional and other problems mentioned earlier. Market share thinking has to be counterbalanced with a market growth orientation, which is a win-win concept and predicated at least in part on coopetition; it is often less costly if an industry collaboratively grows the total market.

Buzzell (1998) has pointed out that one of the biggest gaps that exists in the marketing literature is an understanding of the determinants of market growth. One approach, suggested by Bharadwaj and Clark (1998), highlights the role played by new knowledge creation. As they point out, market growth is typically treated in marketing as an exogenous variable. They propose a model in which marketing and other endogenous actions (such as government policy) stimulate knowledge creation (innovation, invention, discovery), knowledge/use matching, and knowledge dispersion (spillover and dispersal), leading to endogenous market growth. Central to their logic is the increasing returns character of knowledge.

Customer retention or customer outsourcing?

A number of authors have offered competitive strategy typologies. Porter (1980) suggested that business strategies can be classified into three generic types: overall cost leadership, differentiation, and focus. Treacy and Wiersema (1995) proposed that firms pursue either operational excellence, innovation, or customer intimacy. These and other frameworks, while simplifying the complex reality of strategic choices, are becoming less relevant as we begin to disaggregate revenues and costs to the customer or account level. Competitive strategies were developed based on aggregate market behaviors. With better information and accounting systems, we now have information at the individual customer or account level, especially cost information. This has revealed previously hidden subsidies by customers, products, and markets, which create the potential for nonintuitive and nontraditional strategies.

The 80/20 rule is well known, but its implications have not been understood properly because we have only focused on revenues and not looked at the distribution of costs. The low-cost position in Porter's (1980) framework is fundamentally untenable in many industries, especially when customer costs and revenues are not highly correlated. We argue that it is not average cost and average revenue but the distribution of revenues and costs over customers, products, markets, and customers that is key for strategy formulation. Typically, the distribution of revenues is highly nonlinear, while costs are distributed in a more linear relationship with customer size. In other words, the revenue curve slopes down exponentially, while the cost curve slopes down gradually. Nontraditional competitors can exploit this distribution of revenues and costs to their advantage.

Figure 1 shows the distribution of per customer revenues and costs over customers for a typical company. Typically, revenues are sharply skewed from the largest to the smallest customers, while costs tend to decline more gradually. This creates a situation in which a small number of highly profitable customers are in essence subsidizing a larger number of customers on which the company actually loses money. The former are highly attractive targets for focused competitors, while the latter are unprofitable customers that few if any suppliers would want.

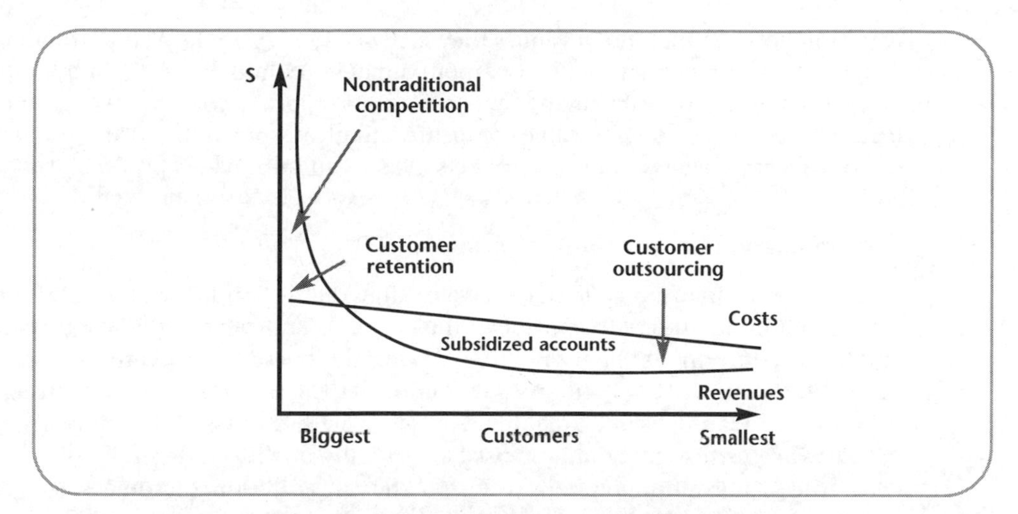

Figure 1 Subsidization across customers

Large companies (which usually have low average costs per customer) are thus vulnerable to targeted entry by smaller competitors that systematically target their most profitable customers, especially if those customers are subsidizing small customers. In regulated industries such as telecommunications and electric utilities, for example, new entrants such as competitive local exchange carriers (CLECs) and power resellers target the most profitable large customers, leaving the incumbent with smaller customers, many of whom cost more to serve than the revenues they generate. Cross-customer subsidies of any kind create such bypass opportunities for savvy competitors. Any time some products or customers or markets subsidize others, there is a potential competitive vulnerability to nontraditional competitors.

In many cases, companies may be unaware that they are subsidizing some customers at the expense of others, making them vulnerable. The marketing discipline needs to develop a theory of subsidization – a strategic understanding of when/how/why to subsidize. This would help companies answer questions such as whether they should have subsidies, how they should manage them, which customer groups should subsidize which others, whether subsidies should exist across products, and so on.

It is important to emphasize that subsidies are not necessarily bad; used strategically, they can turn a competitive vulnerability into a competitive advantage. Telecommunications companies, for example, have found that if they use casual customers to subsidize heavy users, they can eliminate most bypass opportunities for nontraditional competitors. The airline industry, with the use of yield management systems, has come the closest of any industry to using cross-customer subsidies in a strategic manner. Supermarkets and other broad assortment retailers use subsidies in a creative manner; by understanding how customer price sensitivities differ across products, they essentially get customers to cross-subsidize their own purchasing. Customers come to a store in response to loss-leader promotions and then purchase many other products at high markups.

A customer outsourcing strategy is a logical outcome of understanding customer subsidies. For some companies, certain customers are perennial money losers, as they cost more to serve than the revenues they generate. For example, AT&T announced in August 1998 that it loses money on approximately 25 million of its 70 million residential customers. By outsourcing these customers to local phone companies or others (such as electric utilities and cable companies) that can spread the costs of billing and customer service across multiple products, AT&T can improve its profitability.

Vertical integration or virtual integration?

Over the years, many corporations have exhibited a bias in favor of vertical integration, based on the desire to control all the elements and capture the margins at each stage of production (Williamson 1975). Asking the question, "Is Vertical Integration Profitable?" Buzzell (1983) empirically found that the minuses usually outweigh the pluses. The additional capital requirements along with the loss of flexibility associated with it make vertical integration a risky and usually unwise strategy.

Vertical integration typically leads to the subsidization of some stages at the expense of others; the transfer pricing between stages is typically politically driven rather than market based. For example, the most vertically integrated U.S. automaker is General Motors; its internal parts-making divisions are quite profitable (because they have a guaranteed markup) even though the company loses money on each car that it sells. By shielding internal units from market forces, the competitiveness of the company is hurt.

In most industries, vertical integration is becoming less attractive over time; supply can be ensured and marketing costs reduced by using coopetition. Through partnering, buyers and sellers can gain many of the advantages of vertical integration (low transaction costs, assurance of supply, improved coordination, higher entry barriers) without the attendant drawbacks – an approach that is referred to as virtual integration (Buzzell and Ortmeyer 1995).

In addition to vertical partnering up and down the value chain, we are also seeing growth in the area of horizontal partnerships between competitors or between complementary players. However, the theoretical base here is still weak; we have a good grounding on transaction cost analysis, but we do not have a good grounding in relational economics. Similarly, we have good theories on vertical integration (in economics as well as marketing) but not on horizontal integration or alliances.

References

Aaker, David. 1991. *Managing Brand Equity*. New York: Free Press.

Alba, Joseph, John Lynch, Barton Weitz, Chris Janiszewski, Richard Lutz, Alan Sawyer, and Stacy Wood. 1997. "Interactive Home Shopping: Consumer, Retailer, and Manufacturer Incentives to Participate in Electronic Marketplaces." *Journal of Marketing* **61** (Summer): 38–53.

Alderson, Wroe. 1945. "Factors Governing the Development of Marketing Channels." In *Marketing Channels*. Ed. R. M. Clewett. Homewood, IL: Irwin.

Anderson, Eugene W., Claes Fornell, and Donald R. Lehmann. 1994. "Customer Satisfaction, Market Share, and Profitability: Findings From Sweden." *Journal of Marketing* **58**(3): 53–66.

Anterasian, Cathy, John L. Graham, and R. Bruce Money. 1996. "Are U.S. Managers Superstitious About Market Share?" *Sloan Management Review* **37**(4): 67–77.

Arthur, W. Brian. 1996. "Increasing Returns and the New World of Business." *Harvard Business Review* **74**(4): 100–9.

Assael, Henry and A. Marvin Roscoe, Jr. 1976. "Approaches to Market Segmentation Analysis." *Journal of Marketing* **40** (October): 67–76.

Bass, Frank M. 1969. "A New Product Growth Model for Consumer Durables." *Management Science* **15** (January): 215–27.

—. 1995. "Empirical Generalizations and Marketing Science: A Personal View." *Marketing Science* **14**(3): G6–G19.

—and Jerry Wind. 1995. "Introduction to the Special Issue: Empirical Generalizations in Marketing." *Marketing Science* **14**(3): G1–G5.

Bharadwaj, Sundar and Terry Clark. 1998. "Marketing, Market Growth and Endogenous Growth Theory: An Inquiry Into the Causes of Market Growth." Paper presented at the Marketing Science Institute/*Journal of Marketing* Conference on Fundamental Issues and Directions for Marketing, June 5–6. Cambridge, MA.

Blattberg, Robert C., Richard Briesch, and Edward J. Fox. 1995. "How Promotions Work." *Marketing Science* **14**(3): G79–G85.

—, Thomas Buesing, and Subrata Sen. 1980. "Segmentation Strategies for New Brands." *Journal of Marketing* **44** (Fall): 59–67.

Boulding, William and Richard Staelin. 1995. "Identifying Generalizable Effects of Strategic Actions on Firm Performance: The Case of Demand-Side Returns to R&D Spending." *Marketing Science* **14**(3): G222–G231.

Brandenburger, Adam M. and Barry J. Nalebuff 1996. *Coopetition*. New York: Doubleday.

Breyer, Ralph F. 1934. *The Marketing Institution*. New York: McGraw-Hill.

Buzzell, Robert D. 1983. "Is Vertical Integration Profitable?" *Harvard Business Review* **61** (January–February): 92–102.

—1998. "In Search of Marketing Principles." Paper presented at the Academy of Marketing Science Annual Conference on Current Developments in Marketing, May 27–30, Norfolk, VA.

—and Bradley T. Gale. 1987. T*he PIMS Principles: Linking Strategy to Performance*. New York: Free Press.

—and Gwen Ortmeyer. 1995. "Channel Partnerships Streamline Distribution." *Sloan Management Review* **36**(3): 85–96.

Carmody, Deirdre. 1991. "Threats to Mass Circulation on Demographic Landscape." *The New York Times*, January 7.

Carpenter, Gregory S., Rashi Glazer, and Kent Nakamoto. 1998. "Market-Driving Strategy: Toward a New Concept of Competitive Advantage." Paper presented at the Marketing Science Institute/*Journal of Marketing* Conference on Fundamental Issues and Directions for Marketing, June 5–6, Cambridge, MA.

Contractor, Farok J. and Peter Lorange. 1988. "Why Should Firms Cooperate? The Strategy and Economic Basis for Cooperative Ventures." In *Cooperative Strategies in International Business*. Eds. Farok J. Contractor and Peter Lorange. Lexington, MA: Lexington Books.

Converse, Paul D. 1949. "New Laws of Retail Gravitation." *Journal of Marketing* **14** (October): 379–84.

Davis, Stan. 1987. *Future Perfect*. Reading, MA: Addison-Wesley.

Day, George S. 1981. "The Product Life Cycle: Analysis and Application Issues." *Journal of Marketing* **45** (Fall): 60–7.

—. 1998. "What Does It Mean to be Market-Driven?" *Business Strategy Review* 9 (1): 1–14.

Dekimpe, Marnik G. and Dominique M. Hanssens. 1995. "Empirical Generalizations About Market Evolution and Stationarity." *Marketing Science* **14**(3): G122–G131.

Dhalla, N. K. and S. Yuspeh. 1976. "Forget the Product Life Cycle Concept!" *Harvard Business Review* **54** (January–February): 102–10.

Doyle, Peter and John Saunders. 1985. "Market Segmentation and Positioning in Specialized Markets." *Journal of Marketing* **49** (Spring): 24–32.

Gardner, David. 1987. "The Product Life Cycle: A Critical Look at the Literature." In *Review of Marketing*. Ed. Michael J. Houston. Chicago: American Marketing Association.

Ghemawat, Pankaj. 1986. "Sustainable Advantage." *Harvard Business Review* **64** (September–October): 53–8.

Ghosh, Avijit and Samuel Craig. 1983. "Formulating Retail Location Strategy in a Changing Environment." *Journal of Marketing* **47** (Summer): 56–68.

Haley, Russell 1. 1968. "Benefit Segmentation: A Decision-Oriented Research Tool." *Journal of Marketing* **32** (July): 30–5.

Hamel, Gary. 1996. "Strategy as Revolution." *Harvard Business Review* **74** (July/August): 69–82.

—and C. K. Prahalad. 1991. "Corporate Imagination and Expeditionary Marketing." *Harvard Business Review* **69** (July–August): 81–92.

Huff, David L. 1964. "Defining and Estimating a Trading Area." *Journal of Marketing* **28** (July): 34–8.

Hunt, Shelby D. 1976. "The Nature and Scope of Marketing." *Journal of Marketing* **40** (July): 17–28.

Hurley, Robert F. and Tomas M. Hult. 1998. "Innovation, Market Orientation, and Organizational Learning: An Integration and Empirical Examination." *Journal of Marketing* **62** (Summer): 42.

Jacoby, Jacob and Robert W. Chestnut. 1978. *Brand Loyalty: Measurement and Management*. New York: John Wiley.

Jaworski, Bernard J. and Ajay K. Kohli. 1993. "Market Orientation Antecedents and Consequences.' *Journal of Marketing* **57** (Summer): 53–70.

Kalyanraman, Gurumurthy, William T. Robinson, and Glen L. Urban. 1995. "Order of Market Entry: Established Empirical Generalizations, Emerging Empirical Generalizations and Future Research." *Marketing Science* **14**(3): G212–G226.

Kapferer, Jean-Noel. 1994. *Strategic Brand Management: New Approaches to Creating and Evaluating Brand Equity*. New York: Free Press.

Keith, Robert J. 1960. "The Marketing Revolution." *Journal of Marketing* **24** (January): 35–8.

Keller, Kevin Lane. 1993. "Conceptualizing, Measuring and Managing Customer-Based Brand Equity" *Journal of Marketing* **57** (January): 1–22.

Kerin, Roger A. 1996. "In Pursuit of an Ideal: The Editorial and Literary History of the Journal of Marketing." *Journal of Marketing* **60** (Winter): 1.

Kodama, Fumio. 1992. "Technology Fusion and the New R&D." *Harvard Business Review* **70** (July–August): 70–8.

Kohli, Ajay K. and Bernard J. Jaworski. 1990. "Market Orientation: The Construct, Research Propositions, and Managerial Implications." *Journal of Marketing* **54** (April): 1–18.

Kotler, Philip and Ravi Singh. 1981. "Marketing Warfare in the 1980s." *Journal of Business Strategy* **2** (Winter): 30–41.

Kumar, Nirmalya and Lisa Scheer. 1998. "Radical and Incremental Product Innovation Among Market Driven and Market Driving Firms." Paper presented at the Marketing Science Institute/*Journal of Marketing* Conference on Fundamental Issues and Directions for Marketing, June 5–6, Cambridge, MA.

Levitt, Theodore. 1965. "Exploit the Product Life Cycle." *Harvard Business Review* **43** (November–December): 81–94.

Lewis, Peter H. 1998. "Web Concern Gets Patent for Electronic Business Model." *The New York Times*, August 10.

Mahajan, Vijay, Eitan Mueller, and Frank M. Bass. 1995. "Diffusion of New Products: Empirical Generalizations and Managerial Uses." *Marketing Science* **14**(3): G79–G85.

Miller, Greg. 1998. " 'Coopetition' Among Internet Rivals." *Los Angeles Times*, May 11.

Narver, John C. and Stanley E Slater. 1990. "The Effect of a Market Orientation on Business Profitability." *Journal of Marketing* **54** (October): 20–35.

Negroponte, Nicolas. 1995. *Being Digital*. New York: Knopf.

Norton, John A. and Frank M. Bass. 1987. "A Diffusion Theory Model of Adoption and Substitution for Successive Generations of High Technology Products." *Management Science* **33** (September): 1069–86.

—and —. 1992. "Evolution of Technological Generations: The Law of Capture." *Sloan Management Review* **33** (2): 66–77.

Nua Internet Surveys. 1998. http://www.nua.ie/surveys/

Nyquist, Jody D., Mary Jo Bitner, and Bernard H. Booms. 1985. "Identifying Communication Difficulties in the Service Encounter." In *The Service Encounter.* Eds. John Czepiel, Michael Solomon, and Carol Suprenant. Lexington, MA: Lexington Books.

Plummer, Joseph T. 1974. "The Concept and Application of Life Style Segmentation." *Journal of Marketing* **38** (January): 33–7.

Porter, Michael. 1980. *Competitive Strategy: Techniques for Analyzing Industries and Competitors.* New York: Free Press.

Prahalad, C. K. 1995. "Weak Signals Versus Strong Paradigms." *Journal of Marketing Research* **32** (Summer): iii.

—and Gary Hamel. 1990. "The Core Competence of the Corporation." *Harvard Business Review* **68** (May–June): 79–91.

Reibstein, David J. and Paul W. Farris. 1995. "Market Share and Distribution: A Generalization, a Speculation and Some Implications." *Marketing Science* **14** (3): G190–G205.

Reilly, William J. 1931. *The Law of Retail Gravitation.* Austin: University of Texas Press.

Reynolds, Robert B. 1953. "A Test of the Law of Retail Gravitation." *Journal of Marketing* **17** (January): 273–7.

Rogers, Everett. 1962. *Diffusion of Innovations.* New York: Free Press.

Sarkar, Mitrabarun, Brian Butler, and Charles Steinfeld. 1998. "Cybermediaries in Electronic Marketspace: Toward Theory Building." *Journal of Business Research* **41**: 215–21.

Sheth, Jagdish N. 1981. "Psychology of Innovation Resistance: The Less Developed Concept (LDC) in Diffusion Research." In *Research in Marketing,* Vol. 4. Ed. Jagdish N. Sheth. Greenwich, CT: JAI.

—. 1992. "Emerging Marketing Strategies in a Changing Macroeconomic Environment: A Commentary." *International Marketing Review* **9**(1): 57–63.

—and Banwari Mittal. 1996. "A Framework for Managing Customer Expectations." *Journal of Market Focused Management* **1**:137–58.

—,—, and Bruce Newman. 1999. *Customer Behavior Consumer Behavior and Beyond.* New York: Dryden.

—and Atul Parvatiyar. 1992. "Towards a Theory of Business Alliance Formation." *Scandinavian International Business Review* **1**(3): 71–87.

—and S. Ram. 1987. *Bringing Innovation to Market.* New York: John Wiley.

—and Rajendra S. Sisodia. 1995. "Feeling the Heat." *Marketing Management* **4** (Fall): 8–23.

—, David M. Gardner, and Dennis E. Garrett. 1988. *Marketing Theory: Evolution and Evaluation.* New York: John Wiley.

Simon, Hermann. 1994. "Marketing Science's Pilgrimage to the Ivory Tower." In *Research Traditions in Marketing.* Eds. Gilles Laurent, Gary L. Lilien, and Bernard Pras. Boston: Kluwer.

Slater, Stanley F. and John C. Narver. 1995. "Market Orientation and the Learning Organization." *Journal of Marketing* **59** (July): 63–74.

Szymanski, David M., Sundar G. Bharadwaj, and P. Rajan Varadarajan. 1993. "An Analysis of the Market Share–Profitability Relationship." *Journal of Marketing* **57** (Summer): 1.

Treacy, Michael and Fred Wiersema. 1995. *The Discipline of Market Leaders.* Reading, MA: Addison-Wesley.

Tushman, Michael L. and Charles A. O'Reilly 111. 1996. "Ambidextrous Organizations: Managing Evolutionary and Revolutionary Change." *California Management Review* **38** (Summer): 8–30.

—and —. 1997. *Winning Through Innovation: A Practical Guide to Leading Organizational Change and Renewal.* Boston: Harvard Business School Press.

Vaile, Roland S., E. T. Grether, and Reavis Cox. 1952. *Marketing in the American Economy*. New York: Ronald Press.

Williamson, Oliver E. 1975. *Markets and Hierarchies: Analysis and Antitrust Implications*. New York: Free Press.

Winter, Frederick W. 1979. "A Cost-Benefit Approach to Market Segmentation." *Journal of Marketing* **43** (Fall): 103–11.

Wysocki, Bernard, Jr. 1997. "Wealth of Notions." *Wall Street Journal*, January 26.

Zinkham, George M. and Ruby Hirschheim. 1992. "Truth in Marketing Theory and Research: An Alternative Perspective." *Journal of Marketing* **56** (April): 80–8.

Relationship Marketing: The Strategy Continuum

Grönroos, C (1995)

From *Journal of the Academy of Marketing Science*, **23**(4): 252–4

Service firms have always been relationship oriented. The nature of service businesses is relationship based. A service is a process or performance where the customer is involved, sometimes for a long period of time, sometimes only for a short moment, and sometimes on a regular basis, sometimes only as a one-time encounter. There is always a direct contact between a customer and the service firm. This contact makes it possible to create a relationship with the customer, if both parties are interested in such a way of doing business. As service firms, like banks, insurance firms, transportation companies, and retailers, have grown, the masses of customers have made the establishment of true relationships more difficult. In growing service businesses, the customer was turned from a relationship partner into market share statistics.

There are two obvious reasons for this. First, the difficulty to administer a relationship-oriented customer contact when the number of customers is increasing. Second, the growing influence from popular consumer goods-based, nonrelational marketing approaches. The marketing mix management paradigm and its flagship, the 4P model, established itself as the dominating marketing paradigm. At that time, especially during the 1960s and 1970s, this approach to marketing made sense for producers of consumer goods with their nonrelational customer contact. To a considerable degree it makes sense still today, although even in goods marketing a relational approach is called for (e.g., McKenna 1991; Rapp and Collins 1990). The nonmarketing approach did not meet the needs of service firms seeking relational customer contacts. Instead of focusing on the customer contacts, marketing became preoccupied with campaigns and other short-term activities where the interest in getting new customers dominated the task of keeping customers. Marketing was almost totally in the hands of marketing specialists organized in marketing departments. The people in the rest of the organization who in fact took care of the customers by producing and delivering the service to them more and more were forced to pay attention to other aspects of their job than satisfying customers. The relational-based service businesses became mass marketing oriented.

It is quite natural that the seeds of modern relationship marketing first started to grow in service marketing research. In fact, service marketing started to develop as a discipline because the marketing mix management paradigm and some of its key models fitted service firms' customer relations badly (see, for example, Rathmell 1974).

The notion of the need to *market services internally* to the personnel first (Eiglier and Langeard 1976; George 1977, Grönroos 1978; Berry 1981), the *interactive marketing concept* (Grönroos 1979), the *customer relationship life cycle* concept (Grönroos 1982/1983), and the *part-time marketer* notion (Gummesson 1987) are relationship marketing notions and concepts that are derived from the relational customer interface of service firms. Many of these concepts were early developed within what has been called the *Nordic School of Services* (Grönroos and Gummesson 1985; see also Berry and Parasuraman 1993). In a 1983 conference paper, Berry (1983) finally introduced the concept *relationship marketing*.

However, even if the customer contacts of service firms are relational in nature, some contacts are such that no relationships could be established. A traveler who decides to stay at a hotel in a town where he never has been before and does not expect to return is not a profitable target for a relationship approach. Instead, transaction marketing that aims at getting the traveler to choose this particular hotel is probably a good marketing strategy in this case. Moreover, some customers do not wish to get involved in a relational association with a service firm (see Barnes 1994). Clearly there are situations where an orientation toward getting customers or a transaction marketing approach makes more sense than a relationship marketing approach.

A relationship marketing strategy is well applicable in service businesses, whereas a transaction marketing strategy often fits the marketing situation of a consumer goods company. However, there are situations where both types of firms benefit from taking another marketing approach. Of course, there are a number of mixed strategies where the relationship elements or the transaction elements, respectively, dominate. As I in another context (Grönroos 1991) have observed, the marketing strategies available can be seen as a continuum with a relationship-oriented strategy on one end and a transaction-oriented strategy on the other end. In the next section, we shall take a closer look at the implications of this continuum.

The marketing strategy continuum

A relationship type of approach is long term in nature, whereas transaction marketing is more oriented toward short-term goals. One can say that the goal of transaction marketing is to get customers, whereas the goal of relationship marketing is to get *and keep* customers. Keeping customers becomes more important (although getting customers of course is the basis for having any customers to keep) because it is normally less expensive to make a satisfied existing customer buy more compared to what it costs to get a new customer. The economic consequences of reducing the customer defection rate are considerable (Reichheld and Sasser 1990).

The marketing implications across the strategy continuum (relationship versus transaction) are substantially different concerning the dominating marketing orientation, dominating quality function, customer information system, interdependency between business functions, and the role of internal marketing (Grönroos 1991).

Dominating marketing orientation. First of all, a relationship strategy requires that marketing is not restricted to the marketing mix activities. The interactive marketing effect of the production and delivery processes have a profound effect on the inclination of a customer to return. The "part-time marketers" of an organization (Gummesson 1987), who are not part of the marketing department and not reporting to a marketing manager, are the key marketing resources in a relationship marketing strategy. When the part-time marketers, with their dual responsibilities, do their job correctly and in an efficient manner and while doing so make a favorable marketing impact on the customer, they often either make or break the relationship. Of course, they are supported by back-office functions and physical resources, such as information systems and ATMs, but their role in the relationship is paramount. In transaction marketing, their role is more or less negligible. Instead, marketing mix activities, such as advertising campaigns and price offers, form the core of marketing. Such activities are of course not without importance in relationship marketing either, but they should more be seen as supporting interactive marketing and the part-time marketers. Interactive marketing and the part-time marketers are at the heart of relationship marketing.

Dominating quality dimension. Customers' considerations of quality will typically differ depending on what type of strategy the firm uses. In a transaction marketing strategy, it is normally enough if the output has an acceptable quality. The benefits sought by the customers are embedded in the technical solution provided by the core product. *What* the customer gets as the end result of the production process, which in service contexts is called output quality or technical quality, determines the level of satisfaction with quality. However, in order to start developing an ongoing relationship with a customer, the firm must be able to offer a good interaction process as well. All the interactions with the firm, with its contact personnel, information systems, and physical resources, have to support the quality perception of the customer. The *functional quality* or the impact of the interaction process, *how* the service production and delivery process itself is perceived, grows in importance, and in many cases becomes dominating. Of course, the technical quality has to be on an acceptable level, but it is no longer the only quality dimension of importance, and its part of the total perception of quality may even be marginal as long as it remains acceptable. If the part-time marketers are doing a good job and the interactive marketing effect is good, the functional quality impact will be favorable as well. Hence there is an obvious connection between functional quality and interactive marketing.

Customer information system. A firm pursuing a transaction marketing strategy normally has no or limited direct customer contacts. It relies on ad hoc customer satisfaction surveys and market share statistics to get information about the behavior and satisfaction of its customers. The customer base is managed indirectly through information systems that treat customers as numbers. Of course market share measures give important information about the relative number of customers a given firm has, but the firm does not know how satisfied its customers are or the defection rate of its customer base. Ad hoc studies may give additional information about these issues, but a real touch with the customer base is lacking. Market share and ad hoc surveys give a faceless proxy indication of satisfaction or dissatisfaction. Service firms, however, have natural direct contacts with their customers, and hence they can develop direct ways of managing their customer information systems. Customer satisfaction can be monitored by directly managing the customer base. The firm has at least some kind of direct knowledge of how satisfied its customers are. Instead of thinking in anonymous numbers, or market share, it thinks in terms of people with personal reactions and opinions. This of course gives quicker and much more accurate information about how customer satisfaction or dissatisfaction is developing. A firm that applies a relationship marketing strategy should monitor customer satisfaction by directly managing its customer base.

Interdependency between marketing, operations, and human resources. The level of interdependency between functions and departments in an organization depends on whether the firm has chosen a transaction-type strategy or a relationship-type strategy. In transaction marketing where the marketing mix activities dominate and constitute all or most of the elements of the customer relationship, the marketing department can take care of the marketing function. People in other functions and departments do not have to act as part-time marketers. Therefore, the interface between marketing and other functions have limited or no strategic importance to the firm. The situation is quite different for a firm that applies a relationship marketing strategy. There the interactive marketing function becomes critical to success, which requires a good cooperation between marketing and operations. And in order to ensure that the part-time marketers of the operations function accept their marketing role, the human resources function gets involved as well. Hence the interface between at least these three functions becomes important to the success of the firm.

Internal marketing. Preparing the part-time marketers for their marketing tasks is of course a paramount part of a relationship marketing strategy. The firm has to take an active approach to get the commitment to a marketing-like behavior of the personnel and to develop service and communication skills in the organization. The more persons in the firm who are involved in the marketing function as part-time marketers, the greater the need for active internal marketing. Hence it can be concluded that there is limited need for internal marketing in connection with a transaction marketing strategy, whereas a relationship marketing strategy requires a thorough and ongoing internal marketing process.

Conclusion

Few service firms will apply a pure transaction marketing strategy. Even highly standardized service operations include direct contacts with customers, and the customers do perceive the production and delivery process. Hence there are part-time marketers and functional quality effects, so we cannot talk about a pure transaction marketing situation. However, the more standardized the process is, the more dominating is the core service and the technical quality of the outcome of the production and delivery process and the less difficult it is to manage the personnel from a marketing point of view. Firms can position their strategic approach along the strategy continuum, and the more a relationship-type strategy is called for, the more has to be invested in interactive marketing, the functional quality impact, and internal marketing. In such a situation, it is at the same time more important to create information systems where the firm is managing its customer base directly and not relying on market share statistics and ad hoc customer surveys.

References

Barnes, James G. 1994. "The Issues of Establishing Relationships With Customers in Service Companies: When are Relationships Feasible and What Form Should They Take?" Paper presented at the Third Frontiers in services Conference, American Marketing Association and Vanderbilt University, Nashville, TN, October.

Berry, Leonard L. 1981. "The Employee as Customer." *Journal of Retail Banking* (March): 33–40.

—. 1983. "Relationship Marketing." In *Emerging Perspectives on Services Marketing*. Eds.

Leonard L. Berry, G. Lynn Shostack, and Gregory Upah. Chicago, IL: American Marketing Association, 25–8.

Berry, Leonard L. and A. Parasuraman. 1993. "Building a New Academic Field – The Case of Services Marketing." *Journal of Retailing* **69** (Spring): 13–60.

Eiglier, Pierre and Eric Langeard. 1976. *Principes de politique marketing pour les enterprises de service* [Principles of Marketing Policy for Service Firms]. Research report. I.A.E. Université d'Aix-Marseille, France, December.

George, William R. 1977. "The Retailing of Services: A Challenging Future." *Journal of Retailing* **53** (Fall): 85–98.

Grönroos, Christian. 1978. "A Service-Oriented Approach to the Marketing of Services." *European Journal of Marketing* **8**(12): 588–602.

—. 1979. *Marknadsföring av tjänster. En studie av marknadsföringsfunktionen i tjänsteföretag* [The Marketing of Services. A Study of the Marketing Function in Service Firms]. Stockholm, Sweden: Akademilitteratur/Marknadstekniskt centrum.

—. 1983. *Strategic Management and Marketing in the Service Sector.* Cambridge, MA: Marketing Science Institute. (Original work published 1982, Swedish School of Economics and Business Administration, Helsingfors, Finland)

—. 1991. "The Marketing Strategy Continuum: Toward a Marketing Concept for the 1990s." *Management Decision* **29**(1): 7–13.

Grönroos, Christian and Evert Gummesson.1985. *Service Marketing – A Nordic School Perspective.* Research report. Stockholm, Sweden: Stockholm University.

Gummesson, Evert. 1987. "The New Marketing—Developing Long-Term Interactive Relationships." *Long Range Planning* **20**(4): 10–20.

McKenna, Regis. 1991. *Relationship Marketing. Successful Strategies for the Age of the Customer.* Reading, MA: Addison-Wesley.

Rapp, Stan and Tom Collins. 1990. *The Great Marketing Turnaround.* Englewood Cliffs, NJ: Prentice Hall.

Rathmell, John M. 1974. *Marketing in the Service Sector.* Cambridge, MA: Winthrop.

Reichheld, Frederick E and Earl W. Sasser, Jr. 1990. "Zero Defections: Quality Comes to Service." *Harvard Business Review* **68** (September–October): 105–11.

Combining Corporate and Marketing Strategy for Global Competitiveness

White, D S and Griffith, D A (1997)

From *Marketing Intelligence and Planning*, **15**(4): 173–8

Outlines effective corporate strategy-marketing strategy relationships in the context of a behavioural segmentation framework for competing in the global marketplace. Evaluates standard, local and regional market strategies in conjunction with cost-based, customer-based and innovation-based corporate strategies. Highlights key corporate strategy-marketing strategy combinations in a global strategic marketing decision tree. These combinations enhance an organization's ability to compete effectively in global consumer markets. Utilizes corporate examples to emphasize the effectiveness of these combinations. The premiss of this paper is that corporate strategy drives marketing strategy. Concludes that by recognizing the complex interrelationships between corporate and marketing strategy, organizations may achieve global strategic competitiveness.

Introduction

Movement towards a global consumer market has increased the competitive environment of multinational organizations. Due to the increase in competition, organizations have attempted to implement a variety of strategy programmes. In international marketing, managers have focused on the debate between standardization, regionalization and localization. However, marketing strategy implementation is not a question of standardization, regionalization or localization, but is rather an issue of knowing when to utilize each (Huszagh *et al.*, 1986; Levitt, 1983; Quelch and Hoff, 1986; Rau and Preble, 1987).

Effective marketing strategy adoption can be determined by examining the foundation (i.e. core competences) on which the organization operates. By adopting a marketing strategy that is compatible with the multinational's corporate strategy, the organization can achieve a strategic competitive advantage in the global marketplace (Walters, 1986).

This paper provides a conceptualization of successful corporate marketing and behaviour segmentation strategy combinations that have allowed multinational corporations to achieve dominance. Cost-, customer- and innovation-based corporate strategies provide the impetus for defining both international marketing (standardization, localization and regionalization) and target market behaviour segmentation. Finally, the concepts are combined to provide a new conceptualization for determining the most effective marketing strategy to implement, based on the organization's corporate strategy.

Organizational focus as a basis for global competitiveness

Corporate strategy is what positions multinationals in the global marketplace. Corporate strategy is guided by the organization's core competences – those competences on which the multinational operates. Operating strategies are either cost-, customer- or innovation-based (Aaker, 1992; Porter, 1980; Treacy and Wiersema, 1995).

Firms utilizing a *low-cost* strategy provide customers with quality products and services at competitive prices (Aaker, 1992; Porter, 1980; Treacy and Wiersema, 1995). These companies follow an organizational philosophy of leading the industry in price and convenience. Relying on economies of scale and competitive pricing, organizations position themselves in the market as a cost leader. It is important to differentiate the concept of *cost-based* corporate strategy from *pricing* strategy. Whereas the latter seeks to position the product in the consumers' eyes using price as a cue, the former focuses on becoming the most *cost-efficient* producer of the product. Multinationals utilizing this strategy, such as McDonald's, United Parcel Service and Coca-Cola, target customers who are interested more in getting quality products at the lowest possible price with the least possible hassle than in the specific product features or attributes they are buying (Porter, 1980; Treacy and Wiersema, 1995).

Multinationals refining their products and services to meet specific customer needs are following a *customer-based* corporate strategy (Porter, 1980; Treacy and Wiersema, 1995). By redefining their products according to specific market needs, these multinationals are able to establish strong customer relationships. Employing a corporate strategy aimed at understanding their customers, these firms are able to provide a higher level of service and re-establish the level of value expected by their customers. Firms utilizing this strategy are targeting customers who are concerned more with getting exactly what they need than with the price that they pay (Treacy and Wiersema, 1995). Through the redefinition of value in this segment of the marketplace, firms such as Proctor & Gamble, Volvo and Philips have been able to achieve strategic competitive advantages in their respective industries.

Multinationals competing on the basis of *innovation* strive to produce top-of-the-line, cutting-edge products (Aaker, 1992; Porter, 1980; Treacy and Wiersema, 1995). These organizations believe that by fostering an entrepreneurial environment their employees will continually challenge themselves to produce innovative products; the production of innovative products allows the multinational to establish itself as an innovative organization. Utilization of this philosophy means targeting customers who are willing to pay premium prices in order to obtain state-of-the-art products (Treacy and Wiersema, 1995). Firms such as Michelin, Ciba-Geigy and Sony use this strategy to position themselves as innovators throughout the global marketplace.

The different corporate strategies highlight the core competence the organization is using to differentiate itself from its competitors. Not only does the corporate strategy identify how the organization positions itself in the marketplace, it also identifies consumer choice criteria. For example, customers who value innovative products, or low-cost products, can be found throughout the world. Whether the organization is targeting customers in London, Paris, Madrid or Brussels, those utilizing similar choice criteria are known to exist. However, developing and implementing the appropriate marketing strategy within the framework of one's product, core competences and the international competitive environment are crucial.

Segue from corporate to marketing strategy

Standardization proponents have argued from the beginning that consumers are becoming more homogeneous in terms of their wants and needs (Elinder, 1965; Eger, 1987; Fatt, 1967; Levitt, 1983; McNally 1986; Porter, 1986), due most notably to an increase in international television broadcasting and international travel (Eger, 1987; Fatt, 1967; Levitt, 1983; McNally 1986). By standardizing marketing strategy, managers seek to achieve economies of scale (Levitt, 1983; McNally 1987) and brand-image consistency (Eger, 1987; Fatt, 1967; Peebles, 1989).

Champions of *localization* argue that the utilization of a global marketing strategy is based on a flawed assumption: the world population is becoming homogeneous. Localization advocates argue that standardization authors ignore the importance of culture (Wind, 1986). Cultural differences, a fatal omission in the homogenization argument, cannot be ignored and have a significant impact on consumer behaviour (Black, 1986; Locke, 1986). Since cultural differences between individuals and societies are the barriers to standardization, marketers need to identify specific target markets and then service them effectively (Black, 1986; Shao, Shao, and Shao, 1992). Accordingly, scholars are finding that practitioners are customizing their marketing strategies to compete effectively in individual markets (Shao *et al.*, 1992; Sorenson and Wiechmann, 1975).

Advocates of *regional segmentation* strategy contend that the practice of market segmentation in domestic markets is a clear indicator of the ineffectiveness of treating the whole world as a homogeneous market (Baalbaki and Malhotra, 1993; Kreutzer, 1988). Regional market segmentation examines homogeneous segments, those with similar demand functions, across world markets. Assessing the similarities and differences between consumers across markets, this strategy achieves the advantages of both standardization and localization (Baalbaki and Malhotra, 1993; Kale and Sundharshan, 1987; Kreutzer, 1988).

The making of a target market

Behavioural characteristics can be effective for segmenting the consumer market (Hassan and Katsanis, 1991). While a number of behavioural frameworks have been proposed in the literature (for a post-Levitt review, see Hassan and Katsanis, 1991), one developed by Ryans (1969) warrants further examination. This framework may be beneficial in resolving the most controversial debate about international marketing strategy – that of whether to implement standard, regional or local marketing strategies.

Ryans (1969) trichotomized the global market into the international sophisticate, the sophisticate and the provincial. This segmentation is based on behavioural characteristics, rather than any set of demographic characteristics, and includes a wide range of ages, incomes and educational levels within each segment. Ryans (1969) accomplished this by segmenting on the basis of the behavioural characteristic of "degree of cultural sensitivity", which he then uses to select the appropriate advertising strategy whether standardization, regionalization or localization. While this segmentation was applied originally only to advertising strategy, extending it to overall marketing strategy allows organizations to address a broader range of issues.

International sophisticates are a small group of consumers who might be termed "world citizens" (Ryans, 1969). These consumers have an appreciation of other cultures. Beyond their appreciation of other cultures, they are open and receptive to cultural differences and international products. Since these consumers are interested in other cultures and have a great deal of cross-cultural exposure, brand-image consistency is increasingly important to a multinational which is targeting this market segment. The global philosophy of these consumers, plus the heightened sensitivity to brand-image consistency, are the cornerstones of standardization.

The *sophisticate* consumer segment, although intrigued by other cultures, still perceives those other cultures to be socially distant. Overall, these consumers fall somewhere between the global and the ethnocentric in their consumption philosophy. Although this segment is not influenced to the same extent by a global campaign, regional campaigns, the sophisticates consider, may be effective (Ryans, 1969).

Provincial consumers are defined as individuals who lack an interest in, or an appreciation of, other cultures, and consequently exhibit a hesitancy towards purchasing "foreign" products. This hesitancy ensues from an overall ethnocentric consumer philosophy. Hesitant about the unfamiliar in terms of products or advertising, this segment is most receptive to a localized strategy (Ryans, 1969).

Many multinationals which study their market closely find that they are concentrating on one behavioural type; or they may find that individual customer types can be associated with certain products in their product line. As a result, the effective utilization of a behavioural segmentation strategy can provide a multinational with a strategic competitive advantage.

Strategy development for global competitiveness

For an organization to compete in the competitive global marketplace, it must select and implement a marketing strategy that is compatible with its corporate strategy. The multinational operating in the global marketplace must develop a synergistic bond between marketing strategy and corporate strategy. Through the correct strategy combination, a multinational can maximize its own competitive advantage(s), thus allowing it to compete effectively and efficiently throughout the world.

The schema for combining marketing and corporate strategy is illustrated in Figure 1, the global strategic marketing decision tree. By analysing traditional corporate strategies under Ryans' (1969) behavioural characteristic market segmentation typology, multinationals may be able to flexibly implement the appropriate marketing strategy (whether standardization, regionalization or localization), while targeting in an effective way specific consumer segments throughout the world.

Six congruent strategy-target market combinations are identified. The rationale for asserting either congruence or incongruence is twofold:

1 Each strategy combination either does or does not make sense conceptually when real-world considerations are weighed. For example, the control and centralization that is required for a low-cost approach supports a one-size-fits-all standardization strategy and is appropriate for a target market of international sophisticates, whereas low-cost production and standardization targeted for acceptance in a provincial customer market are contradictory.

2 The global strategic marketing decision tree is compelling from a strictly practical position. Examples of leading multinationals combining the six conceptually

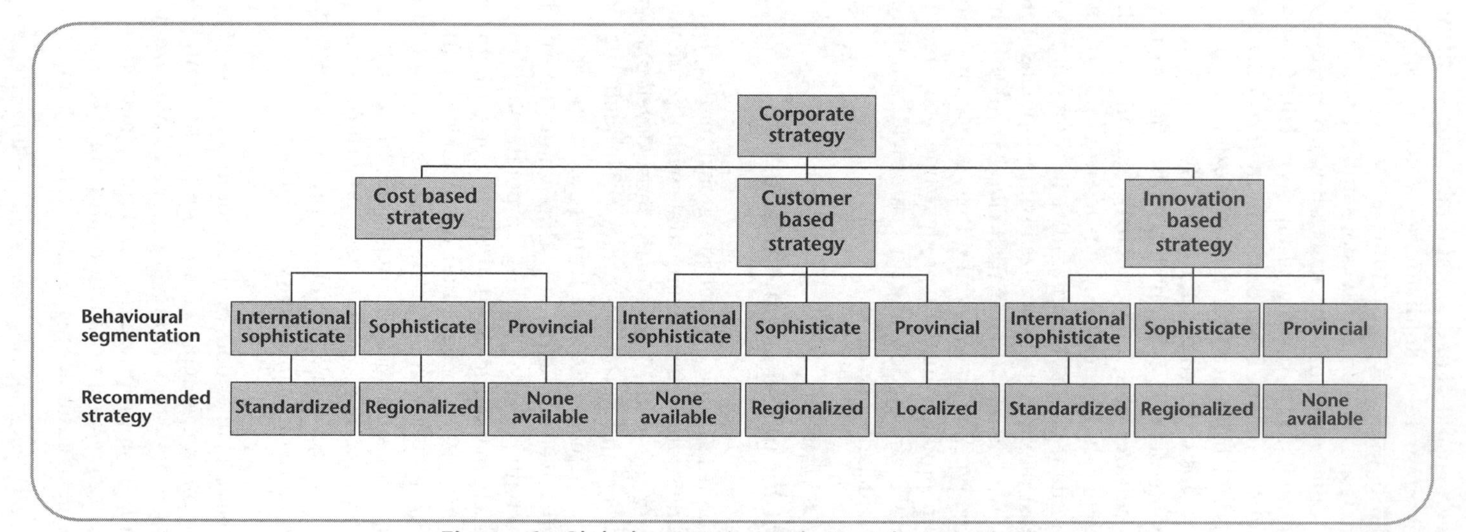

Figure 1 Global strategic marketing decision tree

compatible combinations are abundant, while few or no cases can be found in support of the incongruent combinations.

Four managerial guidelines for formulating and executing multinational strategies are directly reasoned or can be inferred from the global strategic marketing decision tree. Each is consistent and logical in the abstract, while also being supported by corroborating experiences.

Guideline 1: world citizens embrace the cost-effectiveness of standardization

The cost-based strategy indicates not only the corporate focus, but also the type of customer the multinational is targeting. Because the organization is striving for price competitiveness, products produced under this philosophy need to be standardized and made inherently less culturally sensitive.

A standardized marketing strategy has been implemented effectively by McDonald's, United Parcel Service and Coca-Cola when targeting the international sophisticate segment. McDonald's march across continents provides evidence that cost advantages coupled with a unified global marketing strategy produce outstanding results when targeting the international sophisticate markets from Paris to Moscow. UPS and Coca-Cola's adherence to a global marketing strategy designed to capitalize on cost efficiencies, as demonstrated most recently in their sponsorship of the 1996 centennial Olympics competition and the commercials aired during, has enabled them to achieve competitive advantages in their respective industries.

Since these organizations compete on the basis of price and convenience, while targeting the international sophisticate customer type, standardization has been effective. Through standardization, these global organizations have been able to achieve significant cost savings in comparison to their competitors, thereby leading to a competitive advantage.

This strategy combination is in stark contrast to one capable of satisfying the provincial segment. A localized strategy is contrary to the principles of cost-based efficiencies and therefore may not be combined effectively. Cost-based organizations targeting provincial markets find profits lacking. If Coca-Cola began by adapting its product and advertising for each local market, would it be as successful as it is today?

Guideline 2: world citizens follow technological leaders closely

An innovation-based strategy demands an ability continually to produce cutting-edge products that have limited cultural boundedness. Targeting the international sophisticate customer segment with a globalized marketing strategy has proved effective for global industry leaders such as Michelin, Sony and Ciba-Geigy

Michelin is the world's largest tyre company. Movement from a rubber products business back in the 1880s to global dominance today has developed through the effective targeting of *world citizens* by combining innovative products with a global marketing strategy. Who can deny the fact that the maker of the first radial tyre has captured the hearts of consumers around the world with their "baby" campaign?

Sony and Ciba-Geigy have also combined their technological prowess synergistically with global marketing strategies to surpass the expectations of consumers around the world. Sony's humble beginnings in war-ravaged Japan shed little light on the global dominance it would obtain 50 years later by identifying the global electronic market for smaller and more efficient products. Likewise, Johann Rudolf Geigy might never have dreamed back in 1758 that 212 years later his firm would marry Alexander Clavels' 1859 dye works legacy to become a global leader in pharmaceutical and chemicals. The strength born through that unlikely marriage has enabled Ciba-Geigy to develop cutting-edge products with global reach.

These multinationals have combined innovative products/services with a global marketing strategy to target a single global market. Targeting the *world citizens* who demand leading-edge products, has enabled them to position themselves as effective innovators throughout the global marketplace. Since customers in this segment are not averse to other cultures, the utilization of a global strategy has been most effective.

Given the drive for technological prowess, local market adaptation appears counterproductive. A multinational that is destined to compete on product innovation has no choice but to standardize its marketing strategy, and thus focus on the international sophisticate market. Michelin's dominance would surely fade if it were to adopt the customer-based approach of a WPP Group.

Guideline 3: provincials crave that local touch

A customer-based strategy directs organizational resources towards establishing high-value customer relationships. The focus of this strategy is to understand customers' wants and needs, and therefore the multinational must take into consideration the cultural characteristics of each market in which it operates. As a result, product development and customization need to be evaluated on the basis of the product's level of cultural appeal. Within a marketing management framework, this strategy concentrates on tailoring the product to customer needs and hence requires more adaptation across the marketing mix.

The provincial market demands a localized strategy. Roadway and Cable & Wireless have demonstrated the effectiveness of a localization strategy when catering to the specific needs of their customers, with Roadway providing on-site logistical help for its larger clients and Cable & Wireless tirelessly providing customer consultation. This type of customer requires a localized strategy, combined with a corporate strategy aimed at continual tailoring of the product to the customer. With a localized marketing strategy, the marketing management bases also need to be localized. As a result, product, promotion, distribution and pricing need to be tailored for the specific customer in each market.

Enterprises that have developed and enhanced their reputations by exceeding customer expectations use customer preferences to guide marketing strategy. Due to the highly specialized aspects of a customer-based strategy requiring the redefining of product attributes, inefficiencies may be created when firms move away from their guiding principle. The Walt Disney Company is one such example. Disneyland Paris has been less than optimally marketed in Europe. After three-and-a-half years of less than Disney-like performance on a pan-European basis, the entertainment giant is beginning to target specific European markets, such as the UK. The move to a more focused marketing effort should help revitalize Disney's European image.

Guideline 4: a plethora of strategies with which to satisfy sophisticates

Sophisticates are accepting of all. Consider Proctor & Gamble's value-pricing strategy in its pan-European campaign; or Volvo's development of regionally acceptable products providing value-added benefits such as safety; or Philips's pan-European approach to competing on a technological basis – in each case a regionalized strategy has proven effective. These multinationals adhere to the adage of meeting specific customer needs on a regional basis, thus recognizing and incorporating cultural differences into their overall marketing strategy. By targeting the sophisticate segment, which is interested in other cultures, the regionalized marketing strategy has allowed them to achieve benefits of both standardization and localization.

Regionalization occurs with products or services that require some degree of adaptation. A company such as Nestlé, for instance, would suffer greatly if it were to attempt to reap the cost benefits of standardization at the cost of regional acceptance. Additionally, Nestlé's market leadership would most likely erode if it were to attempt to satisfy local needs. Its operating efficiencies lie in satisfying the regional needs of the sophisticate market.

The Achilles heel

The Achilles heel of this entire argument is behaviour segmentation. Marketers have tried for decades to identify behaviour segments within the marketplace. While this has proved futile in many cases, the point here is that the identification of each segment may not be as important as originally thought.

The global strategic marketing decision tree (Figure 1) indicates that marketing strategy derives from the economic advantages of corporate strategy. Given the synergistic combination of the two, a target market behaviour segment is identified. That is to say, once an organization has committed to a particular operating philosophy and marketing strategy, there may be only a few behaviour segments that it can target effectively. Thus, a number of strategic managerial guidelines are presented to help managers identify each.

Implications

The global strategic marketing decision tree can be used by executives to develop ideas and think about the four issues that are critical to establishing and maintaining a competitive organization:

1 On which core competence does/should the organization operate?

2 How might the organization realign its strengths to better position itself?

3 Are the behavioural characteristics of your target market consistent with your core competence?

4 What environmental changes may impact the effectiveness of your current strategy combination?

These inquiries provide a starting-point for international executives to redefine their competitive position in the marketplace. The global strategic marketing decision tree provides a guide of past successful combinations. While the insights provided by the decision tree are illuminating, it is important for international executives to find new means of surpassing old parameters. Perhaps the solution lies in the rapid technological advances occurring in the global telecommunications industry.

References

Aaker, D. (1992), *Strategic Market Management*, 3rd ed., John Wiley & Sons, New York, NY.

Baalbaki, I.B. and Malhotra, N.K. (1993), "Marketing management bases for international market segmentation: an alternate look at the standardization/customization debate", *International Marketing Review*, Vol. 10 No.l, pp. 19–41.

Black, G. (1986), "Think globally sell locally", *Business Marketing* Vol. 71 No. 5, p. 144.

Eger, J.M. (1987), "Global television: an executive overview", *Columbia Journal of World Business*, Vol. 22 No. 3, pp. 5–10.

Elinder, E. (1965), "How international can European advertising be?", *Journal of Marketing*, Vol. 29 No. 2, pp. 7–11.

Fatt, A.C. (1967), "The danger of 'local' international advertising", *Journal of Marketing*, Vol.31 No.l, pp. 60–2.

Hassan, S.S. and Katsanis, L.R (1991), "Identification of global consumer segments: a behavioural framework", *Journal of International Consumer Marketing*, Vol. 3 No. 2, pp. 11–28.

Huszagh, S.M., Fox, R.J. and Day, E. (1986), "Global marketing: an empirical investigation", *Columbia Journal of World Business*, Vol. 20 No. 4, pp. 31–43.

Kale, S.H. and Sundharshan, D. (1987), "A strategic approach to international segmentation", *International Marketing Review*, Vol. 8 No. 3, pp. 31–5.

Kreutzer, R.T. (1988), "Marketing mix standardization: an integrated approach in global marketing", *European Journal of Marketing*, Vol. 22 No. 10, pp. 19–30.

Levitt, T. (1983), "The globalization of markets", *Harvard Business Review*, Vol. 61 No. 3, pp. 92–102.

Locke, WW. (1986), "Global marketing: the fatal flaw: hidden cultural differences", *Business Marketing*, Vol. 71 No. 4, pp. 65, 72–6.

McNally G.J. (1986), "Global marketing: it's not ,just possible – it's imperative", *Business Marketing*, Vol.71 No.4, pp. 64–70.

Peebles, D.M. (1989), "Executive insights don't write off global advertising: a commentary", *Journal of International Marketing*, Vol.6 No.l,pp. 73–8.

Porter, M.E. (1980), *Competitive Strategy*, The Free Press, New York, NY.

Porter, M.E. (1986), "The strategic role of international marketing", *Journal of Consumer Marketing*, Vol.3 No. 2, pp. 17–21.

Quelch, J.A. and Hoff, E.J. (1986), "Customizing global marketing", *Harvard Business Review*, Vol.64 No.3, pp. 59–68.

Rau, PA. and Preble, J.F. (1987), "Standardization of marketing strategy by multinationals ", *International Marketing Review*, Vol.3 No.2, pp. 18–28.

Ryans, J.K. Jr. (1969), "Is it too soon to put a tiger in every tank?", *Columbia Journal of World Business*, Vol. 2 No. 2, pp. 69–75.

Shao, A.T., Shao, L.R and Shao, D.H. (1992), "Are global markets with standardized advertising campaigns feasible?", *Journal of International Consumer Marketing*, Vol. 4 No.3, pp. 5–16.

Sorenson, R.Z. and Wiechmann, U.E. (1975), "To what extent should a consumer goods multinational corporation vary its marketing from country to country?", *Harvard Business Review*, Vol.53 No.3, pp. 38–44,167.

Treacy, M. and Wiersema, E (1995), *The Discipline of Market Leaders*, Addison-Wesley Reading, MA.

Walters, RG.R (1986), "International marketing policy: a discussion of the standardization construct and its relevance for corporate policy", *Journal of International Business Studies*, Vol.17 No.2, pp. 55–69.

Wind, Y. (1986), "The myth of globalization", *Journal of Consumer Marketing*, Vol. 3 No.2, pp. 23–6.

Value-based Marketing

Doyle, P (2000)

Extract from *Value-based Marketing,* **18–23**

Marketing's lost influence

In today's information age marketing professionals should have become more important in the top councils of business. First, the central issue facing all firms now is understanding and adapting to rapidly changing markets – globalisation, new competition, rising customer expectations and the implications of the information revolution on how companies market. Second, marketing, rather than production, skills have become the key to creating competitive advantage. More and more leading branded goods companies follow the lead of the likes of Coca-Cola, Dell, Nike, Bodyshop and Armani in outsourcing all their manufacturing to outside suppliers, often in the developing countries. Others, like General Electric and IBM, are seeing their future not in selling products, but in providing services that offer tailored solutions to the needs of individual customers. Third, marketing performance is the root source of shareholder value. The firm's opportunity to create cash is based first and foremost on its ability to create a competitive advantage that will enable it to attract and retain customers paying satisfactory prices.

But rather than gaining in influence, marketing professionals, whose expertise is in identifying these market opportunities and building customer relationships, appear to have lost influence in the board rooms of industry. A recent survey, for example, found that only 12 of the chief executives of Britain's top 100 companies had experience in a marketing job. Only 57 per cent of larger companies had marketing represented on the board. The survey found that while all companies considered profit at each board meeting, only one in three regularly reviewed customer attitudes to the company and its brands. Several of the major consulting companies have also observed the waning influence of marketing departments in many companies.

Why does the lack of marketing professionalism in the board room matter? It matters because top managers will lack expert guidance on how their customers and competitors' strategies are changing. New market opportunities and threats are unlikely to be recognised speedily and, once recognised, acted upon decisively. If senior management are not focusing on customers and markets, it will mean that other issues fill the agenda. Evidence suggests that managers become preoccupied with short-term budgets, operating rather than strategic issues, and when difficulties arise, retrenchment rather than renewal. Such myopia is, in the long run, antithetical to genuine value-creating strategies.

Several factors account for this paradox of the growing importance of marketing with the lack of influence of marketing professionals in top management. Of fundamental importance has been the failure of the marketing discipline to incorporate the concept of shareholder value. As a result there is no criteria for judging the success of a marketing strategy or comparing alternatives. This in turn means it is difficult to accept marketing recommendations on product policy, pricing, promotions, or, indeed, any element of the marketing mix. All too often marketing managers think a strategy is sensible if it increases sales or market share. But astute top managers know that strategies to maximise market share will very rarely make economic sense. More sophisticated marketing managers will be tempted to use projected profits or return on investment to rationalise their marketing proposals. Unfortunately, this approach has the opposite bias and leads to an under-investment in marketing and a failure to capitalise on opportunities. Modern marketing has not incorporated current strategic valuation techniques and has consequently become marginalised in many board rooms. The marketing disciple lacks the framework for engaging in the strategic debate.

Because the link between marketing strategy and shareholder value has not been made, boards have tended to look at two other more transparent strategies. One has been cost reduction – sometimes disguised by more appealing names such as reengineering, downsizing or right sizing. Unfortunately, in a time of rapid market change, such actions are invariably only palliatives at best. The other common remedy has been acquisition. Acquisitions have broken all records in recent years. They have been seen as a way of generating value by adding top-line growth and by permitting a reduction in average costs. But, again, the evidence is that three out of four acquisitions fail to add value for the acquiring company. Excessive bid premiums, cultural differences between the businesses and a failure to rejuvenate the company's marketing orientation appear to be the major weaknesses.

The failure to place marketing strategy at the centre of the corporate agenda cannot be laid solely at the door of the marketing profession. Financial management has also failed to bridge the marketing–finance interface. Top management still focuses on company accounts that measure only the historical cost of assets and omit internally developed brands and other intangible assets. Yet these marketing assets are now by far the most important sources of shareholder value. The market-to-book ratios for the *Fortune 500* average over 4, implying that over 75 per cent of the value of these companies lies in their brands and other marketing-based intangibles. Companies whose goal is maximising shareholder value need a framework for placing the development and management of marketing assets at the centre of their planning processes. It is these marketing assets – brands, market knowledge and customer and partner relationships – that have become the key generators of long-term profits in today's information age.

Marketing's new opportunity

Shareholder value analysis is becoming the new standard because of increasing realisation of the defects of conventional accounting. As we shall see, accounting profits encourage an excessively short-term view of business. They also encourage an under-investment in information-based assets – staff, brands, and customer and supplier relationships. In today's information age, the accounting focus only on tangible assets makes little sense now that these intangible assets are the overwhelming source of value creation. Shareholder value analysis (SVA) can avoid both these biases. But to achieve its potential, SVA needs marketing. Similarly, marketing needs SVA if it is to make a real contribution to strategy.

Shareholder value needs marketing

SVA is tautological without a marketing strategy. The shareholder value principle is that a business should be run to maximise the return on the shareholders' investment. SVA provides a tool for calculating the shareholder value added from any given growth, profit and investments projections. But what drives these growth, profit and investment requirements is outside the financial model. SVA does not address how managers can develop strategies that can accelerate growth, increase profit margins and lever investments. These are the objectives of marketing strategy. ... SVA was able to identify which of the three strategies presented was best, but developing the innovative dual-branding plan came solely from an understanding of the market dynamics and a creative approach to serving different customer segments.

The heart of SVA is that economic value is created only when the business earns a return on investment that exceeds its cost of capital. From economic theory we know that in competitive markets this will only occur when it has a differential advantage in cost or product superiority. Without a unique advantage, competition will drive profits down to the cost of capital. Creating shareholder value is then essentially about building a sustainable competitive advantage – a reason why customers should consistently prefer to buy from one company rather than others. Marketing provides the tools for creating this competitive advantage. These are frameworks for researching and analysing customer needs, techniques for competitive analysis, and systems for measuring and enhancing consumer preference. Effective marketing input allows SVA to be dynamic and growth orientated. Without it, SVA is static, merely focusing on ways of reducing costs and assets to produce a temporary fillip to cash flow.

The inputs to the SVA model are largely estimates about marketing variables. Key inputs are future sales volumes and prices. The other inputs are costs, investments and the cost of capital. Each of these variables depends on careful analysis and projections of the market. As with all models, the lesson is 'garbage in, garbage out'. Poor judgements about the future behaviour of customers and competitors will make worthless any conclusions from SVA.

SVA only deals with the latter stages of strategic planning. Any decision problem has four steps: (1) perceiving a need to change, (2) identifying alternative courses of action, (3) evaluating the options and (4) making the choice. SVA only provides answers for the last two steps. It does not provide for the continuing analysis of the firm's markets and technologies that is needed to alert management to emerging problems and opportunities. Nor does it suggest alternative strategies – these have to be discovered elsewhere. For example, SVA is not going to alert management to the opportunities of the Internet or identify great new product or distribution ideas. These are most likely to be generated by staff who are close to customers. Just as marketing needs to be augmented to include developments in finance, so finance needs to be extended and broadened to include developments in marketing.

Marketing needs shareholder value

SVA is a great opportunity for marketing professionals. Traditional accounting, by focusing on short-term profits and ignoring intangible assets, marginalises marketing. In contrast, SVA can bring to the fore the real value drivers in today's globally competitive markets. First, SVA roots marketing in a central role in the board-room process of strategy formulation. The language of the modern board is finance. Actions have to be justified in terms of their ability to increase the financial value of the business. In the past marketing has not been able to measure and communicate to other disciplines the financial value created by marketing activities. This has resulted in marketing professionals being undervalued and sidelined. Now SVA offers marketing a direct way to show how marketing strategies increase the value of the firm. It provides the framework and language for integrating marketing more effectively with the other functions in the business.

Second, SVA provides marketing with a stronger theoretical base. Traditionally, marketing has tended to see increasing customer loyalty and market share as ends in themselves. But today, top management requires that marketing view its ultimate purpose as contributing to increasing shareholder value. No longer can marketers afford to rely on the untested assumption that increases in customer satisfaction and share will translate automatically into higher financial performance. This dilemma now suggests a reformulation of the marketing discipline as about developing and managing intangible assets – customer and channel relationships and brands – to maximise economic value. We call this value-based marketing. This view of marketing is theoretically appealing and also places marketing activities in a pivotal role in the strategy formulation process.

Third, SVA encourages profitable marketing investments. Conventional accounting has treated marketing expenditures as costs rather than investments in intangible assets. Because the long-term profit streams generated by such investments are ignored, marketing in many businesses is underfunded. SVA, however, is future orientated; it encourages the long-term effects of marketing expenditures to be explicitly estimated. Brand-building investments that would be discouraged under conventional accounting procedures because they reduce current profits are shown as value creating under SVA.

Finally, SVA penalises arbitrary cuts in marketing budgets. Management have found marketing budgets an easy target when they need to improve short-term profits. For example, cutting brand support will normally boost profitability without significantly affecting sales in the short run. The fact that such policies invariably lead to longer term erosion in market share and price premiums has been ignored. Now SVA gives marketing management the tool to demonstrate that these short-term cuts destroy rather than build value. Informed shareholders are likely to react to *ad hoc* cuts in brand supports by reducing the market value of the company.

The shareholder value principle

In the past ten years more and more leading companies have shifted to adopt shareholder value as the criterion for evaluating strategies and the performance of their managers. This criterion asserts that business strategies should be judged by the economic returns they generate for shareholders, as measured by dividends and increases in the company's share price.

Companies that adopt the shareholder value approach accept two assumptions drawn from contemporary financial theory. The first is that the primary obligation of managers is to maximise the returns for ordinary shareholders of the business. Managers are agents whose task is to act in the interests of the principals – the shareholders with financial ownership rights over the business. The second assumption is about how this is achieved in practice. This states that the stock market value of the company's shares is based on investors' expectations of the cash-generating abilities of the business. This then leads to the definition of the task of management as about developing strategies that maximise the value of these cash flows over time. A company generates cash, i.e. creates value, when its sales exceed its costs (including capital costs).

SVA calculates the total value of a strategy by discounting these cash flows. Discounting reflects that money has a time value. Because cash can earn interest, cash received today is worth more than the same amount received a year or more in the future. Discounting also allows for risk. To take greater risks, investors demand the promise of higher returns. Risk is reflected in the cost of capital used in the discounting formula. The idea of discounting cash flows (DCF) is not new; indeed, it has been the standard for evaluating capital projects for 40 years. But it was not until the 1980s that firms began seriously using DCF for broader strategic planning purposes. It is only now that it is being considered for evaluating marketing strategies.

SVA seeks to identify those strategies that create shareholder value. The stock market's judgement on the expected financial performance of a company is reflected in its market-to-book ratio … . If the market value of the shares exceeds the book value of the firm, it has created value. This ratio is a useful insight for measuring how successful management has been in maximising shareholder value.

To evaluate a new strategy proposed by the management team, the future effects of this strategy must be separated from the results of past strategies and investments. The current share price reflects both the values derived from these past decisions as well as shareholders' expectations about what the current management team will do. To judge the current strategy we need to focus on the incremental effect on shareholder value. The essence of the shareholder value approach is that managers create value when their strategy generates a greater economic return than their cost of capital. The cost of capital is what investors would expect to earn if they invested the funds on their own, in businesses with a similar degree of risk.

Why shareholder value?

The spread of value-based management and SVA has been triggered by the changes brought in by the new information age. One is the enormous growth of equity markets around the world caused by economic expansion and the declining role of government investment in industry. While government investment is motivated by complex political concerns, the objectives of private equity investors are much simpler and clearer. Private investors expect the pension, insurance and mutual funds that invest their money to maximise their performance. This in turn causes the fund managers to increasingly demand value from the companies they invest in.

The modern shareholder value movement started in the USA and the UK but, with the globalisation of trade and capital flows, it is sweeping into other major countries. Companies are now competing internationally not only for customers but also for capital. The most important criterion for attracting equity capital is its expected economic return. The information revolution is also making markets more efficient. Computers and modelling software now make it much quicker to run SVA methodology and test the implications of a company's strategic thinking. The quantity and quality of information available to investors have also increased exponentially in recent years. Finally, the sophistication of modern telecommunications means that money can now travel around the world in seconds. All these trends mean that managers are under increasing scrutiny from the people whose money they are using.

Companies that do not manage for value find capital more difficult and costly to obtain, handicapping their growth potential. They also become vulnerable more quickly. Non-executive shareholders and fund managers are becoming notably more proactive in removing top management when they fail to create value for shareholders. Chief executives recently removed in this way include those at General Motors, IBM, American Express and Kodak in the US, and Marks & Spencer, Mirror Group, Sears and BP in the UK. Finally, acquisition is a potent threat. When a weak market-to-book ratio indicates a 'value gap', i.e. a difference between the value of the company if it were operated to maximise shareholder value and its current value, an invitation appears for an acquirer to bid for it and replace the existing management.

Index

U

V

W

Y

Z